Making Content Comprehensible for Elementary English Learners
The SIOP® Model

Jana Echevarría

California State University, Long Beach

MaryEllen Vogt

California State University, Long Beach

Deborah J. Short

Center for Applied Linguistics, Washington, DC

Academic Language Research & Training, Arlington, VA

Allyn & Bacon

Boston   New York   San Francisco

Mexico City   Montreal   Toronto   London   Madrid   Munich   Paris

Hong Kong   Singapore   Tokyo   Cape Town   Sydney

Executive Editor: Aurora Martínez Ramos
Series Editorial Assistant: Jacqueline Gillen
Marketing Manager: Danae April
Production Editor: Gregory Erb
Editorial Production Service: Nesbitt Graphics, Inc.
Composition Buyer: Linda Cox
Manufacturing Buyer: Megan Cochran
Electronic Composition: Nesbitt Graphics, Inc.
Interior Design: Nesbitt Graphics, Inc.
Photo Researcher: Annie Pickert
Cover Designer: Linda Knowles

For Professional Development resources visit www.pearsonpd.com.

Between the time website information is gathered and then published, it is not unusual for some sites to have closed. Also, the transcription of URLs can result in typographical errors. The publisher would appreciate notification where these errors occur so that they may be corrected in subsequent editions.

Library of Congress Cataloging-in-Publication Data was unavailable at press time.

Photo Credits: p. 3, Bob Daemmrich Photography; p. 25, Robin Sachs/PhotoEdit; p. 55, Courtesy of Jana Echevarría; p. 81, Lindfors Photography; p. 97, Courtesy of Jana Echevarría; p. 119, David Young-Wolff/PhotoEdit; p. 143, Shutterstock; p. 161, Robert Harbison; p. 175, David Mager/Pearson Learning Photo Studio; p. 197, Comstock RF; p. 213, Ellen Senisi; inside front cover, Image 100.

Printed in the United States of America

10 9 8 7 6 5   BRG 13 12 11 10

Allyn & Bacon
is an imprint of

www.pearsonhighered.com   ISBN-10: 0-205-62756-0
                              ISBN-13: 978-0-205-62756-1

For my husband, Casey Vose, for his generosity, support and love.
JE

To my children and grandchildren: Scott, Kevin, Jeff, Karlin, Kyndal,
Kameron, True, Arik, and Emerson for their inspiration.
MEV

To my parents and grandmother, for their tradition of strength
and determination and for their support and encouragement
over the years.
DJS

Jana Echevarría is a Professor Emerita of Education at California State University, Long Beach. She has taught in elementary, middle, and high schools in general education, special education, ESL, and bilingual programs. She has lived in Taiwan, Spain, and Mexico. Her UCLA doctorate earned her an award from the National Association for Bilingual Education's Outstanding Dissertations Competition. Her research and publications focus on effective instruction for English learners, including those with learning disabilities. Currently, she is Co-Principal Investigator with the Center for Research on the Educational Achievement and Teaching of English Language Learners (CREATE) funded by the U.S. Department of Education, Institute of Education Sciences (IES). In 2005, Dr. Echevarría was selected as Outstanding Professor at CSULB.

MaryEllen Vogt is Distinguished Professor Emerita at California State University, Long Beach. Dr. Vogt has been a classroom teacher, reading and special education specialist, district reading resource teacher, and university teacher educator. She received her doctorate from the University of California, Berkeley. A co-author of fourteen books, including the SIOP series and *Reading Specialists and Literacy Coaches in the Real World* (2007), Dr. Vogt has provided professional development in all fifty of the United States, and in eight other countries. She served as President of the International Reading Association in 2004–2005.

Deborah J. Short is a professional development consultant and a senior research associate at the Center for Applied Linguistics in Washington, DC. She co-developed the SIOP® Model for sheltered instruction and has directed national research studies on English language learners funded by the Carnegie Corporation, the Rockefeller Foundation, and the U.S. Dept. of Education. She chaired an expert panel on adolescent ELL literacy and co-wrote a policy report. As the director of Academic Language Research & Training, Dr. Short provides professional development on sheltered instruction and academic literacy around the United States and abroad. She has numerous publications, including the SIOP® book series and five ESL textbook series for Hampton-Brown. She has taught English as a second/foreign language in New York, California, Virginia, and the Democratic Republic of Congo.

contents

4 Comprehensible Input   80

5 Strategies   96

9 Review & Assessment 174

10 Issues of Reading Development and Special Education for English Learners 196

11 Effective Use of the SIOP® Protocol 212

It is hard to believe that over fourteen years have passed since we first began our journey with the SIOP® Model. In the beginning, it would have been hard to believe that a decade later the SIOP® Model would be implemented in districts throughout all 50 states in the United States, and in numerous other countries. Whether you are already familiar with the SIOP® Model or are just now learning about it, we hope that you will find this new elementary edition to be informative, helpful, and most important, beneficial to the English learners (ELs) and other children with whom you work. In the earlier editions of the text, we discussed the need for a comprehensive, well-articulated model of instruction for preparing teachers to work with English learners. From this need, the Sheltered Instruction Observation Protocol (SIOP®) was created. Now, with the widespread use of the SIOP® Model throughout the country, we offer this version, especially written for K–6 educators.

Our work on the SIOP® Model began with reviewing the literature and examining district-produced guidelines for English learners to find agreement on a definition of sheltered instruction, or SDAIE (Specially Designed Academic Instruction in English). A preliminary observation protocol was drafted and field-tested with sheltered teachers. A research project through the Center for Research on Education, Diversity, & Excellence (CREDE) enabled us to engage in an intensive refinement process and to use the SIOP® Model in a sustained professional development effort with teachers on both the East and West Coasts. Through this process of classroom observation, coaching, discussion, and reflection, the instrument was refined and changed, and eventually it evolved into the Sheltered Instruction Observation Protocol, or as it has come to be known, the SIOP® (pronounced sī-ŏp). The SIOP® Model operationalizes sheltered instruction by offering teachers a model for lesson planning and implementation that provides English learners with access to grade-level content standards.

Since the first edition of this book was published, we have continued to refine the SIOP® Model, and in our work with thousands of teachers and administrators throughout the country, our own understanding of effective sheltered instruction/SDAIE and the needs of English learners has grown substantially. We believe, and our research confirms, that when teachers use the SIOP® Model for their planning and teaching of English learners, high-quality and effective sheltered instruction results, and student achievement is improved.

As the authors of this book, we have approached our teaching, writing, and research from different and complementary fields. Jana Echevarría's research and publications have focused on issues in the education of English learners, and on ELs with special education needs, as well as on professional development for regular and special education teachers. MaryEllen Vogt's research interests include improving comprehension, especially in the content areas, content literacy for English learners, and teacher change and development. Deborah Short is a researcher and former sheltered instruction teacher with expertise in second-language development, academic literacy, methods for integrating language and content instruction, materials development, and teacher change.

The strength of our collaboration is that we approach the issue of educating English learners from different perspectives. In writing the book, we each provided a slightly different lens through which to view and discuss instructional situations. But our varied experiences have led us to the same conclusion: Educators need a resource for planning and implementing high-quality sheltered lessons for English learners, and the SIOP® Model is fulfilling this need.

Overview of the Book

Over the years, elementary school teachers have asked for their own SIOP® book, with examples, lessons, instructional activities, and techniques that are especially effective for the ages and needs of the children they teach. In response to these requests, we have revised the original *Making Content Comprehensible for English Learners: The SIOP® Model* (3rd Ed.), and now you have your own book! Obviously, we did not revise or adapt the SIOP® Protocol or SIOP® Model because it is intended as a framework for teaching English learners (as well as all other students) of any age.

What is different in this book is our focus on teaching children in self-contained elementary classrooms (K–6). Increasingly, pre-K teachers are also implementing the SIOP® Model, and for those of you who teach our youngest students, we hope you will find ideas that you can use directly or modify somewhat for your unique situation. Likewise, for those of you who teach in the upper elementary grades (4–6), you will find many ideas for teaching your older English learners in academic English concurrently with your academic content. As always, what is of critical importance is fidelity to the SIOP® Model. Former, recent, and current research studies have shown conclusively that the greater the degree of implementation of the SIOP® Model by teachers, the greater the academic achievement of English learners in their classrooms. To assist you in accessing the information you need from this book so you can be a "high implementer," we provide the following overview.

- **Content and language objectives.** One of the most important aspects of the SIOP® Model is the inclusion of both content and language objectives for each and every lesson. Many teachers have found writing these objectives to be challenging, even as they acknowledge their importance both for their own planning and for their students' understanding of the lesson's content goals and language focus. Therefore, you will find a comprehensive discussion in Chapter 2 (Lesson Preparation) that provides specific guidance for writing a range of content and language objectives, along with recommendations for how to effectively present them orally and in writing to children.

  Some teachers who work with young children who are nonreaders or are in the beginning stages of learning to read have suggested that it doesn't make sense to post (on the board, chart paper, pocket chart, etc,) and then orally review the content and language objectives because the children cannot read them. We strongly disagree with this and encourage pre-K, kindergarten, and first-grade teachers to write and state the objectives very simply, with illustrations or rebus pictures, if needed. We hope the hints for writing content and language objectives in Chapter 2 will be helpful for you as you begin planning SIOP® lessons.

- **Discussion of the eight components and thirty features of the SIOP®.** Each chapter begins with discussion of a component of the SIOP® and its various features. For example, the discussion of lesson planning and preparation is found in the first half of Chapter 2. As you read about each feature in this section, think about how it would "look" in an actual classroom setting and how teachers might use this information to plan and prepare effective SIOP® lessons.

- **Teaching scenarios.** The second half of each chapter includes teaching scenarios. In these vignettes, three teachers, while teaching the same grade level and content, attempt to include the focal SIOP® features, but with varying degrees of success. At the end of each teaching scenario, you will have the opportunity to use that section of the SIOP® to rate the effectiveness of the lesson in implementing the particular SIOP® features. For example, as you read the teaching scenarios in Chapter 2, think about how well the three teachers included the features of the SIOP® component Lesson Preparation in their planning and preparation. Note that the illustrated lessons throughout the book range from grades K–6, and they cover a variety of content areas.

- **Discussion of the three teaching scenarios.** Following the description of the three teachers' lessons, you will be able to see how we have rated the lessons for their inclusion of the SIOP® features of effective sheltered instruction. We provide detailed explanations for the ratings and encourage you to discuss these with others to develop a high degree of inter-rater reliability.

- **Lesson activities.** In each chapter, you will find several activities identified with the icon shown at left as exemplars for implementing the eight components of the SIOP® Model. The activities are all appropriate for elementary classrooms, and some are especially effective for the younger children. Some activities will be familiar because you already use them in your own classroom. We hope you'll be motivated to try the others because they represent best practice—those ideas and activities that are included have been found to be especially effective for English learners.

- **Discussion questions.** Based on input from educators who have used this book, there are discussion questions found at the end of each chapter that reflect actual classroom practice with the SIOP® Model. We hope these questions will promote thinking about your own practice, conversations during professional development, and opportunities for portfolio reflection for preservice university and inservice courses.

- **The SIOP® protocol.** Two versions of the SIOP® protocol are included in Appendix A. The eight components and thirty features of the SIOP® are all the same as in the third edition of *Making Content Comprehensible for English Learners: The SIOP® Model* book.

- **SIOP® lesson plans.** We have been asked frequently for assistance with lesson planning for the SIOP® Model. In this edition, we have included four different formats for lesson plans (see Appendix B); we hope you will find one that is useful for you. In Chapters 2 and 5, you will also find complete plans for two of the lessons featured in the chapter scenarios (for Ms. Chen and Mrs. Abbas). In Chapter 6, you will find another lesson plan written for a technology class. These lesson plans are written with different formats, grade levels, and subject areas. (For additional sample lesson plans, see www.siopinstitute.net; *99 Ideas and Activities for Teaching English Learners with the SIOP® Model*, (Vogt & Echevarría, 2008); *Implementing the SIOP® Model with Effective Professional Development and Coaching* (Echevarría, Short, & Vogt, 2008); *The SIOP® Model for Teaching Mathematics to English Learners* (Echevarría, Vogt, & Short, in press); *The SIOP® Model for Teaching Science to English Learners* (Short, Vogt, & Echevarría, in press); *The SIOP® Model for Teaching History-Social Studies to English Learners* (Short, Vogt, & Echevarría, in press); and *The SIOP® Model for Teaching English/ Language Arts to English Learners* (Vogt, Echevarría, & Short, in press).

- **Discussion of reading development and special education for English learners.** In our work with the SIOP® Institutes and in district trainings, we have heard many educators ask questions about English learners who have reading or learning problems and are struggling academically because of them. Based on the published report of the National Literacy Panel on Language-Minority Children and Youth (August & Shanahan, 2006a), and the Response to Intervention (RTI) initiative, we have updated Chapter 10 with information and recommendations that we hope you will find helpful in SIOP® Model program design and implementation for students with special needs.

- **SIOP® Model research.** In Appendix C, you will find an overview of the findings from the original SIOP® Model research as well as a brief description of recent and current (at the time of this writing) national research studies on the SIOP® Model. We would greatly appreciate hearing about any additional SIOP® studies you are involved with or know about.

- **CD-ROM.** On the inside back cover, you will find a CD with video vignettes of classroom teachers whose instruction exemplifies each of the eight SIOP® components. Keep in mind that even though the CD clips illustrate particular components, you will see a number of features present in each clip. We hope these vignettes will promote reflection and discussion with your colleagues. In addition, you will find brief video clips of the authors speaking about aspects of the SIOP® Model.

Overview of the Chapters

The first chapter in the book introduces you to the pressing educational needs of English learners and to sheltered instruction. In Chapters 2 through 9, we explain the SIOP® Model in detail, drawing from educational theory, research, and practice to describe each component and feature of the SIOP® protocol. Teaching scenarios drawn from K–6 classroom lessons of sheltered instruction teachers follow. The features of the SIOP® Model that pertain to each chapter are included for the lesson descriptions in the teaching scenarios. After you read about each of the elementary teachers' lessons, use the SIOP® protocol to rate on the 0 to 4 rubric the degree to which the features are present. The classroom scenarios reflect a different grade level and content area in each chapter and are linked to core curriculum objectives and standards. All the classrooms include English learners, and many also include native English speakers.

In Chapter 10, we discuss the special needs of English learners who have reading problems and learning disabilities. You may wish to read this chapter before you delve into the SIOP® Model, especially if you have had little experience teaching English learners. It will assist you in situating the SIOP® Model in "real" classrooms with English learners who have a wide variety of academic and literacy abilities and needs. Chapter 11 provides a discussion of scoring and interpreting the SIOP® protocol, explaining how the instrument can be used holistically to measure teacher fidelity to the model and strategically to guide the teacher in planning lessons for one or more targeted SIOP® components. A full lesson from one research classroom is described and rated, revealing areas of strength and areas for improvement that can guide the teacher in future planning and teaching.

As you read each scenario in the chapters that follow, reflect on how effectively the teacher is meeting the linguistic and academic needs of English learners, especially as related to the SIOP® features being described. If you were observing this teacher's lesson, how would you rate it along the five-point SIOP® rubric? Is a particular feature clearly evident in the lesson, thus receiving a rating of 4? Or is the respective feature somewhat evident, thus receiving a 2? Or is it clear that the teacher has not modified teaching practices at all to accommodate the needs of ELs, with the lesson thus receiving 0? Compare your assessment of the lessons with our discussion at the conclusion of the teaching scenarios.

In the appendixes, you will find the Sheltered Instruction Observation Protocol (SIOP®), both the comprehensive and the abbreviated versions. You will also find four lesson planning formats to guide your lesson design and implementation and an overview of research on the SIOP® Model. The book concludes with a Glossary of terms related to the instruction of English learners.

Acknowledgments

Many educators throughout the United States have contributed to this book through their work as SIOP® teachers, bilingual specialists, curriculum coordinators, school and district administrators, and professional developers. We thank them for their insights and critical analyses of the SIOP® Model and protocol. We also appreciate the contributions of those who have participated in the SIOP® Institutes throughout the country (for more information, see www.siopinstitute.net). At each of these institutes, we gain new understanding about our work from those who participate in them.

We also thank the many teachers and administrators in whose schools we have conducted research on the SIOP® Model, both past and present. Their willingness to let us observe and discuss their teaching of English learners has enhanced our understandings and validated our work. The contributions of these fine educators to the ongoing development of the SIOP® Model are many, and we are grateful for their continued interest and encouragement.

We acknowledge a special group of expert teachers who have worked for many years with the SIOP® Model. They are the original cohort of National Faculty of the SIOP® Institute. They have provided input, a critical eye, many exceptional teaching ideas, and unconditional support. They include Melissa Castillo, John Seidlitz, Nicole Teyechea McNeil, Wanda Holbrook, Alvaro Hernandez, Martha Trejo, Kendra Moreno, and Karlin LaPorta.

We found the comments and suggestions from our reviewers to be of great help and we thank them: Julia S. Austin, University of Alabama at Birmingham; Danny Brassell, California State University, Dominguez Hills; Carla Chavez, Prairie Park Elementary School (KS); Lisa De Maagd, Taft Elementary School (MI); Jodi Grubb, Pittsfield Elementary School (NH); and Socorro Herrera, Kansas State University. We also appreciate the ongoing support, assistance, and patience of our Allyn & Bacon team, especially that of our editor, Aurora Martínez Ramos.

The original SIOP® work was supported under the Education Research and Development Program, PR/Award No. R306A60001, the Center for Research on Education, Diversity, & Excellence (CREDE), as administered by the former Office of Educational Research and Improvement, now the Institute for Education Studies (IES), National Institute on the Education of At-Risk Students (NIEARS), and U.S. Department of Education (ED). The contents, findings, and opinions expressed here are those of the authors and do not necessarily represent the positions or policies of IES, NIEARS, or ED.

Finally, we express appreciation to our families, whose support has enabled us to pursue our professional interests.

je mev djs

chapter 1

Introducing Sheltered Instruction

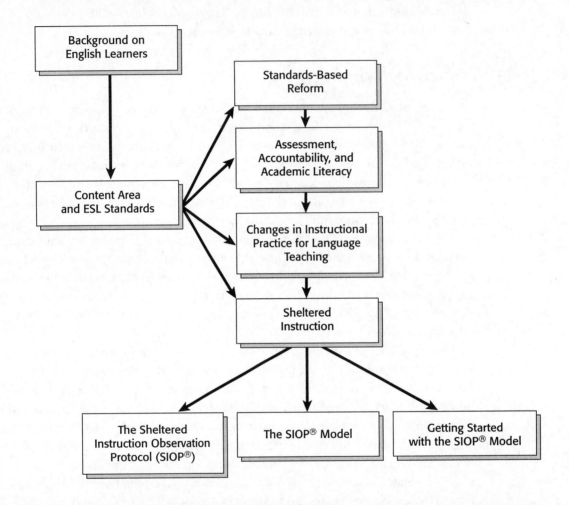

Background on
English Learners

Standards-Based
Reform

Content Area
and ESL Standards

Assessment,
Accountability, and
Academic Literacy

Changes in Instructional
Practice for Language
Teaching

Sheltered
Instruction

The Sheltered
Instruction Observation
Protocol (SIOP®)

The SIOP® Model

Getting Started
with the SIOP® Model

Objectives

After reading, discussing, and engaging in activities related to this chapter, you will be able to meet the following content and language objectives.

Content Objectives

Distinguish between content-based ESL and sheltered instruction.

List characteristics of English learners that may influence their success in school.

Explain the development of the SIOP® Model.

Language Objectives

Discuss the challenges of school reform and its effect on English learners.

Develop a lexicon related to sheltered instruction.

"Hola prima," called Graciela to her cousin, Jocelyn, on the playground "¡Ayuda con mi tarea!" Graciela asked her cousin for help with a homework assignment. "Cúal es el problema?" replied Jocelyn. Graciela went on to explain that she had to write a paper about recycling. She had to write an action plan, but she didn't know what an action plan was.

The two girls are cousins from Central America who entered fourth grade in Bray Elementary School together seven months earlier. They were placed in different classes in this suburban setting, but because the fourth-grade science teachers all did the same project, Jocelyn knew how to help her cousin. She explained that they had already started to work on that project. They had looked through the trash can in the lunchroom and found many things that could be recycled. They are creating a bulletin board with vocabulary and pictures about recycling. They had watched two videos, one about neighborhood families recycling and one about a recycling plant. They were going to make paper the next day. "We have to make a poster with our partner telling why it is important to recycle," Jocelyn told her cousin. "We made a list in class of reasons and I decided to try to stop pollution in the sea. Ms. Sylvan showed us two posters from last year's class. Then she bookmarked some websites for me to look at. Some of them are in Spanish and you can listen to people talking about pollution and recycling. What did you do in class?"

Graciela explained that one day the teacher had talked to them for a long time about what recycling is and why it is important. "She told us to take notes when she talked, but it was hard. She talked too fast and she didn't write anything on the board. Then we read a few

4

pages in our science textbook and answered questions yesterday. Today she gave us this sheet and told us to start writing our ideas." Graciela showed her cousin the assignment:

> Think of a recycling project. What needs to be improved in your school or town? Write an action plan proposing the school board or the town council take steps to alleviate the problem or introduce a new program.

Jocelyn shook her head slowly as she looked at the paper. "I know what we can do. Let's go ask Ms. Sylvan. She just came out of the cafeteria."

Graciela and Jocelyn have experienced different teaching styles in their fourth-grade classrooms. Graciela's teacher uses a teacher-directed approach with an emphasis on mini-lectures and textbook reading. She provides little scaffolding for her English learners, indeed little scaffolding for any of her students. Recycling, a topic that lends itself easily to visuals and other realia, hands-on materials, field trips, and more is not brought alive in her classroom. Nor was a model for the action plan presented. Ms. Sylvan, on the other hand, provides a range of activities that help students understand the concept of recycling and see its application in their everyday lives. Her lessons built background and vocabulary for the fourth-graders and gave them hands-on experiences. She tapped into the students' different learning modes and supported her English learners with access to websites in their native language.[1] Her lessons reveal a great deal of preparation that will lead to the success of all her students.

Jocelyn is luckier than a number of English learners (ELs). She has a teacher who provides effective instruction as she learns content through English, a new language. If more teachers learn the techniques that Ms. Sylvan uses, then many more ELs will have a chance to develop academic literacy in English and be successful in elementary school. But it will take significant effort on the part of schools, districts, and universities to make this happen for Graciela and other students like her.

Consider the following statistics. Although many refer to the dire situation in high school, we know that the foundation for academic success is laid in the elementary schools. If students do not learn to read and read to learn by the upper elementary grades, we know they will experience significant academic achievement challenges in middle and high school.

- More than 80 percent of our elementary limited English proficient students are second- or third-generation Americans; 56 percent of our secondary students are (Capps et al., 2005; Batalova, Fix, & Murray, 2005).

- We continue to have achievement gaps between native English speakers and those learning English. On the 2007 National Assessment of Education Progress (NAEP) 4th Grade Reading test, the average score for English learners was 36 points lower than the average score for non-English learners. On the NAEP 8th Grade Reading test, the average score for ELs was 42 points lower than the average score for non-ELs (Lee, Grigg, & Donahue, 2007).

---

[1]For more information about a unit on recycling designed for classes with English learners, see Syvanen, 2000.

- On the 2007 National Assessment of Education Progress (NAEP) 4th Grade Mathematics test, the average score for English learners was 25 points lower than the average score for non-English learners. On the 2007 National Assessment of Education Progress (NAEP) 8th Grade mathematics test, the average score for ELs was 37 points lower than the average score for non-ELs (Lee, Grigg, & Dion, 2007).

- Only 4 percent of eighth-grade ELs and 20 percent of students classified as "formerly EL" scored at the proficient or advanced levels on the reading portion of the 2005 National Assessment for Educational Progress (Perie, Grigg, & Donahue, 2005). This means that 96 percent of the eighth-grade limited English proficient (LEP) students scored *below* the Basic level.

- A dramatic, lingering divide in achievement exists between Caucasian students and those from culturally and linguistically diverse groups on state and national measures of achievement (California Dept. of Education, 2004; Grigg, Daane, Jin, & Campbell, 2003; Kindler, 2002; Siegel, 2002).

- A recent five-year, statewide evaluation study found that English learners with 10 years of schooling in California had less than a 40 percent chance of meeting the criteria to be redesignated as fluent English proficient (Parish et al., 2006).

- Only 30 percent of all secondary students read proficiently, but for students of color, the situation is worse: 89 percent of Hispanic students and 86 percent of African American middle and high school students read below grade level (Perie, Grigg, & Donahue, 2005).

- Only 10 percent of young adults who speak English at home fail to complete high school, but the percentage is three times higher (31 percent) for young adult English learners. If ELs reported speaking English with difficulty on the 2000 U.S. Census, their likelihood of completing high school was 18 percent. However, if they reported speaking English very well, their likelihood of graduating rose to 51 percent (NCES, 2004).

- Since the No Child Left Behind (NCLB) Act was implemented in 2001, there has been an increase in the number of high school ELs not receiving a diploma because they failed high-stakes tests despite fulfilling all other graduation requirements (Biancarosa & Snow, 2004; Edley & Wald, 2002; Kober et al., 2006; McNeil et al., 2008).

A number of recent reports have focused attention on the academic literacy crisis in U.S. schools, particularly for adolescent learners, but they offer very little guidance on how best to meet the varied and challenging literacy needs of ELs. Reports such as *Reading Next* (Biancarosa & Snow, 2004), *Reading to Achieve* (National Governors Association, 2005), and *Creating a Culture of Literacy* (National Association of Secondary School Principals, 2005) have looked at research, student performance, and promising practices. Only *Double the Work* (Short & Fitzsimmons, 2006) has specifically addressed this student population but primarily from a policy perspective.

We need our students like Graciela to be successful in school and beyond. In the long run, such success will benefit the communities in which these students live and the national economy as a whole. This book, *Making Content Comprehensible for Elementary English Learners,* offers a solution to one aspect of school reform needed for English learners' acquisition of English and academic achievement, namely, classroom instruction. It introduces a research-based model of sheltered instruction (SI) and demonstrates through classroom vignettes how the model can be implemented well.

Sheltered instruction is an approach for teaching content to English learners (ELs) in strategic ways that make the subject matter concepts comprehensible while promoting the students' English language development. It also may be referred to as SDAIE (specially designed academic instruction in English). Sheltering techniques are used increasingly in schools across the United States, particularly as teachers prepare students to meet high academic standards. However, in the past, the use of these techniques had been inconsistent from class to class, discipline to discipline, school to school, and district to district. The model of SI presented here mitigates this variability and provides guidance as to what constitutes the best practices for SI, grounded in more than two decades of classroom-based research, the experiences of competent teachers, and findings from the professional literature.

The goal of this book is to prepare teachers to teach content effectively to English learners while developing the students' language ability. The professional development model evolved from the Sheltered Instruction Observation Protocol (SIOP®), seen in Appendix A, an instrument originally used by researchers to measure teacher implementation of SI. Through subsequent research conducted by the National Center for Research on Education, Diversity, & Excellence (CREDE), the SIOP® Model was field tested and the protocol became a training and observation instrument that codifies and exemplifies the model. The SIOP® Model may be used as part of a program for preservice and inservice professional development, as a lesson planner for sheltered content lessons, and as a training resource for faculty. The protocol can be used as an observation measure for site-based administrators, supervisors of student teachers, and researchers who rate lessons.

The book is intended for teachers of linguistically and culturally diverse students in K–6 settings, university faculty who prepare such teachers, site-based administrators, and others who provide technical assistance or professional development to K–6 schools. Our research shows that both language and content teachers can implement the SIOP® Model fully to good effect. The model is suited for content-based ESL classes and grade-level elementary classrooms that are part of a program of studies for English learners. Together these SIOP® classes are proving to be a promising combination when implemented throughout an elementary school.

Demographic Changes

Each year, the United States becomes more ethnically and linguistically diverse, with more than 90 percent of recent immigrants coming from non-English-speaking countries. From the 1989–1990 school year through 2005–2006, the number of identified students with limited English proficiency in public schools (K–12) grew 149 percent while total enrollment increased by only 21.5 percent (National Clearinghouse for English Language Acquisition, 2008). Thus, the proportion of English learners in the schools is growing even more rapidly than the actual numbers. In 2005–2006, more than five million school-age children were identified as limited English proficient (LEP, a federal designation)—greater than 10 percent of the K–12 public school student population.

The rise in immigrant students conforms to the increase in the immigrant population in the United States. The U.S. Census Bureau determined that in 1999, 20 percent of school-age children had at least one parent who was an immigrant and 5 percent of the students were immigrants themselves (Jamieson, Curry, & Martinez, 2001). When race or origin is considered, 65 percent of Hispanic students and 88 percent of Asian and Pacific Islander students had at least one immigrant parent.

According to Ruiz-de-Velasco & Fix (2000), the geographic distribution of immigrants is concentrated in urban areas, primarily in six states that account for three-fourths of all immigrant children: California (35 percent), Texas (11.3 percent), New York (11 percent), Florida (6.7 percent), Illinois (5 percent), and New Jersey (4 percent). However, the states with the fastest-growing LEP student populations are not the same as the top six traditional immigration states. For example, North Carolina experienced a 500 percent growth between 1993 and 2003, and Colorado, Nevada, Nebraska, Oregon, Georgia, and Indiana all had more than 200 percent increases in that time period (Batalova, Fix, & Murray, 2005). Changes in the geographic distribution of ELs present new challenges to the numerous districts in these new destination states that have not served these students in the past. Academic programs are not well-established; sheltered curricula and appropriate resources are not readily available; and most important, many teachers are not trained to meet the needs of these second language learners. Furthermore, many ELs are in linguistically segregated schools. More than half of the LEP students in elementary and secondary schools are in schools where more than 30 percent of the student population is identified as limited English proficient.

While the number of students with limited proficiency in English has grown exponentially across the United States, their level of academic achievement has lagged significantly behind that of their language-majority peers. As the statistics presented at the beginning of this chapter indicate, there exists growing evidence that most schools are not meeting the challenge of educating these students well. The lack of success in educating linguistically and culturally diverse students is problematic because federal and state governments expect *all* students to meet high standards and have adjusted national and state assessments as well as state graduation requirements to reflect new levels of achievement and to accommodate requirements of the No Child Left Behind Act (2001). In order for students whose first language is not English to succeed in school and become productive members of our society, they need to receive better educational opportunities in U.S. schools.

English Learner Diversity

To develop the best educational programs for ELs, we need to understand their diverse backgrounds. These learners bring a wide variety of educational and cultural experiences to the classroom as well as considerable linguistic differences, and these characteristics have implications for instruction, assessment, and program design. Once we know their backgrounds and abilities in their native language, we can incorporate effective techniques and materials in our instructional practices.

All English learners in schools today are not alike. They enter U.S. schools with a wide range of language proficiencies (in English and in their native languages) and of subject matter knowledge. In addition to the limited English proficiency and the approximately 180 native languages among the students, we also find diversity in their educational backgrounds, expectations of schooling, socioeconomic status, age of arrival, personal experiences while coming to and living in the United States, and parents' education levels and proficiency in English. All these factors impinge on the type of programs and instructional experiences the students should receive in order to succeed in school.

At one end of the spectrum among immigrant students, we find some elementary-age ELs who had strong academic backgrounds before they came to the United States and entered our schools. Some of them are above equivalent grade levels in the school's curricula, in math and science, for example. They are literate in their native language and may have already begun study of a second language. For these students, much of what they need is English language development so that, as they become more proficient in English, they can transfer the knowledge they learned in their native country's schools to the courses they are taking in the United States. A few subjects, such as social studies, may need special attention because these students may not have studied them before. Of all the EL subgroups, these students have the greatest likelihood of achieving educational success if they receive appropriate English language and content instruction in their schools.

At the other end, some immigrant students arrive at our schoolhouse doors with very limited formal schooling—perhaps due to war in their native countries or the remote, rural location of their homes. These students have weak literacy in their native language (i.e., they cannot read or write), and they may not have had schooling experiences such as sitting at desks all day, changing teachers per subject, or taking district or national tests. They have significant gaps in their educational backgrounds, lack knowledge in specific subject areas, and often need time to become accustomed to school routines and expectations. These ELs with limited formal schooling and below-grade-level literacy are most at risk for educational failure. They are entering U.S. schools with weak academic skills at the same time that schools are emphasizing rigorous, standards-based curricula and high-stakes assessments.

We also have students who have grown up in the United States but speak a language other than English at home. More than 80 percent of preK–5 ELs were born in the United States; that is, they are second- or third-generation immigrants (Capps, et al., 2005). Some of the students in this group are literate in their home language, such as Mandarin, Arabic, or Spanish, and just need to add English to their knowledge base in school. Others, however, have yet to master either English or the home language. There are also large numbers of second- and third-generation LEP adolescents who continue to lack proficiency in English in secondary school, suggesting that many LEP children are not learning the language well even after many years in U.S. schools.

So far, we have been discussing English learners' individual characteristics and the roles they play in educational attainment. Sociocultural factors also have an influence. Poverty level, for example, is a key predictor of school success. Research has shown that poorer students, in general, are less academically successful (Glick & White, 2004). Some ELs come from middle- and upper-class homes, but according to the 2000 U.S. Census, immigrant youth are more likely to be poor than non-immigrants. For instance, 68 percent of the LEP students in grades preK–5 live in families with incomes 185 percent below the poverty line compared with 36 percent of English proficient children (Capps et al., 2005). Some immigrant ELs are also undocumented, a factor that affects both socioeconomic status and postsecondary educational options. Mobility is another factor that can impinge on school success. Glick and White (2004) found that students with a previous move were twice as likely not to complete high school as those who had not moved. Home language experiences, on the other hand, can support academic literacy development (August & Shanahan, 2006). Ethnicity, however, does not appear to be an important factor in second language (L2) educational achievement (Ima & Rumbaut, 1989).

Given the variability in these students' backgrounds, it is clear that there is no simple, one-size-fits-all solution. They need different pathways for academic success. To meet this challenge, fundamental shifts need to occur in teacher development, program design, curricula and materials, and instructional and assessment practices.

School Reform and Accountability in the Twenty-First Century

The educational landscape has shifted in the past two decades. While the focus on standards-based instruction has been growing since the National Governors Association agreed to promote national education goals in 1989 and the National Council of Teachers of Mathematics issued the first curriculum standards for mathematics in that same year, the advent of the No Child Left Behind (NCLB) Act of 2001 has operationalized the goal of high standards and has held schools more accountable for the success of all of their students. States now have standards for mathematics, reading, language arts, English language development, and science, and implement high-stakes tests based on these standards. NCLB calls for annual testing of reading and mathematics achievement for all students in Title I schools in grades 3–8 and once again in high school. Science testing is also required at least once during the grade 3–5 span, the grade 6–9 span, and the grade 10–12 span. English learners are not only included in these assessment measures if enrolled in Title I schools but must also undergo additional testing of their English language development. While they are designated as limited English proficient, they must be tested yearly in grades K–12. Each state, with the approval of the U.S. Department of Education, sets benchmarks for achievement, and students are expected to make adequate yearly progress on all of these assessments.

As Coltrane (2002) points out, this act offers advantages and disadvantages to ELs. On the positive side, standards-based reform has increased academic rigor for all students with a push for academic literacy. This is beneficial for ELs, so teachers integrate content and language development in their lessons. To help teachers do this effectively, more and more districts are offering professional development on this topic. The requirement that districts disaggregate their test scores to measure progress of LEP students can also have a favorable impact in the long term. If schools do not show that all categories of students, including LEP students, are making annual yearly progress as a group over three years, corrective actions can be taken. This situation has led to improved program designs for English learners, new or revised curricula, and enhanced teacher professional development.

Nonetheless, there are negative implications. ELs, especially those at beginning levels, are learning this challenging content in a language they do not speak, read, or write proficiently. The high-stakes tests therefore are more often a test of their English knowledge than their content knowledge or skills (Coltrane, 2002; Menken, 2008). Furthermore, most of the standardized tests that states use have been designed for, and normed on, native English speakers who have spent their educational careers in U.S. schools. Thus, even in elementary school English learners are at a disadvantage.

In addition, the Center on Education Policy reports that twenty-three states require exit exams to graduate from high school, with three more states following suit by 2012 (Zabala, Minnici, McMurrer, & Briggs, 2008). Kober and colleagues (2006) reported that ELs have lower pass rates on these exit exams and lower graduation rates than native speakers, even with test accommodations such as directions provided in their native language and use of bilingual dictionaries or glossaries. Only three of the twenty-three states with these exit exams offer alternative measures specifically designed for English learners (Zabala et al., 2008).

NCLB calls for highly qualified teachers in every core academic classroom, it does not require elementary classroom or content teachers with LEP students to have any educational background in ESL methodology or second language acquisition theory. Specific qualifications for teachers of "core academic subjects"—English, reading/language arts, mathematics, science, foreign languages, civics and government, economics, arts, history, and geography—are designated by the states, which primarily focus on teachers having a deep understanding of the content area (typically demonstrated by holding a degree in the content area or passing a specialized exam). Despite the rapidly growing numbers of these students, only four states at the time of this writing have policies that require all teachers in preservice programs to have an understanding of how to teach ELs effectively: Arizona, California, Florida, and New York.

The situation at the inservice level has not been any better. In the 1999–2000 Schools and Staffing Survey (National Center for Education Statistics, 2002), 41.2 percent of the 2,984,781 public school teachers reported teaching LEP students, but only 12.5 percent had had eight or more hours of training in the past three years. Eight hours is not even a minimum amount for effective training. A recent survey that sampled teachers in twenty-two small, medium, and large districts in California (Gandara, Maxwell-Jolly, & Driscoll, 2005) found similar results. In the five years prior to the survey "43 percent of teachers with 50 percent or more English learners in their classrooms had received no more than one inservice that focused on the instruction of English learners" (p. 13). Fifty percent of the teachers with somewhat fewer students (26–50 percent English learners in their classes), had had no, or only one, such inservice.

Given that LEP students are more than 10 percent of the student population now, and their proportion of the total student population increases each year, the current status of teacher preparation and development is inadequate for the educational needs of English learners. Indeed, the most desired professional development that the elementary teachers in the California survey (Gandara et al., 2005) wanted was training in reading and writing in English, English language development methods, and instructional strategies. Unfortunately, at present, many English learners receive much of their instruction from classroom teachers or aides who have not had appropriate professional development to address their second language development needs or to make content instruction comprehensible. This situation hinders their academic success.

Because most state certification does not require it and most teacher preparation institutions are not developing all teacher candidates so they can teach linguistically and culturally diverse students appropriately, school districts try to compensate. However, moving toward ongoing, sustained professional development and away from ineffective, one-shot workshops has been a slow process. Research shows that professional development approaches that improve teaching include the following: sustained, intensive development with modeling, coaching, and problem solving; collaborative endeavors for educators to share knowledge; experiential opportunities that engage teachers in actual teaching, assessment, and observation; and development grounded in research but also drawing from teacher experience and inquiry, connected to the teachers' classes, students, and subjects taught (Borko, 2004; Darling-Hammond, 1998; Darling-Hammond & McLaughlin, 1995; NCTAF, 1997).

English learners also have difficulty in school when there is a mismatch among program design, instructional goals, and student needs. Historically, schools offered ESL or bilingual education programs to ELs with specially trained teachers, yet kept those teachers and students separate from regular school programs. Depending on school or state policy and resource availability, ELs were schooled in ESL or bilingual classes and were not a concern of the regular content or classroom teacher until they exited the language support program. In theory, the ELs would make that transition when they were proficient in English and able to perform subject area course work in English-medium classrooms. In practice, however, students would exit before they are proficient in academic English, for several reasons: (1) the number of these students increased without a comparable increase in certified teachers, so it became impossible to relegate the education of these students to separate, specialized classes; (2) policies have been enacted in which the number of years that students are permitted access to language support services is quite limited, such as in Massachusetts, Arizona, and California, where the goal is to move students into regular classrooms after one year.

These policies are misguided if ELs are moved into classrooms lacking well-trained teachers and appropriate curricula and materials. Research shows that conversational fluency develops inside and outside the classroom and can be attained in one to three years (Thomas & Collier, 2002). However, the language that is critical for educational success—academic language (Cummins, 2000)—is more complex and develops more slowly and systematically in academic settings. It may take students from four to seven years of study, depending on individual and sociocultural factors, before they are proficient in academic English (Collier, 1987; Hakuta, Butler, & Witt, 2000; Lindholm-Leary & Borsato, 2006; Thomas & Collier, 2002). In their national research study, Thomas and Collier found that there is a large achievement gap between ELs and native English speakers across most program models. For this gap to be closed with bilingual/ESL content programs, students must gain three to four more NCE (normal curve equivalent) points each year than native English speakers gain. The only way to do that is to have well-implemented, cognitively challenging, not segregated, and sustained programs of five to six years' duration. Typical programs of two to three years are ineffective in closing the large achievement gap.

When policies and programs are in place that complement the research on second-language acquisition, we see more positive outcomes. For example, recent analyses from New York City and the states of New Jersey, Washington, and California reveal that former English learners outperformed students as a whole on state tests, exit exams, and graduation rates (DeLeeuw, 2008; New York City Department of Education, 2004; State of New Jersey Department of Education, 2006; Sullivan et al., 2005). These results indicate that when English learners are given time to develop academic English proficiency in their programs and are exited (and redesignated) with criteria that measure their ability to be successful in mainstream classes, they perform, on average, as well or better than the state average on achievement measures.

Academic Literacy

The foundation of school success is academic literacy in English. Although not understood by many educators, age-appropriate knowledge of the English language is a prerequisite in the attainment of content standards. We learn primarily through language, and use language to express our understanding. As Lemke (1988, p. 81) explained,

> . . . educators have begun to realize that the mastery of academic subjects is the mastery of their specialized patterns of language use, and that language is the dominant medium through which these subjects are taught and students' mastery of them tested.

Defining academic language or academic literacy has been of interest to educators and researchers in the field of second language acquisition and literacy. Most of the definitions incorporate reading, writing, listening, and speaking skills as part of academic language and refer to a specialized academic register of the formal written and spoken code. Although there is not yet a single agreed-upon definition, each one considers how language is used in school to acquire new knowledge and foster success on academic tasks (Bailey, 2007; Gibbons, 2002; Schleppegrell, 2004; Short, 2002). Without proficient oral and written English language skills, students are hard pressed to learn and demonstrate their knowledge of mathematical reasoning, science skills, social studies concepts, and so forth.

Relationship to Second Language Learning

Academic language is used by all students in school settings, native English speakers (referred to as English-only students or EOs) and English learners alike. However, this type of language use is particularly challenging for English learners who are beginning to acquire English at the same time that school tasks require a high level of English usage. Participation in informal conversation demands less from an individual than joining in an academic discussion (Cummins, 2000). While the distinction isn't completely clear-cut, it is widely accepted that the language skills required for informal conversation differ from those required for academic processes such as summarizing information, evaluating perspectives, and drawing conclusions. Certainly, one may converse in a cognitively demanding way—such as debating a current event that requires significant knowledge of both sides of the topic and use of high-level academic language—but that is not the typical social conversation. The distinction becomes clearer when we consider that students have the ability to converse in English without needing a strong repertoire of academic language skills. In many instances, English learners appear to speak English well, in hallways, on playing fields, and in small talk before a lesson begins, but struggle to use English well in classroom lessons or on tests. This situation occurs because they have not yet acquired a high level of academic language, which tends to be cognitively demanding and highly decontextualized (Cummins, 1984).

Role in Schooling

The relationship between literacy proficiency and academic achievement grows stronger as grade levels rise—regardless of individual student characteristics. Language use becomes more complex and more content-area specific (Biancarosa & Snow, 2004). English learners must develop literacy skills for each content area *in* their second language as they simultaneously learn, comprehend, and apply content area concepts *through* their second language (Garcia & Godina, 2004).

Specifically, English learners must master academic English, which includes semantic and syntactic knowledge along with functional language use. Using English, students, for example, must be able to read and understand the expository prose found in textbooks and reference materials, write persuasively, argue points of view, and take notes from teacher lectures or Internet sites. They must articulate their thinking skills in English—make hypotheses and predictions, express analyses, draw conclusions, and so forth. In their classes, ELs must pull together their emerging knowledge of the English language with the content knowledge they are studying in order to complete the academic tasks. They must also learn *how* to do these tasks—generate the format of an outline, negotiate roles in cooperative learning groups, interpret charts and maps, and such. These three knowledge bases—knowledge of English, knowledge of the content topic, and knowledge of how the tasks are to be accomplished—constitute the major components of academic literacy (Short, 2002).

Although we have yet to determine how best to teach academic language to English learners, there is agreement that it should be done and should include a focus on the lexical, semantic, and discourse levels of the language as they are applied in school settings. Analyses of academic language used in assessments by Bailey and Butler (2007) found that there appears to be content-specific language (such as technical terms like *latitude* and *longitude,* and phrases like "We hypothesize that . . .") and general, or common core, academic language (such as how to structure an argument and use persuasive language) that is useful across curriculum areas. Similarly, there are general academic tasks that one needs to know how to do to be academically proficient (e.g., create a timeline) and more specific tasks (e.g., write a scientific laboratory report). They argue teachers and curricula should pay attention to this full range of academic language. As a result, the enhancement of ELs' academic language skills should enable them to perform better on assessments. This conclusion is bolstered by an older study: Snow et al. (1991) found that performance on highly decontextualized (i.e., school-like) tasks, such as providing a formal definition of words, predicted academic performance, whereas performance on highly contextualized tasks, such as face-to-face communication, did not.

Reviews of Research

In recent years, two major syntheses of the research on the education of English learners have been conducted, both with an eye toward academic literacy. The National Literacy Panel on Language-Minority Children and Youth (hereafter NLP) (August & Shanahan, 2006a) analyzed and synthesized the research on these learners with regard to English literacy attainment. Many of the studies that the thirteen-member expert panel examined looked at the reading and writing skills needed for successful schooling. The panel considered second language literacy development, crosslinguistic influences and transfer, sociocultural contexts, instruction and professional development, and student assessment. Figure 1.1 summarizes the findings of the NLP panel that appeared in the executive summary (August & Shanahan, 2006b).

The second major review was conducted by researchers from the National Center for Research on Education, Diversity & Excellence (CREDE), the former federally funded

FIGURE 1.1 *Research Findings from the National Literacy Panel on Language-Minority Children and Youth*

1. English language learners (ELLs) benefit from instruction in the key components of reading as defined by the National Reading Panel (NICHD, 2000) as phonemic awareness, phonics, fluency, vocabulary, and text comprehension.

2. Instruction in these five components is necessary but not sufficient to teach ELLs to read and write proficiently in English. Oral language proficiency is needed also, so ELLs need instruction in this area.

3. Oral proficiency and literacy in the student's native language (L1) will facilitate development of literacy in English, but literacy in English can also be developed without proficiency in the L1.

4. Individual student characteristics play a significant role in English literacy development.

5. Home language experiences can contribute to English literacy achievement, but on the whole, the research on the influence of sociocultural factors is limited.

(August & Shanahan, 2006b)

research center. Their focus was on oral language development, literacy development (from instructional and cross-linguistic perspectives), and academic achievement. Both syntheses led to similar findings.

Some of the findings that are closely related to the topics in this book are the following:

- Processes of second language (L2) literacy development are influenced by a number of variables that interact with each other in complex ways (e.g., L1 literacy, L2 oralcy, socioeconomic status, and more).

- Certain L1 skills and abilities transfer to English literacy: phonemic awareness, comprehension and language learning strategies, and L1 and L2 oral knowledge.

- Teaching the five major components of reading (NICHD, 2000) to English learners is necessary but not sufficient for developing academic literacy. ELs need to develop oral language proficiency as well.

- Oralcy and literacy can develop simultaneously.

- Academic literacy in the native language facilitates the development of academic literacy in English.

- High-quality instruction for English learners is similar to high-quality instruction for other, English-speaking students, but ELs need instructional accommodations and support to fully develop their English skills.

- English learners need enhanced, explicit vocabulary development.

More information on these findings and their implications for developing academic literacy can be found in August & Shanahan (2006a), Genesee et al. (2006), Goldenberg (2008), and Short & Fitzsimmons (2007).

Changes in Instructional Practice for English Learners

The ESL profession has always been sensitive to student needs, and the evolution of ESL methodologies has been a dynamic process over the past five decades (Short, 2006; Stoller, 2004). Teachers have realized that students would benefit from new instructional approaches and have adjusted pedagogical practice and the content of the curriculum over time. But ESL and bilingual teachers alone cannot provide the necessary educational opportunities these learners need.

In the first half of the twentieth century, most language teaching relied on the direct method of instruction or a grammar translation approach. Yet by the 1950s, direct method and grammar translation languished and audiolingual methods surfaced. In the 1970s and after, the audiolingual method was displaced by the communicative method for ESL teaching, preparing students to use functional language in meaningful, relevant ways. As districts implemented communicative curricula, students were given opportunities to discuss material of high interest and topicality, which in turn motivated them to learn and participate in class. Students were encouraged to experiment with language and assume greater responsibility for their learning.

The communicative approach engendered the content-based ESL approach. Viewing the grade-level curricula as relevant, meaningful content for ELs, educators have developed content-based ESL curricula and accompanying instructional strategies to help better prepare the students for their transition to mainstream classes. Content-based ESL classes, in which all the students are ELs, are taught by language educators whose main goal is English language skill development but whose secondary goal is preparing the students for the mainstream, English-medium classroom (Cantoni-Harvey, 1987; Crandall, 1993; Mohan, 1986; Short, 1994). The sophistication of the material presented necessarily varies according to the language proficiency of the students in class, but nonetheless this material addresses key topics in grade-level subjects.

In content-based ESL, content from multiple subject areas is often presented through thematic or interdisciplinary units. For example, in a first-grade classroom, one theme might be "Life on a Farm." While students learn such language-related elements as names of animals, adjectives, and the present continuous tense, they also solve addition and subtraction problems, read poems and sing songs about farm animals, and discuss the food chain, thus exploring objectives from mathematics, language arts, music, and science. Some young English learners may share stories from their families about living on farms in their countries of origin. For the fifth-grade classroom, a theme such as "urbanization" might be selected, and lessons could include objectives drawn from environmental science, geography, social studies, and mathematics. Students with less proficiency might take field trips around a local city and create maps, transportation routes, and brochures. Advanced students might learn to use reference materials and computers to conduct research on the development of cities and their respective population growth. They might study persuasive language to debate advantages and disadvantages to urbanization. English learners may contribute to this topic because some have lived in cities or rural settings overseas. Some may have experienced moving from small towns to large cities and can express their opinions about the differences.

In general, content-based ESL teachers seek to develop the students' English language proficiency by incorporating information from the subject areas that students are likely to study or from courses they may have missed if they are fairly new to the school system. Whatever subject matter is included, for effective content-based ESL instruction to occur, teachers need to provide practice in academic skills and tasks common to mainstream classes (Chamot & O'Malley, 1994; Mohan, Leung, & Davison, 2001; Short, 2002).

Content-based ESL instruction, however, has not been sufficient to help all ELs succeed academically. So the ESL profession developed the SI approach in conjunction with content teachers, and this process was accelerated by the educational reform movement. Through SI, which is described in more detail in the next section, ELs would participate in subject area classes with grade-level objectives delivered through modified instruction that made the information comprehensible to the students. In elementary schools, the ELs might be considered part of a sheltered instruction (SI) or SDAIE program, with the overall goal of teaching content to students learning English through a developmental language approach. SI is generally taught by elementary classroom teachers rather than ESL specialists and can be offered to students of all levels of English proficiency.

Sheltered instruction is an approach that can extend the time students have for getting language support services while giving them a jump start on the content subjects they will need for academic success. SI is *not* simply a set of additional or replacement instructional techniques that teachers implement in their classrooms. Instead, it draws from and complements methods advocated for both second language and mainstream classrooms. For example, some techniques include cooperative learning, connections to student experiences, targeted vocabulary development, slower speech and fewer idiomatic expressions for less proficient students, use of visuals and demonstrations, and use of adapted text and supplementary materials (Short & Echevarria, 2004).

Content-based ESL and SI are favored methods for ELs today, as reflected in the national English language proficiency (ELP) standards developed by the Teachers of English to Speakers of Other Languages (TESOL). Four of the five standards in the *PreK–12 English language proficiency standards* (TESOL, 2006) are specifically geared to the academic language of the core subject areas. Standards 2, 3, 4, and 5 state, "English language learners communicate information, ideas, and concepts necessary for academic success in the area of _____": language arts (#2), mathematics (#3), science (#4), and social studies (#5), respectively. By late 2008, nineteen states had adopted English language proficiency standards (ELP) similar to TESOL's, known as the WIDA (World-Class Instructional Design and Assessment) standards and the companion ELP test, ACCESS for ELLs® (ACCESS: Assessing Comprehension and Communication in English State to State for English Language Learners), to guide and measure annual gains in English language proficiency (WIDA consortium, 2007). To help their ELs meet the WIDA ELP standards, districts in these states, among others, are training teachers in content-based ESL and SI approaches, especially in the SIOP® Model, which we discuss later in this chapter.

SI plays a major role in a variety of educational program designs (Duff, 2005; Genesee, 1999). It may be part of an ESL program, a late-exit bilingual program, a two-way bilingual immersion program, a newcomer program, or a foreign language immersion program. In some districts, it is the name of the language support program itself. For students studying in content-based ESL or bilingual courses, SI often provides the bridge to the mainstream, and the amount of SI provided should increase as students move toward transition out of these programs. Any program in which students are learning content through a nonnative language should use the SI approach.

In some schools, SI is provided to classes composed entirely of ELs. In others, a heterogeneous mix of native and nonnative English speakers may be present. Bilingual, ESL, and grade-level classroom teachers may be the instructors for these classes (Sheppard, 1995). Ideally, all elementary school teachers would be trained in areas such as second language acquisition and ESL methodology although, as mentioned earlier, often that is not the case. At the high school level, sheltered content courses are generally delivered by content teachers so that students may receive the core content, not elective, credit required for graduation.

Research has shown, however, that a great deal of variability exists in the design of SI courses and the delivery of SI lessons, even among trained teachers (August & Hakuta, 1997; Berman et al., 1995; Sheppard, 1995) and within the same schools. Some schools, for instance, offer only SI courses in one subject area, such as social studies, but not in other areas ELs must study. It was our experience as well, after two decades of observing SI teachers in class, that one SI classroom did not look like the next in terms of the teacher's instructional language; the tasks the students have to accomplish; the degree of interaction that occurs between teacher and student, student and student, and student and text; the amount of class time devoted to language development issues versus assessing content knowledge; the learning strategies taught to and used by the students; the availability of appropriate materials; and more. This situation was the impetus for our research in the mid 1990s: to develop a valid, reliable, and effective model of SI.

In retrospect, this lack of consistency across SI classes was somewhat predictable. Sheltered curricula for different areas were few in number and varied widely from school district to school district. Commercial publishers offered a relatively small amount of instructional and pedagogical resources for sheltered courses. There was no model to follow. Teachers were encouraged to pick and choose techniques they enjoyed or believed work best with their students, and very few teachers were specially prepared to be SI teachers through undergraduate or graduate work. Few systematic and sustained forms of professional development were available for SI teachers.

The Sheltered Instruction Observation Protocol

The first version of the Sheltered Instruction Observation Protocol (SIOP®) was drafted in the early 1990s in order to exemplify the model of SI we were developing. We used it exclusively as a research and supervisory tool to determine if observed teachers incorporated key sheltered techniques consistently in their lessons. The preliminary instrument was field-tested with sheltered teachers and refined according to teacher feedback and observations in the classrooms. This early draft, like subsequent ones, pulled together findings and recommendations from the research literature with our professional experiences and those of our collaborating teachers on effective classroom-based practices from the areas of ESL, bilingual education, reading, language and literacy acquisition, discourse studies, special education, and classroom management. We sought to determine which combination of best practices in one instructional framework would yield positive achievement results for English learners.

In 1996, the National Center for Research on Education, Diversity & Excellence (CREDE) was funded by the Office of Educational Research and Improvement, U.S. Department of Education, and we designed a study on SI for its research program. The goals of the research project were to (1) develop an explicit model of sheltered instruction; (2) use that model to train teachers in effective sheltered strategies; and (3) conduct field experiments and collect data to evaluate teacher change and the effects of sheltered instruction on LEP students' English language development and content knowledge. (See Appendix C for a discussion of the research study and its findings.) The project built

FIGURE 1.2   *SIOP® Terminology*

SIOP® Model = the lesson planning and delivery system

SIOP® protocol = the instrument used to observe, rate, and
provide feedback on lessons

---

on preliminary versions of the SIOP® protocol as a small cohort of teachers worked with the researchers to refine the features further: distinguishing between effective strategies for beginner, intermediate, and advanced English learners; determining "critical" versus "unique" sheltered teaching strategies; and making the SIOP® more user friendly.

Over the course of the next three years, and with an expanded team of teachers from districts on both the East and West Coasts, the SIOP® continued to be refined, strengthened, and used for professional development with research project teachers (Short & Echevarria, 1999). A substudy confirmed the SIOP® protocol to be a valid and reliable measure of the SIOP® Model (Guarino et al., 2001). During this time, the teacher-researcher cohort suggested that the SIOP® become more than an observation protocol. They recommended that it become a lesson planning and delivery system as well. "If you are going to rate our lessons based on the protocol, shouldn't we use it to plan our lessons?" one of the teachers asked. And so the SIOP® term now refers to both the observation instrument for rating the fidelity of lessons to the model (as shown in Appendix A) and, as will be explained in detail in the following chapters, the instructional model for lesson planning and delivery. Figure 1.2 shows the terminology we will be using in this book to distinguish between these two uses. In addition, we will use SIOP® as a modifier to describe teachers implementing the model (SIOP® teachers) and lessons incorporating the thirty features (SIOP® lessons). The SIOP® term therefore refers to both the observation instrument for researchers, administrators, and teachers to match the implementation of a lesson to the model of instruction and the instructional model for teachers to plan and deliver lessons.

Specifically, the SIOP® protocol provides concrete examples of the features of SI that can enhance and expand teachers' instructional practice. The protocol is composed of thirty features grouped into eight main components: Lesson Preparation, Building Background, Comprehensible Input, Strategies, Interaction, Practice & Application, Lesson Delivery, and Review & Assessment. These components emphasize the instructional practices that are critical for second language learners as well as high-quality practices that benefit all students.

The six features under Lesson Preparation examine the lesson planning process, including the language and content objectives, the use of supplementary materials, and the meaningfulness of the activities. Building Background focuses on making connections with students' background experiences and prior learning and developing their academic vocabulary. Comprehensible Input considers adjusting teacher speech, modeling academic tasks, and using multimodal techniques to enhance comprehension. The Strategies component emphasizes teaching learning strategies to students, scaffolding instruction, and promoting higher-order thinking skills. The features of Interaction remind teachers to encourage elaborated speech and to group students appropriately for language and content development. Practice & Application provides activities to practice and extend language and content learning while Lesson Delivery ensures teachers present a lesson that meets the planned objectives. In the Review &

Assessment component, four features consider whether the teacher reviewed the key language and content concepts, assessed student learning, and provided feedback to students on their output.

From 1999 to 2002, the researchers field-tested and refined the SIOP® Model's professional development program, which incorporates key features of effective teacher development as recommended by Darling-Hammond (1998). The program includes professional development institutes (see *www.siopinstitute.net*), videotapes of exemplary SIOP® teachers (Hudec & Short, 2002a, 2002b), facilitator's guides (Echevarria & Vogt, 2008; Short, Hudec, & Echevarria, 2002), and other training materials.

Since that original CREDE SIOP® study, other research studies have been undertaken or are in progress (see Appendix C). In addition, school districts have conducted evaluations on their implementation of the model. (See *Implementing the SIOP® Model Through Effective Professional Development and Coaching,* Echevarria, Short & Vogt, 2008, for district information.)

The SIOP® Model

To learn about SIOP® implementation schoolwide, please view the corresponding video clip (Chapter 1, Module 1) on the accompanying CD.

As noted, the SIOP® Model described in this book is the product of several research studies conducted by the authors since the early 1990s. It is grounded in the professional literature and in the experiences and best practice of the researchers and participating teachers who worked collaboratively on developing the observation instrument that codifies it. The theoretical underpinning of the model is that language acquisition is enhanced through meaningful use and interaction. Through the study of content, students interact in English with meaningful material that is relevant to their schooling. Because language processes, such as listening, speaking, reading, and writing, develop interdependently (Genesee et al., 2006; August & Shanahan, 2006a), SIOP® lessons incorporate activities that integrate those skills.

In effective SIOP® lessons, language and content objectives are systematically woven into the curriculum of one particular subject area, such as fourth-grade language arts, social studies, algebra, or life science. Teachers generally present the regular, grade-level subject curriculum to the students through modified instruction in English, although some special curricula may be designed for students with significant gaps in their educational backgrounds or very low literacy skills. Teachers must develop the students' academic language proficiency consistently and regularly as part of the lessons and units they plan and deliver (Echevarria & Graves, 2007; Echevarria & Short, in press; Short, 2002). The SIOP® Model we have developed shares many techniques found in high-quality, nonsheltered teaching for native English speakers, but it is characterized by careful attention to the English learners' distinctive second language development needs.

Accomplished SIOP® teachers modulate the level of English used with and among students and make the content comprehensible through techniques such as the use of visual aids, modeling, demonstrations, graphic organizers, vocabulary previews, adapted texts, cooperative learning, peer tutoring, and native language support. They make specific connections between the content being taught and students' experiences and prior knowledge, and they focus on expanding the students' vocabulary base. Besides increasing students' declarative knowledge (i.e., factual information), SIOP® teachers highlight and model procedural knowledge (e.g., how to accomplish an academic task like writing a science report or conducting research on the Internet) along with study skills and learning strategies (e.g., note-taking and self-monitoring comprehension when reading).

In effective SIOP® lessons, there is a high level of student engagement and interaction with the teacher, with other students, and with text, which leads to elaborated discourse and critical thinking. Student language learning can be promoted through social interaction and contextualized communication as teachers guide students to construct meaning and understand complex concepts from texts and classroom discourse (Vygotsky, 1978). Students are explicitly taught functional language skills as well, such as how to negotiate meaning, confirm information, argue, persuade, and disagree. Teachers introduce them to the classroom discourse community and demonstrate skills like taking turns in a conversation and interrupting politely to ask for clarification. Through instructional conversations and meaningful activities, students practice and apply their new language and content knowledge.

SIOP® teachers also consider their students' affective needs, cultural backgrounds, and learning styles. They strive to create a nonthreatening environment where students feel comfortable taking risks with language. They socialize ELs to the implicit classroom culture, including appropriate behaviors and communication patterns. SIOP® teachers engage in culturally responsive teaching and build on the students' potentially different ways of learning, behaving, and using language (Bartolome, 1994). They also plan activities that tap into the auditory, visual, and kinesthetic preferences of the students. Many effective SIOP® teachers consider the multiple intelligences of their students as well, and provide a variety of assignments that might appeal to the logical/mathematical child, the musical child, the artist, and those with other intelligences (Gardner, 1993).

Depending on the students' proficiency levels, SIOP® teachers offer multiple pathways for students to demonstrate their understanding of the content. For example, teachers may plan pictorial, hands-on, or performance-based assessments for individual students, group tasks or projects, oral reports, written assignments, portfolios, and more common measures such as paper and pencil tests and quizzes to check student comprehension and language growth. In this way, teachers can receive a more accurate picture of most English learners' content knowledge and skills—through an assortment of assessment measures than through one standardized test (TESOL, 2001). Otherwise, student performance may be perceived as lack of mastery of the content when it is actually the normal pace of the second language acquisition process (Abedi & Lord, 2001; Solano-Flores & Trumbull, 2003).

The SIOP® Model is also distinguished by use of supplementary materials that support the academic text. These may include related reading texts (e.g., picture books, big books), graphs and other illustrations, models and other realia, audiovisual and computer-based resources, adapted text, and the like. The purpose of these materials is to enhance student understanding of key topics, issues, and details in the content concepts being taught through means other than teacher lecture or textbook prose. Supplementary materials can also aid teachers in providing information to students with mixed proficiency levels of English. Some students in a mixed class may be able to use the textbook while others may need an adapted text.

The SIOP® Model has been designed for flexibility and tested in a wide range of classroom situations: those with all ELs and those with a mix of native and nonnative

English speakers, those with students who have strong academic backgrounds and those with students who have had limited formal schooling, those with students who are recent arrivals and those who have been in U.S. schools for several years, those with students at beginning levels of English proficiency and those with students at advanced levels. The research evidence shows that the SIOP® Model can improve the academic literacy of ELs. In the original CREDE research, using an assessment of student expository writing (using pre- and postmeasures), students who participated in classes taught by teachers trained in the SIOP® Model improved their writing skills significantly more than students in classes with non-SI-trained teachers. In the more recent New Jersey SIOP® study, students with SIOP®-trained teachers made statistically significant gains in their average mean scores for oral language, writing, and total proficiency on the IDEA Proficiency Test (IPT), which had been the state assessment of English language proficiency, compared to a comparison group of ELs (Center for Applied Linguistics, 2007).

It is important to recognize that the SIOP® Model does not require teachers to throw away their favored techniques or add copious new elements to a lesson. Rather, this model of SI brings together *what* to teach by providing a framework for *how* to teach it. It reminds teachers to select and organize techniques that facilitate the integration of district- or state-level standards for ESL and for specific content areas.

Implementing the SIOP® Model: Getting Started

To hear the authors discuss the SIOP® model, please view the corresponding video clips (Chapter 1, Modules 2 and 3) on the accompanying CD.

The implementation of the SIOP® Model is one key to improving the academic success of English learners: Preservice teachers need it to develop a strong foundation in SI; practicing teachers need it to strengthen their lesson planning and delivery and to provide students with more consistent instruction. Site-based supervisors and administrators use it to train and coach teachers, and conduct classroom observations. Teacher education faculty also use the SIOP® Model in their methods courses and in student teacher supervision. As the SIOP® Model has become more broadly established across the United States and abroad, several applications have been put into practice:

- Teacher lesson plan checklist and self-assessment tool
- Research observation tool for fidelity of model implementation
- Supervision and observation tool for student teachers
- Classroom observation tool for administrators
- Program of professional development

If you are a teacher, you may begin using the SIOP® Model as a guide to teaching high-quality sheltered instruction. You may want to assess your areas of strength and your areas for improvement. As you consider your self-assessment, you may decide to focus on one component at a time. If you are unfamiliar with comprehensible input techniques, you may want to practice implementing them as a first step. Or you may need to become accustomed to writing language and content objectives (see Chapter 2) and the way those objectives influence sheltered lessons (see Chapters 8 and 9). As your proficiency in one area of the SIOP® Model is attained, other components of the model should be added to your teaching repertoire. Once you are familiar with the features in the individual components, you should use the SIOP® protocol as a lesson plan checklist to write your lessons and reflect on them after teaching. A new resource (Vogt & Echevarria, 2008) offers a multitude of teaching ideas and activities for enhancing SIOP® components in your lessons. In addition, books detailing SIOP® lessons for English-language arts, mathematics, history/social studies, and science are available (Vogt, Echevarria, & Short, in press; Echevarria, Vogt, & Short, in press; Short, Vogt, & Echevarria, in press; Short, Vogt, & Echevarria, in press).

If you are a coach, staff developer, or university field-experience supervisor, you need to understand that learning to implement the SIOP® Model is a process. Not all features will be observed to a high degree in the beginning stages. Working through the SIOP® Model systematically over time will be the most effective way to ensure it will become internalized and present in the elementary teachers' regular classroom practice. We encourage coaches and supervisors to use a collaborative approach with teachers who are implementing SI, including conferencing about observations, setting goals for implementing other features of the model, reflecting on progress in using the SIOP® Model, and so forth. The protocol is an excellent tool for targeted and productive discussions between a teacher and a supervisor. Another new resource, *Implementing the SIOP® Model Through Effective Professional Development and Coaching,* (Echevarria, Short, & Vogt, 2008) offers additional tips for professional development and coaching drawn from the experiences of school districts around the United States that have been implementing the SIOP® Model successfully for several years.

In some districts, school administrators are using the SIOP® protocol in a checklist format when they observe teachers. They mark if the feature is present or absent. It is important to note that we designed the protocol as an observation tool, not an evaluation instrument. The protocol is best used to rate the lesson being delivered and determine how faithful it is to the complete SIOP® Model. Administrators should not use the protocol for teacher evaluation, especially while the teachers are learning the model. To change their regular lesson style to the SIOP® Model, teachers must take some risks. Because the process takes time and is challenging, lessons should not be scored during the process. Additional considerations about implementing the SIOP® Model in a school from an administrator's perspective can be found in a third new resource, *The SIOP® Model for Administrators* (Short, Vogt, & Echevarria, 2008).

If you are a researcher, you can measure teachers' level of implementation of the SIOP® Model using the protocol. Because it is the only empirically validated, instructional approach for English learners at the time of this writing, more and more school districts are turning to the SIOP® Model for their staff development plan. However, it is important to determine if the investment in the SIOP® Model is paying off for the students' achievement. One way to check is to see if the teachers who are high implementers of the model are the ones whose students make the most progress.

Summary

Students who are learning English as an additional language are the fastest-growing segment of the school-age population in the United States, and almost all candidates in teacher education programs will have linguistically and culturally diverse students in their classes during their teaching careers. However, most of these future teachers—as well as most practicing teachers—are not well prepared to instruct these learners. Given school reform efforts and increased state accountability measures, this lack of teacher preparation puts ELs at risk of educational failure.

This book describes and illustrates a research-based, professional development model of SI, an effective approach for teaching both academic language and content to ELs that can increase English learners' chances of success in school. The SIOP® Model has been used with positive outcomes in several long-term, collaborative, professional development programs to train and coach teachers in implementing effective SI in their classes in urban, suburban, and rural districts around the United States. (See Appendix C.) The model is operationalized in the SIOP® protocol.

The SIOP® Model does not mandate cookie-cutter instruction, but it provides a framework for well-prepared and well-delivered sheltered lessons for any subject area. As SIOP® teachers design their lessons, they have room for creativity and the art of teaching. Nonetheless, critical instructional features must be attended to for teachers to respond appropriately to the unique academic and language development needs of these students. As you read through this book, you will have the opportunity to explore ways to enhance, expand, and improve your own instructional practice through use of the SIOP® Model.

Discussion Questions

1. Consider the English learners in one elementary school class. Identify the individual and sociocultural factors that may influence the educational success of these students. In what ways might SIOP® Model instruction help them?

2. How would you characterize the type(s) of instruction offered to English learners in your school or schools you know: a pull-out program with a traditional ESL or content-based ESL curriculum, a self-contained regular grade-level classroom with all ELs, a regular grade-level classroom with ELs and native English speakers and an ESL teacher who co-teaches (i.e., pushes in), and/or a regular grade-level classroom with ELs and native English speakers and no additional language support? Provide evidence of your characterization in terms of curricula and instruction. Are the ELs successful when they exit English language support programs and are in regular classrooms without support, either in the upper elementary grades or in middle school? Explain.

3. Many classroom teachers, whether they had special training in ESL methods or in second language acquisition, fail to take advantage of the language learning opportunities for young ELs in their classes. Why do you think this is so? Offer two concrete suggestions for these teachers to enhance their students' language development.

4. Look at one of your own lesson plans. Which characteristics of the SIOP® Model do you already incorporate? Consider the components and features of the model as found in Appendix A.

Lesson Preparation

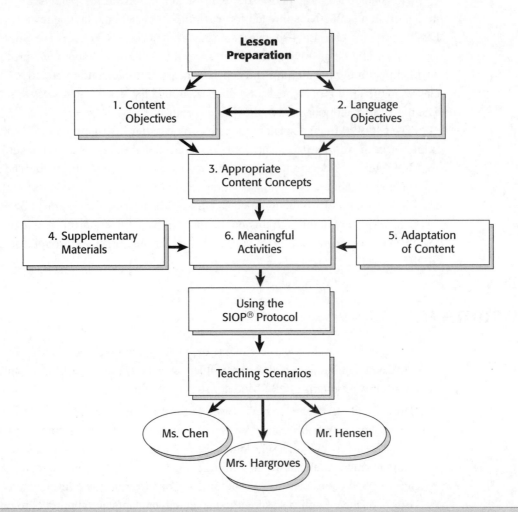

In this and subsequent chapters, we offer an explanation of each component and feature on the SIOP® (Sheltered Instruction Observation Protocol) protocol. Each chapter begins with the explanation of the SIOP® component, offers classroom activities, and then follows with descriptions of the same lesson taught by three different teachers. The lessons throughout the book are on varied topics and at different elementary grade levels.

This chapter introduces the first component of the SIOP® Model, Lesson Preparation. Following the background information and the rationale for each of the six features in this component, you will find an overview of the lesson topic and then teaching scenarios involving three teachers. As you read these, think about the SIOP® features that have been previously described, and prepare to rate the lessons according to them. Reflect on how effectively the teacher is meeting the needs of English learners (ELs) in relation to each feature. At the conclusion of the teaching scenarios, we offer our assessment of the teachers' efforts to shelter content instruction, and we invite you to compare your appraisal to ours.

Background

As we all know, lesson planning is critical to both a student's and a teacher's success. For maximum learning to occur, planning must produce lessons that enable students to make connections between their own knowledge and experiences and the new information being taught (Rumelhart, 2004). With careful planning, we make learning meaningful and relevant by including appropriate motivating materials and activities that foster real-life application of concepts studied.

Traditionally, to meet the needs of students who struggled with grade-level reading materials, texts have been rewritten according to readability formulae or lexile levels (Gray & Leary, 1935; Ruddell, 2005; Stenner & Burdick, 1997). The adapted texts included controlled vocabulary and a limited number of concepts, resulting in the omission of critical pieces of information. We have learned that if students' exposure to content concepts is limited by vocabulary-controlled materials, the amount of information they learn over time is considerably less than that of their peers who use grade-level texts. The result is that the "rich get richer and the poor get poorer" (Stanovich, 1986). That is, instead of closing the gap between native English speakers and ELs, the learning gap is increased and eventually it becomes nearly impossible to close. Therefore, it is imperative we plan lessons that are not negatively biased for students acquiring English and that include age-appropriate content and materials.

This component, Lesson Preparation, is therefore very important to the SIOP® Model. If properly prepared, a lesson will include most of the SIOP® features in advance. It is then up to the teachers and class to accomplish them as the lesson unfolds. However, when planning, teachers have asked how they can meet all thirty features in a given period. We explain that a SIOP® lesson may be single day or multiday in length. Over the course of several days, all thirty features should be met. See Vogt and Echevarria (2008, pp. 8–9) for a SIOP® lesson-planning flow chart.

As teachers learn the model, we strongly encourage them to write out lessons in detail. They may use the SIOP® protocol as a checklist to ensure they incorporate all of the features. In addition, they may want to try one or more of the lesson plan templates we have included in Appendix B or the templates in Chapter 7 of *Implementing the SIOP® Model Through Effective Professional Development and Coaching* (Echevarria, Short, & Vogt, 2008). All of these templates have been used successfully in classrooms.

"How do I start implementing the lessons?" is a frequent question from teachers new to the SIOP® Model. We suggest that elementary school teachers begin with one subject area so they do not have to write multiple SIOP® lessons for each day. In some cases, teachers may learn the SIOP® Model over time, component by component, and they build their lesson plans in the same way. Once teachers have internalized the model, they may write less detailed lesson plans. They will find that creating SIOP® lessons across subject areas is easier once they have mastered the SIOP® Model in one area.

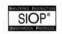 ## SIOP® FEATURE 1:
Content Objectives Clearly Defined, Displayed, and Reviewed with Students

In effective instruction, concrete content objectives that identify what students should know and be able to do must guide teaching and learning. For the most part, these objectives support school, district, or state content standards and learning outcomes. Frequently, in texts and teachers' guides, content objectives and state standards are complex and not written in a manner that is accessible to ELs. This is often the case for standards written for elementary grades. Teachers may or may not present them to students. In other cases, standards are too generic or broad, such as "Describe the phases of the water cycle and interpret the impact of human use of water as a resource on the cycle." Given either situation, it is important to write lesson-level objectives (something that can be taught and learned in a lesson or two) and use student-friendly language that suits the age and proficiency levels in the class. Even if young English learners in kindergarten and first grade cannot read the written objectives yet, the objectives should be posted with simple phrasings, key words, illustrations or rebuses, and read aloud. The bottom line for English learners is that content objectives need to be written in terms of what students will learn or do; be stated simply, orally and in writing; and tied to specific grade-level content standards (Echevarria & Graves, 2007). Also, it may be necessary to limit content objectives to only one or two per lesson to reduce the complexity of the learning task.

Most of us learned about the importance of writing and teaching to content objectives early in our professional preparation. However, it is often easy to overlook sharing the objectives, orally and in writing, with students. One of the sheltered teachers who was learning the SIOP® Model explained her growing awareness of the importance of clearly stated content objectives that are displayed for ELs:

> The objectives are still going on in my class. They're on the board every day and the students are getting used to seeing them, reading them out loud, and evaluating whether or not we achieved them at the end of each class. I still have questions about the wording and what's a good objective . . . but that will come with time and more discussion and study. I just wanted to say that defining the objectives each day definitely brings more focus to my planning and thinking, and it helps bring order to my classroom procedures. So far, it has not been too burdensome and the habit is definitely forming.

Teachers use different approaches when they present the objectives to the class. One teacher asked the students to focus on the verbs in the statements and generated a discussion about what they would be doing in the lesson. Another teacher asked student partners to discuss one objective at a time and to try to determine what it meant. The student pairs shared their explanations with the class. As needed, the teacher paraphrased or gave examples.

Examples of content objectives and language objectives, discussed below, can be found throughout each chapter in this book, in the *99 Ideas and Activities for Teaching English Learners with the SIOP® Model* (Vogt & Echevarria, 2008) resource, in lesson plans presented in *Science for English Language Learners* (Fathman & Crowther, 2006) in *Helping English Language Learners Succeed in Pre-K-Elementary Schools* (Lacina, Levine, & Sowa, 2006), and on the websites www.cal.org and www.siopinstitute.net.

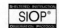

SIOP® FEATURE 2:
Language Objectives Clearly Defined, Displayed, and Reviewed with Students

While carefully planning and delivering content objectives, SIOP® teachers must also incorporate in their lesson plans activities that support students' academic language development (Short, 1999). This hallmark of the SIOP® Model, the incorporation of language objectives in every lesson, has been endorsed by Gersten and colleagues (2007) in a recent

FIGURE 2.1 *Process-to-Performance Verbs*

Process-Oriented ----->----->----->	Performance-Oriented
Explore	Define
Listen to	Draft
Recognize	Write
Discuss in small groups	Give an oral presentation
	Edit

research-based practice guide for ELs in elementary grades. Recommendation 4 of that document from the U.S. Department of Education states: "Ensure that the development of formal or academic English is a key instructional goal for English learners, beginning in the primary grades" (p. 16). As with content objectives, language objectives should be stated clearly and simply, and students should be informed of them, both orally and in writing.

When considering which language objectives to include in a lesson and how to write them, it is important to keep in mind that acquiring a second language is a process. As such, language objectives may cover a range from process-oriented to performance-oriented statements so that students have a chance to explore, and then practice, before demonstrating mastery of an objective. The following objectives from a SIOP® language arts class show the progression of objectives that might be taught over one week:

Students will be able to

1. Recognize similes in text (day 1)

2. Discuss the functions of similes (day 2)

3. Write three similes (day 3)

4. Write a paragraph that describes a setting using similes (days 4–5)

For the first lesson, students learn to recognize similes in text, perhaps by focusing on the key words *like* and *as*. Then in the next lesson, they develop an understanding of the purpose of similes. Only after that are they tapped to generate their own similes, first in decontextualized sentences, then in a paragraph.

Figure 2.1 displays possible verbs for objective statements that reflect this process-to-performance continuum.

When determining language objectives, it is also important to distinguish between receptive and productive language skills. English learners tend to develop receptive skills (listening and reading) faster than productive skills (speaking and writing), but all the skills should be worked on in a unified way. Students don't have to learn to speak, for instance, before they learn to read and write (August & Shanahan, 2006a). Moreover, we cannot ignore oral language practice and focus our objectives only on reading and writing. We know from research (Goldenberg, 2008; Guthrie & Ozgungor, 2002) that the absence of planned speaking practice—be it formal or informal—by ELs in content class-rooms is detrimental to the development of academic English. Gibbons (2003) argues that skillful teachers should take advantage of oral interaction to move students from informal, everyday explanations of a content topic (e.g., a scientific process) to the more special-ized academic register of the formal written and spoken code. Schleppegrell and col-leagues (Schleppegrell, 2004; Schleppegrell, Achugar, & Orteíza, 2004) have conducted linguistic analysis of the lexical and grammatical forms that construe meaning in written and spoken school discourse and have identified implications for instruction. SIOP® teachers might make the development of specialized grammar and lexical forms part of their scope and sequence of language objectives.

A wide variety of language objectives can be planned according to the goals and activities in the lesson. In some cases, language objectives may focus on developing students' vocabulary, which is of critical importance for English learners who have to close significant gaps in their academic vocabulary knowledge. Other lessons may lend themselves to developing phonemic awareness or reading comprehension skills, or helping students to brainstorm, draft, revise, and edit a text. Students also benefit from objectives that highlight functional language use such as how to request information, present opinions, negotiate meaning, provide detailed explanations, and so forth. Higher-order thinking skills, such as articulating predictions or hypotheses, stating conclusions, summarizing information, and making comparisons, can be tied to language objectives, too. Sometimes specific grammar points can be taught as well; for example, learning about capitalization when studying famous historical events and persons, or teaching word parts to help ELs develop new vocabulary. These ideas will be expanded upon in the next section.

Teachers are interested in sources of language objectives. The first place to start is the national or state English language proficiency [ELP] standards (also known as English language development [ELD] or English as a second language [ESL] standards). National standards for English language proficiency have been developed by the Teachers of English to Speakers of Other Languages (TESOL) association. Four of the five standards in the *Pre-K–12 English language proficiency standards* (TESOL, 2006) address the academic language of the core subject areas and therefore offer an excellent resource for SIOP® language objectives. Nineteen states have adopted a common set of English language development standards similar to TESOL's and formed the WIDA (World-Class Instructional Design and Assessment) Consortium. This consortium has compiled a list of "Can Do" descriptors that can help teachers identify the kind of language tasks students should be able to perform according to five differing levels of English proficiency. (To view these descriptors, go to http://www.wida.us/standards/CAN_DOs/)

Other resources include the state English language arts standards and state content standards that include a strand focused on communication. Ideas for objectives will be found in all of these official documents as well as in local district curricula, especially for elementary reading and language arts. Instructional materials are another source. By reviewing textbooks and other materials, you can see if there are language skills and academic vocabulary that students need to develop in order to comprehend the information.

One final critical source for successful SIOP® lesson implementation is your colleagues. If you are a grade-level classroom teacher, pair up with an ESL or bilingual teacher. Tap his or her expertise for language topics and knowledge of the ELs' academic language needs. (The recent book from the National Science Teachers Association, *Science for English Language Learners* [Fathman & Crowther, 2006] is an excellent resource. Each chapter was a collaboration between a language specialist and a science educator. It includes science lessons with language and content objectives.) If you are an ESL teacher, you have a plethora of language objectives at your disposal. You need to partner with one or more grade-level classroom teachers to identify content objectives they perceive their ELs need assistance with and align them to your language ones.

To see an example of integrating language objectives, please view the corresponding video clip (Chapter 2, Module 1) on the accompanying CD.

You may want to focus on thematic units to cover a variety of content topics or focus on one subject area per quarter. (See Lacina, Levine, and Sowa, 2006, for examples of collaboration between elementary ESL and classroom teachers.)

Remember, as you teach and assess these language objectives in your lessons, you can plan for multilevel responses from the students according to their proficiency in English. For example, you might use group response techniques (e.g., thumbs-up/thumbs-down) for students who are in the early stages of English language development. For students who are more proficient English speakers, incorporate activities that involve partner work and small group assignments so that ELs can practice their English in a less threatening setting. When possible, accept approximations and multiple word responses rather than complete sentences because this supports English development. However, it is also appropriate to require ELs, depending on their level of proficiency, to give answers in one or two complete sentences. This requirement helps develop language skills because it advances students beyond what may be their comfort zone in using English.

Writing Content and Language Objectives

To see an example of writing content and language objectives in lessons, please view the corresponding video clip (Chapter 2, Module 2) on the accompanying CD.

All the content and language objectives should evolve from the lesson topic and be part of the instructional plan. After a teacher writes content and language objectives, posts them, and discusses them with the students at the start of class, at some point in the lesson explicit instruction must be provided on these objectives. Students would then have opportunities to practice with the objectives and be assessed on their progress toward meeting them at the close of the lesson. In other words, each objective is what we want the students to learn, and each needs explicit attention. An objective is not a by-product of an activity but the foundation of one.

Content objectives as mentioned earlier are usually drawn from the state subject area standards. Consider this standard of learning from Virginia: "Students will investigate and understand the basic needs and life processes of plants and animals." It is too broad to be addressed in one lesson, but it is written in a straightforward manner. Surprisingly, however, it is an objective for kindergarten. Posting this objective word for word in the kindergarten classroom would not be successful. How might you rewrite it to present to five- and six-year-olds? You might write the following on a lesson plan: "Students will identify parts of a tree and their functions"; but for the students you might write on the board, "Identify parts of a tree. Tell what the parts do." When you explain it, you might elaborate, "Today you will learn about parts of a tree (show a picture or drawing). You will be able to identify the parts (point to the different parts) and tell what the parts do (explain that leaves make food for the tree)."

After you have rewritten the state standard as an appropriate content objective for the kindergartners, you will need to plan the lesson and determine a language objective. One teacher we worked with combined the science lesson with a reading of *The Giving Tree* (Silverstein, 1988). For his language objective, he decided on "Students will listen to *The Giving Tree* and act out the story miming vocabulary words (trunk, branch, leaf)." He explained to the students that they would listen to a story, look at the pictures, name the parts of the tree, and then act out parts of the tree when he read the story again. In this lesson, he would therefore reinforce the skill of listening for specific information and have students physically demonstrate their understanding of vocabulary terms.

Although incorporating language objectives in all content lessons is a hallmark of the SIOP® Model, it is a challenging proposition for many classroom teachers. It requires a new way of thinking about their subject, specifically both the written and spoken discourse. It also requires them to know their students' proficiency levels so the language objectives can be targeted to what the students need to learn about the academic language of social studies, science, or mathematics but not be at a level too high for their current understanding. Note that even if you have students with mixed levels of English proficiency in class, we do not suggest you write different language objectives for each proficiency level. Instead, write an objective that all students should attain based on the content concepts in the lesson but adjust the intended outcomes (such as the work product) to match the students' ability levels. Some students may master the objective by the end of the lesson; others will be at some point on a path toward mastery.

Because elementary classroom teachers usually have their students for the full day, they have some flexibility in teaching the language objectives. With careful planning, a language objective introduced in the science lesson can be reinforced in the language arts lesson, particularly if there is a complex grammatical or usage construct to convey to the students. However, the SIOP® Model does not support eliminating language objectives from the content lessons because they could be covered in the language arts or reading time. It is important instead to have language and content objectives for each subject so the children have explicit instruction targeting how the academic language is used within each subject area.

Content-based ESL teachers who may have pull-out or push-in assignments sometimes face the opposite challenge. They are familiar with language objectives and often have a syllabus that systematically introduces them to students. They need assistance in identifying appropriate content objectives to add to their lessons. In a similar way to classroom teachers, they may feel unprepared for in-depth instruction on a content topic. For these reasons, we advocate that classroom and language teachers collaborate closely as they prepare lessons and help their students meet language and content goals.

The six categories in Figure 2.2 on the following pages (adapted from Short, Hudec, & Echevarria, 2002) offer a starting point for generating language objectives. Teachers need to think about how language will be used in their lesson: in their speech, in class discussion, in the reading assignments, in the lesson activities. Then given the content topic and an understanding of the students' degree of academic language acquisition, the teacher writes an objective that complements the topic and can be explicitly addressed in the lesson. Sample objectives listed in Figure 2.2 could be incorporated into several lessons throughout a third grade math unit on geometry.

Sometimes the language and content objectives may be closely linked as in the following upper elementary math lesson:

- Students will solve word problems using a two-step process.
- Students will write a word problem for a classmate to solve requiring a two-step process.

The first statement is the content objective. It focuses on a mathematical procedure. The second is the language objective, wherein students practice mathematical writing skills.

FIGURE 2.2 *Categories and Examples for Developing Language Objectives*

Consider these six categories as a starting point for generating a language objective. Think about your content topic and how language will be used in your lesson: in your speech, in the reading assignments, and in the lesson activities. Given the content topic and your understanding of the students' degree of academic language acquisition, write an objective that complements the topic and that can be addressed explicitly in the lesson. Examples of language objectives are listed below and could occur over several lessons in a third-grade mathematics unit on geometry.

- **Key Vocabulary** refers to the **technical terms, concept words, and other words** needed to discuss, read, or write about the topic of the lesson (e.g., names of important people, places, and events; scientific and mathematical terms; social studies or health concepts) can become language objectives. The "other words" subset includes process words and words like comparatives (e.g., *both, are similar, greater than*), conjunctions (e.g., *so, but, however*), and transition phrases (e.g., *first, next, after that, during the second phase*).

    An example objective is

    Students will be able to define the terms *geometric figure, two-dimensional, three-dimensional, and congruent* **orally and in writing.**

    Therefore, in this lesson, the teacher will spend time making sure English learners become familiar with these definitions and can use them, with support as needed.

- **Language Functions** refer to the ways students use language in the lesson. The lesson may call for students to describe, compare, or predict, for example. Some state standards are organized in this way and are a good source for ideas.

    An example objective is

    Students will be able to compare geometric figures and describe characteristics that are similar or different.

    If a lesson focuses on language functions, the teacher will spend time teaching or reviewing the purpose and procedures for the targeted language use. In this case, the teacher might provide sentence starters or sentence frames (e.g., The two triangles are congruent because _____. Both figures have _____ so they are similar.).

- **Language Skills** are the reading, writing, listening, and speaking skills students need to learn. Skills should be taught directly, practiced, and reviewed. The skills need to link to the topic of the lesson. In a language arts class, for example, will students need to read and determine a main idea? In social studies, will they need to listen to an audio or video recording and identify the speaker's point of view regarding an historical conflict? In science class, will they have to record their observations during an experiment?

    An example objective is

    Students will be able to listen to teacher descriptions in order to draw different types of parallelograms.

    In this lesson on geometric figures, the teacher may teach listening comprehension skills, orally describing attributes of figures (e.g., this figure has four right angles and four equal sides) and asking students to draw the shapes or construct them on a geoboard.

- **Grammar or Language Structures** can be taught when they are prevalent in the written or spoken discourse of the class. They might include questioning patterns, past or future tense verbs, paragraph writing, pronoun usage, or sentence formation. Structural clues for words like roots (-form-), prefixes (semi-,) and suffixes (-tion) can be addressed in this category as well.

    An example objective is

    Students will be able to use comparative phrases, such as *greater than, larger than, smaller than, less than,* **and** *equal to* **orally and in writing when describing geometric figures and angles.**

    The teacher might introduce or review these phrases and also show the appropriate mathematical symbols (i.e., >, <, and =). The purpose is to do more than have students understand the concept of relative proportions; they need to be able to articulate the differences and similarities.

- **Lesson Tasks** are a source for language objectives as well. Teachers consider what language is embedded in a lesson assignment that could be pulled forth and turned into explicit instruction in language. Will the student need language to play a particular role in a cooperative learning group? Will the students have to take notes or explain a procedure to one another?

(Continued)

FIGURE 2.2 *Continued*

An example objective is

Students will be able to record real-life examples of three-dimensional figures and describe their uses.

This example shows how a language objective can be built around an application task. In this task, students look for real-life examples of three-dimensional shapes (e.g., a soccer ball is a sphere, a salt shaker is a cylinder), then record how the shape is used and for what purpose.

- **Language Learning Strategies** may include corrective strategies (e.g., reread confusing text), self-monitoring strategies (e.g., make and confirm predictions), prereading strategies (e.g., relate to personal experience), or language practice strategies (e.g., repeat or rehearse phrases, visualize). Teaching students with Latin-based native languages to consider cognates when they see new academic terms is a very powerful strategy as well.

An example objective is

Students will be able to represent data in a bar graph.

Because interpreting graphs and charts are important skills in the content areas, the teacher may teach students how to convert data (e.g., a list of the number of squares, rectangles, and rhombuses found in an illustration) into a graphic representation. Similarly, in a separate lesson, the teacher will want to teach students how to interpret graphs and charts, orally and in writing.

At other times, the language objective might extend the content knowledge as in this grade 6 geography lesson:

- Students will be able to (SWBAT) identify specific landforms on a map of South America.
- SWBAT present an oral report about one landform and its influence on a country's history.

For language arts and reading teachers, teasing apart language and content objectives can be tricky. Certain curriculum concepts like *plot* and *setting* are clearly ingredients for language arts content objectives, but some potential objectives like "produce writing that conveys a clear point of view and maintains a consistent tone" could be either a language or a content objective. We encourage language arts and reading teachers nonetheless to consistently identify a content and a language objective for each lesson, even if some might be placed in either category. Because we are aiming for whole-school implementation of the SIOP® Model, having students recognize and expect both types of objectives across all their classes is a valuable goal.

 The following objectives are from a fifth-grade language arts class. Which one is the content objective and which is the language objective? Justify your answer.

- SWBAT use descriptive adjectives to write sentences about the characters.
- SWBAT compare traits of two characters in a story.

You are an ESL teacher who pushes into a first-grade classroom in which one-third of the students are beginning or intermediate-level English learners. Your co-teacher has asked for your help preparing students for an upcoming unit on motion. The state standard is "The student will investigate and understand that objects may vibrate and produce sound when they move." You intend to present a lesson to build background on this topic. Write a language and content objective for this class.

As you write your objectives, keep the verbs in Figure 2.3 in mind. Although the verbs are not exclusive to one type or another, they are more common to the category presented. Over time, add to this list to further distinguish between the content and language goals of your lesson.

FIGURE 2.3   *Verbs for Writing Content and Language Objectives*

Verbs for Content Objectives	Verbs for Language Objectives
Identify	Listen for
Solve	Retell
Investigate	Define
Distinguish	Find the main idea
Hypothesize	Compare
Create	Summarize
Select	Rehearse
Draw conclusions about	Persuade
.	Write
.	.
.	.
	.

Once you have written your content and language objectives, you might use this checklist to evaluate them:

—— The objectives are observable.

—— The objectives are written and presented in language the students can understand.

—— The content objective is related to the key concept of the lesson.

—— The language objective promotes student academic language growth (it is not something most students already do well).

—— The language objective connects clearly with the lesson topic or lesson activities.

—— I have a plan for assessing student progress on meeting these objectives during the lesson.

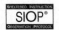

SIOP® FEATURE 3:
Content Concepts Appropriate for Age and Educational Background

SIOP® teachers must carefully consider the content concepts they wish to teach and use district curriculum guidelines and grade-level content standards as guides. In SIOP® classrooms, this entails ensuring that, although materials may be adapted to meet the needs of English learners, the content is not diminished. When planning lessons around content concepts, consider the following: (1) the students' first language (L1) literacy, (2) their second language (L2) proficiency, (3) their reading ability, (4) the cultural and age appropriateness of the L2 materials, and (5) the difficulty level of the material to be read (Gunderson, 1991, p. 21).

In some cases, students with major gaps in their educational backgrounds may be placed in newcomer programs or specialized classes that pull objectives and content concepts from earlier grades to provide the foundational knowledge the students need to perform grade-level work successfully and catch up to their classmates (Short & Boyson, 2004). In general, it is inappropriate to use the curriculum materials and books from much earlier grades. Students in high school who are developing literacy for the first time should not be reading about "doggies and birdies," for example. Other materials should be found, and if necessary, the teacher should provide the scaffolding needed to understand the content concepts. Ideally, specialized courses would be developed to accelerate their learning, such as FAST Math developed by Fairfax County (VA) Public Schools (Helman & Buchanan, 1993), which can help students gain several years' worth of mathematics instruction in one subject area in six months to one year.

Additionally, reflect on the amount of background experience needed to learn and apply the content concepts and include ways to activate students' prior knowledge related to them. For example, fourth-grade students typically learn about magnetism, yet some ELs may not have the requisite background knowledge to understand this concept. Rather than diminish the content, use what prior knowledge students do have, perhaps about attraction, and then explicitly build background information as a foundation for their understanding of magnetism.

Providing adequate background requires teachers to perform a *task analysis*—a process in which you carefully analyze the requisite knowledge a student must possess to understand what is being taught. The purpose is to lessen the gap between what a student knows and what he or she must learn. This can be accomplished by modifying the lesson to include substantial background building, or through a small-group minilesson that precedes the regular whole-class lesson (Vogt, 2000). This minilesson provides a "jump start" by reviewing key background concepts, introducing vocabulary, leading a picture or text "walk" through the reading material, engaging in simulations or role-plays, or using hands-on experiential activities. The jump-start minilesson develops context and gives access to children who may lack appropriate background knowledge or experience with the grade-level content concepts. In heterogeneous classes in which ELs study with native English speakers, peer tutors can be used to teach some of the requisite background information as well.

You are the one to decide when to modify content concepts by providing extensive background building for the whole class, or by teaching a brief jump-start lesson to a small group. If you have a large number of English learners who are in the early stages of language development, you may need to include extensive background building. If you have a small group of ELs who have intermediate language proficiency, the jump-start minilesson may provide sufficient scaffolding and access to the content concepts. Alternately, in situations in which an ESL teacher and a content teacher work collaboratively with the same group of students, the ESL teacher can offer lessons that build background and vocabulary before the ELs study the topic in their regular or sheltered content class.

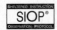

SIOP® FEATURE 4:
Supplementary Materials Used to a High Degree

To see an example of a lesson with high usage of supplementary materials, please view the corresponding video clip (Chapter 2, Module 3) on the accompanying CD.

Information that is embedded in context allows English learners to understand and complete more cognitively demanding tasks. Effective SIOP® instruction involves the use of many supplementary materials that support the core curriculum and contextualize learning. This is especially important for students who do not have grade-level academic backgrounds and/or who have language and learning difficulties. Because lectures and pencil-and-paper activities centered on a text are often difficult for these students, remember to plan for supplementary materials that will enhance meaning and clarify confusing concepts, making lessons more relevant. Fortunately, many elementary instructional programs, for mathematics and reading, for instance, are now offered with supplementary materials, including trade books at different reading levels, manipulatives, picture cards, and so on.

A variety of supplementary materials also supports different learning styles and multiple intelligences because information and concepts are presented in a multifaceted manner. Students can see, hear, feel, perform, create, and participate in order to make connections and construct personal, relevant meanings. Supplementary materials provide a real-life context and enable students to bridge prior experiences with new learning.

Examples of supplementary materials that can be used to create context and support content concepts include the following:

- **Hands-on manipulatives:** These can include anything from counter chips for math to microscopes for science to globes for social studies. Manipulating objects physically can reduce the language load of an activity; beginning students in particular can still participate and demonstrate their understanding.

- **Realia:** These are real-life objects that enable students to make connections to their own lives. Examples include play money (coins and bills) for a unit on money, or nutrition labels on food products for a health unit.

- **Pictures:** Photographs and illustrations depict nearly any object, process, or setting, and magazines, commercial photos, and hand drawings can provide visual support for a wide variety of content and vocabulary concepts and can build background knowledge.

- **Visuals:** These can include overhead transparencies, models, graphs, charts, timelines, maps, props, and bulletin board displays. Students with diverse abilities often have difficulty processing an inordinate amount of auditory information and are aided with visual clues.

- **Multimedia:** A wide variety of multimedia materials are available to enhance teaching and learning. These range from simple tape recordings to videos, DVDs, interactive CD-ROMs, and an increasing number of resources available on the World Wide Web. Brief video clips at www.unitedstreaming.com are effective tools. For some students and tasks, media in the students' native language may be a valuable source of information. It is important to preview websites for appropriateness and readability, especially when using them with beginning and intermediate-level students.

- **Demonstrations:** Demonstrations provide visual support and modeling for ELs. If you have a lesson task that includes supplementary materials, then you can scaffold information by carefully planning demonstrations that model how to use the materials and follow directions. Students can then practice these steps in groups or alone, with you or other experienced individuals nearby to assist as needed.

- **Related literature:** A wide variety of fiction and nonfiction can be included to support content teaching. The literature enables readers to create what Rosenblatt (1991) refers to as an "aesthetic response." This type of literature response is characterized by personal feelings about what is read. Aesthetic responses to literature promote more reading of literature, and hopefully, a deeper understanding of the concepts that are depicted—what Rosenblatt refers to as a *transactional experience.* Many elementary classroom teachers create libraries in their rooms with trade books on key topics. Students can read these as supplements to the textbook. They offer a more relaxing way to look at a topic in more depth.

- **Hi-lo readers:** Some publishers are now offering classic literature as well as fiction and nonfiction selections in a hi-lo format. The stories are of high interest but lower readability levels and tend to include many visuals. Some books are grouped thematically and can accompany different content areas and language arts courses. They are useful for students at lower proficiency levels in English.

- **Adapted text:** A type of supplementary reading material that can be very effective for English learners, as well as struggling readers, is adapted text. Without significantly diminishing the content concepts, a piece of text (usually from a grade-level textbook) is adapted to reduce the readability demands. Complicated, lengthy sentences with specialized terminology are rewritten in smaller chunks. Definitions are given for difficult vocabulary, if possible, in context. Please note that we are not advocating "dumbing down" the textbook, an approach that in the past yielded easy-to-read materials with virtually no content concepts left intact. Rather, we suggest that the major concepts be retained and just the readability level of the text be reduced.

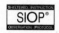

SIOP® FEATURE 5:
Adaptation of Content to All Levels of Student Proficiency

In many schools, teachers are required to teach from textbooks that are too difficult for English learners to read. We have previously mentioned the problem of "watering down" text to the point where all students can read it; content concepts are frequently lost when the text is adapted in this way. We also know ELs cannot be expected to learn all content information by listening to lectures.

Therefore, we must find ways to make the text and other resource materials accessible for all students, adapting them so that the content concepts are left intact. Several ways of doing this have been recommended for students who have reading difficulties (Readance, Bean, & Baldwin, 2001; Ruddell, 2005; Vacca & Vacca, 2004; Vogt, 1992), and they work equally well for ELs. These approaches can be used throughout a lesson, as a prereading instructional strategy, as an aid during reading, and as a postreading method for organizing newly learned information.

Suggestions for adapting content to make it more accessible include the following:

- **Graphic organizers:** These are schematic diagrams that provide conceptual clarity for information that is difficult to grasp. They help students identify key content concepts and make relationships among them (McLaughlin & Allen, 2002). Graphic organizers also provide students with visual clues they can use to supplement written or spoken words that may be hard to understand. Prior to reading, students can use the organizers as a guide and as a supplement to build background for difficult or dense text. When used concurrently with reading, they focus students' attention and help them make connections between concepts (e.g., Venn diagram), take notes (e.g., T-chart), and understand the text structure (e.g., a timeline informs students the text will be organized chronologically). When used after reading, graphic organizers can be employed to record personal understandings and responses (Buehl, 2009). Graphic organizers include story or text structure charts, Venn diagrams, story or text maps, timelines, discussion webs, word webs, clusters, thinking maps, and so forth. Vogt & Echevarria (2008) include a number of templates for these graphic organizers.

- **Outlines:** Teacher-prepared outlines equip students with a form for note-taking while reading dense portions of text, thus providing scaffolded support. These are especially helpful if major concepts, such as the Roman numeral level of the outline, are already filled in. The students can then add other information to the outline as they read. For some students, an outline that is entirely completed may be helpful to use as a guide to reading and understanding the text. Figure 2.4 shows an example of a scaffolded outline for a reading from a fifth-grade text on the circulatory system.

FIGURE 2.4 *Scaffolded Outline*

The Circulatory System

   I. Major Organs
      A. Heart
         1. Pumps blood throughout the body
         2. _____
      B. _____
         1. _____
         2. _____

  II. Major Vessels
      A. Artery
         1. Takes blood away from heart
         2. _____
      B. Vein
         1. _____
         2. _____
      C. _____
         1. Connects arteries and veins
         2. _____

 III. Types of Blood Cells
      A. Red blood cells
         1. _____
      B. _____
         1. Fights disease
      C. Platelets
         1. _____

- **Leveled study guides:** These study guides, usually for grade 3 and higher, are designed specifically for diverse students' needs. All students are expected to master the key concepts in the text; however, depending on students' language and literacy development, the leveled study guides are written differently. For some students who can easily read the text material, the study guides extend and enrich the subject material and they include challenging questions or tasks. For other students, leveled study guides lead them through the material with definitions and "hints" for unlocking the meaning, and they include fewer challenging questions and tasks. For some ELs and struggling readers, the study guides may include brief summaries of the text along with more manageable questions and tasks. Questions, tasks, and statements on the leveled study guides can be marked with asterisks as follows (from most manageable to most challenging):

*All students are to respond to these questions/statements/tasks

**Group 1 students are required to complete these questions/statements/tasks

***Group 2 students are required to complete these questions/statements/tasks

Of course, the option to try the more challenging questions or statements should be open to all students.

- **Highlighted text:** A few literature anthologies or content textbooks may be marked and reserved for students acquiring English and/or for those with delayed literacy development. Overriding ideas, key concepts, topic sentences, important vocabulary, and summary statements are highlighted (by the teacher or other knowledgeable person) prior to the students using the books. Students are encouraged first to read only the highlighted sections. As confidence and reading ability improve, more of the unmarked text is attempted. The purpose of highlighted text is to reduce the reading demands of the text while still maintaining key concepts and information.

- **Taped text:** Key portions (such as the highlighted text just mentioned) or the entire text is recorded, and students are encouraged to listen to the tape while they follow along in the book. For some students, multiple exposures to the taped text may result in a more thorough understanding. Ideally, tapes should be available for both home and school learning center use.

- **Adapted text:** As mentioned earlier in this chapter, text adaptation involves rewriting selected sections of text that contain key concepts and information. Although time consuming, rewriting text is an effective modification of curricular materials because information is organized in small sequential steps. Short, simpler sentences are rewritten from long, complex ones. An example of a complex sentence from a science text follows: "Electrons have negative electric charges and orbit around the core, nucleus, of an atom." A simple adaptation of this sentence is, "Electrons have negative charges. They orbit around the core. The core of the atom is called the nucleus."

   Ideally, rewritten paragraphs should include a topic sentence with several supporting details. Maintaining a consistent format promotes easier reading for information-seeking purposes. All sentences included in the rewritten text should be direct and relevant to the subject. In the following example, a paragraph of original text is taken from an anthology theme in a reading series (Cooper et al., 2003). This passage was excerpted from a piece of nonfiction literature, *Into the Mummy's Tomb,* written by Nicholas Reeves.

Original text: "Tutankhamen's mummy bore a magnificent mask of burnished gold, which covered its face and shoulders. Its headcloth was inlaid with blue glass. The vulture and cobra on its forehead, ready to spit fire at the pharaoh's enemies, were of solid gold" (p. 237).

We have rewritten the original text as follows:

Adapted text: "King Tutankhamen's mummy wore a grand mask, made of very shiny gold. It covered the face and shoulders of the body. The part of the mask over the forehead looked like a gold headcloth. Blue glass was set into the headcloth. Shapes of a vulture (a type of bird) and a cobra (a type of snake) were above the eyes on the mask. They were solid gold. The artist made them look like they could attack the pharaoh's (King Tut's) enemies."

Obviously, adapting text like this takes time and is not easy to do. Note here that the adapted version is slightly longer than the original, which often happens when definitions are included. If you have a large number of ELs in your classroom, adapted text can be very beneficial, and it is worth the time and effort to provide students with more accessible material. Be sure to have a colleague read the adapted text to make sure it clarifies rather than confuses the content.

- **Jigsaw text reading:** Originally designed as a cooperative learning activity for all students, Jigsaw works well with English learners when there is a difficult-to-read text. One or two members from each cooperative learning group come together to form a new group of "experts." Assign each new "expert" group a different section of the text to be read. This group reads the text orally taking turns; partners read to each other, or group members read the text silently. Following the reading, each "expert" group reviews and discusses what was read, determining the essential information and key vocabulary. You need to check carefully with each "expert" group to make sure all members understand the material they have read.

  After you feel sure that the "experts" know their assigned information, they return to their original groups and teach fellow group members what they learned. This process scaffolds the learning of ELs because in both groups they are working with others to understand the text. Some classmates may have more background information on the topic. Text can be read with other students, reducing the demands of lengthy sections. Depending on English proficiency, ELs may join an "expert" group individually or with a partner. It is important that you form the "expert" groups rather than letting the students choose their own group members.

- **Marginal notes:** As with highlighted text, you may wish to reserve a few textbooks for English learners and struggling readers. Print marginal notes directly in the margin of the textbook pages or duplicate notes on a handout that students can put alongside a page they are reading. The marginal notes or handout should include hints for understanding the content, key concepts, and/or key vocabulary and definitions. The notes, whether in the textbook's margin or on a handout, are similar to the ones often found in teachers' guides.

  Most marginal notes deal specifically either with content (e.g., "Xylem carries water. Phloem carries food."), or with hints for reading a passage (e.g., "This paragraph explains why General George Armstrong Custer believed he could win the Battle of Little Big Horn. As you read it, think about whether his reasons make sense."). Marginal notes reduce ambiguity as well as the reading difficulty of the text, making it more accessible and less intimidating.

You may be thinking that marginal notes create an unnecessary burden for the teacher. Please note that once you have completed a set for one textbook, whether in the margins or on handouts, teaching assistants (parent volunteers, other adults, or capable students) can copy them in other student texts. Obviously, this type of scaffolding works only when you have extra textbooks you can write in or when you can assign specific books to particular students.

- **Native language texts:** If some students are literate in their first language, texts written in that language may be used to supplement a textbook or clarify key concepts. Students may conduct research using native language materials and share the information with classmates in English. Increasingly, the Internet offers native language websites, especially for the more commonly taught languages, and authentic materials such as newspapers can be found online. For students who are not literate in their L1, but have oral skills, native language broadcasts, podcasts, and audio books may be additional sources of information.

SIOP® FEATURE 6:
Meaningful Activities That Integrate Lesson Concepts with Language Practice Opportunities

To the extent possible, lesson activities should be planned to promote language development in all skills while ELs are mastering content objectives. We want to provide oral and written language practice that is relevant to the lesson concepts, but remember that all activities that generate language practice do not need to be identified as language objectives.

Students are more successful when they are able to make connections between what they know and what they are learning by relating classroom experiences to their own lives. These meaningful experiences are often described as "authentic" because they represent a reality for students. That is, classroom experiences mirror that which actually occurs in the learner's world. Authentic, meaningful experiences are especially important for ELs because they are learning to attach labels and terms to things already familiar to them. Their learning becomes situated rather than abstract when they are provided with the opportunity to actually experience what they are learning about.

Too often, however, English learners are relegated to activities that are not meaningful and are unrelated to the content and activities pursued by the other English-proficient students in their classes. It is essential that content standards that apply to students with English proficiency also apply to ELs, and that the planned activities reflect and support these standards.

Consider a class of fourth-grade students studying insects, butterflies in particular. While the rest of the class learns the scientific names and habitats of varied kinds of butterflies, the teacher has the ELs color and cut out pictures of butterflies to make a butterfly mobile. This activity is neither authentic nor meaningful for these young learners. And in this example, the teacher obviously has not provided meaningful activities that support the grade-level science content standards.

Using the SIOP® Protocol

As you learn to use the SIOP® protocol, both for your own teaching and for coaching other teachers, it is important that you rate each feature as reliably as possible. That is, you need to develop consistency in your rating by having a clear understanding of each feature and how it "looks" during a sheltered lesson. Therefore, it is very important that you discuss with other teachers and/or supervisors how you determined your ratings on the various SIOP® features for the lessons depicted in this book. Some schools have group meetings to discuss the ratings, while other teachers work with a partner to establish reliability. You will probably notice that some ratings for the features will seem quite obvious to you (usually those that fall on 0, 1, or 4 on the scale), while others will be more challenging. As we learned to use the SIOP® protocol in many classroom settings and with many lessons, we developed consistency in our ratings. With practice and discussion about the ratings you give, you will do the same.

Although we organized this book so that you can score the lessons as you read, in real life, you may not want to give scores on each feature, especially as teachers are learning to implement the model. You can record comments and note if a feature is present or absent, and then use the protocol to offer targeted feedback. You will also notice that five of the thirty features have an NA option (see Appendix A). After years of research we determined that those five (such as Adaptation of Content, in Lesson Preparation) might not need to be included in every SIOP® lesson. Adaptation of Content, for example, may not be needed in a class with advanced ELs. Chapter 11 provides more explanation on scoring and interpreting the SIOP® protocol.

The Lesson

The lesson described below is intended to teach fourth-grade children about the Gold Rush, in particular, about the trails taken by the pioneers. (For more examples of lesson and unit plans in social studies, see Short, Vogt, & Echevarria, in press.)

UNIT: The Gold Rush (Fourth Grade)

The classrooms described in the teaching scenarios in this chapter are all in a suburban elementary school with heterogeneously mixed students. English learners represent approximately 30 percent of the student population, and the children speak a variety of languages. In the fourth-grade classrooms of teachers Ms. Chen, Mrs. Hargroves, and Mr. Hensen, the majority of the ELs are at the intermediate stage of English fluency.

As part of the fourth-grade social studies curriculum, Ms. Chen, Mrs. Hargroves, and Mr. Hensen have planned a unit on the California Gold Rush. The school district requires the use of the adopted social studies series, although teachers are encouraged to supplement the text with primary source materials, literature, and realia. The content topics for the Gold Rush unit include westward expansion, routes and trails to the West, the

UNIT: The Gold Rush (Fourth Grade) *continued*

people who sought their fortunes, hardships, settlements, the discovery of gold, the life of miners, methods for extracting gold, and the impact of the Gold Rush.

Each of the teachers has created several lessons for this unit, beginning with a lesson plan (approximately 55 minutes) on routes and trails to the West. Specifically, the content of this lesson covers the Oregon Trail, the Overland Trail, and the Route Around Cape Horn.

Teaching Scenarios

To demonstrate how Ms. Chen, Mrs. Hargroves, and Mr. Hensen prepared their first lesson on the trails west, we visit them in their fourth-grade classrooms. As you read, think of the SIOP® features for Lesson Preparation: content objectives, language objectives, content concepts, supplementary materials, adaptation of content, and meaningful activities.

Ms. Chen

As Ms. Chen began the first day's lesson on the Gold Rush, she referred students to the content objectives written on the board: (1) Find and label the three main routes to the West on a map; (2) tell one or two facts about each of the three trails. After reading the content objectives aloud, Ms. Chen then explained the language objectives: (1) Write sentences explaining how the three routes to the West were given their names; (2) tell how the structure of some words gives clues to their meaning.

Next, Ms. Chen asked the students to brainstorm why people would leave their comfortable homes and travel great distances to seek their fortunes. She listed their responses on the board and then asked the students to categorize the words or phrases, using a List-Group-Label activity. The children determined the following categories: For Adventure, To Get Rich, For a Better Life. Examples of phrases under the first category included *riding in a wagon train, seeing new places, climbing mountains, becoming a gold miner,* etc.

Ms. Chen then assigned her students a quick-write about the Gold Rush. She distributed two or three picture books on the topic for each of the table groups (four or five children per group) and directed students to use their background knowledge, the brainstormed categories, and the books to generate a brief paragraph on the Gold Rush. Students were encouraged to work quietly together with a partner, and each pair was expected to have a brief paragraph written for later whole-class discussion.

While the rest of the class were preparing their quick-writes, Ms. Chen asked the six English learners with very limited English proficiency to meet her at the table in the back of the room. For seven to ten minutes, she provided the small group of students with a jump start for the Gold Rush unit they were about to begin. She introduced key vocabulary with illustrations and simple definitions, led the students through a picture and text walk of two picture books and the textbook chapter, showed the trails on the U.S. map, and talked about where the pioneers began their journey and where they were heading in California. Ms. Chen showed the students some chunks of fool's gold (iron pyrite) and asked them how they thought the gold miners were able to get the gold from the earth. After the brief jump-start lesson, Ms. Chen convened the entire class for a brief discussion of the quick-writes and a whole-class introduction to the unit. Several of the groups volunteered to share their quick-writes with the entire class.

Ms. Chen then referred to the key vocabulary she had previously written on the board: Oregon Trail, Overland Trail, Route Around Cape Horn. She asked students to think about the names of the trails they were going to be reading about, and she asked, "Why are streets given their names?" She then asked students to call out some of the names of streets on which they lived. They offered First Street, River Avenue, Main Street, and Mill Creek Road, among others. Ms. Chen then suggested that trails, routes, streets, avenues, and highways are often named after geographical landmarks. She explained that often we learn about places and surrounding areas by examining their names.

Following a shared reading of the social studies text, Ms. Chen asked the students to examine the map of the United States on the wall and try to determine why the three main trails to the West were named as they were. The children volunteered appropriate ideas for the first one, the Oregon Trail. Ms. Chen then wrote "Over + land = Overland." One child said, "I get it! They went over the land!" The teacher reinforced this by pointing out the "over the land" route on the wall map. She then wrote "Route Around Cape Horn" on the board and asked students to think about the name's meaning while directing them to look at the map. One child said, "See, the land looks kind of like a horn. And they had to sail around it!" To check understanding, Ms. Chen asked each student to tell a partner in a complete sentence why the three western routes were given their respective names. These reasons were shared with the others in their groups.

Next, Ms. Chen distributed a duplicated map of the United States to each group. She asked three students to come to the wall map and point to the Route Around Cape Horn, the Overland Trail, and the Oregon Trail. She then modeled with transparencies how to locate and color in the trails, and then directed the students to work together as a team to complete their groups' maps.

In the few remaining minutes, Ms. Chen distributed a skeleton outline of the chapter that students would complete individually the following day. The outline had subheadings labeled for each of the trails: "Location," "Characteristics," "Challenges," and "Advantages." She told the groups they would have about ten minutes to begin working on the outline, using their maps and their text chapter. Ms. Chen wrapped up the lesson by reviewing the content and language objectives and by having several students report a number of facts about each of the trails.

On the SIOP® form in Figure 2.5, rate Ms. Chen's lesson on each of the Lesson Preparation features.

Mrs. Hargroves

Mrs. Hargroves began her lesson on the trails west by stating, "Today you'll learn about the Oregon Trail, the Overland Trail, and the Route Around Cape Horn. We'll also be working on maps, and I want you to color the Overland Trail a different color from the

FIGURE 2.5 *Lesson Preparation Component of the SIOP® Model: Ms. Chen's Lesson*

4	3	2	1	0
1. **Content objectives** clearly defined, displayed, and reviewed with students		**Content objectives** for students implied		No clearly defined **content objectives** for students
2. **Language objectives** clearly defined, displayed, and reviewed with students		**Language objectives** for students implied		No clearly defined **language objectives** for students
3. **Content concepts** appropriate for age and educational background level of students		**Content concepts** somewhat appropriate for age and educational background level of students		**Content concepts** inappropriate for age and educational background level of students
4. **Supplementary materials** used to a high degree, making the lesson clear and meaningful (e.g., computer programs, graphs, models, visuals)		Some use of **supplementary materials**		No use of **supplementary materials**
5. **Adaptation of content** (e.g., text, assignment) to all levels of student proficiency		Some **adaptation of content** to all levels of student proficiency		No significant **adaptation of content** to all levels of student proficiency NA
6. **Meaningful activities** that integrate lesson concepts (e.g., interviews, letter writing, simulations, models) with language practice opportunities for reading, writing, listening, and/or speaking		**Meaningful activities** that integrate lesson concepts, but provide few language practice opportunities for reading, writing, listening, and/or speaking		**No meaningful activities** that integrate lesson concepts with language practice

color you use for the Cape Horn route. When you learn about the Oregon Trail, you'll complete the map with a third color. By the time you're finished, you should have all three routes drawn on the map using different colors." She held up a completed map for the students to see as an example.

Mrs. Hargroves then presented a brief lecture on the trails west, using the map in the textbook to point out where the pioneers traveled. She referred students to pictures in the book and answered questions. She read the chapter title and the first few paragraphs about the trails west and then assigned the remainder of the chapter as independent reading. She suggested that if students had difficulty with any words, they should hold up their hands and she would circulate to give assistance.

After about twenty minutes, Mrs. Hargroves asked students to stop reading. She distributed the U.S. maps and colored pencils and asked the students to work with a partner to complete their maps by locating and coloring in the three trails. When most were finished, Mrs. Hargroves asked three of the students to show and explain their maps to the other students. All maps were then submitted for a grade. At the conclusion of the lesson, students were given the following writing assignment for homework: "If you had been a pioneer, which trail would you have chosen? Why?"

On the SIOP® form in Figure 2.6, rate Mrs. Hargroves's lesson on each of the Lesson Preparation features.

Mr. Hensen

Mr. Hensen began his lesson on westward expansion by introducing the topic and asking how many children had been to California. He then asked, "How did you get to California? Did you go by car? By plane? By boat? Or did you go by wagon train? Today you're going to learn how the pioneers made their voyages to California." Mr. Hensen then showed a brief video on the westward expansion. At the end of the video, he introduced the terms Oregon Trail, Overland Trail, and Route Around Cape Horn, and then read aloud two paragraphs from the textbook that described the routes. Then he numbered off the students to form six new groups and quickly moved students into the groups. With their team members, students did a Jigsaw activity for the remainder of the chapter, and when they had finished reading, everyone returned to their original home groups to report on what they had read. The ELs with limited English proficiency were partnered with other students during the Jigsaw reading activity.

Mr. Hensen then wrote the names of the three trails on the board, and on his wall map he pointed out where the pioneers had traveled along the three routes. He directed the groups to divide the three trails, with one or two students in each group drawing the Oregon Trail and the other students drawing either the Overland or Cape Horn trails. Their next task was to tell the other students in their group how to draw and color their maps, using the map in the text and the language on the board as a guide. Mr. Hensen circulated through the room while the children completed the mapping activity, assisting as necessary. At the lesson's conclusion, students were directed to pass in their maps. Those maps that were not finished were assigned as homework.

On the SIOP® form in Figure 2.7, rate Mr. Hensen's lesson on each of the Lesson Preparation features.

FIGURE 2.6 *Lesson Preparation Component of the SIOP® Model: Mrs. Hargroves's Lesson*

4	3	2	1	0
1. **Content objectives** clearly defined, displayed, and reviewed with students		**Content objectives** for students implied		No clearly defined **content objectives** for students
2. **Language objectives** clearly defined, displayed, and reviewed with students		**Language objectives** for students implied		No clearly defined **language objectives** for students
3. **Content concepts** appropriate for age and educational background level of students		**Content concepts** somewhat appropriate for age and educational background level of students		**Content concepts** inappropriate for age and educational background level of students
4. **Supplementary materials** used to a high degree, making the lesson clear and meaningful (e.g., computer programs, graphs, models, visuals)		Some use of **supplementary materials**		No use of **supplementary materials**
5. **Adaptation of content** (e.g., text, assignment) to all levels of student proficiency		Some **adaptation of content** to all levels of student proficiency		No significant **adaptation of content** to all levels of student proficiency **NA**
6. **Meaningful activities** that integrate lesson concepts (e.g., interviews, letter writing, simulations, models) with language practice opportunities for reading, writing, listening, and/or speaking		**Meaningful activities** that integrate lesson concepts, but provide few language practice opportunities for reading, writing, listening, and/or speaking		No **meaningful activities** that integrate lesson concepts with language practice

FIGURE 2.7 *Lesson Preparation Component of the SIOP® Model: Mr. Hensen's Lesson*

4	3	2	1	0
1. **Content objectives** clearly defined, displayed, and reviewed with students		**Content objectives** for students implied		No clearly defined **content objectives** for students
4	3	2	1	0
2. **Language objectives** clearly defined, displayed, and reviewed with students		**Language objectives** for students implied		No clearly defined **language objectives** for students
4	3	2	1	0
3. **Content concepts** appropriate for age and educational background level of students		**Content concepts** somewhat appropriate for age and educational background level of students		**Content concepts** inappropriate for age and educational background level of students
4	3	2	1	0
4. **Supplementary materials** used to a high degree, making the lesson clear and meaningful (e.g., computer programs, graphs, models, visuals)		Some use of **supplementary materials**		No use of **supplementary materials**
4	3	2	1	0 NA
5. **Adaptation of content** (e.g., text, assignment) to all levels of student proficiency		Some **adaptation of content** to all levels of student proficiency		No significant **adaptation of content** to all levels of student proficiency
4	3	2	1	0
6. **Meaningful activities** that integrate lesson concepts (e.g., interviews, letter writing, simulations, models) with language practice opportunities for reading, writing, listening, and/or speaking		**Meaningful activities** that integrate lesson concepts, but provide few language practice opportunities for reading, writing, listening, and/or speaking		No **meaningful activities** that integrate lesson concepts with language practice

Discussion of Lessons

1. *Content Objectives Clearly Defined, Displayed, and Reviewed with Students*

Ms. Chen: 4

Mrs. Hargroves: 2

Mr. Hensen: 1

During their planning, Ms. Chen, Mrs. Hargroves, and Mr. Hensen approached the task of writing and delivering content objectives in different ways.

A review of Ms. Chen's lesson plan book indicated the following objectives for her first lessons on the Gold Rush: "The learner will be able to 1) identify the three main routes to the West on a map; 2) state at least one distinct fact about each of the three trails." She wrote the content objectives on the whiteboard and she clearly, explicitly, and simply stated them in a manner that was comprehensible to her students: "Find and label the three main routes to the West on a map; and tell one or two facts about each of the three trails." (See Figure 2.8 for Ms. Chen's lesson plan.) Her lesson received a "4."

Mrs. Hargroves wrote a content objective in her plan book but not on the board, and she orally stated what she wanted her students to learn and do. However, her English learners might have had difficulty understanding what the purpose was for the activities they were to do. She did state her objectives in simple terms, and some students may have inferred that the purpose for the lesson was the coloring activity rather than learning where the trails and routes were. Further, the content objectives were not written on the board or overhead for the students to see. Her lesson was rated "2."

A review of Mr. Hensen's lesson plan book revealed no content objectives for the Gold Rush lesson on routes and trails. He did not define any content objectives for the students, but just began the lesson with a brief discussion and the video. Some students may have been able to infer the purpose of the map work, but English learners may have been unaware of the purpose of these assignments. His lesson received a "1."

2. *Language Objectives Clearly Defined, Displayed, and Reviewed with Students*

Ms. Chen: 4

Mrs. Hargroves: 0

Mr. Hensen: 2

The three teachers incorporated language objectives into their lesson planning and delivery to varying degrees.

Ms. Chen wrote the following language objectives on the board and she read them orally to her students: 1) Write sentences explaining how the three routes to the West were given their names; 2) tell how the structure of some words gives clues to their meaning. Ms. Chen provided opportunities for students to meet the objective by encouraging class and small-group discussion, by assigning sentences about the three trails, and by having each student convey important facts related to the lesson. Further, she scaffolded students' understandings of the names of the routes and trails by having them examine the names of familiar street names, and she led them through an analysis of the names of the historical routes, such as "over + land." She pointed out the compound word and supported students' approximations. At the end of the

FIGURE 2.8 *Ms. Chen's SIOP® Lesson Plan*

Date: Feb. 10–11   Grade/Class/Subject: 4 – SS

Unit/Theme: Gold Rush   Standards: History—Social Source 4.3

Content Objective(s): Students will find and label 3 routes to West on map;

Tell 1–2 facts about each trail

Language Objective(s): Students will write sentences explaining how 3 routes got

their names; Explain how word structure gives clues to meaning

Key Vocabulary
Oregon Trail
Overland Trail
Route around Cape Horn

Supplementary Materials
Picture books   Outlines
Iron Pyrite
Transp. w/ US map

SIOP Features

Skel.
Outline
Jumpstart

Preparation
- ✓ Adaptation of Content
- ✓ Links to Background
- ✓ Links to Past Learning
- ✓ Strategies incorporated
  List / Group / Label

Integration of Processes
- ✓ Reading
- ✓ Writing
- ✓ Speaking
- ✓ Listening

Scaffolding
- ✓ Modeling Transp.
- ✓ Guided practice
- ___ Independent practice
- ✓ Comprehensible input

Application
- ✓ Hands-on maps
- ✓ Meaningful
- ✓ Linked to objectives
- ✓ Promotes engagement

Grouping Options
- ✓ Whole class
- ✓ Small groups
- ___ Partners
- ✓ Independent

Assessment
- ✓ Individual
- ✓ Group
- ✓ Written
- ___ Oral

Min.	Lesson Sequence
	1. Content/lang. obj.
5	2. Brainstorm — Why would people leave their homes to seek fortunes?
	3. List – Group – Label
10	4. EOs — Quick Write: Gold Rush
	5. ELs — Jumpstart text/fool's gold/pictures
5	6. Quick Write Share Out
	7. Intro. Vocabulary: Why are streets given their names?
10	8. Shared reading — p. 124–128
10	9. On map — show trails – How did they get their names?, Discuss word structure
	10. Pass out U.S. maps —
	11. Model on transp. — Have kids color
5	12. Skeleton Outline — Work in groups – fill in categories –
10	(Start, if time)

Reflections:

It felt a little rushed, but everyone finished the maps. Next time, save Skeleton outlines for 2nd day. Kids loved the fool's gold!

lesson, she orally reviewed the language objectives for the students. Her lesson was rated a "4."

Mrs. Hargroves did not include any language objectives in her lesson plan and she did not suggest any to the students. She did not discuss the meanings of the names or terms used in her demonstration and explanations, nor did she encourage her students to use the terminology and concepts during discussion. Further, Mrs. Hargroves expected students to read the textbook with very little support. Her instruction was conveyed mostly orally, and she expected students to complete the writing assignment as homework with no modeling or assistance. Her lesson received a "0."

Although Mr. Hensen had no stated language objectives, he did write key vocabulary on the board. He scaffolded the mapping activity and the text reading by having the children work in groups and by having each group member explain the map and key words to the others. This activity was appropriate for beginning English learners because they were supported by each other, and their oral explanations were not "public," for the entire class. The lesson would have been more effective had Mr. Hensen explained his language objectives to the children, emphasizing the importance of listening carefully and of giving clear directions. Though one purpose of the lesson was to build listening and speaking skills, the children were not informed of these objectives either orally or in writing. His lesson was rated a "2."

3. *Content Concepts Appropriate for Age and Educational Background Level of Students*

Ms. Chen: 4

Mrs. Hargroves: 4

Mr. Hensen: 4

Each of the teaching scenarios indicates that the three fourth-grade teachers, Ms. Chen, Mrs. Hargroves, and Mr. Hensen, were teaching a unit on the Gold Rush. The content concepts were appropriate because they are congruent with the fourth-grade state and district standards for the social studies curriculum in the district where the teachers are employed. Each lesson was rated a "4."

4. *Supplementary Materials Used to a High Degree*

Ms. Chen: 4

Mrs. Hargroves: 1

Mr. Hensen: 3

Ms. Chen used the following supplementary materials: picture books on the Gold Rush, fool's gold, the wall map of the United States, and transparencies to model how students might color the trails on their maps. Her lesson received a "4" on this feature.

Mrs. Hargroves, on the other hand, used only the wall map and the textbook during her lecture and when the students were coloring their maps. She did not demonstrate, model, or show visuals or other resources to support student learning other than the illustrations in the textbooks. Because Mrs. Hargroves delivered the content orally, some English learners may have had difficulty making connections between the lecture and the illustrations and maps in their books. Her lesson received a "1."

Mr. Hensen's video enabled his English learners and other students to connect with the pioneers in the Gold Rush, and his use of the wall map enhanced student learning about the location of the three trails. His lesson was rated "3."

5. *Adaptation of Content to All Levels of Student Proficiency*

Ms. Chen: 4

Mrs. Hargroves: 0

Mr. Hensen: 3

Ms. Chen adapted the grade-level content for her English learners and struggling readers in a number of ways. First, she had students brainstorm, categorize, and then quick-write information about the Gold Rush. She then provided a "jump start" for her English learners by preteaching the lesson concepts and key vocabulary. She also had a variety of picture books that were easier to read and more comprehensible than the textbook. In addition, she used a skeleton outline that included key information. The students used this outline to organize their understanding of the content concepts. Her lesson was rated "4."

Mrs. Hargroves did not adapt the content for her English learners, other than by lecturing on the topic. Without any supplementary support except the pictures in the textbook and her oral reading of the first few paragraphs, the ELs may have had difficulty learning key concepts just by listening and reading independently. Further, Mrs. Hargroves did not paraphrase or clarify important points during her lecture, nor did she explain or define key language or vocabulary before or during reading. Her lesson plans made no mention of other ways to adapt the content or text. Her lesson received a "0."

Mr. Hensen provided access to the textbook content through the Jigsaw activity and the video. He grouped the students for their reading so that they read with the support of others and then conveyed what they had learned to another group of students. He also had the students complete their work on the maps in small groups, and he encouraged them to help each other with the assignment. His lesson was rated "3."

6. *Meaningful Activities That Integrate Lesson Concepts with Language Practice Opportunities*

Ms. Chen: 4

Mrs. Hargroves: 2

Mr. Hensen: 4

Recall that Ms. Chen asked students to brainstorm what they knew about the Gold Rush in order to activate and build background. She later asked them to name the streets they lived on. The purpose of this was to make the names of geographic locations meaningful, such as familiar street names, as well as routes to California. Her jump-start activity for the English learners included picture walks and discussion of key vocabulary, and the students were able to see and hold fool's gold, which simulated the feel and look of gold. The picture books supported their learning, and the skeleton outline provided a meaningful way to summarize the key concepts. Students located and colored in the trails on the U.S. maps after watching modeling by Ms. Chen. Her lesson received a "4."

Mrs. Hargroves's lesson plan included her lecture, the mapping activity, and the independent reading. Locating the trails by coloring the map was meaningful for students if they understood what they were doing; however, if they were unable to access the text or the lecture, the mapping activity may have been irrelevant. Mrs. Hargroves's lesson received a "2." It was teacher-centered, with lecture and independent seat work the predominant activities. She expected students to complete the homework assignment based only on the information they could gather from the lecture and text. If students did not understand the lecture or comprehend the chapter, it is unlikely they were able to write a meaningful essay on what they learned.

Mr. Hensen activated prior knowledge and background when he asked which students had traveled to California. He also showed the video on the westward expansion, incorporated a Jigsaw reading activity, and had the students complete and explain their maps in triads. All of these activities helped make the content concepts more comprehensible for his English learners, and were considered to be meaningful and appropriate. His lesson was rated a "4."

Summary

We view Lesson Preparation as a critical foundation for delivering a high-quality SIOP® lesson. Thoughtful planning leads to effective teaching—but a great plan does not always guarantee a great lesson for English learners. They require sensitive teachers who realize that curriculum must be grade-level appropriate, based on content standards and learning outcomes. Moreover, all SIOP® lessons need attention to language with at least one objective devoted to furthering the ELs' academic English development. If children lack background knowledge and experience with content concepts, effective sheltered teachers provide it through explicit instruction and they enhance student learning with appropriate supplementary materials. They provide scaffolded support by adapting dense and difficult text. They situate lessons in meaningful real-life activities and experiences that involve students in reading, writing, and discussion of important concepts and ideas.

These principles of effective sheltered instruction should be reflected in teachers' lesson plans. As we explore the other features of the SIOP® Model and see how teachers apply many other important principles in their classrooms, remember that the first step in the instructional process is comprehensive and thoughtful lesson design.

Discussion Questions

1. What are some advantages to writing both content objectives and language objectives for students to hear and see? How might written objectives affect teacher and student performance in the classroom?

2. Think of a lesson you have recently taught or one you might teach. What would be an appropriate content objective and language objective for that lesson?

3. In many elementary schools, one ESL teacher supports English learners from several classrooms, sometimes across different grade levels. How can the ESL and grade-level classroom teachers collaborate to share the responsibility for teaching both language and content objectives to these students? Co-plan a mini-unit in which some lessons will be taught by the ESL teacher and others by the grade-level classroom teacher.

4. Many teachers in sheltered settings rely on paper-and-pencil tasks or lectures for teaching concepts. Think of a curricular area (e.g., science, language arts, math, social studies) and discuss some meaningful activities that could be used to teach a concept in that area. What makes each of these activities "meaningful" and how would they provide language practice?

5. Begin writing a SIOP® lesson. Identify the topic and content and language objectives. Find or create supplementary materials and adapted content as needed. Determine at least one meaningful activity the students can engage in during the lesson. Decide how many class periods will be needed to complete the lesson. When you finish, share your initial lesson plan with a colleague and garner feedback. Revise your lesson.

chapter 3

Building Background

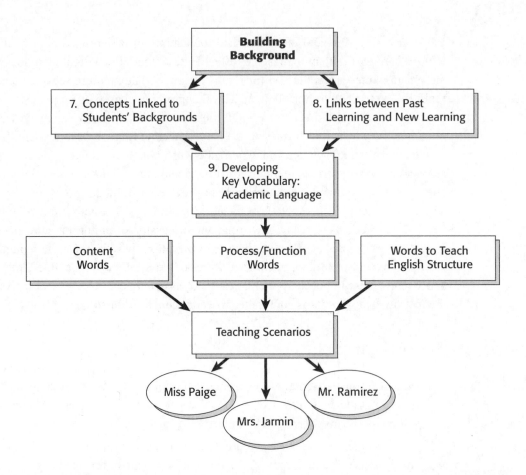

Objectives

After reading, discussing, and engaging in activities related to this chapter, you will be able to meet the following content and language objectives.

Content Objectives

Identify techniques for connecting students' personal experiences and past learning to lesson concepts.

Define the key elements of academic vocabulary (content words, process/function words, and words to teach English structure) and describe its importance for English learners.

Language Objectives

Write a lesson plan incorporating activities that build background and provide explicit links to students' backgrounds, experiences, and past learning.

Identify the academic language in a SIOP® lesson and select key vocabulary words to emphasize.

Background

Have you ever been teaching a lesson that you carefully prepared but with which your students cannot connect? As you are explaining new concepts, you observe confused faces, off-task behaviors, and maybe some students mumbling to each other. While there may be several reasons why your students don't understand what you are explaining, one common cause is a mismatch between what your students have learned and experienced and the concepts that you're teaching. English learners, in particular, are frequently at a disadvantage because their schooling experiences (whether they have had little schooling or exceptional schooling) may be considerably different from U.S. educational contexts. For example, the K–6 curriculum may be quite different from country to country, and depending on circumstances, some students may have experienced interrupted schooling, especially if they have been refugees. English learners may not have learned the academic language and key vocabulary necessary for understanding content information. It is important that we not assume that all students lack knowledge of academic language; some students may know academic language well in their native language, but not in English.

Effective teaching takes students from where they are and leads them to a higher level of understanding (Krashen, 1985; Vygotsky, 1978). Students learning English must have ample opportunity to use the target language (English); to hear and see comprehensible English; and to read, write, and speak the new language within the context of subject matter learning. But there is a caveat to this: *the language must be meaningful.* It is not only the amount of exposure to English that affects learning, but the quality as well.

As we will discuss in the next few chapters of this book, effective SIOP® teachers present information in a way that students can understand, bearing in mind their language development needs and any gaps in their educational experiences. New information is tied to students' background and experiences, and learning strategies are used to scaffold students' acquisition of knowledge and skills (see Chapter 5 for a detailed discussion). All students benefit from scaffolded instruction, but it is a necessity for English learners. This chapter focuses on *Building Background,* which is closely tied to Lesson Preparation and the teacher's assessment of the students' knowledge of and experience with the topic at hand.

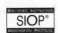

SIOP® FEATURE 7:
Concepts Explicitly Linked to Students' Background Experiences

During the past three decades, researchers have investigated how highly proficient readers and writers process new information (Baumann, 2005; Carrell, 1987; Dole, Duffy, Roehler, & Pearson, 1991). It is a widely accepted notion among experts that a reader's "schemata"—knowledge of the world—provide a basis for understanding, learning, and remembering facts and ideas found in stories and texts. Individuals with knowledge of a topic have better recall and are better able to elaborate on aspects of the topic than those who have limited knowledge of the topic (Brown, 2008; Chiesi, Spilich, & Voss, 1979; Vogt, 2005).

The importance of background experiences are expressed in the following ways:

> Schemata are the reader's concepts, beliefs, expectations, processes—virtually every-thing from past experiences—that are used in making sense of things and actions. In reading, schemata are used in making sense of text; the printed work evoking the reader's associated experiences, and past and potential relationships. (John McNeil)
>
> When reading, the learner forms meaning by reviewing past experiences that given images and sounds evoke. (Edmund Huey)

Christen & Murphy (1991) suggested that when readers lack the prior knowledge necessary to read, three major instructional interventions need to be considered: (1) teach vocabulary as a prereading step, (2) provide meaningful experiences, and (3) introduce a conceptual framework that will enable students to develop appropriate background information.

Teach Vocabulary During the Prereading Stage
In this chapter, we present ideas for teaching vocabulary before and during a lesson. Some studies suggest that a limited number of words should be taught per lesson or per week, and those words should be key words in the text (Beck, Perfetti, & McKeown, 1982). Others recommend teaching ELs the meanings of basic words, such as those that native English speakers know already (Diamond & Gutlohn, 2006; Stahl & Nagy, 2006). In SIOP® lessons, teachers select words that are critical for understanding the text or material and provide a variety of ways for students to learn, remember, and use those words. In that way, students develop a core vocabulary over time (Blachowicz & Fisher, 2000; Graves & Fitzgerald, 2006).

Provide Meaningful Experiences
Connecting students' experiences to a text they will read, developing background knowledge, and teaching key vocabulary are all effective ways to increase comprehension

and achievement (Biemiller, 2005; Echevarria, Short, & Powers, 2006; Stahl & Nagy, 2006).

Introduce a Conceptual Framework

This can be accomplished by using techniques such as graphic organizers and chapter previews. As students begin to develop a conceptual framework for their own learning and understanding, they build a repertoire of background experiences from which to draw.

One of the challenges of teaching English learners is that students in the same class vary in the amount of prior knowledge they possess related to a topic. Christen and Murphy (1991) suggest that students generally fall into three categories: much, some, or little prior knowledge. Based on students' levels, the teacher makes specific instructional decisions and differentiates instruction for each level. Some ideas for differentiation include using and teaching superordinate concepts, definitions, analogies, and linking words for students who have much prior knowledge; using and teaching examples, attributes, and defining characteristics for students who have some prior knowledge; and using and teaching associations, morphemes (e.g., base words and word roots), sound-alikes, and firsthand experiences for students who have little prior knowledge.

Children from culturally diverse backgrounds may struggle with comprehending a text or concept presented in class because their schemata do not match those of the culture for which the text was written (Jiménez, Garcia, & Pearson, 1996; Anderson, 1984). In the United States, most school reading materials, such as content area texts, rely on assumptions about students' prior knowledge, especially related to curriculum. Many ELs emigrate from other countries and bring an array of experiences that are quite different from those of the majority culture in the United States, and some have gaps in their education. Even for those English learners born in the United States, culture may have an impact on reading comprehension. As a teacher reads, "The barking dog ran toward the boy on the bike," do all children get a sense of fear or danger? Anderson (1994) questions whether we can assume that "when reading the same story, children from every subculture will have the same experience with the setting, ascribe the same goals and motives to characters, imagine the same sequence of actions, make predictions with the same emotional reactions, or expect the same outcomes" (pp. 480–481).

As an actual example, a second-grade teacher in a large urban district began teaching map skills, a state history–social studies standard for second grade, by having students identify on a grid some familiar locations and features of their school. The next step of the teacher's lesson plan was to focus on the children's local community and the location and features of the police and fire departments, city hall, post office, community hospital, and so forth. Finally, she planned to work on another social studies standard by talking with the children about those individuals in the community that "make a difference." She intended to connect their contributions with those of some of the historical figures students had learned about previously.

The teacher thought that focusing on the features and locations of the local community would be a relatively simple task for her students. She soon realized, however, that the task was quite difficult for many students, especially her immigrant English learners and others who had scarcely ventured from their own city blocks during their lifetimes. Although the ocean was just a few blocks away, the teacher discovered that some of her young students had never seen it. Also, while many children heard and saw ambulances and fire trucks race frequently by their apartment buildings, they had not seen a fire

To see an example of the importance of building background, please view the corresponding video clip (Chapter 3, Module 1) on the accompanying CD.

department or hospital. These children were unable to engage in a class discussion of the community beyond the school, and they lacked the knowledge and experience to sketch a map of it or describe some of the people who worked within their community, except for the small market that was down the street from the school.

This teacher quickly realized that she needed to rethink her lesson plans for this unit, begin again and determine what her students knew about the concept of "community," including the one in which they lived. Not surprisingly, her students' backgrounds and experiences varied widely. For some who had a large extended family, this defined their "community." For others, they described their community as their home, church, and school. For still others, who had attended the ballet and theater, who regularly shopped with their family at large local malls, and who had siblings who participated in Scouts or Camp Fire, their understanding of "community" was quite different.

Teachers of English learners need to be aware that what may appear to be poor comprehension and a lack of skills may in fact be a lack of experience or a failure to activate background knowledge assumed by a message or a text (Bransford, 1994). Through the SIOP® Model, we urge teachers to activate students' background knowledge explicitly, provide linkages from their experiences to the key concepts, and build additional background when there are gaps. The interactive emphasis of the SIOP® Model (see Chapter 6 for specific features) enables teachers to elicit students' prior knowledge and discuss ideas, issues, concepts, or vocabulary that are unfamiliar to them, in order to develop necessary background information.

Instructional Implications

As you begin to write SIOP® lessons with techniques to develop students' background knowledge, reflect on the following questions:

To hear a teacher talk about how the SIOP® model has affected her teaching, please view the corresponding video clip (Chapter 3, Module 3: Techniques) on the accompanying CD.

- What is meant by activating prior knowledge?
- What is meant by building background?
- How do these terms differ instructionally?

In the past, we have used the terms *activating prior knowledge* and *building background* somewhat synonymously. However, we now believe there are some instructional differences that need to be considered when teaching English learners. All students have prior knowledge, gained from schooling and life experiences, and teachers can informally assess what students know and can do, as well as any mismatches in schemata through brainstorming, structured discussion, quick-writes, and techniques such as the familiar KWL (Ogle, 1986).

However, if some ELs have little or no prior knowledge about a content topic (e.g., "our community"), brainstorming about it may not be helpful because the brainstormed terms, names, and places may be unfamiliar to some children. Therefore, it is of critical importance that teachers build background using techniques that fill in the gaps, and help students connect what they do know with what is being taught. And when teachers' explanations are made more concrete with supplementary materials (e.g., photos, models, illustrations, etc.), students are more likely to make the appropriate connections.

To see an example of activating prior knowledge, please view the corresponding video clip (Chapter 3, Module 2) on the accompanying CD.

Additional activities that activate prior knowledge and/or build background include

 Read a Big Book, story, picture book, or Readers Theater play about the topic;

Use the Insert Method (adapted from the RWCT Project of the International Reading Association; Vogt & Echevarria, 2008). This activity is appropriate for grades 3–6 and all subject areas. First, duplicate a nonfiction article written at an appropriate level on the topic you're teaching, one per student. In pairs, children read the article. While reading, they insert the following codes directly into the text:

- A check mark (✓) indicates a concept or fact that is already known by the students.
- A question mark (?) indicates a concept or fact that is confusing or not understood.
- An exclamation mark (!) indicates something that is unusual or surprising.
- A plus sign (+) indicates an idea or concept that is new to the reader.

When the partners finish reading and marking the text, they share their markings with another pair of students. If any misconceptions or misunderstandings are cleared up, then the question mark is replaced with an asterisk (*). When groups finish working, the whole class discusses what they have read and learned with the teacher;

Pretest with a Partner (Vogt & Echevarria, 2008). This activity is helpful for students in grades 2–6 and is appropriate for any subject area. The purpose of Pretest with a Partner is to allow English learners the opportunity to preview at the beginning of a lesson or unit the concepts and vocabulary that will be assessed at the conclusion of the lesson or unit. Distribute one pretest and pencil to each pair of students. The pretest should be similar or identical to the posttest that will be administered later. The partners pass the pretest and pencil back and forth between one another. They read a question aloud, discuss possible answers, come to consensus, and write an answer on the pretest. This activity provides an opportunity for students to activate prior knowledge and share background information, while the teacher circulates to assess what students know, recording gaps and misinformation. For grades 3 and 4, be sure to model the process several times before asking children to work independently.

Plot Chart (Vogt & Echevarria, 2008). Many (if not most) young English learners are unfamiliar with the fairy tales that are referred to and practiced (for reading fluency and comprehension) in U.S. schools. For children in pre-K to third grade, the Plot Chart provides an opportunity for ELs to learn common fairy tales, and to learn about the elements of short stories, such as character and plot development.

For pre-K–2, use four simple boxes on a graphic organizer with the headings *Somebody, Wanted, But, So.* For older children, use a more complex graphic organizer with five boxes: *Somebody, Wanted, So, But, So,* In the end. The Plot Chart is also great for children who may have a learned a similar fairy tale in their home language but don't know the English version. Older students who are literate in their first language can write and compare both versions on two Plot Charts. (Did you know that the Cinderella story is found in many, many versions and languages throughout the world, and was shared with children long before Walt Disney's version?)

Example:	Somebody:	*Goldilocks*
	Wanted:	*Some food and a place to rest.*
	So:	*She stopped at the bears' house.*
	But:	*The bears were not home.*
	So:	*Goldilocks found some food that was too hot or too cold, and beds that were too hard or too soft.*
	In the end:	*Goldilocks found porridge (or food) and a bed that was just right! Then the bears came home and found her.*

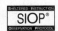

SIOP® FEATURE 8:
Links Explicitly Made Between Past Learning and New Concepts

It is also important for teachers to make explicit connections between new learning and the material, vocabulary, and concepts previously covered in class. Research clearly emphasizes that for learning to occur, new information must be integrated with what students have previously learned (Rumelhart, 1980). The teacher must build a bridge from previous lessons and concepts to today's lesson. Many students do not automatically make such connections, and all students benefit from having the teacher explicitly point out how past learning is related to the information at hand (Tierney & Pearson, 1994).

Explicit links between past learning and new learning can be made through a discussion—such as, "Who remembers what we learned about _____? How does that relate to our chapter?"—or by reviewing graphic organizers, previously used class notes, transparencies, or PowerPoint slides related to the topic. By preserving and referring to photos, word banks, illustrations, charts, maps, and graphic organizers, teachers have tools for helping students make critical connections. This is particularly important for ELs who receive so much input through the new language. An explicit, if brief, review of prior lessons focuses on the key information they should remember.

SIOP® FEATURE 9:
Key Vocabulary Emphasized (e.g., introduced, written, repeated, and highlighted for students to see)

Vocabulary development, critical for English learners, is strongly related to academic achievement (Saville-Troike, 1984; Hart & Risley, 2003; Biemiller, 2005; Manzo, Manzo, & Thomas, 2005). In addition, for over 80 years, we have known of the powerful relationship between vocabulary knowledge and comprehension (Baumann, 2005; Stahl & Nagy, 2006). According to Graves & Fitzgerald (2006, p. 122), systematic and comprehensive vocabulary instruction is necessary for English learners because

- content area texts that students must read include very sophisticated vocabulary;
- reading performance tests given to English learners rely on wide-ranging vocabulary knowledge;

- English learners' vocabulary instruction must be accelerated because ELs are learning English later than their native-speaking peers;
- English learners' acquisition of deep understandings of word meaning is very challenging.

Academic Language (or English) and Academic Vocabulary

Many English learners who have been educated in their native countries come to school in the United States with well-developed vocabularies and an understanding of academic language. Currently, the terms *academic language* and *academic English* are being widely used to describe academic vocabulary and language use in U.S. classrooms, though Stahl & Nagy (2006) refer to it as "literate English." Within the SIOP® Model, we refer to academic vocabulary as having three key elements:

1. **Content Words**: These are the key vocabulary words, terms, and concepts associated with a particular topic being taught (e.g., for the American Revolutionary War: *Redcoats, democracy, Patriots, freedom of religion, Shot Heard Round the World, Paul Revere*, etc.);

2. **Process/Function Words**: These are the words that have to do with functional language (e.g, how to request information, justify opinions, state a conclusion, etc.), language used in the classroom for processes and tasks (e.g., *share with a partner, discuss, line up, graph, list, classify*, etc.), and language processes (e.g., *scan, skim, question, debate, argue, summarize*, etc.). Other kinds of words that are included in this category include transition words (*therefore, in conclusion, moreover, furthermore*, etc.), and sequence words (*first, then, next, finally, at last*, etc.).

3. **Words and Word Parts That Teach English Structure**: These are words that enable students to learn new vocabulary, primarily based upon English morphology. Biemiller (2004) suggests students in grade 12 know about 175,000 words with roots; of these, about 15,000 are known by a majority of students. Additionally, students through grade 6 acquire approximately 800–1,200 root words per year. These estimates are based upon *The Living Word Vocabulary* by Dale & O'Rourke (1981). There is no way that English learners can realistically learn all the words they need to know through instruction and memorization. Therefore, all teachers, elementary and secondary alike, must help students learn that many English words are formed with roots and base words joined to prefixes and suffixes. For example, if a science teacher is teaching photosynthesis, he can help students learn the meaning of *photosynthesis* by introducing the meaning of the root, *photo-* (light). By comparing the words *photosynthesis, photocopy, photograph, photography, photoelectron, photofinish*, and *photogenic*, students can see how these English words are related by both spelling and meaning (Bear, Invernizzi, Templeton, & Johnston, 2007).

To assist with teaching English word structure, especially for those who are not English or language arts teachers, we include in Figure 3.1 some of the most common Latin roots that are found in thousands of English words. The fourteen roots with asterisks provide the meaning of over 100,000 words! By adding suffixes to many of the

FIGURE 3.1 *Common Word Roots*

There are hundreds of Latin word roots that are used frequently with prefixes and suffixes. This is only a partial list of the most frequently used roots. The roots with asterisks (*) are the fourteen roots that provide clues to the meaning of over 100,000 words.

Port: to carry
Import, export, portable, transport, porter, deport, report, support, portal, important, importantly, unimportant

Form: to shape
Reform, deform, inform, information, transform, conform, formula, formal, informal, formality, informative

Rupt: to break
Rupture, disrupt, disruptive, disruption, abruptly, bankrupt, corruption, erupted, eruption, interrupt

Tract: to draw or pull
Tractor, attract, abstract, contract, retract, contractual, detract, distract, extract, subtract, tractable, intractable, traction, protract, protractor

*Scrib or script: to write
Scribble, ascribe, describe, description, conscript, inscribe, inscription, superscription, prescribe, prescriptive, script, scripture, transcribe, transcript, transcription

*Spec or spect: to see, watch, observe
Spectator, spectacular, spectacle, respect, spectrum, specter, disrespect, inspect, inspector, retrospective, species, special, specimen

Stru or struct: to build
Structure, structural, construct, construction, destructive, reconstruct, instruct, instructor, obstruct, instrument, construe

Jac or jec or ject: to throw, lie
Dejected, rejection, adjective, conjecture, eject, injection, interjection, object, objective, project, rejection, adjacent

Dic or dict: to say, tell
Dictate, dictator, predict, diction, dictation, contradict, contradictory, edict, indicate, indict, indictment

Flect or flex: to bend
Flex, flexible, flexibility, deflect, inflection, reflect, reflexive, reflective, reflector, circumflexion

Ped or pod: foot (*ped* is Latin; *pod* is Greek)
Pedestrian, pedestal, podium, pedometer, centipede, pedal, expedition, impede, podiatry, podiatrist

*Mit or miss: to send
Mission, missile, missive, admit, admission, commit, dismissed, emissary, intermission, intermittent, remiss, remit, remittance, submit, submission, transmit, transmission, emit, permit, permission, permissive

*Tend or tens or tent: to stretch, strain
Intend, intention, intently, extended, tense, intense, pretense, tension, intensity, attention, inattention, unintentionally, distend, detention, détente

*Ten, tent, or tain: to have, hold
Tenant, tenable, tenacity, tenacious, contents, contended, discontented, contentment, intent, maintain, retain, retentive

*Plic or ply: to fold
Implicit, implicitness, explicit, explicate, implication, replicate, complicated, application, ply, apply, imply, reply

*Fer: to bring, bear, yield
Refer, reference, confer, conference, inference, suffer, transfer, defer, differ, difference, fertile, fertilize, fertilization, circumference, odoriferous

Aud: to hear
Audible, auditory, audience, audio, audiotape, audiovisual, audition, auditorium

Vis: to see
Visual, visa, visor, vision, visible, visitor, visitation, visualize, invisible, evident, provide, providence

Cred: to believe
Credit, credential, credible, incredible, creditable, accredit, credence, incredulity

*Duc, duce, or duct: to lead
Conduct, deduct, educate, induce, introduction, produce, reduce, reduction, reducible, production

Pel or puls: to drive, push, throw
Impulse, compel, compulsion, expel, propel, dispel, impulsive, pulsate, compulsive, repel, repellent

*Fac, fact, fic, or fect: fact, manufacture, faculty, facility, facile, facilitate, satisfaction, factor, beneficiary, amplification, certificate, confection, affect, defective, disinfect, efficacy, magnificent, personification, proficient, sufficient

FIGURE 3.1 *Continued*

Vert or vers: to turn
Convert, convertible, revert, reversible, extrovert, introvert, divert, avert, aversion, aversive, vertigo

Capit or capt: head, chief, leader
Capital, decapitate, capitol, capitalize, captain, caption, recapitulate

*Cept, cap, ciev, or ceit: to take, to seize, to receive
Capable, capsule, captive, captor, capture, accept, deception, exception, intercept, conception, receptable, susceptible, perceptive, precept, receive, receipt, deceive, deceit

Pend or pens: to hang
Pendant, suspend, suspense, pendulum, pending, dependent, perpendicular, appendix

*Pos, pon, or pose: to put, place, set
Compose, composite, dispose, disposable, oppose, component, postpone, proponent, deposit, compound, depose, proposal, preposition, disposal, exposition, exponent, expose, impose, suppose, opponent, proposition, position

*Sist, sta, or stat: to stand, endure
Persist, consistent, consist, desist, assist, resist, assistant, insist, stamina, constant, circumstance, distant, obstacle, standard, substance

Greek Combining Forms

Beginning: auto, phono, photo, biblio, hydro, hyper, hypo, tele, chrom, arch, phys, psych, micro, peri, bi, semi, hemi, mono, metro, demo

Ending: *graph, gram, meter, *ology, sphere, scope, crat, cracy, polis

Examples: photograph, microscope, hemisphere, telegram, chronometer, physiology, metropolis, perimeter, archeology, bibliography, democracy, autocrat

Compiled by M.K. Henry, 1990.

---

words that are included with each root (e.g., *disrespectful, extraction, informed*), you can increase further the number of words on this list.

We urge caution about sharing this list with students. It is not included here as a list for having students memorize roots, words, and their meanings. Instead, use what students already know about words: If they know how the words *import, export, portable, transport,* and *porter* are all related (they all have to do with carrying something), they can transfer that knowledge to learning the meanings of *important* (carrying value) and *unimportant* (not carrying value). These roots and words should be used for your reference and for helping students understand how roots work in the English language. (For more information about word parts—morphemes—and English structure, see Bear et al., 2007, and Bear, Helman, Invernizzi, Templeton, & Johnston, 2007).

Another source of words for teaching vocabulary is found in a scheme designed by Beck, McKeown, and Kucan (2002). They describe three tiers of words often taught in U.S. schools:

1. Tier One words are common words, such as simple nouns, verbs, high-frequency words, and sight words. Most students know these words conversationally, and it is usually isn't necessary to focus on them, except for young children who are learning to read. While Beck, McKeown, and Kucan (2002) recommend teachers focus primarily on Tier Two words in their vocabulary lessons, we urge a caution. Teachers of English learners need to be careful that they not assume their students know the Tier One words; newcomers and emergent speakers especially may need explicit instruction and practice with these words. Depending on their ages, they are likely to know the Tier One words in their native language, but they'll most likely need help in learning them in English.

2. Tier Two words are commonly found in school texts but not in general conversation. Stahl and Nagy (2006) refer to them as "Goldilocks words—words that are not too difficult, not too easy, but just right" (p. 133). These are also considered to be the words students need to know for comprehending school texts and achieving academically, and they should be taught explicitly to English learners, and most native-speaking students.

3. Tier Three words are uncommon words, found rarely in school texts except in particular contexts, such as a discussion of a specific content-related topic. While these words may be interesting, fun to know, and unique to a particular topic, it is recommended that teachers not spend a great deal of time on them. When a Tier Three word is included only once or twice in a story, for example, it's fine to mention the word in its particular context, but then move on.

With all this serious discussion about words and vocabulary development, it's very important to remember that learning about words and playing with words can be great fun, for English learners and native speakers alike. Stahl and Nagy (2006) discuss the importance of developing students' "word consciousness." Word consciousness "is a phrase used to refer to the interest in and awareness of words that should be part of vocabulary instruction. In other words, motivation plays an important role in vocabulary learning, as it does in any other kind of learning" (p. 137). Activities in which students manipulate words, sort words, laugh and giggle about funny words, and choose words they want to know about are as important for vocabulary growth as the more scholarly aspects of vocabulary teaching and word learning. For example, see if you don't chuckle or eye-roll with the following (Stahl & Nagy, 2006, pp. 147–148):

- A bicycle can't stand alone because it is two-tired.
- Time flies like an arrow. Fruit flies like a banana.
- A chicken crossing the road is poultry in motion.
- Those who get too big for their britches will be exposed in the end.

And how about some of these homographs:

- We polish the Polish furniture.
- He could lead if he would get the lead out.
- The present is a good time to present the present.
- I did not object to the object.

As elementary teachers, probably you are familiar with many wonderful picture books that celebrate and play with words. For English learners, as well as children who struggle with learning to read, using these books to poke fun at the idiosyncrasies of the English language can decrease some of the frustration in learning the language. Some of our favorites include:

- *The Boy Who Loved Words* by Roni Schotter (2006; Schwartz & Wade Books/Random House); for grades 2–5; Winner of the Parents' Choice 2006 Gold Award
- *Fancy Nancy* (there is a series of Fancy Nancy books) by Jane O'Connor (2005; HarperCollins Publisher); for ages 4–8

- *Miss Alaineus: A Vocabulary Disaster* by Debra Frasier (Paperback 2007; Voyager Books); best for upper-grade students
- *Donovan's Word Jar* by Monalisa Degross (1994; paperback 1998; HarperCollins Publisher); for upper grades: the story is about a third-grade boy

Vocabulary Instruction

In a synthesis of twenty years of research on vocabulary instruction, Blachowicz and Fisher (2000) determined four main principles that should guide instruction:

1. *Children should be active in developing their understanding of words and ways to learn them.* Such ways include use of semantic mapping, word sorts (see Figure 3.2a and 3.2b, pp. 66–67), Concept Definition Maps (see Figure 3.3, p. 69), and developing strategies for independent word learning.

2. *Children should personalize word learning* through practices such as Vocabulary Self-Collection Strategy (VSS) (Ruddell, 2007), mnemonic strategies, and personal dictionaries.

3. *Children should be immersed in words* by rich language environments that focus on words and draw students' attention to the learning of words. Word walls, personal word study notebooks and dictionaries, and comparing/contrasting words with the same morphemic element (e.g., photograph, photosynthesis, photogenic) aid students in recognizing and using the words around them.

4. *Children should build on multiple sources of information to learn words through repeated exposures.* Letting students see and hear new words more than once and drawing on multiple sources of meaning are important for vocabulary development.

There is little benefit to selecting 10 or 15 or 20 isolated vocabulary terms and asking ELs to copy them from the board and look up their definitions in the dictionary, (Allen, 2007, Fisher & Frey, 2008b), many of the words in the definitions are also unfamiliar to these students, rendering the activity meaningless. Although using the dictionary is an important school skill to learn, the task must fit the students' learning needs. The number of terms should be tailored to the students' English and literacy levels, and they should be presented in context, not in isolation. The *Oxford Picture Dictionary for the Content Areas* and related books (Kauffman & Apple, 2000) are excellent resources for contextualizing terms. There are numerous, excellent picture dictionaries for elementary children. For students with minimal literacy skills, using the dictionary to find words can serve to reinforce the concept of alphabetizing and it familiarizes them with the parts of a dictionary; however, defining words should not be the only activity used. Effective SIOP® teachers support the understanding of dictionary definitions so that the task is meaningful for students. In fact, many effective teachers introduce dictionary skills to students by using words that are already familiar to them.

There are a myriad of meaningful and useful ways that vocabulary can be taught to English learners. The following section describes approaches to vocabulary development and word study that are especially helpful to ELs. When used regularly, they provide students with multiple exposures to key language and vocabulary through meaningful practice and review.

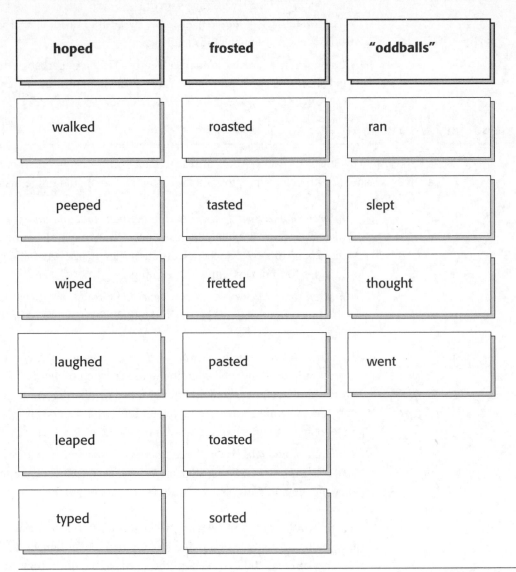

hoped	frosted	"oddballs"
walked	roasted	ran
peeped	tasted	slept
wiped	fretted	thought
laughed	pasted	went
leaped	toasted	
typed	sorted	

FIGURE 3.2a *Word Sorts: Past Tense*

Word Sorts During a Word Sort, students categorize words or phrases that have been previously introduced into groups predetermined by the teacher (Bear, Invernizzi, Templeton, & Johnston, 2004). Words or phrases are typed on a sheet of paper (46-point type on the computer works well). Students cut the paper into word strips and then sort the words according to meaning, similarities in structure, derivations, or sounds.

For example, a variety of words in the past tense are listed in mixed order on a sheet of paper (see Figure 3.2a). After you orally read and then have children chorally read the words, ask them to cut out each of the words and sort them according to spelling pattern and ending sound. You might wish to differentiate here by having your fluent speakers and capable readers determine for themselves several possibilities for sorting, such as by ending sound, by words that end in "e" before the "ed" ending is added, and so forth. These children then could do a "word hunt" (Bear et al., 2007) to search for additional words that fit the varied patterns they have identified.

For your English learners and struggling readers, you may wish to engage in a small-group lesson with the sorts to teach and reinforce how the past tense is formed in

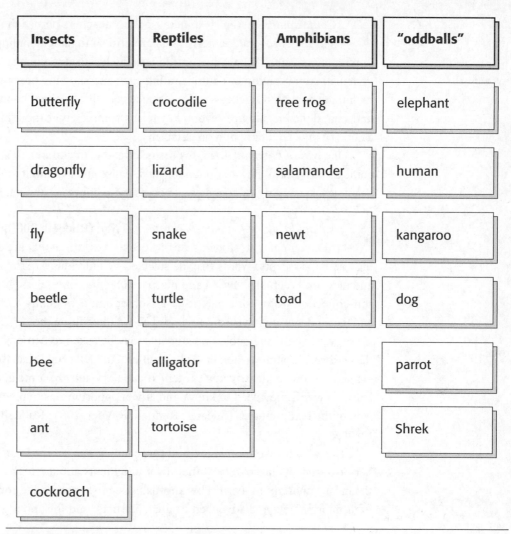

Insects	Reptiles	Amphibians	"oddballs"
butterfly	crocodile	tree frog	elephant
dragonfly	lizard	salamander	human
fly	snake	newt	kangaroo
beetle	turtle	toad	dog
bee	alligator		parrot
ant	tortoise		Shrek
cockroach			

FIGURE 3.2b   *Word Sorts: Content Vocabulary*

English words. Contextualize the sorts by providing sentences in which the words are used. For very young students, teachers provide the words on word cards to eliminate the inordinate amount of time required for children to cut the words themselves.

Other examples of Word Sorts involve words and phrases related to the content concepts being taught, and sounds (such as open/long and closed/short sounds). After students cut apart the words and phrases, sort them into groups, and identify an appropriate label for each, if they are able to do so (see Figure 3.2b,). Consider the ways you could differentiate this activity: (1) Provide labels for students who may be unfamiliar or shaky with English words for concepts being reviewed; (2) students for whom this content sort is quick and easy could be directed to www.Wikipedia.org (the free online encyclopedia) and investigate further what distinguishes insects, reptiles, and amphibians; (3) students could add more columns to the sort (such as mammals and birds) and fill in the columns with appropriate information, using books, Wikipedia, or other resources. Adding the "oddball" column in sorts encourages children to think about both examples and non-examples during the classification activity.

Contextualizing Key Vocabulary SIOP® teachers peruse the material to be learned and select several key terms that are critical to understanding the lesson's most important concepts. The teacher introduces the terms at the outset of the lesson, systematically defining or demonstrating each and showing how that term is used within the context of the lesson. Experienced SIOP® teachers know that having students understand the meaning of several key terms completely is more effective than having a cursory understanding of a dozen terms.

One way of contextualizing words is to read with children in small groups and, as they come across a term they do not understand, pause and explain it to them, using as many examples, synonyms, or cognates as necessary to convey the meaning.

Vocabulary Self-Collection Strategy (VSS) (Ruddell, 2007) Following the reading of a content text, students self-select several words that are essential to understanding content concepts. Words may be selected by individuals, partners, or small groups, and they are eventually shared and discussed by the entire class. A class list of vocabulary self-collection words for a particular lesson or unit is mutually agreed on by the teacher and the students, and these are reviewed and studied throughout. They also may be entered into a word study notebook, and students may be asked to demonstrate their knowledge of these words through written or oral activities. Ruddell (2007) has found that when students are shown how to identify key content vocabulary, they become adept at selecting and learning words they need to know, and, given opportunities to practice VSS, comprehension of the text improves (Shearer, Ruddell, & Vogt, 2001; Ruddell & Shearer, 2002; Stahl & Nagy, 2006).

The VSS is an effective method for teaching and reviewing content vocabulary because students learn to trust their own judgments about which content words are the most important to learn. This approach is most appropriate for students who are high-intermediate and advanced English learners, and for upper grade (4–6) students.

Personal Dictionaries Similar to VSS, personal dictionaries are created as an individual vocabulary and spelling resource for children at all levels of English proficiency, and are generally used with students who have intermediate and advanced English proficiency. ELs read together in pairs or small groups and write unknown words they encounter in their personal dictionaries. The teacher works with each group and discusses the words students have written in their dictionaries, providing correction or clarity as needed. For young children (K–2), have them draw a picture to help them remember key words.

Word Wall During a lesson, key vocabulary is reviewed with a word wall where relevant content vocabulary words are listed alphabetically, usually on a large poster, sheet of butcher paper, or pocket chart (Cunningham, 2004). Originally designed as a method for teaching and reinforcing sight words for emergent readers, word walls are also effective for displaying content words related to a particular unit or theme. The words are revisited frequently throughout the lesson or unit, and students are encouraged to use them in their writing and discussions.

Cunningham (2004) recommends that teachers judiciously select words for a word wall and that the number be limited to those of greatest importance. We would add that teachers should resist the temptation to have multiple word walls in one classroom because the walls quickly become cluttered with words that are difficult to sort through, especially for ELs. One word wall, carefully maintained and changed as needed, is what we recommend. Some teachers, with students' input, regularly remove words from a word wall to keep the number of words reasonable. Every Friday, or every other Friday, for example, the children jointly decide which words they no longer need on the wall. Word wall posters can also be kept and stored for later reference or review.

For English learners, it is helpful to have an illustrated word wall, whenever possible. Granted, some abstract words and concepts are difficult to portray through illustrations or photos (e.g., *freedom* or *democracy*). However, many words can be depicted with simple illustrations that serve as reminders of their meanings.

Concept Definition Map The Concept Definition Map is a great way to learn and remember content vocabulary and concepts (Buehl, 2009). For example, in one classroom, the first-grade children were learning about families as their teacher read aloud and discussed several picture books about different kinds of families, including *My Family* by Debbie Bailey and Susan Huszar (1998, Annick Press); *The Family Book* by Todd Parr (2003, Little, Brown Books for Young Readers); and *Five Little Monkeys Jumping on the Bed* by Eileen Christelow (1989, Clarion). At the beginning of the day's lesson, the teacher introduced a partially completed Concept Definition Map (see Figure 3.3), with the word *Family* in the center box. As the children discussed the different kinds of

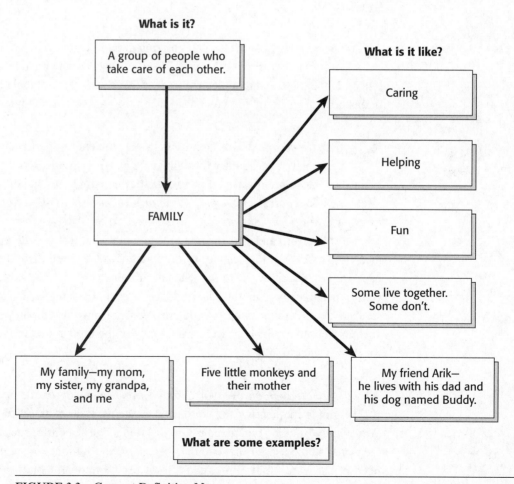

FIGURE 3.3 *Concept Definition Map*

families they read about, the teacher began filling in some of the boxes in a large Concept Definition Map on chart paper. The next day, after one more story, the children completed their own maps, and used them to write sentences about their own and other families. The teacher honored the fact that English learners, including those who were recent immigrants, knew about families and could contribute what they knew during the class discussions, even if they didn't know some of the English words for the familiar concepts.

For upper-grade teachers, even though the Concept Definition Map is a simple graphic organizer, it can be used to discuss complex concepts such as *freedom, democracy, revolution*, or *evolution*, and literary terminology (such as *symbolism* or *irony*). The Concept Definition Map is also an excellent prewriting activity for teaching summarizing. Children begin the summarizing process by organizing content concepts in the graphic organizer. Then sentences can be created from the information in the Concept Definition Map and subsequently written into paragraph form.

Cloze Sentences Cloze sentences can be used to teach and review content vocabulary. Students read a sentence that has strong contextual support for the vocabulary word that has been omitted from the sentence. Once the meaning of the word is determined and possible replacement words are brainstormed, the teacher (or a student) provides the correct word. For example, "The largest state in the United States, ———, is sometimes, called America's last frontier because it is so vast and most of it is undeveloped (Alaska)."

List–Group–Label This categorizing activity can also be completed as a List–Group–Label activity (Vacca & Vacca, 2004) in which students brainstorm words related to the topic and then determine possible categories or labels for the words. The brainstormed words are then reviewed when they are rewritten under the various labels.

Word Generation This activity helps EL students and others learn and/or review new content vocabulary through analogy. For example, write "-port" on the board. Invite students to brainstorm all the words they can think of that contain "port." Examples might include *report, import, export, important, portfolio, Port-a-Potty, Portland, deport, transport, transportation, support, airport*, and so on. Analyze the meaning of each brainstormed word and ask students to figure out what words containing "-port" might mean ("to carry"). If they cannot figure it out, it's fine to tell them the meaning. Then go back and revisit each word to see if the definition "to carry" has something to do with the word's meaning. Note that we did not define "port" first; rather, we recommend that students generalize meanings of content words from words that they already know that contain the same syllable or word part. Many of the roots found in Figure 3.1 can be used for Word Generation.

Word Study Books A Word Study Book is a student-made personal notebook containing frequently used words and concepts. Bear et al. (2007) recommend that the Word Study Book be organized by English language structure, such as listing together all the words studied so far that end in -tion, -sion, and -tation. We support this notion and believe that Word Study Books can also be used for content study where words are grouped by meaning.

Vocabulary Games Playing games like Pictionary and Scrabble can help students recall vocabulary terms. Word searches for beginning English speakers and crossword puzzles for more proficient speakers are additional vocabulary development tools. Software programs are available for teachers or students to create crossword puzzles.

Self-Assessment of Levels of Word Knowledge (Diamond & Gutlohn, 2006, p. 5) As English learners are acquiring vocabulary, it may be helpful for them to self-assess their knowledge of new words. Dale (1965) described four levels of word knowledge that can be used to describe the extent of a person's understanding of words:

1. I've never heard or seen the word before.
2. I've seen or heard the word before, but I don't know what it means.
3. I vaguely know the meaning of the word, and I can associate it with a concept or context.
4. I know the word well.

With effective vocabulary instruction and repeated exposures to unfamiliar vocabulary, knowledge of the words increase and they move up the levels from 1 to 4. When teachers introduce the four Levels of Word Knowledge to students, they can self-assess their word knowledge as words are introduced and studied.

The Lesson

UNIT: *Mrs. Frisby and the Rats of NIMH* (Sixth Grade)

The lessons described in this chapter take place in an urban elementary school with a large population of ELs. The number of ELs in this school enables classes to be grouped homogeneously by students' English proficiency levels. Students in all three classes described here are a heterogeneous mix of native English Speakers and ELs with varied levels of English proficiency. Many of the ELs emigrated from rural areas in Latin America and have low literacy levels due to interrupted schooling experiences.

As part of a literature course, Miss Paige, Mrs. Jarmin, and Mr. Ramirez are required to teach a variety of American literature. The first book in the series is *Mrs. Frisby and the Rats of NIMH*, and the teachers will spend one week to ten days on the unit. The story is about Mrs. Frisby, a field mouse, who is worried about her younger son, Timothy. He has had pneumonia and is too weak and frail to be moved. But if the Frisbys don't move immediately, they'll all be killed. Mrs. Frisby hears about the wonderful Rats of NIMH who are strong, smart, and able to do almost anything. The story chronicles the adventures of the family and the Rats of NIMH.

The goals for this unit include (1) students will read an extended text, and (2) students will use their prior knowledge as a tool for understanding the text. Although these may seem somewhat vague, the teachers felt strongly that these students need to have the experience of reading an extended text, even a challenging one, because materials written at their literacy levels tend to be short, simple stories. They believe that with appropriate instruction, the ELs will be able to participate in reading the novel. The teachers are planning to introduce the novel by showing the video version of the story. Seeing the video prior to reading the text will provide students with an overall understanding of the story and will provide exposure to new vocabulary associated with the text. Following the viewing of the video, the teachers will introduce the text, which the class will read together. The teachers may provide activities of their choosing to reinforce the concepts and vocabulary covered in the story. (For more examples of lesson and unit plans in language arts, see Vogt, Echevarria, & Short, in press.)

Teaching Scenarios

The teachers have prepared their own plans for teaching the unit on *Mrs. Frisby and the Rats of NIMH*. Their individual approaches to teaching the unit and SIOP® ratings are described below.

Miss Paige

Miss Paige began the first lesson of the unit by asking, "Have you ever seen a rat?" and showing the class a picture of one. The students were quite interested in this topic and readily shared their experiences. She then talked with the students about how in some stories and novels, animals take on human characteristics, such as in *Charlotte's Web* (E. B. White, 1974), a book many students had read or listened to in grade 4. She asked students for other examples of stories or books that had animals who behaved like humans. Two students, both English learners, mentioned books they had read in their native languages before moving to the United States. Miss Paige then introduced a semantic map that had the word *survival* written in the center. She asked, "What are some words and ideas you can think of that have to do with survival?" As students orally provided their ideas, she clustered them on the chart: *Survivor TV show, escaping a tsunami, September 11, earthquakes, animals' need for food and water*, and so forth. She then asked students to discuss with a partner the following question: "What would you do if a member of your family was very ill, but you had to move in order to survive?" The students and Miss Paige had a brief and lively discussion about what students thought they would do. Miss Paige then introduced *Mrs. Frisby and the Rats of NIMH*, written by R. C. O'Brien & Z. Bernstein (1986). She told her students that in this book a family of rats who behaved like humans would face the problem of survival. She then began showing the video of *Mrs. Frisby and the Rats of NIMH*.

After watching the video, Miss Paige showed a transparency listing ten key terms from the story that she was certain some students would not know. As she pointed to each word, she asked the class if they knew what the word meant. At least one student knew the meaning of two of the ten vocabulary terms, indicating that Miss Paige had done an adequate job of selecting key vocabulary words for which the students needed direct instruction. She discussed each term and wrote a brief definition next to the word on the transparency. Next, Miss Paige began reading the first chapter of the book with her students. While reading chapters in the book throughout the course of the unit, she made it a practice to pause every few paragraphs to check for understanding, elaborate, define words, and paraphrase parts of the story. Occasionally she reminded students of something they had discussed in another lesson. For example, when Mrs. Frisby is described as a widow, Miss Paige said, "Who remembers what a widow is? We talked about that word when we read *The Witches* by Roald Dahl. Remember the grandma who was a widow? What does that mean?" Then Miss Paige wrote the word on a piece of chart paper that she continued to use as a word wall throughout the unit, adding words the students identified as unfamiliar throughout the course of the unit.

On the SIOP® form in Figure 3.4, rate Miss Paige's lesson for each of the Building Background features.

Mrs. Jarmin

At the beginning of the first lesson of the unit, Mrs. Jarmin began by telling the class that they would be reading an interesting book in which the main characters were rats. Then Mrs. Jarmin asked, "Who has ever seen a rat?" Several students told of their experiences

FIGURE 3.4 *Building Background Component of the SIOP®: Miss Paige's lesson*

4	3	2	1	0	NA
7. **Concepts explicitly linked** to students' background experiences	**Concepts loosely linked** to students' background experiences			**Concepts not explicitly linked** to students' background experiences	

4	3	2	1	0
8. **Links explicitly made** between past learning and new concepts	**Few links made** between past learning and new concepts			**No links made** between past learning and new concepts

4	3	2	1	0
9. **Key vocabulary emphasized** (e.g., introduced, written, repeated, and highlighted for students to see)	**Key vocabulary** introduced, but not emphasized			**Key vocabulary** not introduced or emphasized

seeing rats or having them as pets. Then Mrs. Jarmin told the class that they would see a video based on the novel *Mrs. Frisby and the Rats of NIMH*, and that they would read the book after seeing the video.

Before showing the video, Mrs. Jarmin wanted to teach the students some terms they would encounter during the unit. Working with small, rotating groups, she introduced reciprocal teaching (Palinscar & Brown, 1984) by posting the following words on a chart: *predicting, clarifying,* and *questioning.* Mrs. Jarmin distributed three index cards that described each of the three terms to each student in the group. First she asked students to look at the card that gave guidelines for predicting. She read, "Let's look at the title." Mrs. Jarmin paused and asked the students what the title was. The students showed her the title of the book. She continued reading, "Look at all the visual clues on the page." Again she stopped to make sure the students understood and she asked the meaning of "visual clues." Because the students weren't sure, she told them the phrase means pictures, graphs, and the like. Then she read, "What do you think we'll be reading about?" Mrs. Jarmin told the students to follow the guidelines and tell her what they predicted the book would be about. (See Figure 3.5.)

She reiterated the information on the card, telling the students to look at the title, look at the pictures, and think about what they'd be reading about. She left the group to think while she checked on another group. When she returned she said, "What do you think we'll be reading about? I . . ." A student began his sentence with, "I think we'll be reading about some rats." Mrs. Jarmin asked him to explain how he came to that answer and then replied, "Good. Who has more information they want to share?" One student made a comment about the mice. The teacher wrote the words *mice* and *rats* on the board and asked what the story would be about. Some students seemed confused about those words so the teacher asked them to look at the title. They had a brief discussion about how mice and rats differ. Once the distinction was made, they moved on to the card about clarifying.

Mrs. Jarmin read, "One of the words I wasn't sure about was _____." She then distributed a photocopy of the summary of the story to the students and told them to use

---

Predicting

Let's look at the title. Look at all the visual clues on the page. What do you think we'll be reading about?

Clarifying

One of the words I wasn't sure about was _____.

Questioning

What is the story about?

FIGURE 3.5 *Activity Based on Reciprocal Teaching*
(Palinscar and Brown, 1984)

a highlighter to identify the words they didn't understand. The teacher circulated among other groups as the students read the summary and highlighted unfamiliar words. When she returned, she asked the students to tell her their highlighted words as she wrote them on the board. She said, "Let's see if there are other words that can be used in place of the highlighted words. We'll see which words we already know and the ones we don't know we'll look up in the thesaurus. A thesaurus is a book that is like a dictionary that helps us clarify words." The words the students didn't know were:

Vocabulary Word List

NIMH–　　　a place

Scarce–　　　_____

Asparagus–　a vegetable

Frail–　　　_____

Abandoned–　left behind

The group went through the list, with Mrs. Jarmin asking if anyone knew the meaning of the words. One student recognized that NIMH is the name of a place and that asparagus is a vegetable, so the teacher wrote those definitions beside the words. Because nobody knew the meaning of *frail* and *scarce*, Mrs. Jarmin drew a line, indicating that the students would find those words in the thesaurus. Then the students looked up each word together. The first student to find the word called out to the others the page number on which the word was found. As a group, the students decided on a word or two to denote meaning. When they finished defining all the words, the teacher drew their attention to the final card about questioning. She read, "What is the story about?" and said, "Now that we have made some predictions about the story and we've clarified some terms, what do you think this story will be about?"

The students were now familiar with making predictions about a story and knew one way to clarify words they didn't understand. So before starting the video, Mrs. Jarmin showed a transparency on the overhead projector that listed ten words she identified as key vocabulary. Each group of students was asked to look up two of the words in their thesaurus. The class discussed the synonyms that the students read, and Mrs. Jarmin wrote a short definition next to each word on the overhead. She then told the students to copy the words on a piece of paper and to put a check next to each word as they heard it while watching the video. At the conclusion of the video, she asked students which vocabulary words they had heard and marked. Mrs. Jarmin wrote those words on a word wall and then reviewed with the class the meaning of each word, providing synonyms and drawing a picture, if necessary, to convey meaning as they had done in the clarifying exercise. (The word wall remained posted throughout the reading of the novel, and Mrs. Jarmin often drew students' attention to one of the posted words as they came across it in the text.)

After viewing the video, Mrs. Jarmin and the class began reading the story. Mrs. Jarmin paused after the first chapter and brought out a Venn diagram from an earlier lesson that illustrated the way fiction and fantasy are similar, although not all fiction involves fantasy. She asked the students how they would describe this story so far, as fiction or as fantasy. Looking at the descriptors listed on the Venn diagram, they decided the story was fantasy. Mrs. Jarmin then told the students that, especially because fantasy can sometimes be confusing, they would construct a graphic organizer as they proceeded through the story to keep track of the characters, as well as to provide visual clues for plot events and vocabulary in the story. She asked students to think of words to describe the characters Timothy, Martin, Cynthia, Teresa, and Mrs. Frisby, from the first chapter. As students mentioned adjectives describing the characters, Mrs. Jarmin began writing them on chart paper as a graphic organizer.

Mrs. Jarmin and the class continued this same type of process until they had completed the novel.

On the SIOP® form in Figure 3.6 rate Mrs. Jarmin's lesson on each of the Building Background features.

Mr. Ramirez

Mr. Ramirez began the first lesson of the unit by distributing the text to the students. He asked what the students thought the book would be about, and they suggested that it would be something about rats. He told them that they would first watch a video based on the book before actually reading the text. He gave an oral summary of the video to provide some background before showing it. He showed the video, then told the students they would begin reading the book the next day.

Mr. Ramirez began the second day's lesson by writing twenty vocabulary terms on the board. He told the students that they were to copy each term in their notebooks and look up the definition of each term in the dictionary. The students spent the second day completing this activity. Most students worked independently, although sometimes they would ask a friend for help.

FIGURE 3.6   *Building Background Component of the SIOP®: Mrs. Jarmin's Lesson*

4	3	2	1	0	NA
7. **Concepts explicitly linked** to students' background experiences		**Concepts loosely linked** to students' background experiences		**Concepts not explicitly linked** to students' background experiences	
4	3	2	1	0	
8. **Links explicitly made** between past learning and new concepts		**Few links made** between past learning and new concepts		**No links made** between past learning and new concepts	
4	3	2	1	0	
9. **Key vocabulary emphasized** (e.g., introduced, written, repeated, and highlighted for students to see)		**Key vocabulary** introduced, but not emphasized		**Key vocabulary** not introduced or emphasized	

The third day of the unit Mr. Ramirez read the first chapter with the students. While reading, he asked a number of comprehension questions, cleared up one student's confusion about which character was ill, and reviewed the chapter completely after reading it with the students. He continued this process throughout the book. At the conclusion of the unit, he gave the class an exam to check their understanding.

On the SIOP® form in Figure 3.7, rate Mr. Ramirez's lesson on each of the Building Background features.

FIGURE 3.7   *Building Background Component of the SIOP®: Mr. Ramirez's lesson*

4	3	2	1	0	NA
7. **Concepts explicitly linked** to students' background experiences		**Concepts loosely linked** to students' background experiences		**Concepts not explicitly linked** to students' background experiences	
4	3	2	1	0	
8. **Links explicitly made** between past learning and new concepts		**Few links made** between past learning and new concepts		**No links made** between past learning and new concepts	
4	3	2	1	0	
9. **Key vocabulary emphasized** (e.g., introduced, written, repeated, and highlighted for students to see)		**Key vocabulary** introduced, but not emphasized		**Key vocabulary** not introduced or emphasized	

Discussion of Lessons

7. *Concepts Explicitly Linked to Students' Background Experiences*

Miss Paige: 4

Mrs. Jarmin: 2

Mr. Ramirez: 1

Miss Paige's lesson received a "4" on the SIOP® for this feature. She elicited information about students' knowledge of rats, but more important, she discussed how animals in stories and novels sometimes take on human characteristics. She also asked students for examples of books they knew that had animals behaving as people. Miss Paige introduced a central theme in the novel, survival, by having students brainstorm words and concepts they knew related to the theme. A novel such as *Mrs. Frisby and the Rats of NIMH* may be difficult for English learners to understand, yet by linking the topic to their own experiences, the teacher helped to enhance student comprehension.

Mrs. Jarmin's lesson received a "2" on the SIOP® for this feature. She made an effort to activate the students' prior knowledge, but it was not done in an explicit or systematic way. While Miss Paige organized the information using a semantic map for students to see and make reference to later, Mrs. Jarmin merely conducted a verbal discussion of a few students' experiences. ELs benefit from visual clues given during a discussion, and Mrs. Jarmin did not provide any visual assistance for those learners with limited English proficiency. Further, she did not organize the information in a useful way that would make the information accessible and meaningful to all the students in class.

Mr. Ramirez's lesson received a "1" on the SIOP® for this feature. Although the video did provide background information for the students, Mr. Ramirez did not provide students with an adequate introduction to the video or the book. While he attempted to provide some background before showing the video, there is little benefit for English learners to hear only an oral explanation of new, unknown information. Further, he did not provide any opportunity to link the students' background or experiences to the unit by tapping into what they already knew.

8. *Links Explicitly Made between Past Learning and New Concepts*

Miss Paige: 3

Mrs. Jarmin: 4

Mr. Ramirez: 0

Miss Paige made several links to past learning by discussing books students had read or listened to (e.g., *Charlotte's Web* and *The Witches*). She also developed a word wall that assisted students' learning by reminding them of the meaning of words used in the story.

Mrs. Jarmin provided a direct link between past learning and new learning by showing the Venn diagram, and she also began constructing a graphic organizer that will be an important tool for activating students' knowledge as they proceed through the book. Each day the students will be oriented to the characters in the story and will be reminded of events covered in the book.

Mr. Ramirez did not make any attempt to link previous learning to what the students were currently reading about, nor did he establish any system for reviewing the material during subsequent lessons.

9. *Key Vocabulary Emphasized*

Miss Paige: 1

Mrs. Jarmin: 4

Mr. Ramirez: 0

Although Miss Paige wrote on a transparency a number of key vocabulary terms and discussed them, there was no further reference to the list nor did she have students copy the list for their own reference. It became a vocabulary-building activity done in isolation of any context, rendering it less effective than if she had used the transparency throughout the unit, reviewing and repeating the words and having them available for students to see.

Mrs. Jarmin took time to introduce students not only to the story and associated vocabulary, but also to ways of "doing school." The introduction took only fifteen minutes or so, and it presented some valuable skills that are required in school but not always explicitly taught. Also, she made new vocabulary words meaningful by defining terms before watching the video, then asking students to identify the terms within the context of the video. The words were written, posted, and referred to frequently. In this way, the key vocabulary terms became an integral part of the unit.

Mr. Ramirez's lesson did a poor job of developing students' vocabulary in any authentic way. First, rather than selecting a manageable number of key terms, twenty words were selected. The teacher didn't discuss the terms with the students or support their understanding of new vocabulary. Given these students' low literacy and English proficiency levels, an optimal number of new terms would range from five to twelve. The large number of terms, coupled with the vocabulary contained within the definitions, becomes overwhelming. Second, considering the students' academic and English proficiency levels, copying terms from the board and looking up their definitions in the dictionary is not meaningful. Frequently this type of exercise results in papers filled with misspelled words and incomplete sentences because the majority of words— both the vocabulary terms and their definitions—are unfamiliar to these students. Finally, the more decontextualized the activity, the more problematic learning becomes. That is, the more directly related the activity is to the learning objective, the more likely it is that student learning will take place. In this lesson, the activity was not closely aligned to the context of the story. Both the vocabulary terms and their multiple definitions were unfamiliar to the students, as was the formal lexicon of the dictionary that was supposed to clarify the terms. The activity, although probably well-intentioned, had little or no meaning for these students.

Summary

The importance of building background has been well established in the research literature, and is one of the easier components of the SIOP® to incorporate into teaching. Taking a few minutes to jump-start students' schemata and past learning, to explicitly find out what they know or have experienced about a topic, and then explicitly linking their knowledge directly to the lesson's objectives will result in greater understanding for English learners. English learners may have an especially difficult time with academic language, the vocabulary necessary for academic achievement. Therefore, it is of critical importance that the key vocabulary necessary for mastering content and language objectives be explicitly taught and reviewed regularly. Three types of academic vocabulary focused on in the SIOP® Model include content words, process/function words, and words that teach English structure. The traditional method of copying words and writing definitions is ineffective. Activities such as preteaching vocabulary words by highlighting them in context, posting and frequently reviewing words, using visuals to provide concrete meanings, and engaging students in interactive practice with words are effective ways to promote academic language development for English learners.

Discussion Questions

1. Some educators argue the importance of connecting new information to English learners' own cultural backgrounds in order to make content concepts meaningful. Others disagree, stating that students relate more to popular American influences (e.g., television shows) than they do to their parents' traditional cultural practices. What are some merits and problems with both positions? What about ELs born in the United States who have never lived in their native cultural setting?

2. Think about a joke or cartoon that you didn't understand, such as from a late-show monologue or a political cartoon. Why was it confusing or unamusing? What information would you have needed for it to make sense? What are the implications for teaching content to all students, including English learners?

3. If you are creating a SIOP® lesson, how will you activate children's prior knowledge and build background? What connections to past learning can you make? What are your key vocabulary words and how will you teach them?

chapter 4

Comprehensible Input

Comprehensible Input

10. Appropriate Speech

11. Clear Explanation of Academic Tasks

12. A Variety of Techniques Used

Teaching Scenarios

Mr. Edwards

Mr. Hernandez

Mrs. Monroe

Objectives

After reading, discussing, and engaging in activities related to this chapter, you will be able to meet the following content and language objectives.

Content Objectives

Explore techniques for presenting content information in ways that students comprehend.

Review various ways to model and provide directions for academic tasks.

Language Objectives

Discuss modifications to teacher speech that can increase student comprehension.

Write the steps needed for students to perform an academic task and have a partner perform each step.

While many of the features of the SIOP® Model are indicators of effective instruction for all students, this component comprises some of the features that make SIOP® instruction different from "just good instruction." An effective SIOP® teacher takes into account the unique characteristics of English learners. For these students, the teacher makes verbal communication more understandable by consciously attending to students' linguistic needs. Making the message understandable for students is referred to as comprehensible input (Krashen, 1985). Comprehensible input techniques are essential to help English learners understand what the teacher is saying, and these techniques should be evident throughout the lesson.

Background

Children who are learning rigorous content material in a language they do not speak or understand completely require specialized teaching techniques to make the message understood. Effective SIOP® teachers understand that acquiring a new language takes time and is facilitated by many "clues" and appropriate speech. Comprehensible input is achieved when teachers pay attention to the unique linguistic needs of ELs and consistently incorporate these techniques into their daily teaching routines.

Comprehensible input is much more than simply showing pictures as visual clues during a lesson. It involves a conscious effort to make the lesson understandable through a variety of means. Communication is made more understandable through speech that is appropriate to students' proficiency levels. The teacher enunciates and speaks more slowly, but in a natural way, for students who are beginning English speakers. More repetition may be needed for beginners and, as students gain more proficiency in English, the teacher adjusts her speech for the students' levels. Teachers will increase students' understanding by using appropriate speech coupled with a variety of techniques that will make the content clear. We will discuss a number of ways to achieve comprehensible input in the next sections. In the scenarios that follow later in the chapter, you will see examples of teachers who use comprehensible input techniques to varying degrees of effectiveness. Further examples of comprehensible input techniques are seen in the classroom footage on the CD.

SIOP® FEATURE 10:
Speech Appropriate for Students' Proficiency Levels

To hear a student describe the importance of appropriate speech, please view the corresponding video clip (Chapter 4, Module 1) on the accompanying CD.

For this feature, speech refers to (1) rate and enunciation and (2) complexity of speech. The first aspect addresses *how* the teacher speaks and the second aspect refers to *what* is said, such as level of vocabulary used, complexity of sentence structure, and use of idioms.

Students who are at the beginning levels of English proficiency benefit from teachers who slow down their rate of speech, use pauses, and enunciate clearly while speaking. As students become more comfortable with the language and acquire higher levels of proficiency, a slower rate isn't as necessary. In fact, for advanced and transitional students, teachers should use a rate of speech that is normal for a regular classroom. Effective SIOP® teachers adjust their rate of speech and enunciation to their students' levels of English proficiency.

Likewise, students will respond according to their proficiency level. The following example illustrates the variation in responses that may be expected when students at different levels of English proficiency are asked to describe the setting in a story:

- Beginning: "Cold day."
- Early Intermediate: "The day is cold and there is snow."
- Intermediate: "The day is very cold and heavy snow is falling."
- Advanced: "It is a cold, winter day and it is snowing more heavily than usual."
- Transitional: "The unusually heavy snow on the day the story takes place causes a number of problems for the characters."

SIOP® teachers carefully monitor the vocabulary and sentence structure they use with ELs in order to match the students' proficiency levels, especially with students at beginning levels of English proficiency. With students at intermediate and advanced levels, teachers should frequently ask students to explain their answers; say it another way; ask why, how, or what if; and require students to connect words, phrases, and short sentences into compound sentences that represent their ideas and thoughts. In this way, students not only use the language but think about how to use it as well.

Idioms—common sayings that cannot be translated exactly—create difficulty for students who are trying to make sense of a new language. Some common idioms include "below the belt" for unfair; "put one's foot down" meaning to be firm; "see eye to eye" for being in agreement; "get the hang of" meaning to become familiar with; and "get a person's back up" indicating to make someone annoyed. English learners are better served when teachers use language that is straightforward, clear, and accompanied by a visual representation.

Paraphrasing and repetition are useful practices that enhance understanding. English learners require repeated exposures to a word in order to hear it accurately because they often lack the auditory acuity to decipher sounds of English words. In addition, they need to see and hear the words used repeatedly, preferably in a variety of ways. Brain research tells us that repetition strengthens connections in the brain (Jensen, 2005).

Cognates are often useful in promoting comprehension for students whose native language has a Latin base. For example, using "calculate the total number of pennies" (*calcular* in Spanish) may be easier for some students to understand than "figure out the total number of pennies." (See Vogt and Echevarria, 2008, for more examples of cognates.)

SIOP® teachers also use simple sentence structures like subject–verb–object with beginning students and reduce or eliminate embedded clauses. For example, in a history lesson, the teacher may use the following complex sentence structure that is difficult to understand: "English colonists brought free enterprise, the idea of owning and controlling their own businesses, from England but because England's leaders wanted the colonies' financial support, laws were passed to limit the free enterprise system in the colonies." It might be better stated as, "English colonists brought the idea of owning and controlling their own businesses from England. This idea is called free enterprise. England's leaders wanted the colonies' financial support, so laws were passed to limit the free enterprise system in the colonies." Reducing the complexity of language is effective but should be used judiciously; oversimplification of spoken or written language eliminates exposure to a variety of sentence constructions and language forms (Crossley, McCarthy, Louwerse, & McNamara, 2007).

Using appropriate speech patterns and terms that are easier for ELs to understand contributes to comprehensible input.

SIOP® FEATURE 11:
Clear Explanation of Academic Tasks

To see an example of clear instructions, please view the corresponding video clip (Chapter 4, Module 2) on the accompanying CD.

English learners at all levels (and native English speakers) perform better in academic situations when the teacher gives clear instructions for assignments and activities. The more practice students have with the types of tasks found in content classes, the better they will perform in class and the better prepared they will be when they exit the language support program. It is critical for ELs to have instructions presented in a step-by-step manner, preferably modeled or demonstrated for them. Ideally, a finished product such as a business letter, a research report, or a graphic organizer is shown to students so that they know what the task entails. Oral directions should always be accompanied by written ones so ELs can refer back to them at a later point in time as they complete the assignment or task. Students with auditory processing difficulties also require clear, straightforward instructions posted for them to see.

According to case study data collected from ELs in sheltered classes (Echevarria, 1998), middle school students were asked what their teachers do that makes learning easier or more difficult. The following are some student comments:

- "She doesn't explain it too good. I don't understand the words she's saying because I don't even know what they mean."
- "She talks too fast. I don't understand the directions."
- "He talks too fast. Not patient."
- "It helps when he comes close to my desk and explains stuff in the order that I have to do it."

It is reasonable to assume that elementary age students would express much the same sentiment if they were able to articulate it in the same way. These students' comments illustrate the importance of providing a clear explanation of teachers' expectations for lessons, including delineating the steps of academic tasks. This point cannot be over-stated. In our observations of classes, many "behavior problems" are often the result of students not being sure what they are supposed to do. A cursory oral explanation of an assignment can leave many students without a clue as to what to do to get started. In pri-mary grades, the result may be that students bother their neighbor or play at their desk, while in the upper grades, students may talk aloud or distract friends. The teacher, frus-trated with all the chatter, scolds students, exhorting them to get to work. However, stu-dents do not know *how* to get to work and often don't know how to articulate that fact to the teacher. Bottom line: making expectations clear to students contributes to an efficient and effective classroom (Gibson & Hasbrouck, 2008).

An example of a clear explanation comes from a reading selection about community. The story contains lots of words about people, places, and things in the community. The teacher writes on the board:

1. Read the story together.
2. Read word cards with your partner.
3. Place each card in a column: people, places, things.
4. Tell your partner why the card goes in the column.

The teacher goes over each step of the lesson, showing visuals with each step, for example, the text, word cards, and paper with three columns. After reading the story together, the teacher points to the steps and tells them that they have completed the first part, now they work with their partners. In this way, if students didn't understand, weren't paying attention, or simply forget, they have the written steps to guide them and keep them on task. Depending on the group, the teacher may need to model one or more of the steps for comprehension.

In the area of writing, students need to be shown very specifically—and have opportunities to practice what has been clearly explained—the essential elements of good writing. Showing students what constitutes good writing, explaining it clearly, and providing opportunities to practice will result in improved writing (Schmoker, 2001). For intermediate and advanced speakers, focused lessons on "voice" or "word choice" may be appropriate, while beginning speakers benefit from models of complete sentences using adjectives or forming a question.

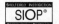

SIOP® FEATURE 12:

A Variety of Techniques Used to Make Content Concepts Clear

Effective SIOP® teachers make content concepts clear and understandable for English learners through the use of a variety of techniques that make content comprehensible. We have observed some teachers who teach the same way for English learners as they do for native English speakers, except that they use pictures for ELs. We believe that the actual teaching techniques a teacher uses have a greater impact on student achievement than having a lot of pictures illustrating content concepts. High-quality SIOP® lessons offer students a variety of ways for making the content accessible to them. Although it might be impossible for teachers to present a variety of interesting hands-on lessons that include visuals to illustrate every concept and idea in the curriculum each period of every day, there does need to be sufficient planning to incorporate such techniques and activities throughout the week's lessons.

Some techniques include:

Use gestures, body language, pictures, and objects to accompany speech. For example, when saying, "We're going to learn about the three forms of water," the teacher holds up three fingers. Showing one finger she says, "One form is liquid," and shows a glass of water. Holding up two fingers she says, "the second form is ice," and shows an ice cube. Holding up three fingers she says, "and the third form is steam," and shows a picture of a steaming cup of coffee. These simple gestures and visual aids assist students in organizing and making sense of information that is presented verbally.

To see an example of effective techniques, please view the corresponding video clip (Chapter 4, Module 2) on the accompanying CD.

Provide a model of a process, task, or assignment. For example, as the teacher discusses the process of water turning to ice, she shows or draws a model of the process as it is being described. When students are later instructed to record conditions under which the change in ice from a solid to a liquid is accelerated or slowed, the teacher shows an observation sheet that is divided into three columns on the overhead projector. The teacher has a number of pictures (e.g., lamp, sun, and refrigerator), which depict various conditions such as heat and cold. She demonstrates the first condition, heat, with a picture of the sun. She models how students will describe the condition in the first column (e.g., heats). Then she asks students what effect the sun, or heat, has on ice. They answer and in the second column she records how the ice changed (e.g., melted), and in the third column she indicates if the process was accelerated or slowed by the condition (e.g., accelerated). Providing a model as the students are taken through the task verbally eliminates ambiguity and gives the message in more than one way. Students are then able to complete the rest of the worksheet.

Preview material for optimal learning. When students' attention is focused on the specific information they will be responsible for learning in the lesson, students are able to prepare themselves for the information that is coming, making it more comprehensible for them. Further, they have an opportunity to access prior knowledge and make the connections that they will need to understand the lesson.

Allow alternative forms for expressing their understanding of information and concepts. Often ELs have learned the lesson's information but have difficulty expressing their understanding in English, either orally or in writing. Hands-on activities and symbolic representation, such as pictures, pictographs, maps, and diagrams, can be used to reinforce the concepts and information presented, with a reduced linguistic demand on these students.

Use multimedia and other technologies in lessons. Teachers may use overhead transparencies, PowerPoint slides, or relevant websites as supplements to a presentation. In so doing, they not only provide more visual support but also model the use of the technology.

Provide repeated exposures to words, concepts, and skills. English learners are learning through a new language, and in order for the input to be comprehensible, they need repetition. However, excessive practice of a single word or skill can become monotonous and defeat the purpose. Jensen (2005) discusses a process for introducing material repeatedly in a variety of ways. He suggests introducing terms and skills well in advance of learning the material (pre-exposure); explicitly previewing the topic at the start of the lesson; exposing students to the target information (priming); reviewing the material minutes after students have learned it; and allowing students to revise or reconstruct information hours, days, or weeks after the lesson to revisit the learning. Research indicates that teachers ought to provide students with the specifics of what they need to learn—the key details of the unit—and then find ways to expose students to the details multiple times (Marzano, Pickering, & Pollock, 2001).

Use sentence strips. This common technique can be used in a variety of ways at all grade levels. In reading/language arts, students can review events in a story by writing each event on a sentence strip, then sequencing the strips to retell the story. This technique can be applied in science to sequence steps in an experiment or in math to sequence the steps for problem solving.

Scaffold language by chunking information into smaller bits, asking questions about it and talking about it. In reading/language arts, compare and contrast books and genres through discussion and meaningful questioning. These techniques will improve children's language proficiency by using language just beyond their independent speaking abilities while at the same time making information more comprehensible.

Use graphic organizers effectively. New ideas and concepts presented in a new language can be overwhelming for English learners. Graphic organizers (GOs) take the information, vocabulary, or concept and make it more understandable by showing the key points graphically. To paraphrase the saying "a picture is worth a thousand words," a graphic organizer can capture and simplify a teacher's many potentially confusing words. While GOs are used commonly in school, they are most effective when they match the task and lead to attaining the lesson's objectives. So if the task is learning definitions, then the GO would be:

| | is a | | that | |

Especially for preschool or kindergarten, GOs can be simple, such as a problem/solution chart or a web with a topic with descriptor words. For older students, especially those with learning challenges, some more elaborate GOs such as a Concept Diagram have improved student performance (Deshler & Schumaker, 2006). See Vogt & Echevarria (2008) for many SIOP®-appropriate graphic organizers.

Audiotape texts for comprehension. A taped version of the text not only allows for multiple opportunities to hear the text, but the reader who records can modify it to proficiency levels. The same passage may be read more slowly with clear enunciation for beginning speakers, or synonyms may be substituted for difficult words.

The techniques we suggest in the SIOP® are critical for providing meaningful, understandable lessons to students learning English, including adapting the content to students' proficiency levels (Chapter 2), highlighting key vocabulary (Chapter 3), using scaffolding techniques and providing opportunities for students to use strategies (Chapter 5), and providing activities that allow students to apply newly acquired content and language knowledge (Chapter 7).

The Lesson

Unit: Land Forms (Third Grade)

The following lessons take place in an urban elementary school where English learners make up 35% of the school population. In the classrooms described, there is a mix of language proficiency levels represented, ranging from beginning speakers to advanced English speakers. Students have varying levels of literacy in their native languages.

Third-grade teachers Mr. Edwards, Mr. Hernandez, and Mrs. Monroe are all teaching a unit on life forms in different environments to meet the standard, *Students know examples of diverse life forms in different environments, such as oceans, deserts, tundra, forests, and wetlands.* The third-grade teachers typically plan similar lessons so all students are learning the same material. The three classes had previously learned the name of five land forms: oceans, tundra, deserts, forests, and wetlands. Also, the students had Googled each of the terms on computers and found some information about each type of environment. (For more examples of lesson and unit plans in science, see Short, Vogt, & Echevarria, in press.)

Teaching Scenarios

Mr. Edwards

The previous day, each student made cards with a drawing of an environment on the front (e.g., tundra, forests) and a definition of the environment on the back. In addition, they brainstormed together things that they enjoy doing and eating. Mr. Edwards made a T-chart of things to do on the left column and things to eat on the right column.

The lesson began with Mr. Edwards asking students to recall the names of environments they had talked about the previous day. He wrote words on the board as students began calling out words such as *oceans, deserts,* and others they had researched on the computer. Mr. Edwards asked the students to take out the cards they had made. He then pointed to a word he'd written on the board and told students to hold up the corresponding card. He did this for each of the five words.

Pointing to the objectives on the board, Mr. Edwards and the class read in unison the lesson's content and language objectives: Students will write five words that belong together. Students will create a country and use those five words to label land forms. The language objective was: Students will discuss categories of words with teams.

Standing by an easel with chart paper, Mr. Edwards said that the class would complete the first part of the unit by writing five words that went together and then creating a country of their own with various life forms and environments. He spoke clearly and slowly enough so that all students could understand. He frequently used think-alouds to make information clear to students: for example, "What do I mean by creating a country? Well let's see. What are some of the things we listed yesterday that we like to do or eat?" He gestured toward the T-chart and then he said, "Well, I like to read so I'm going to make a 'Book Country.'" He then drew a large picture of an open book on the chart paper. Above it he drew a web GO (center circle with five lines extending out from it) and wrote *Book* in the center. He said, "I'm thinking to myself, 'Hmmm, these are categories, things that go together.' For example, red, blue, yellow green are . . . (students answered in unison, "Colors") or triangle, hexagon, circle . . . (students answered, "Shapes"). What words would go together with book? Talk with your teams."

Students were seated in groups of three, and each group huddled together and talked. After a couple of minutes, Mr. Edwards asked which words they had discussed and called on names he drew from sticks in a can. As students said words such as *author*, *illustrator*, *words*, *pages* and *title*, Mr. Edwards wrote them on the GO, on the lines extending from the word, *Book*. Under each word, he wrote a different environment (e.g., forests, tundra). Next, he asked students to generate words that went together using the topic, *basketball* then *hamburgers*.

Mr. Edwards pointed to the GO and showed them again how the words around *Book* were words that went together. Then he told the class that they needed to think of something they liked to do or eat: "You can think of something yourself or use the T-chart to give you ideas." He passed out white construction paper and told the groups to work together to generate words that went together. Students began drawing their individual web GO and wrote a word in the center. Teams helped each other think of words until all students had completed a web GO. They used Spanish and English while interacting.

Students then played a guessing game. A student volunteered to read his or her descriptor words and the class guessed the topic word. When they finished playing the game, Mr. Edwards went over to the chart paper and labeled a few areas on his "book country" using the environment words. He told students that the following day, they would draw a picture to represent their topic word and add the environments to it, illustrating the five types of environments they were studying.

On the SIOP® form in Figure 4.1, please rate Mr. Edwards's lesson on each of the Comprehensible Input features.

Mr. Hernandez

As part of his daily routine, Mr. Hernandez wrote the day's objectives on the board: Your job today is to define each environment (*oceans*, *deserts*, *tundra*, *forests*, and *wetlands*); write a sentence using each word. He began the lesson by asking who remembered what they studied the previous day. A number of hands went up and as he called on students, responses varied

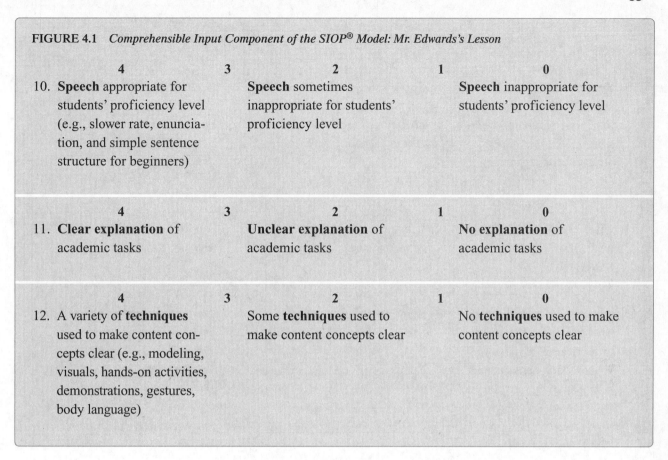

FIGURE 4.1 *Comprehensible Input Component of the SIOP® Model: Mr. Edwards's Lesson*

4	3	2	1	0
10. **Speech** appropriate for students' proficiency level (e.g., slower rate, enunciation, and simple sentence structure for beginners)		**Speech** sometimes inappropriate for students' proficiency level		**Speech** inappropriate for students' proficiency level

4	3	2	1	0
11. **Clear explanation** of academic tasks		**Unclear explanation** of academic tasks		**No explanation** of academic tasks

4	3	2	1	0
12. A variety of **techniques** used to make content concepts clear (e.g., modeling, visuals, hands-on activities, demonstrations, gestures, body language)		Some **techniques** used to make content concepts clear		No **techniques** used to make content concepts clear

from "worked on computers" to "learned about oceans." Mr. Hernandez pointed to the objective and said, "You're right, we learned a little something about different environments and today we're going to write a definition of each environment and then use it in a sentence." He pointed to the board where he had written the five types of environments. He said, "Let's say these words together after I read each one: *oceans, deserts, tundra, forests, and wetlands.*" He modeled the pronunciation of each word and students repeated it after him.

Then he asked students to take out their notes from the previous day. (He had provided a worksheet with each word followed by several lines on which students wrote notes they acquired from the Internet search.) The class had a brief discussion of each environment, contributing facts from their notes. During the discussion, Mr. Hernandez used his normal speaking style, which was fine for fluent English speakers but was too fast for others; many of the complex sentence structures he used were lost on beginning and advanced beginning speakers.

Mr. Hernandez wrote sentence frames on the board: A _____ has _____. It is found _____. The life forms there include _____. He told the students to use the frames as a way to define the environments. He said that they could use their notes and work with a partner if they wanted.

Some students took out paper and began writing the sentence frames, filling in the blanks with words from their notes. Others copied what was on the board but then were

FIGURE 4.2 *Comprehensible Input Component of the SIOP® Model: Mr. Hernandez's Lesson*

4	3	2	1	0	NA
10. **Speech** appropriate for students' proficiency level (e.g., slower rate, enunciation, and simple sentence structure for beginners)		**Speech** sometimes inappropriate for students' proficiency level		**Speech** inappropriate for students' proficiency level	

4	3	2	1	0	NA
11. Clear **explanation** of academic tasks		**Unclear** explanation of academic tasks		**No** explanation of academic tasks	

4	3	2	1	0	NA
12. **A variety of techniques** used to make content concepts clear (e.g., modeling, visuals, hands-on activities, demonstrations, gestures, body language)		Some **techniques** used to make content concepts clear		No **techniques** used to make content concepts clear	

off task, talking with others. A few students didn't have paper and sat quietly looking at their notes from the previous day.

After 10 minutes, Mr. Hernandez asked for volunteers to read their definitions. Several students had completed one or two definitions and read what they had written. Mr. Hernandez told the rest of the class to hurry and finish because they still needed to write sentences using the terms.

Mr. Hernandez circulated around the class and provided assistance to the many students who seemed confused about what to do. With only 10 minutes remaining before the bell, Mr. Hernandez told the students to write a sentence using each word. He gave an example orally, "I like swimming in the ocean."

On the SIOP® form in Figure 4.2, please rate Mr. Hernandez's lesson on each of the Comprehensible Input features.

Mrs. Monroe

After reading the content and language objectives to the class, Mrs. Monroe asked students to take out their graphic organizer (GO) from the previous day's lesson. Students each had a five-column GO with the name of an environment at the top of each column (e.g., ocean, tundra) and six bullets below on which students had recorded facts from their Internet search. The class was set up in pods of six desks, and Mrs. Monroe gave the students five minutes to work with their assigned partners to fill in any bullet points that were missing. Students eagerly began discussing each category and checking to be sure their facts were correct. At the sound of a bell, students looked up. She asked if any group needed help. A student raised her hand and said that she and her partner needed one more fact about forests. Mrs. Monroe asked the class for help, and she called on a pair, who provided the information.

Next, a picture of an environment was placed in the center of each pod of desks and students were given poster board. Mrs. Monroe directed students' attention to an easel, where she had a completed poster about ice environments. It had a drawing of icebergs at the top and had information about the environment, including a description of life forms. She told the students that they would make a similar poster of the environment pictured at their desks. On the overhead projector she had the steps of the process they would follow:

1. Each group has two minutes to choose two artists for the drawing, a pair that selects the most informative points from their GOs, a student who organizes the information about life forms from the GOs, and a writer/facilitator who keeps students on task and then writes the information on the poster as it is dictated.
2. After roles are assigned, you will have 15 minutes to complete the task.
3. Once the information is written on the poster, the drawing will be glued to the poster.

As Mrs. Monroe went step by step through the task, she enunciated clearly and repeated words that some students may not have been familiar with. She was careful to make sure all students understood; she asked group by group if they had questions. Then she sounded the bell and held up two fingers saying, "You have two minutes to assign roles." She pointed again to step 1 on the screen. Students were familiar with this type of activity because they often worked in teams with assigned roles.

Once roles were established, Mrs. Monroe pointed to step 2 and asked for a volunteer to read it. Then the groups got to work. Students were engaged in their part of the assignment and when the bell sounded, most groups were done. Mrs. Monroe asked if anyone needed another minute and two groups raised their hands. She said that they had two minutes to complete it, and in the meantime collected the other three posters and hung them around the room. When the final two groups were done, she hung their posters as well. Next to the posters was chart paper.

Mrs. Monroe asked, "Who knows what we're going to do?" Hands shot up and she said, "Ok, what?" and most of the children shouted, "Gallery Walk!" Although the students had done the activity before, Mrs. Monroe walked over to a poster and asked a series of questions to confirm that students understood that they were to write questions or comments about the poster on the chart paper. She repeated the process with another poster, and then told the students to stand and quietly walk to their poster. At the sound of the bell, students circled the perimeter of the classroom, going from poster to poster, reading the information, and writing questions and comments. Mrs. Monroe's bell signaled the pace of the walk, allowing students enough time at each poster.

When they were done and everyone was seated, she praised their good work and told them they would address the questions and comments in the next day's lesson.

On the SIOP® form in Figure 4.3, please rate Mrs. Monroe's lesson on each of the Comprehensible Input features.

FIGURE 4.3 *Comprehensible Input Component of the SIOP® Model: Mrs. Monroe's Lesson*

4	3	2	1	0
10. **Speech** appropriate for students' proficiency level (e.g., slower rate, enunciation, and simple sentence structure for beginners)		**Speech** sometimes inappropriate for students' proficiency level		**Speech** inappropriate for students' proficiency level

4	3	2	1	0
11. **Clear explanation** of academic tasks		**Unclear** explanation of academic tasks		**No** explanation of academic tasks

4	3	2	1	0
12. A variety of **techniques** used to make content concepts clear (e.g., modeling, visuals, hands-on activities, demonstrations, gestures, body language)		Some **techniques** used to make content concepts clear		No **techniques** used to make content concepts clear

Discussion of Lessons

10. Speech Appropriate for Students' Proficiency Levels (Rate and Complexity)

Mr. Edwards: 4

Mr. Hernandez: 2

Mrs. Monroe: 4

The lesson description indicates that the three teachers varied in their attention to the unique linguistic needs of the English learners in their classes.

Mr. Edwards used clear, well articulated speech. He slowed his rate of speech and enunciated clearly for beginning speakers and adjusted his speech for more fluent English speakers. He used a natural speaking voice but paid attention to his rate of speed and enunciation. Because there were many beginning and advance beginning speakers, he selected words that were appropriate to their level of proficiency. He said, "There are categories, words that go together," which helped define a word (categories) that some students may not have known. He also used an oral cloze technique by listing words and then saying, "These are all _____." And students completed the sentence.

Although Mr. Hernandez attempted to make his speech understandable for students when he modeled correct pronunciation of the terms, overall he ignored the variety of language proficiency levels in his class. With few exceptions, he used his usual speaking style, which was difficult for many students to understand.

Mrs. Monroe used appropriate speech herself, accommodating the variety of English proficiency levels in her class. She enunciated and spoke clearly for beginning speakers and called on more advanced speakers to answer more complex questions.

11. Clear Explanation of Academic Tasks

   Mr. Edwards: 4

   Mr. Hernandez: 0

   Mrs. Monroe: 4

Making your expectations crystal clear is one of the most important aspects of teaching, and when working with English learners, explicit, step-by-step directions can be critical to a lesson's success. It is difficult for almost any student (or adult!) to remember directions given orally, and oral directions may be incomprehensible to many English learners. A lesson is sure to get off to a rocky start if students don't understand what they are expected to do. Written procedures provide students with a guide and help keep students engaged and involved in academic tasks, thus reducing behavior issues.

In Mr. Edward's class, students were engaged throughout the lesson because he modeled and practiced each step before having students do it independently. In this case, he didn't have to write the steps of a procedure on the board because of extensive demonstration. The visual model was in front of the class to assist those students who may not have understood completely the oral explanation. Also, the use of think-alouds helped students understand what they were supposed to do. Finally, if beginning English speakers needed clarification, Spanish speakers provided support.

Mr. Hernandez told students that they would define the terms and use each in a sentence but he didn't say *how* they were to do it, which resulted in disengagement. First, the sentence frames he provided were more of an informal definition and may have been confusing for students who associate *definition* with the language one finds in the dictionary. Further, few third graders were able to use information from random notes to complete the frames—and English learners were much less so. Demonstration of a step-by-step process was needed, beginning by telling students to take out a clean paper on which to complete the task. Neglecting small details such as this can derail an assignment, as seen in this case.

Every minute in Mrs. Monroe's class, students knew what they should be doing and how to get it done. She modeled extensively and made certain that all students understood her expectations. The steps of the activity were posted for students to see and refer to, and a model of the completed poster was shown before asking students to complete their own versions. She made sure assignment of roles was secured in the groups and gave concrete time limits for the activities. Overall, she did an outstanding job of ensuring all students could participate at maximum levels, regardless of their language proficiency.

12. A Variety of Techniques Used

   Mr. Edwards: 4

   Mr. Hernandez: 1

   Mrs. Monroe: 4

Concepts become understandable when teachers use a variety of techniques, including modeling, demonstrations, visuals, and body language. Throughout his lesson, Mr. Edwards consistently pointed at visual aids such as the white board, T-chart, and the GO on chart paper; used gestures; and provided students with hands-on materials. He utilized picture cards of the five environments to make the review of the words more understandable and provided individual GOs so students could create their own "country" based on their background experiences.

Mr. Hernandez, on the other hand, used few techniques to make the lesson's content or his expectations clear. The visuals (terms written on the board; sentence frames) and hands-on materials (notes) he did have were fairly ineffective because he failed to show students their purpose or how they could be used. For example, he didn't model how students were to complete the sentence frames, and for beginning speakers in particular, the sentence frames didn't provide a scaffold as intended because these children didn't understand what Mr. Hernandez wanted them to do. First, he should have talked in much more depth about the notes the students had taken the previous day and checked for understanding. He didn't have a clue how well or poorly students took notes from the Web search. Second, he needed to provide an example of how to use the information from their notes with the sentence frames. On an overhead or on the board, he could have asked a student to read information from his or her notes. Using student-generated information, he could have completed a sample sentence frame. This process should have been repeated several times in any number of creative ways: asking one student to read to a partner and the other student to complete a frame, or Mr. Hernandez could have given some information statements and had students work alone or in groups to complete the frames. Finally, he didn't even make clear something as simple as where students were supposed to write the definitions—on their notes? On another sheet of paper? Mr. Hernandez left many students wondering what to do. The contrast between Mr. Hernandez's lesson and the other teachers' lessons is striking. Often it isn't that students can't do the work or won't do it, but rather that they are unsure *how,* and sufficient scaffolds aren't provided to empower them to succeed.

Mrs. Monroe used modeling (finished product), demonstration (walking from poster to poster demonstrating where to write comments), visuals (overhead projector, pictures of environments), hands-on activities (poster, Gallery Walk), and gestures (holding up fingers, pointing). Her lesson exemplifies how decontextualized paper-and-pencil tasks can be transformed into comprehensible, interesting activities.

Summary

Although ELs learn in many of the same ways as fluent English-speaking students, they do require special accommodations to make instruction understandable (August & Shanahan, 2006). Effective SIOP® teachers constantly modulate and adjust their speech when teaching English learners to ensure that the content is comprehensible. Concepts are taught using a variety of techniques, including modeling, gestures, hands-on activities, and demonstrations, so that students understand and learn the content material. Finally, effective SIOP® teachers provide explanations of academic tasks in ways that make clear what students are expected to accomplish and that promote student success.

Discussion Questions

1. Have you recently been in a situation where you were not an "insider," and therefore you didn't understand what was being said? Compare that situation and your feelings about it to the way language is used in classrooms where there are English learners. As a teacher, what can you do to make sure all students are able to follow a lecture or discussion?

2. Many times in classrooms, discipline problems can be attributed to children not knowing what they're supposed to be doing. What are some ways that a teacher can avoid having students who are confused about accomplishing academic tasks?

3. If you have traveled in another country, or if you are an English learner, reflect on difficulties you had in understanding others. What are some techniques people used to try to communicate with you? What are some techniques you can use in the classroom?

4. Using the SIOP® lesson you have been developing, add to it so that the Comprehensible Input features in the lesson are enhanced.

chapter 5

Strategies

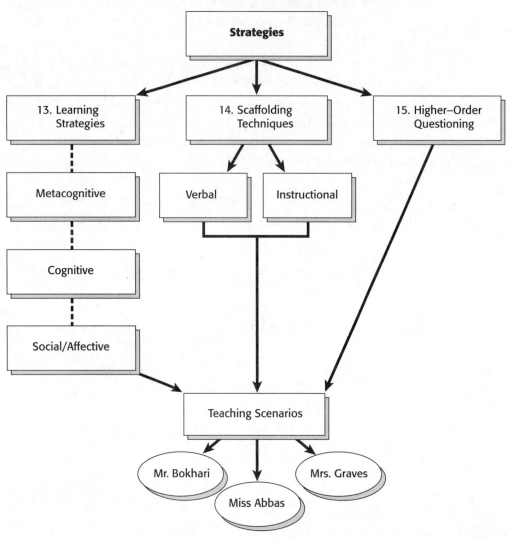

Objectives

After reading, discussing, and engaging in activities related to this chapter, you will be able to meet the following content and language objectives.

Content Objectives

Select learning strategies appropriate to a lesson's objectives.

Incorporate explicit instruction and student practice of metacognitive and cognitive strategies in lesson plans.

Identify techniques for scaffolding verbal, procedural, and instructional understanding.

Language Objectives

Identify language learning strategies to use with students.

Discuss the importance of asking higher-order questions of students of all English proficiency levels.

Write a set of questions with increasing levels of difficulty on a topic.

Up to this point, we have discussed elements of effective planning, background building, and comprehensibility for English learners (ELs). This chapter examines how we teach students to access information in memory, help them connect what they know to what they are learning, assist them in problem solving, and promote retention of newly learned information. This involves the explicit teaching of learning strategies that facilitate the learning process. Techniques and methods for learning and retaining information are systematically taught, reviewed, and assessed in effective SIOP® classrooms.

The lessons on Saving Our Planet found later in this chapter illustrate how three fifth-grade teachers incorporate the teaching of strategies into their classrooms.

Background

As introduced in Chapter 3, researchers have learned that information is retained and connected in the brain through "mental pathways" that are linked to an individual's existing schemata (Anderson, 1984; Barnhardt, 1997). If the schemata for a particular topic are well developed and personally meaningful, new information is easier to retain and recall, and proficient learners initiate and activate their associations between the new and old learning.

In cognitive theory, this initiation and activation are described as the mental processes that enhance comprehension, learning, and retention of information. Competent language learners actively engage these cognitive skills, and researchers know these learners are effective, in part, because they have special ways of processing the new information they are learning. These mental processes are called *learning strategies* because they are "the special thoughts or behaviors that individuals use to help them comprehend, learn, or retain new information" (O'Malley & Chamot, 1990, p. 1).

SIOP® FEATURE 13:
Ample Opportunities Provided for Students to Use Learning Strategies

There is considerable evidence that explicitly and carefully teaching students a variety of self-regulating strategies improves student learning and reading (Afflerbach, Pearson, & Paris, 2008; Fisher, Frey, & Williams, 2002; Neufeld, 2005; Pressley, 2000; 2002; 2005; Shearer, Ruddell, & Vogt, 2001). Self-regulated learning "emphasizes autonomy and control by the individual who monitors, directs, and regulates actions toward goals of information acquisition, expanding expertise, and self-improvement" (Paris, 2001, p. 89).

Three types of learning strategies have been identified in the research literature (O'Malley & Chamot, 1990). These include:

1. **Metacognitive Strategies.** The process of purposefully monitoring our thinking is referred to as metacognition (Baker & Brown, 1984). Metacognition is characterized by (1) matching thinking and problem-solving strategies to particular learning situations, (2) clarifying purposes for learning, (3) monitoring one's own comprehension through self-questioning, and (4) taking corrective action if understanding fails (Dermody & Speaker, 1995). The use of metacognitive strategies implies awareness, reflection, and interaction, and strategies are used in an integrated, interrelated, and recursive manner (Dole, Duffy, Roehler, & Pearson, 1991; Pressley, 2000). Studies have found that when metacognitive strategies are taught explicitly, reading comprehension is improved (Duffy, 2002; McLaughlin, 2003; Snow, Griffin & Burns, 2005; Vogt & Nagano, 2003).

2. **Cognitive Strategies.** Along with metacognitive strategies, cognitive strategies help students organize the information they are expected to learn through the process of self-regulated learning (Paris, 2001). Cognitive strategies are directly related to individual learning tasks and are used by learners when they mentally and/or physically manipulate material, or when they apply a specific technique to a learning task (Pressley, Johnson, Symons, McGoldrick, & Kurita, 1989; Slater & Horstman, 2002). Previewing a story prior to reading, establishing a purpose for reading, consciously making connections between personal experiences and what is happening in a story, taking notes during a lecture, completing a graphic organizer, and creating a semantic map are all examples of cognitive strategies that learners use to enhance their understandings (McLaughlin & Allen, 2002).

FIGURE 5.1 *Continuum of Strategies*

Teacher-Centered	Teacher-Assisted	Peer-Assisted	Student-Centered
Lecture	Drill and practice	Role playing	Rehearsal strategies
Direct instruction	Discovery learning	Peer tutoring	Repeated readings
Demonstration	Brainstorming	Reciprocal teaching	Selective underlining
Recitation	Discussion	Cooperative learning	Two-column notes
			Elaboration strategies
			Mental imagery
			Guided imagery
			Creating analogies
			Organizational strategies
			Clustering
			Graphic organizers
			Outlining

Muth & Alvermann, 1999

3. **Social/Affective Strategies.** These are identified in the research literature on cognitive psychology as the social and affective influences on learning (O'Malley & Chamot, 1990). For example, learning can be enhanced when people interact with each other to clarify a confusing point or when they participate in a group discussion or cooperative learning group to solve a problem.

In a somewhat different scheme, Muth and Alvermann (1999, p. 233) suggest there is a continuum of strategies that occurs during the teaching–learning process (see Figure 5.1)—from teacher-centered, teacher-assisted, peer-assisted, and student-centered.

The ultimate goal is for students to develop independence in self-monitoring and self-regulation through practice with peer-assisted and student-centered strategies. Many English learners, however, have difficulty initiating an active role in using these strategies because they are focusing mental energy on their developing language skills. Therefore, effective SIOP® teachers scaffold ELs by providing many opportunities for them to use a variety of learning strategies that have been found to be especially effective.

Whatever strategies are emphasized, learned, and used, it is generally agreed that they should be taught through explicit instruction, careful modeling, and scaffolding (Duffy, 2002). Additionally, Lipson and Wixson (2008) suggest that teaching a variety of strategies is not enough. Rather, learners need not only *declarative* knowledge (What is a strategy?) but also *procedural* knowledge (How do I use it?), and *conditional* knowledge (When and why do I use it?). When teachers model strategy use and then provide appropriate scaffolding while children are practicing strategies, they are likely to become more effective strategy users (Fisher, Frey, & Williams, 2002; Pressley & Woloshyn, 1995).

When teaching learning strategies, effective SIOP® teachers employ a variety of approaches, such as the following:

Mnemonics: A memory system often involving visualization and/or acronyms. For example, to help students remember how to spell some challenging words, here are some helpful and fun mnemonics. Hopefully, they'll also remember the phrases!

Because: Big Elephants Can Always Understand Small Elephants

Arithmetic: A Rat In The House May Eat The Ice Cream

Geography: General Eisenhower's Oldest Girl Rode A Pony Home Yesterday

Rhythm: Rhythm Helps Your Two Hips Move

Necessary: Not Every Cat Eats Sardines (Some Are Really Yummy)

Argument: A Rude Girl Undresses; My Eyes Need Taping!

Ocean: Only Cats' Eyes Are Narrow

Potassium: One tea; two sugars

Desserts: Two Sugars Sweet

These mnemonics were found on the website *www.fun-with-words.com*. Additional mnemonics, word games, tongue twisters, and other spelling and vocabulary ideas are also available on the website.

SQP2RS ("Squeepers"): An instructional framework for teaching content with expository texts that includes the following steps (Vogt, 2000; Vogt, 2002; Vogt & Echevarria, 2008):

1. <u>S</u>urvey: Children preview and scan the text to be read for about one minute to determine key concepts that will be learned. For grades K–2, preview the book with your students. Informational Big Books work great.

2. <u>Q</u>uestion: In groups, children generate questions likely to be answered by reading the text; teacher posts student questions on chart paper and marks with multiple asterisks those that are frequently suggested by the groups. If you teach young children, you will need to teach how questions are formulated in English.

3. <u>P</u>redict: As a whole class, students come up with three or four key concepts they think they will learn while reading; the predictions are based on the previously generated questions, especially those marked with asterisks. Model this step frequently with young children.

4. <u>R</u>ead: While reading (with partners or small groups, or with the teacher in a small group), students search for answers to their generated questions and confirm or disconfirm their predictions; sticky notes or strips are used to mark answers to questions and spots where predictions have been confirmed.

5. <u>R</u>espond: Students answer questions (not necessarily in writing) with partners or group members and formulate new ones for the next section of text to be read (if the text is lengthy); teacher leads discussion of key concepts, clarifying any misunderstandings.

6. <u>S</u>ummarize: Orally or in writing, alone or with a partner or group, students summarize the text's key concepts, using key vocabulary where appropriate.

Read Miss Abbas's lesson in this chapter to see Squeepers in action.

GIST: This summarization procedure assists students in "getting the gist" from extended text (Cunningham, 1982; as cited in Muth & Alvermann, 1999).

GIST stands for Generating Interactions between Schemata and Texts. Together, students and teacher read a section of text (150 to 300 words) printed on a transparency or hand-out. After reading, assist students in underlining ten or more words or concepts that are deemed most important to understanding the text. List these words or phrases on the board. Without the text, together write a summary sentence or two using as many of the listed words as possible. Repeat the process through subsequent sections of the text. When finished, write a topic sentence to precede the summary sentences; the end result can be edited into a summary paragraph. Generally, GIST is effective for children who can read extented text in grade 2, and for all students in grades 3 and up.

Rehearsal strategies: Rehearsal is used when verbatim recall of information is needed (McCormick & Pressley, 1997; Muth & Alvermann, 1999). Visual aids, such as flashcards, engage students during rehearsal; and cognitive strategies, such as underlining and note-taking, help students commit information to memory.

Graphic organizers: These are graphic representations of key concepts and vocabulary. Teachers present them as schematic diagrams of information being taught, and students use them to organize the information they are learning. Barton, Heidama, & Jordan (2002) recommend the use of graphic organizers to help students comprehend math and science textbooks. Examples include Venn diagrams, timelines, flow charts, semantic maps, and so forth. See Buehl (2009) and Vogt and Echevarria (2008) for more examples.

Comprehension strategies: Dole, Duffy, Roehler, and Pearson (1991) and Baker (2004) recommend that students' comprehension of text is enhanced when teachers incorporate instruction that includes strategies such as prediction, self-questioning, monitoring, determining importance, and summarizing. These strategies were identified in what has come to be known as the "proficient reader research" because (1) proficient readers use them in all kinds of text; (2) they can be taught; and (3) the more they are taught explicitly and practiced, the more likely students are to use them independently in their own reading. In their studies involving diverse readers, Duffy (2002) and Fisher, Frey, and Williams (2002) report that reading test scores can be elevated through explicit scaffolded instruction of these and other similar metacognitive strategies.

Directed Reading-Thinking Activity (DRTA): DR-TA (Stauffer, 1969; Ruddell, 2007; Vogt & Echevarria, 2008) is a very effective activity for encouraging strategic thinking while students are reading or listening to narrative (fiction) text. It is especially effective in grades K–8 with the steps given below; only the difficulty level of the text changes. Reading materials, including Big Books, are rich, interesting, and if possible, cliff-hanging stories in which there is some question as to how the story may end. Throughout the reading of a story or book, the teacher and students stop periodically and contemplate predictions about what might follow logically in the next section of the text. Begin the lesson with a question about what the children think the story or book will be about, based on the title. As children respond, include a variety of probes, such as:

- "With a title like . . . , what do you think this story will be about?"
- "Let's read to find out."
- Revisit predictions: "Did . . . happen? If not, why not?"

- "What do you think is going to happen next? What makes you think so?"
- "Where did you get that idea?"
- "What made you think that?"
- "Tell me more about that . . . "

It is important that teachers revisit previously made predictions after chunks of text are read so that students come to understand how predictions (and their confirmation or disconfirmation) affect their comprehension. Children can vote on which predictions are most likely and explain why, as they focus their thinking on character (and author) motivations, problems characters face, reasons for characters' behaviors, and how the plot unfolds. Note that DR-TA is also effective for the upper grades with longer novels, with chapter-to-chapter discussions focusing on what students think will happen, what really happened, and why.

CALLA: One of the most widely accepted methods for teaching learning strategies to English learners is the Cognitive Academic Language Learning Approach (CALLA) created by Chamot and O'Malley (1987, 1994). It is an instructional model for content and language learning that incorporates student development of learning strategies. Developed initially for intermediate and advanced ESL students in content-based ESL classes, it has had wider application over the years in sheltered classes as well. The CALLA method incorporates the three previously identified categories of learning strategies: metacognitive, cognitive, and socioaffective. Through carefully designed lesson plans tied to the content curriculum, teachers explicitly teach the learning strategies and have students apply them in instructional tasks. These plans are based on the following propositions (Chamot & O'Malley, 1994, p. 196):

1. Mentally active learners are better learners.
2. Learning strategies can be taught.
3. Learning strategies transfer to new tasks.
4. Academic language learning is more effective with learning strategies.

SIOP® FEATURE **14**:
Scaffolding Techniques Consistently Used, Assisting and Supporting Student Understanding

To see MaryEllen Vogt explain scaffolding, please view the corresponding video clip (Chapter 5, Module 1) on the accompanying CD.

Scaffolding is a term associated with Vygotsky's (1978) notion of the Zone of Proximal Development (ZPD). In essence, the ZPD is the difference between what a child can accomplish alone and what he or she can accomplish with the assistance of a more experienced individual. In the classroom, teachers scaffold instruction when they provide substantial amounts of support and assistance in the earliest stages of teaching a new concept or strategy, and then gradually decrease the amount of support as the learners acquire experience through multiple practice opportunities (Vacca, 2002).

For example, when teaching learning strategies, the gradual release of responsibility is manifested when teachers consciously include the following practices (adapted from Brown, 2008, p. 541):

- Emphasize the role of personal choice, effort, and persistence in enacting strategies.

- Motivate students' strategy use by showing how applying strategies improves comprehension.

- Highlight the vital role of prior knowledge activation and connection in comprehension.

- Explain the benefits of strategy use in general and the value of using specific strategies.

- Mentally model (e.g., think-aloud) to make thinking apparent to children.

- Provide guided and independent practice so that students learn to use strategies when cued by a diverse array of goals, needs, task demands, and texts.

- Promote independent strategy use by shifting responsibility for using strategies to students as quickly as they can do so.

Two types of scaffolding can be used effectively with English learners. One is *verbal scaffolding*, in which teachers, aware of ELs' existing levels of language development, use prompting, questioning, and elaboration to facilitate students' movement to higher levels of language proficiency, comprehension, and thinking. Effective teacher–student interaction promotes confidence when it is geared to a student's language competence. The following are examples of verbal scaffolding:

- **Paraphrasing**—restating a child's response in order to model correct English usage

- **Using think-alouds**—carefully structured models of how effective strategy users think and monitor their understandings (Baumann, Jones, & Seifert-Kessell, 1993); for example, when teaching children how to preview a chapter, the teacher might think aloud as follows: "When I'm preparing to read a chapter or article, I ask myself, 'What is the main concept I'm supposed to learn? If I look at the big bold heading at the top of the page, I'll get an idea. The heading might be black, or it could be another color. I see here that it's _____.' Now I need to look at the other headings on the pages to see if they will help me figure out what I'm supposed to learn. Usually I think about what I already know about the topic. If I know something about it, it helps me understand better."

- **Reinforcing contextual definitions**—an example is "Aborigines, the people native to Australia, were being forced from their homes." The phrase "the people native to Australia" provides a definition of the word "Aborigines" within the context of the sentence.

- **Providing correct pronunciation by repeating students' responses**—When teachers repeat English learners' correct responses, enunciating carefully and naturally, students have another opportunity to hear the content information, and correct English pronunciation and inflection are reinforced.

- **Slowing speech, increasing pauses, and speaking in phrases**—Teachers provide scaffolding for ELs' language acquisition when they slow down the rate of speech, pause between phrases, and allow students the wait time they may need to process information in English (see Chapter 4 for more information about Comprehensible Input).

In addition to this important verbal scaffolding, effective teachers incorporate instructional approaches that provide *procedural scaffolding*. These include, but are not limited to, the following:

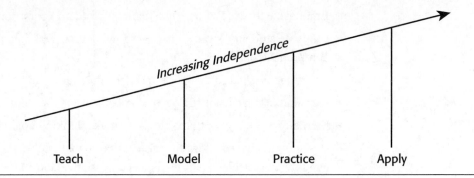

FIGURE 5.2 *Scaffolding Model: Teach, Model, Practice, Apply*

1. Using an instructional framework that includes explicit teaching, modeling, and practice opportunities with others, and expectations for independent application (see Figure 5.2)

2. One-on-one teaching, coaching, and modeling

3. Small group instruction with children practicing a newly learned strategy with another, more experienced student

4. Partnering or grouping students for reading activities, with more experienced readers assisting those with less experience (Nagel, 2001)

In addition, teachers can use *instructional scaffolding* to enhance student learning. For example, graphic organizers can be used as a prereading tool to prepare children for the content of a textbook chapter or a story. The organizer can also be used to illustrate a chapter or a story's text structure, such as comparative or chronological (Vogt & Echevarria, 2008). Think of how the graphic organizers are used in this book and how they assist you in comprehending and organizing the text content.

SIOP® FEATURE 15:
A Variety of Questions or Tasks That Promote Higher-Order Thinking Skills

To see how a teacher leads students into asking higher level questions while teaching key vocabulary, note how Ms. Hollingsworth scaffolds her students' learning. See Chapter 5, Lesson Introduction on the accompanying CD.

Another way that effective SIOP® teachers can promote strategy use is by asking questions that promote critical thinking (Fordham, 2006). More than 40 years ago, Bloom and colleagues (1956) introduced a taxonomy of educational objectives that includes six levels: Knowledge, Comprehension, Application, Analysis, Synthesis, Evaluation. This taxonomy was formulated on the principle that learning proceeds from concrete knowledge to abstract values, or from the denotative to the connotative. Educators adopted this taxonomy as a hierarchy of questioning that, when used in the classroom, elicits varied levels of student thinking.

In 2001, D. R. Krathwohl (who originally worked with Benjamin Bloom) and colleagues published a revised taxonomy: *Taxonomy for Learning, Teaching, and Assessing: A Revision of Bloom's Taxonomy of Educational Objectives* (see Anderson & Krathwohl, 2001). In the revised taxonomy the six levels (simplified here) include:

1. Remember
   a. Recognizing
   b. Recalling

2. Understand
   a. Interpreting
   b. Exemplifying
   c. Classifying
   d. Summarizing
   e. Inferring
   f. Comparing
   g. Explaining

3. Apply
   a. Executing
   b. Implementing

4. Analyze
   a. Differentiating
   b. Organizing
   c. Attributing

5. Evaluate
   a. Checking
   b. Critiquing

6. Create
   a. Generating
   b. Planning
   c. Producing

Whichever taxonomy teachers choose to use for their lessons, it is important that they carefully plan higher-order questions prior to lesson delivery. It is just too difficult to think of higher-order questions "on your feet."

In fact, researchers have found that of the approximately 80,000 questions the average teacher asks annually, 80 percent of them are at the Literal or Knowledge level (Gall, 1984; Watson & Young, 1986). This is especially problematic with English learners. As children are acquiring proficiency in English, it is tempting to rely on simple questions that result in yes/no or other one-word responses.

It is possible, however, to reduce the linguistic demands of responses while still promoting higher levels of thinking. For example, in a study of plant reproduction, the following question requires little thought: "Are seeds sometimes carried by the wind?" A nod or one-word response is almost automatic if the question is understood. A higher-level question such as the following requires analysis: "Which of these seeds would be more likely to be carried by the wind: the round one or smooth one? Or this one that has fuzzy hairs? Why do you think so?" Encouraging students to respond with higher levels of thinking requires teachers to consciously plan and incorporate questions at a variety of levels.

Teachers can also assist children in becoming strategic when they teach them how to determine levels of questions they are asked. For example, if a student recognizes that a question is at the literal level, he'll know the answer can be found right in the text. Similarly, if he identifies a question as inferential, he'll know he'll have to "think and search" or read between the lines to find the answer. This process has been named QAR (question-answer relationships) (Raphael, 1984; Raphael, Highfield, & Au, 2006). See a detailed explanation in Vogt and Echevarria, 2008.

When students are able to determine levels of questions, they can be taught to ask their own questions of varying levels. This complements the goal of developing hypotheses using the scientific method, and it also benefits the research skills older students must learn and practice. For example, Burke (2002) explains the importance of older students writing their own research questions *before* they use the Internet to find information so that they "steer" rather than "surf" for answers. Also, QAR is a powerful addition to SQP2RS (p. 100), when students are writing their questions.

Successful learners know how to use question-asking to help them construct meaning while they read (Taboada & Guthrie, 2006). They ask questions and challenge what the author says if something does not make sense to them. Beck and McKeown (2002, 2006), recommend using the instructional approach Questioning the Author (QtA) to develop students' comprehension of textbook material, which sometimes can be disjointed and lacking in connections between ideas and key concepts. QtA values the depth and quality of students' interactions with texts, and their responses to authors' intended meanings. It assists students in developing the ability to read text closely, as if the author were there to be questioned and challenged. We encourage you to learn more about both QAR and QtA in order to enhance your students' comprehension of text material and to assist them in developing self-regulating strategies related to questioning. (See Vogt and Echevarria, 2008, pp. 79–81, for QAR bookmarks.)

The Lesson

The lesson described in this chapter is taken from a fifth-grade reading/language arts theme titled Saving Our Planet.

UNIT: Saving Our Planet (Fifth Grade)

The three classrooms described in the teaching scenarios in this chapter are heterogeneously mixed with native English speakers and English learners with varied levels of fluency. The elementary school is in a suburban community with Hispanic English learners constituting approximately 55% of the student population. There are also small numbers of English learners representing other language groups.

Mr. Bokhari, Miss Abbas, and Mrs. Graves are each teaching a reading/language arts unit on Saving Our Planet. The district-adopted reading series is used for most of the instruction for this unit, but teachers are encouraged to supplement the series with relevant trade books when appropriate. For the following two-period lesson, the fifth grade teachers chose a beautiful informational trade book available in multiple copies from the school library. The book titled *Earth From Above For Young Readers* by Yann Arthus-Bertrand and Robert Burleigh (Harry N. Abrams, Inc., Publishers, 2001), includes stunning photographs taken from the air of interesting and beautiful countries around the world, some of which are in ecological danger. A brief and informative description accompanies each photograph.

The teachers' lessons are designed to address the following state standards for reading comprehension (grade 5):

- Understand how text features (e.g., format, graphics, sequence, diagrams, illustrations, charts, maps) make information accessible and usable.

- Discern main ideas and concepts presented in texts, identifying and assessing evidence that supports those ideas.

- Draw inferences, conclusions, or generalizations about text and support them with textual evidence and prior knowledge.

- Distinguish facts, supported inferences, and opinions in text.

(For more examples of lesson and unit plans in language arts, see Vogt, Echevarria, & Short, in press.)

The following teaching scenarios take place during the fourth and fifth days of the six-day unit on Saving Our Planet.

Teaching Scenarios

To demonstrate how Mr. Bokhari, Miss Abbas, and Mrs. Graves planned instruction for the students, including their English learners, we look at how each designed a two-day lesson using the trade book, *Earth from Above For Young Readers*.

Mr. Bokhari

Mr. Bokhari began his lesson by distributing two copies of the trade book to the six table groups, which included either four or five students in each group. His 17 English learners were mixed heterogeneously in the class of 33 students. He asked the students, in pairs or triads, to thumb through the book and to use the photos and other textual features (e.g., titles, maps, and illustrations) to predict what these had to do with the unit theme, Saving Our Planet. One student in each group was to be the recorder who would jot the group's thoughts, and the other group members were to be ready to explain orally how they came up with their predictions. Mr. Bokhari then asked the students to orally report their findings as he wrote them on the white board. Next, he asked the table groups to determine which photographs of six countries depicted in the book they would like to read about, three countries for each pair or triad. Once the children made their selections, they orally read the descriptions of their three countries by taking turns. Students were then directed to find the most important information in each of the three descriptions and write a three-sentence summary. Mr. Bokhari encouraged the students to make connections between what they had been learning about the planet Earth and what they were going to read in the book. Next, the partners and triads read their sentences to each other when their group members had completed the summaries. During the second day of the lesson, Mr. Bokhari reviewed each group's summaries and then asked the groups to describe their chosen photographs by orally reading their summaries to the other class members. Each group then voted on their favorite photograph in the book, and a spokesperson gave an oral rationale for the group's choice.

On the SIOP® form in Figure 5.3, rate Mr. Bokhari's lesson on each of the Strategies features.

Miss Abbas

Miss Abbas began the lesson by introducing to her 31 students (of whom 22 were English learners at varied levels of English proficiency) the content and language objectives that she had written on sentence strips and placed in a pocket chart (see following lesson

FIGURE 5.3 *Strategies Component of the SIOP® Model: Mr. Bokhari's Lesson*

4	3	2	1	0
13. Ample opportunities provided for students to use **learning strategies**		Inadequate opportunities provided for students to use **learning strategies**		No opportunity provided for students to use **learning strategies**

4	3	2	1	0
14. **Scaffolding techniques** consistently used, assisting and supporting student understanding (e.g., think-alouds)		**Scaffolding techniques** occasionally used		**Scaffolding techniques** not used

4	3	2	1	0
15. A variety of **questions or tasks that promote higher-order thinking skills** (e.g., literal, analytical, and interpretive questions)		Infrequent **questions or tasks that promote higher-order thinking skills**		No **questions or tasks that promote higher-order thinking skills**

plan—Figure 5.6—for the objectives). She distributed two copies of the book *Earth From Above for Young Readers* to each table group, and reviewed previously taught academic language (*environment, prediction, summarize*). She then reviewed the steps to SQP2RS ("Squeepers"), a process designed to engage students in critical and strategic thinking while reading challenging informational and expository texts (see p. 100). Previously, Miss Abbas had taught, modeled, and provided practice with each of the six sequential steps in Squeepers, so students were able to begin the process with a quick review. Also in an earlier lesson in the reading series, the children had noted on a world map with sticky notes places on Earth where there are current and potential environmental problems. Miss Abbas referred to this map on the wall as she introduced the book title that she had distributed, and reminded students of environmental issues they have previously discussed. She then directed students to remember these as they began to **Survey** this new book to determine what they thought they would learn by reading it and by examining carefully the large photographs and other illustrations. The survey continued for about two to three minutes.

Miss Abbas stopped the surveying, and then directed her students to work with a partner to write two or three **Questions** they thought they might find answers to by reading some of the descriptions in the book that accompanied the photographs. Miss Abbas jotted these questions on chart paper, noting with asterisks which questions were asked by more than one group of students. From the questions, the class next predicted five important concepts or ideas they thought they would learn from this book (**Predict**).

Because this book is an informational text that can be challenging for some students, including English learners, Miss Abbas read aloud the first two brief descriptions about New Calcedonia and Botswana. She modeled how to review the class list of posted questions to see if any had been answered at this point. When students read a sentence about how hunters pose dangers for elephants in Botswana, several students immediately remarked that this was similar to what they had read earlier in the week when they learned about other endangered species. All partner/triad groups noted this sentence with a sticky note. Miss Abbas then directed the pairs and triads to **Read** quietly together the descriptions of Mali, Indonesia, Argentina, Côte d'Ivoire, and Brazil. She selected these particular photographs and descriptions because each includes mention of an environmental problem. As students read together, they noted with their sticky notes those sentences that answered their posted questions, as well as some that described an environmental concern. If students finished the reading task, they were encouraged to continue looking through the book, reading about places of interest.

When everyone was finished, Miss Abbas asked each set of partners or triads to return to the country descriptions, as well as the introductory descriptions that Miss Abbas had read aloud, and find important words related to their unit on Saving Our Planet (VSS: Vocabulary Self-Collection Strategy, p. 106). These VSS words were shared with other table members and ultimately with the class, and as Miss Abbas and the students discussed the meanings, the words were posted on chart paper for future reference.

Miss Abbas then directed students back to the questions they had earlier generated to see which had been answered and which remained unanswered. Also, during this **Response** time, the children reported what they had discovered while reading and showed in their books where they had marked important information with the sticky notes. They checked their predictions to see if they had been confirmed, and discussed why some were not, such as the author didn't include certain information in the descriptions.

Next, each set of pairs or triads was asked to **Summarize** in writing (the length depending on levels of English proficiency) the key concepts that had been discussed and learned. Students were encouraged to use in their summaries the chart papers with the questions, predictions, and pages that had been noted with sticky notes, and the key vocabulary that had been selected during VSS. Miss Abbas spot-checked throughout this final step in SQP2RS to make sure each individual was contributing to the group summary.

To prepare the students for the next day's activity, Miss Abbas taught the meaning of the word *persuade* by providing examples of how someone was trying to persuade another (e.g., persuading someone to buy a particular product, to go on a diet, or vote for a candidate for office). Finally, Miss Abbas assigned the following questions for students to take home and discuss with their parents or caregivers during the evening. She indicated that the next day's discussion during their reading/language arts block would focus on the responses to the questions. Each group would pool their responses and argue for the environmental issue they think is most important.

- Of the environmental problems described in the book we read today, which do you think are the most important for Saving our Planet? Why do you think so?
  a. Vegetation unable to grow in salt water (New Calcedonia).
  b. Animals like elephants becoming endangered by humans (Botswana).
  c. Agricultural land being used poorly and unwisely (Indonesia).
  d. Whales killed for the oil in their bodies (Argentina).
  e. Hydroelectric dams flooding needed agricultural land (Côte d'Ivoire).
  f. Climate changes resulting because of logging in the Amazon forests (Brazil).

On the SIOP® form in Figure 5.4, rate Miss Abbas's lesson on each of the Strategies features.

FIGURE 5.4   *Strategies Component of the SIOP® Model: Miss Abbas's Lesson*

4	3	2	1	0
13. Ample opportunities provided for students to use **learning strategies**		Inadequate opportunities provided for students to a use **learning strategies**		No opportunity provided for students to use **learning strategies**
14. **Scaffolding techniques** consistently used, assisting and supporting student understanding (e.g., think-alouds)		**Scaffolding techniques** occasionally used		**Scaffolding techniques** not used
15. A variety of **questions or tasks that promote higher-order thinking skills** (e.g., literal, analytical, and interpretive questions)		Infrequent **questions or tasks that promote higher-order thinking skills**		No **questions or tasks that promote higher-order thinking skills**

Mrs. Graves

Mrs. Graves began her lesson by distributing the two trade books to each table group (28 students; 16 of whom were English learners at varied levels of proficiency). She asked each student to complete a quick write based on the cover photo of the book and the following prompts: *Where do you think this photograph was taken? Where do you think the people on the walkway are going?* (Note: The colorful photograph, taken from high in the sky, is of Yellowstone Park's hot springs with tourists walking by on a wooden walkway.) After students completed the quick-write, Mrs. Graves asked each child to read his or her writing to the others at their tables. Some students wrote paragraphs, while others wrote only a few words. A few students wrote nothing.

Next, Mrs. Graves directed students to look through the book with other students in their group, find their favorite photographs, and try to figure out what the photos were all about. Because many of the students had reading problems and/or were limited English speakers, Mrs. Graves had students identify the page numbers of their favorite photos, and then she read aloud the descriptions for their favorites. This activity took the entire period on the first day, and most students enjoyed looking at the pictures.

During the second day of the lesson, students were directed to complete independently a Venn Diagram, comparing and contrasting any two photos and countries described in *Earth From Above.* Students had completed Venn Diagrams frequently, so they began working when the graphic organizers were distributed. Mrs. Graves said that the students could talk to each other quietly but they were to work independently. She collected graphic organizers at the end of the period so that she could generate a grade for the two-day lesson.

On the SIOP® form in Figure 5.5, rate Mrs. Graves's lesson on each of the Strategies features.

FIGURE 5.5 *Strategies Component of the SIOP® Model: Mrs. Graves's Lesson*

4	3	2	1	0
13. Ample opportunities provided for students to use **learning strategies**		Inadequate opportunities provided for students to use **learning strategies**		No opportunity provided for students to use **learning strategies**

4	3	2	1	0
14. **Scaffolding techniques** consistently used throughout lesson, assisting and supporting student understanding (e.g., think-alouds)		**Scaffolding techniques** occasionally used		**Scaffolding techniques** not used

4	3	2	1	0
15. A variety of **questions or tasks that promote higher-order thinking skills** (e.g., literal, analytical, and interpretive questions)		Infrequent **questions or tasks that promote higher-order thinking skills**		No **questions or tasks that promote higher-order thinking skills**

Discussion of Lessons

13. *Ample Opportunities Provided for Students to Use Learning Strategies*

Mr. Bokhari: 3

Miss Abbas: 4

Mrs. Graves: 1

Mr. Bokhari's lesson received a 3 for the learning strategies feature. His students were required to make predictions about the content of the book they were going to read. After reading, the children evaluated the importance of the factual information in the descriptions of the three countries they had selected. While Mr. Bokhari asked the students to "make connections" to earlier learning, he did not provide an example of what he meant, so some ELs (and other students) had difficulty doing this task. Finally, students were asked to summarize the information they had read and orally share it with their table group and ultimately the entire class. Mr. Bokhari's lesson would have been stronger had he asked the students to return to their earlier predictions and confirm or disconfirm them after they had read the text selections.

Miss Abbas's lesson received a 4 for the learning strategies feature because students engaged in using cognitive, metacognitve, and affective strategies throughout. During SQP2RS (Squeepers), students predicted, reexamined their predictions later in the lesson,

FIGURE 5.6 *Miss Abbas's Lesson Plan*

Key: SW = Students will; TW = Teacher will; HOTS = higher-order thinking skills (questions and tasks)

Unit: Saving Our Planet	**Grade: 5**	**Teacher:** Miss Abbas

SIOP® Lesson: Comparing environmental issues in seven countries outside the United States

Reading/Language Arts Content Standards (Comprehension):

2.1 Understand how text features (e.g., format, graphics, sequence, diagrams, illustrations, charts, maps) make information accessible and usable.

2.3 Discern main ideas and concepts presented in texts, identifying and assessing evidence that supports those ideas.

2.7 Draw inferences, conclusions, or generalizations about text and support them with textual evidence and prior knowledge.

2.8 Distinguish facts, supported inferences, and opinions in text.

Key Vocabulary: TW review *environment, prediction, summarize.* Teach meaning of *persuade;* In VSS, SW find key words and phrases in the descriptions.

HOTS:

Of the environmental problems described in the book we read today, which do you think are the most important for Saving our Planet? Why do you think so?

a. Vegetation unable to grow in salt water because of human-made floods (New Calcedonia).

b. Animals like elephants becoming endangered by humans (Botswana).

c. Agricultural land being used poorly and unwisely (Indonesia).

d. Whales killed for the oil in their bodies (Argentina).

e. Hydroelectric dams flooding needed agricultural land (Côte d'Ivoire).

f. Climate changes resulting from logging in the Amazon forests (Brazil).

Visuals/Resources: Yann, Arthus-Bertrand & Burleigh Robert. (2001). *Earth From Above For Young Readers.* New York: Harry N. Abrams, Inc., Publishers.

World map, sticky notes, chart paper, markers, binder paper, copies of questions for homework.

Connections to Prior Knowledge and Past Learning; Building Background:

● Review steps to SQP2RS (Squeepers): Who remembers the steps?

● Review unit theme by referring to world map and sticky notes placed there last week indicating places where serious environmental problems are currently occurring, including the United States.

● Complete the Survey, Question, Predict steps of SQP2RS to narrow focus and build background.

● Introduce book and share introductory information about the photographer, Yann Arthus-Bertrand.

● Review the differences between a *fact* and an *opinion*.

Content Objectives:	**Meaningful Activities: Lesson Sequence**	**Review and Assessment:**
1. You will use photographs, maps, and illustrations to predict important information about environmental concerns in several different countries.	● TW post and orally explain content and language objectives. ● TW briefly review meanings of words previously taught: *environment, prediction, summarize.* ● TW review steps of SQP2RS ● TW distribute copies of books, two/table group. ● Introduce the photographer and author: Introduction (pp. 6–9). ● TW review how to do a quick survey of informational text (2–3 min). ● In partners or triads, SW write 2–3 questions generated from the survey. TW post questions on	Add 1-2 minutes to Survey if questions are lacking in substance. Review how to ask appropriate questions based on the text information (Practice and Application).
2. You will identify key information in written descriptions of five environmental problems.		
3. You will select what you think is the most important environmental issue facing us today.		

FIGURE 5.6 *Continued*

Language Objectives:

1. You will listen to two and will read five descriptions of environmental problems in the world.

2. You will write a brief summary about the environmental issues you read about.

3. You will try to *persuade* others about the environmental issue you think is most important by saying:

   "I am going to *persuade* you that the environmental issue that is most important for saving our planet is: _____ because _____."

   My reason is a (*fact*) or (*opinion*).

---

chart paper; mark with asterisks the questions generated by more than one group (i.e., 4 asterisks for a question asked by four groups).

- SW predict 3–4 most important concepts we will discuss and learn. TW post on chart paper.

- TW read first two descriptions of New Calcedonia (pp. 10–11) and Botswana (pp. 12–13).

- SW read about Mali (pp. 16–17), Indonesia (pp. 28–29), Argentina (pp. 38–39), Côte d'Ivoire (pp. 44–45), Brazil (pp. 62–63), using sticky notes for noting key ("most important") information.

- VSS: SW find 2–3 vocabulary words or phrases in the seven descriptions that are related to Saving Our Planet Examples: p. 45: *"The vegetation was submerged."* What happened to the plants when the dam was built? Or p. 62: *"Here, as elsewhere, people must weigh the good results against the bad."* What is the meaning of *weigh* in this sentence? (Practice and Application)

- TW will list words/phrases on white board. Explain/discuss as necessary.

- TW lead discussion on posted questions and spots in text with sticky notes. Check back on earlier predictions to see if they were confirmed or disconfirmed (Practice and Application).

- TW review how to use the key information from charts, maps, photographs; VSS words and phrases; and descriptions marked with sticky notes to write brief summaries (suggest at each table which partners or triads need to write paragraphs, which need to write good sentences).

- TW reminds students to take summaries home along with homework questions.

- TW distribute and read aloud questions for homework discussion at home and in class tomorrow. Review the meanings of *fact, opinion.* Teach the meaning of *persuade.* Review sentence stem in language objectives. Chorally read the sentence starter several times for practice. Each student's job tomorrow is to try to *persuade* the others in his or her table group which is the most important environmental issue affecting the countries we read about. You can include your parents' or caregivers' opinions, too. Remember the differences between *facts* and *opinions* when you're trying to *persuade* others.

Check to see if predictions include most important information; if not, add another 1-min. survey.

Spot-check while students are quietly reading to each other to see what they're marking with sticky notes.

Spot-check to make sure all partners or triads are finding key vocabulary and/or phrases. Help with pronunciation and meanings, if necessary.

Are students able to answer their own questions? If not, why not?

Model with think-aloud how to take information from charts, map, and create 2–3 summary statements together with class. Circulate and spot-check while students are writing summaries paragraphs or sentences.

Check understanding of questions, and vocabulary *fact, opinion, persuade.*

Model pronunciation of sentence starter; listen during choral reading.

Ask for student examples of *facts* and *opinions* as review.

Wrap-up:

- Review the three key concepts about the environmental issues identified in the book descriptions: (1) humans flooding agricultural land, (2) animals being endangered by humans, (3) world climate changes because of humans.

- Review key vocabulary on VSS poster; review the meaning of *persuade.*

- Review content and language objectives by showing fingers: 1 = I met this objective, 2 = I'm getting close to meeting the objective, but need more practice; (3) I'm still confused and need some more help.

Lesson plan format created by Melissa Castillo & Nicole Teyechea generated questions about the reading materials, identified important information with sticky notes, read together and noted key points, selected key vocabulary, and wrote a partner or triad summary. Finally, everyone was asked to evaluate the relative importance of six environmental issues found throughout the world. Miss Abbas also encouraged her students to make connections with past learning.

Mrs. Graves's lesson received a 1 for the learning strategies feature. While she attempted to engage the students in making predictions from the cover of the book, many of the English learners (and other students as well) knew little of Yellowstone Park's hot springs, and therefore they were disengaged because they had no idea what the photograph was. Mrs. Graves also asked the students to evaluate their favorite photo of the 34, but because the students weren't expected to read or really learn much of anything from the accompanying descriptions for the photos, the task was more about looking at interesting pictures than engaging in strategic thinking.

14. *Scaffolding Techniques Consistently Used, Assisting and Supporting Students*

Mr. Bokhari: 2

Miss Abbas: 4

Mrs. Graves: 2

Mr. Bokhari missed several opportunities to provide scaffolding for his English learners and struggling readers, and therefore his lesson received a 2 for the scaffolding feature. While he did have the students work in heterogeneous groups allowing them to work together and help each other, he did not remind the children how to use the textual features in the book to guide their predictions about the course content. He also could have scaffolded the group's selections of their countries by limiting the number so the task was more manageable, especially because some of the descriptions and photos aren't directly related to the unit theme. Instructional time was not used well by some groups because there were 34 descriptions with appealing photographs in the book, and several groups had a difficult time making their selections. The entire lesson would have been more effective if Mr. Bokhari had modeled exactly what the students were to do, including how to make their selections, how to forge connections with prior learning, and how to use their notes to create their oral summaries. These directions, as well as criteria for selecting the most important information in the descriptions, should have been written and posted for the students' use. This type of scaffolding is critical for English learners and other children who struggle, but it is also helpful for all students.

Miss Abbas's lesson received a 4 for the scaffolding feature. Throughout her lesson, she provided the following scaffolds: (1) posting and orally explaining the lesson's content and language objectives; (2) reviewing essential academic language (*prediction, summarize, environment*), and teaching what could be new academic language to English learners (*persuade*); (3) reviewing the steps to SQP2RS (Squeepers); (4) grouping students heterogeneously in pairs or triads; (5) reviewing an earlier lesson by referring back to the world map; (6) introducing the photographer and author information from the book's introduction; (7) encouraging students to survey the text prior to reading; (8) listing the student-generated questions on chart paper and indicating with asterisks which questions had been asked by multiple groups, thereby narrowing the focus of the topic to important information; (9) limiting to five the number of descriptions that groups would read; (10) modeling by reading aloud the first two descriptions before the students read the others; (11) allowing students to find their VSS words, a process Miss Abbas frequently included in lessons after she initially taught the children how to find important words; (12) reviewing and discussing the questions the students had earlier generated; (13) adjusting the final written summary assignment according to the ELs' proficiency levels; (14) allowing all students to use their notes, charts, map, and Squeepers questions and predictions during the group summary writing; and (15) previewing the key question for the following day and allowing students to discuss this with family members at home. Because of the extensive scaffolding throughout the lesson, the children were able to complete the assigned tasks.

Mrs. Graves's lesson received a 1 for the scaffolding feature because her attempts to assist the students actually may have hindered their learning. For example, she assigned a quick write for everyone. While this activity is generally considered to be an effective way to activate students' prior knowledge about a topic, it was inappropriate for the selected book because the cover photo was taken from the air and is somewhat difficult to figure out even for those familiar with Yellowstone Park. The quick write proved especially difficult for the ELs, not only because of their levels of English proficiency, but also because of their lack of prior knowledge about what they were viewing. A more effective activity would have been to allow the students to talk together about the cover photo and pool their ideas and predictions. In addition, many English learners have a very challenging time listening for an entire period while the teachers reads content material aloud. While Mrs. Graves believed she was supporting her ELs by reading the descriptions, in reality, the children were unable to follow what she was saying, even when they had the text in front of them. Remember that there were only two books for each table group so many students had nothing to look at during the teacher's read-aloud. Finally, even though the students had prior practice with the Venn Diagram graphic organizer, expecting them to complete one based on the photos and the teacher's oral reading of the descriptions was unreasonable, especially when the students could not work together. It appears that the grade, not student mastery of clearly stated objectives, was Mrs. Graves's goal for the lesson.

15. *A Variety of Questions and Tasks That Promote Higher-Order Thinking Skills*
>   Mr. Bokhari: 2
>
>   Miss Abbas: 4
>
>   Mrs. Graves: 1

Mr. Bokhari's lesson received a 2 for the tasks that required the students to engage in higher order thinking. Something to think about as you plan lessons according to the SIOP protocol is that, even when teachers include higher order questions and tasks, if an adequate amount of scaffolding isn't included in the lesson, some students will not be engaged in critically thinking. Even the best lesson plan that promotes higher order thinking will be ineffective in execution if students are unable to complete the tasks that are assigned. This is precisely why the scaffolding feature is included in the Strategies component. See Chapter 8 for a complete discussion of this and other issues during lesson delivery.

Miss Abbas's lesson received a 4 for the higher order thinking questions and tasks she planned. The steps of SQP2RS (Squeepers) promote critical thinking when students are engaged in predicting, questioning, monitoring their comprehension (when they are searching for answers to their questions and confirming/disconfirming predictions), determining what's really important, and summarizing. Keep in mind that the Squeepers technique can be used with students of all ages, including pre-K and K. The steps remain the same; the text is what changes according to age, English proficiency, and reading level. Also note that the final question of Miss Abbas's lesson that was to be discussed at home and the following day is written at the highest level of Bloom's Taxonomy (Evaluation).

Mrs. Graves's lesson received a 1 for the final feature in the strategies component. The initial questions in the lesson (*Where do you think this photograph was taken? Where do you think the people on the walkway are going?*) are thought-provoking, but the manner in which they were asked (the quick write) was inappropriate given the varied English proficiency levels. Having the students orally read their quick writes in front of all classmates is also an ineffective (and frankly deleterious) practice, especially when children are acquiring a new language and/or are having difficulty with reading. Sharing a quick write with a partner or triad is very different from reading in front of an "audience" of peers. Finally, while Venn Diagrams are intended to promote critical thinking (comparing and contrasting), when assigned as Mrs. Graves did without interaction and as a silent independent task, the graphic organizer became just another classroom ditto.

Summary

We frequently remind teachers, "Just because your students can't read well doesn't mean they can't think!" A similar adage to this might be said of English learners: "Just because they can't speak English proficiently doesn't mean they can't think!"

In this chapter, we have described how to promote critical and strategic thinking for all students, but most especially for ELs. Learning is made more effective when teachers actively assist students in developing metacognitive, cognitive, and social/affective strategies, those that promote self-monitoring, self-regulation, and problem solving. We believe that students with developing English proficiency should not be denied effective, creative, and generative teaching while they are learning the language. Therefore, it is imperative that all teachers provide English learners with sufficient scaffolding, including verbal supports such as paraphrasing and frequent repetition, and instructional supports such as the appropriate use of graphic organizers and opportunities to work with more experienced individuals in flexible groups. While English learners are developing English proficiency, teachers must remember to include in their lessons higher-order questions that promote critical thinking.

Discussion Questions

1. Describe a learning situation you participated in or observed in which the teacher modeled how to do something. Describe a recent lesson in which you modeled a process, directions students were to follow, or steps for an experiment. What did you have to do to ensure that students could follow your instruction? What worked and what didn't? How could you have made things more clear?

2. The concept of scaffolding may be somewhat new for you. The definition in the glossary may be helpful, as may be the following construction analogy. Picture

a high-rise building as it is under construction. As new stories are added, scaffolding is built along the outside of the previously constructed story (or level). This scaffolding allows access for the construction workers—they need to be able to get into the upper stories in order to continue the building process.

Think of a content topic that you must teach that is challenging to students acquiring English as a second (or multiple) language. What types of scaffolds must you put in place for your students to successfully access your content and language objectives?

3. Here's a factual question a teacher might ask based on a social studies text: "Who was the first president of the United States?" Given the topic of the presidency, what are several additional questions you could ask that promote higher-order thinking? Why is it important to use a variety of questioning strategies with English learners? Use one of the taxonomies (Bloom's or Anderson & Krathwohl's) to guide you.

4. Using the SIOP® lesson you have been developing, add meaningful activities that develop learning strategies. Determine how to scaffold ELs' access to your objectives. Write several higher order thinking questions/tasks.

Interaction

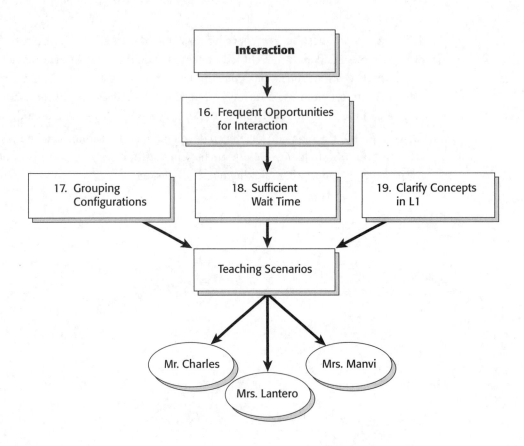

Objectives

After reading, discussing, and engaging in activities related to this chapter, you will be able to meet the following content and language objectives.

Content Objectives

Select from a variety of activities that promote interaction and incorporate them into lesson plans.

Design grouping patterns that support lesson content and language objectives.

Identify techniques to increase wait time.

Identify resources to support student clarification in the native language.

Language Objectives

Explain in writing the purpose of student–student interaction for language development.

Describe techniques to reduce the amount of teacher talk in a lesson.

Practice asking questions that promote student elaboration of responses.

For young English learners to become fluent in academic English, we need to provide structured opportunities in all subject areas to practice using the language. Because of the large number of English learners in schools today, *all* teachers are teachers of English, even in subjects like science, math, or social studies; the integration of language development across the curriculum is vital. For students learning English, teachers must create ample opportunities to practice using *academic* language, not simply social uses of language. It is recommended that English learners as young as kindergarten spend about 90 minutes per week working together in pairs, practicing and extending material already taught (Gersten, Baker, Shanahan, Linan-Thompson, Collins, & Scarcella, 2007). And the language must be meaningful to students; it is not just the quantity of exposures to English that affects learning, but it is the quality as well (Wong-Fillmore & Valadez, 1986).

Background

"Use it or lose it" is a saying that conveys what we know from our own experience in learning a second language. If one doesn't practice using the language, it is difficult to maintain it. But what about learning a language in the first place—does speaking it help to develop the language? The answer is a resounding "Yes!" The role that conversation plays in the process of second language teaching and learning is clear (Day, 1998). But discussion also offers important benefits for learning in general. As Gerald Graff puts it, "Talk—about books and subjects—is as important educationally as are the books and subjects themselves" (2003, p. 9).

The issue is, why are there so few opportunities for students to interact in typical classrooms? Studies indicate that, in most classrooms, teachers dominate the linguistic aspect of the lesson, leaving students severely limited in terms of opportunities to use language in a variety of ways (Goodlad, 1984; Marshall, 2000). In a study of programs for ELs (Ramirez, Yuen, Ramey, & Pasta, 1991), it was found that the classes were characterized by excessive teacher talk. When students were given an opportunity to respond, it usually involved only simple information-recall statements, restricting students' chance to produce language and develop complex language and thinking skills. In our own work, we observe teachers doing a significant amount of talking at students rather than providing the impetus for a discussion or sharing, then allowing students to talk to one another.

There are many benefits to having students actively engaged in interaction around subject matter. Some include:

- **Deeper understanding of text.** When teachers use thoughtful questioning to promote discussion, it encourages children to discuss what the passage is about and to think about the text at deeper levels (Echevarria, 1995; Goldenberg, 1992–1993).

- **Oral language development.** Being exposed to and interacting with language that is just beyond their independent speaking level moves students to higher levels of language proficiency.

- **Brain stimulation.** Interesting, engaging activities, including discussions, play an important role in learning. When students are engaged, more of the pleasure structures in the brain are activated than when students are simply asked to memorize information (Poldrack, Clark, Pare-Blagoev, Shohamy, Creso Moyano, Myers, & Gluck, 2001).

- **Increased motivation.** Interaction with others is an important component of reading instruction that increases motivation and comprehension (Guthrie & Ozgungor, 2002).

- **Reduced risk.** The typical question-answer sessions where teachers call on students may be threatening to students, particularly those unprepared to respond. Some students cannot focus on the content in this setting because it triggers the brain's "threat response" (Jensen, 2005). Students talking in pairs or small groups minimizes the risk and allows ideas to flow more easily.

- **More processing time.** Students need time to process after learning. Direct instruction should be limited to short increments followed by time for discussion.

- **Increased attention.** Use of pairs or teams can heighten attention levels. Students may be asked to work together to compare/contrast material learned, group and regroup the material, resequence it, or retell it from another point of view (Marzano, Pickering, & Pollock 2001).

To see an example of eliciting interaction, please view the corresponding video clip (Chapter 6, Module 1) on the accompanying CD.

Unfortunately, these practices tend not to be prevalent in classrooms with English learners.

We find that it is both interesting and helpful to analyze actual transcripts from lessons to demonstrate the kind of teacher dominance that is so prevalent in classrooms. The following transcripts are from a pilot SIOP® study (Echevarria, Greene, & Goldenberg, 1996) in sixth-grade social studies classes. The teachers were videotaped teaching the same content about consumerism to English learners, the first using a typical approach found in mainstream classes and the other using the SIOP® Model approach. Both classes had approximately twenty-five students, and in this lesson, students were learning how to read labels on clothing and on a bottle of antiseptic.

Mainstream Lesson

TEACHER: Look at the piece of clothing at the bottom. It says *(he reads)*, "This shirt is flame-resistant," which means what?

STUDENT: Could not burn.

STUDENT: Won't catch fire.

TEACHER: It will not burn, won't catch fire. Right *(continues reading)*. "To retain the flame-resistant properties"—what does "to retain" mean?

STUDENT: *(unintelligible)*

TEACHER: To keep it. All right. *(He reads)*, "In order to keep this shirt flame-resistant wash with detergent only." All right *(he reads)*. "Do not use soap or bleach. Tumble dry. One hundred percent polyester." Now, why does it say, "Do not use soap or bleach"?

STUDENT: 'Cause it'll take off the . . .

TEACHER: It'll take off the what?

STUDENTS: *(fragmented responses)*

TEACHER: It'll take off the flame-resistant quality. If you wash it with soap or bleach, then the shirt's just gonna be like any old shirt, any regular shirt, so when you put a match to it, will it catch fire?

STUDENT: No.

TEACHER: Yes. 'Cause you've ruined it then. It's no longer flame-resistant. So the government says you gotta tell the consumer what kind of shirt it is, and how to take care of it. If you look at any piece of clothing: shirt, pants, your shirts, um, your skirts, anything. There's always going to be a tag on these that says what it is made of and how you're going to take care of it. Okay. And that's for your protection so that you won't buy something and then treat it wrong. So labeling is important. All right. Let's review. I'll go back to the antiseptic. What did we say indications meant? Indications? Raise your hands, raise your hands. Robert?

STUDENT: What's it for.

TEACHER: What is it for, when do you use this? Okay. What do directions, what is that for, Victor?

STUDENT: How to use . . .

TEACHER: How to use. Okay, so indications is when you use it *(holds one finger up)*, directions is how you use it *(holds another finger up)*, and warnings is what?

STUDENTS: *(various mumbled responses)*

TEACHER: How you don't use it. This is what you don't do.

The teacher in this case tended to finish sentences for the students and accept any form of student comment without encouraging elaborated responses. In examining the exchanges, what did the teacher do when students gave partial or incorrect answers? He answered the question himself. Students learn that they can disengage because the teacher will continue with the "discussion."

TEACHER: Most clothing must have labels that tell what kind of cloth was used in it right? Look at the material in the picture down there *(points to picture in text).*[1] What does it say, the tag right there?

STUDENT: The, the, the . . .

TEACHER: The tag right there.

STUDENT: *(Reading)* "Flame-resis . . . "

TEACHER: Resistant.

STUDENT: "Flame-resistant. To retain the flame-resistant properties, wash with detergent only. Do not use soap or bleach. Use warm water. Tumble dry."

TEACHER: "One hundred percent . . . "

STUDENT: "Polyester."

TEACHER: Now, most clothes carry labels, right? *(pointing to the neck of her sweater).* They explain how to take care of it, like dry clean, machine wash, right? It tells you how to clean it. Why does this product have to be washed with a detergent and no soap or bleach?

STUDENT: Because clothes . . .

TEACHER: Why can't you use something else?

STUDENTS: *(several students mumble answers)*

STUDENT: *(says in Spanish)* Because it will make it small.

TEACHER: It may shrink, or *(gestures to a student)* it may not be . . . what does it say?

STUDENT: It's not going to be able to be resistant to fire.

TEACHER: Exactly. It's flame-resistant, right? So, if you use something else, it won't be flame-resistant anymore. How about the, uh, look at the *antiseptic (holds hands up to form a container)*—the picture above the shirt, the antiseptic?

STUDENT: Read it?

TEACHER: Antiseptic *(Teacher reads)* and other health products you buy without a prescription often have usage and warning labels. So what can you learn from this label? Read this label quietly please, and tell me what you can learn from the label. Read the label on that antiseptic. *(Students read silently.)*

TEACHER: What can you learn from this label?

STUDENT: It kills, oh I know.

TEACHER: Steve?

STUDENT: It kills germs.

STUDENT: Yeah, it kills germs.

TEACHER: It kills germs. You use it for wounds, right? What else?

STUDENTS: *(various enthusiastic responses)*

---

[1]The teacher explained then that they would be doing an activity in which they would read labels for information.

TEACHER: One person at a time. Okay, hold on. Veronica was saying something.

STUDENT: It tells you in the directions that, you could use it, that like that, 'cause if you use it in another thing, it could hurt you.

TEACHER: It could hurt you. Okay, what else? Ricardo?

STUDENT: If you put it in your mouth, don't put it in your mouth or your ears or your eyes.

TEACHER: Very good. Don't put it in your mouth, ears, and eyes. Okay, for how many days should you use it? No more than what?

STUDENT: No more than ten days.

STUDENT: Ten days.

TEACHER: So don't use it—you have to follow what it says so don't use it more than ten days. Now, the next activity you're going to do . . .

The SIOP® teacher allowed for a balance of teacher-to-student talk and encouraged student participation. She asked questions, waited for students' responses, and restated or elaborated on the responses. In this case, what did the teacher do to elicit answers to the question? She scaffolded the answer by encouraging the students to think about it, prompting them to give their responses.

The features of the SIOP® Model within the Interaction component are designed to provide teachers with concrete ways of increasing student participation and developing English language proficiency.

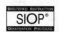

SIOP® FEATURE 16:
Frequent Opportunities for Interaction and Discussion

Oral Language Development

To see an example of student-to-student interaction, please view the corresponding video clip (Chapter 6, Module 1) on the accompanying CD.

This SIOP® feature emphasizes the importance of balancing linguistic turn-taking between the teacher and students, and among students. It also highlights the practice of encouraging students to elaborate their responses rather than accepting yes/no and one-word answers, even for the youngest learners.

The findings of the National Literacy Panel on Language Minority Children and Youth (August & Shanahan, 2006) revealed the important relationship between oral proficiency in English and reading and writing proficiency. Specifically, reading comprehension skills and writing skills are positively correlated with oral language proficiency in English (Geva, 2006), two areas that are particularly challenging for English learners. Solid reading comprehension is the foundation for achievement in nearly every subject area in school, and writing proficiency in English is an essential skill as well.

There has long been recognition that language, cognition, and reading are intimately related (Tharp & Gallimore, 1988). As one acquires new language, new concepts are developed. Think about your own language learning with respect to understanding computer functions. Each new vocabulary word and term you learn and understand (e.g., *hard drive, memory,* and *gigabyte*) is attached to a concept that in turn expands your ability to think about how a computer works. As your own system of word-meaning grows in complexity, you are more capable of using the self-directed speech of verbal thinking ("Don't forget to save it on the hard drive."). Without an understanding of the words and the concepts they represent, you would not be capable of thinking about (self-directed speech) or discussing (talking with another) computer functions.

Reading comprehension is inseparable from language development. Because an understanding of language makes acquiring knowledge possible, deriving meaning from texts in English will be extremely challenging for English learners who may have difficulty reading unfamiliar words or comprehending their meaning.

Researchers who have investigated the relationship between language and learning suggest that interactive approaches—where there is more balance in student talk and teacher talk—are effective in promoting meaningful language learning opportunities for English learners (Cazden, 2001; Echevarria, 1995b; McIntyre, Kyle, & Moore, 2006; Saunders & Goldenberg, 1992; Tharp & Gallimore, 1988; Walqui, 2006). Sometimes called instructional conversations (ICs), this mode of instruction emphasizes active student involvement and meaningful language-based teaching. Instructional conversations have been defined as having a number of elements (Goldenberg, 1992–1993) that are consistent with other discussion-based methods (Wilen, 1990). Essentially it is talking about text, which provides opportunities for using language to learn language and concepts. An instructional conversation (IC) approach differs from typical teaching because most instructional patterns in classrooms involve the teacher asking a question, the student responding, the teacher evaluating the response and asking another question (Cazden, 2001). In contrast, the typical format of an IC begins with the teacher introducing the group to a theme or idea related to the text, then relating the theme to students' background experiences. Next, the teacher shows the text to be read and asks prediction questions. As the text is read, it is "chunked" into sections to provide maximum opportunity for discussion, constantly relating the theme and background experiences to a text-based discussion. Figure 6.1 illustrates the contrast in approaches.

This conversational approach is particularly well-suited to English learners who, after only a few years in school, frequently find themselves significantly behind their peers in most academic areas, usually due to low reading levels and underdeveloped language skills. IC provides a context for learning in which language is expressed naturally through meaningful discussion.

A rich discussion, or conversational approach, has advantages for teachers as well. Through discussion a teacher can more naturally activate children's background knowledge as they are encouraged to share their knowledge of the world and about how

FIGURE 6.1   *Contrast Typical Instruction with IC*

Typical Instruction	*Instructional Conversation*
Teacher-centered	Teacher facilitates
Exact, specific answers evaluated by the teacher	Many different ideas encouraged
No extensive discussion	Oral language practice opportunities using natural language
Skill-directed	Extensive discussion and student involvement
Easier to evaluate	Draw from prior or background knowledge
Check for understanding	Student level of understanding transparent
Mostly literal level thinking and language use	Fewer black and white responses
	Mostly higher level thinking and language use

language works. When teachers and students interact together, it fosters a supportive environment and builds teacher–student rapport. Also, when working in small groups with each child participating in the discussion, teachers are better able to determine each child's level of understanding; weak areas are made transparent.

As mentioned previously, however, teachers typically do most of the talking in class. Of course, teachers have knowledge to share and discuss with children, but consistent teacher dominance reduces the opportunities children have to participate fully in lessons by discussing ideas and information, and practicing English as they express their ideas, opinions, and answers.

Effective SIOP® teachers structure their lessons in ways that promote student discussion, and they strive to provide a more balanced linguistic exchange between themselves and their students. It can be particularly tempting for teachers to do most of the talking when students are not completely proficient in their use of English, but these students are precisely the ones who need opportunities to practice using English the most.

Effective SIOP® teachers also encourage elaborated responses from students when discussing the lesson's concepts. The teacher elicits more extended student contributions by using a variety of techniques that will take students beyond simple yes or no answers and short phrases (Echevarria, 1995b; Goldenberg, 1992–1993). Some of these techniques include asking students to expand on their answers by saying, "Tell me more about that"; and by asking direct questions to prompt more language use such as, "What do you mean by . . ." or "What else. . . ." Another technique is to provide further information through questions such as "How do you know?" "Why is that important?" "What does that remind you of?" Other techniques include offering restatements such as "In other words . . . is that accurate?" and by frequently pausing to let students process the language and formulate their responses. Some teachers call on other students to extend a classmate's response.

It takes time and practice for these techniques to become a natural part of a teacher's repertoire. The teachers with whom we've worked report that they had to consciously practice overcoming the temptation to speak for students or to complete a student's short phrase. The preceding transcript showed how the first teacher spoke for students instead of encouraging students to complete their thoughts. The following segment from the transcript provides another example:

TEACHER: What do "directions" . . . what is that for, Victor?

STUDENT: How to use . . .

TEACHER: How to use. Okay, so "indications" is when you use it, "directions" is how you use it, and "warnings" is what?

STUDENTS: *(various mumbled responses)*

TEACHER: How you don't use it. This is what you don't do.

In this segment, the mainstream teacher could have encouraged a more balanced exchange between himself and the students. First, he did not encourage students to completely express their thoughts; he accepted partial and mumbled answers. Second, he answered for the students, dominating the discussion. It is easy to imagine how students could become disinterested, passive learners in a class in which the teacher accepts minimal participation and does the majority of the talking.

The SIOP® teacher approached students–teacher interaction differently:

TEACHER: What can you learn from this label?

STUDENT: It kills, oh I know.

TEACHER: Steve?

STUDENT: It kills germs.

STUDENT: Yeah, it kills germs.

TEACHER: It kills germs. You use it for wounds, right? What else?

STUDENTS: *(various enthusiastic responses)*

TEACHER: One person at a time. Okay, hold on. Veronica was saying something.

STUDENT: It tells you in the directions that, you could use it, that like that, 'cause if you use it in another thing, it could hurt you.

TEACHER: It could hurt you. Okay, what else? Ricardo?

STUDENT: If you put it in your mouth, don't put it in your mouth or your ears or your eyes.

TEACHER: Very good. Don't put it in your mouth, ears, and eyes. Okay, for how many days should you use it? No more than what?

STUDENT: No more than ten days.

STUDENT: Ten days.

TEACHER: So don't use it—you have to follow what it says, so don't use it more than ten days. Now, the next activity you're going to do . . .

The SIOP® teacher let the students have time to express their thoughts (e.g., student says, "It kills . . . It kills germs."). The teacher could have completed the sentence for the student, but she waited for him to complete his answer. Also, the SIOP® teacher encouraged and challenged the students more than the mainstream teacher did by asking twice, "What else?" Finally, the teacher nominated students who volunteered to talk and repeated what they said so that the class could hear a full response (e.g., Veronica).

Effective SIOP® teachers plan instruction so that students have opportunities to work with one another on academic tasks, using English to communicate. Through meaningful interaction, students can practice speaking and making themselves understood. That implies asking and answering questions, negotiating meaning, clarifying ideas, giving and justifying opinions, and more. Students may interact in pairs, triads, and small groups. Literature circles, think-pair-share, Jigsaw readings, debates, and science experiments are only a sample of the types of activities teachers can include in lessons to foster student–student interaction. An interactive approach has been shown to improve the achievement of young English learners with learning disabilities (Echevarria, 1995b) as well as typically developing fourth-grade EL students (Saunders & Goldenberg, 2007).

Other Opportunities for Interaction

Interaction need not always be oral. Students can interact with teachers through dialogue journals, sharing ideas and learning from the teacher who models appropriate written text.

Using technology, students can interact with each other through a class electronic list, shared research files on a school network, or a planned pen pal e-mail exchange with another class elsewhere in the world.

In a discussion of the importance of movement for learning at all ages, Jensen (2005) suggests a number of games such as rewriting lyrics to familiar songs in pairs or teams as a content review, then performing the song; playing Simon Says using content such as "Point to Rome. Point to the first country the Romans conquered," etc.; or role-plays, charades, or pantomime to review main ideas or key points.

Students may interact by sharing their expertise. For example, in an activity called Expert Stay Stray, students work on an assignment in small groups, such as completing a chart summarizing the key points from a unit of study. Students in the group number off. The teacher calls a number, e.g., #4, and student #4 takes his or her group's chart and goes to another table and shares the information with the new group. Then the student remains with the new group as the teacher calls another number, for example, #1. Student #1 takes the chart of the student who shared (#4)—which encourages students to listen carefully—and goes to a new group and shares the information from the chart. This activity provides students with an opportunity to discuss the information while completing the chart, then to share the information orally while others listen attentively, and to paraphrase someone else's explanation of the chart. It can be adapted to any content area or grade level.

Start the class each day with students in pairs and have them tell each other the day's content objective. Then they move to find another partner and tell them the language objective.

Dinner Party (or Birthday Party for K–2) is an activity appropriate for all levels and most content areas. For instance, in language arts, children would respond to the prompt: "Suppose you could have a dinner party for the authors or poets that we have studied. Whom would you invite? Why would you select them? What would be the seating order of the guests at your table, and why would you place them in that order? What do you think the guests would talk about during dinner? Include specific references to the authors' lives and works in your response." The purpose is for students to act out the questions by assuming personas, such as characters in stories, scientists, historical figures, or artists. During each dinner or birthday party, specific content must be included and the characters must respond to each other as realistically and accurately as possible (Vogt & Echevarria, 2008).

A complete lesson that illustrates interaction is seen in Figure 6.2a. A technology teacher on the Arizona-Mexico border, Steve Young, uses an interactive SIOP® approach for making difficult concepts understandable. In this lesson, he uses a visual representation of the four functions of a computer (Figure 6.2b) tying the concepts to something students can relate to: eggs. Eggs are stored in the refrigerator as data are stored on the hard drive. Cooking eggs is like processing data. The output from a computer is information and for the eggs, it is the finished product—cooked eggs.

After students have been taught the four functions of a computer and the related terms, they complete a classification activity (Figure 6.2c) as practice/application.

FIGURE 6.2a   *SIOP® Lesson Plan: Four Functions of a Computer*

LESSON TOPIC: *Four Functions of a Computer*

OBJECTIVES

Content
Identify the Four Functions of a computer (Storage, Input, Processing, and Output). Classify computer components according to their functions.

Language
Discuss the difference between long-term and short-term storage.
Distinguish data from information.

CONCEPTS
Data is what the computer understands.
Information is what humans understand.
Data must be processed to become information.
In order for data to be processed it must be in short-term memory.

MATERIALS
Old computer to remove parts from. Four boxes. Four Functions Graphic Organizer (Figure 6.2b). Categorize This worksheets (Figure 6.2c). Cloze summary

STRATEGIES/ACTIVITIES
Think-Pair-Share, Categorize This (classifying), Cloze summary

VOCABULARY
Prior Vocabulary: *Keyboard, Monitor, Printer, Microphone, Speakers, CPU*
Content Vocabulary: *Storage, Input, Processing, Output, Data, Information, RAM, Hard Drive*
Process Vocabulary: *Identify, Function, Distinguish, Relate, Classify*

MOTIVATION (*Building background*)
The teacher says: *How many of you have a kitchen at home? Think right now about what you use your kitchen for, and when you've thought of at least one function, tell your neighbor. When you and your neighbor have thought of three functions, things you use your kitchen for, one of you stand up to share your ideas with the class.* (When students stand, the teacher calls on students to solicit the responses: keeping food, cooking, and eating. On the board or on the computer projection screen the words *food, keeping food, cooking,* and *eating* are displayed. Next to food, teacher writes "input"; next to "keeping," "storage"; next to "cooking," "processing"; next to "eating," "output.") *How many of you have cooked eggs? I'm going to show you how the four functions of a computer are just like cooking eggs.*

PRESENTATION
(Language and content objectives, comprehensible input, strategies, interaction, feedback)

Objectives are presented after background is built, and content words and process words are introduced. Previous vocabulary words, which consist of the basic parts of a computer system, are reviewed.

The teacher says the following:
Let's get back to the eggs. Tell your neighbor where you keep your eggs. The refrigerator? Good. Tell your neighbor what a refrigerator is for. Keeping things in? Good.

Another word for what you keep or put things in is "storage." Everyone say "storage." The refrigerator is for storage. What's the refrigerator for? Tell your neighbor one or two other things you use for storage in your kitchen.

The computer needs storage, too. Discuss with your neighbor why the computer needs storage. Where do you think the computer stores, or keeps, the things you save? Think about it and tell your neighbor what you think . . .

(The teacher selects a pair to remove the hard drive from the parts computer and pass it around to everyone. Then he asks someone to classify the hard drive by placing it in one of the four boxes that are labeled *storage, input, processing,* and *output.*)

Discuss with your neighbor which one of your vocabulary words is what is stored on the hard drive. Stand up when you think you know. Data, very good. You know what data is when we are talking about computers. It's ones and

---

FIGURE 6.2a *Continued*

zeroes. That's all the computer understands. What's the only thing the computer understands? What do we call the ones and zeroes the computer understands?

Data is raw like the egg you are going to cook. Would you eat a raw, uncooked egg? No? Well, you won't be able to understand data either unless the computer cooks it for you.

Where do you put everything you get out of the refrigerator before you cook it? Tell your neighbor where you place the ingredients you are going to use as you cook . . . The counter? The table? Good. The refrigerator is long-term storage and the counter or table is short-term storage. We put things on the counter or table to use them but we don't leave them there.

The computer has a counter or table too for short-term storage. It's called RAM, random access memory. When you open a document you want to work with, the computer moves it from the hard drive to RAM. (The RAM picture is now displayed on the graphic organizer.) *This is what RAM looks like. Who wants to find the RAM in our parts computer and take it out for us to see?*

So look at the document you have opened right now on your computer. Is it in long-term or short-term storage? Is it in RAM or on the hard drive?

Let's talk about the eggs again. Tell your neighbor where you got them. Tell your neighbor where you placed them while you got the pan out and the butter or oil to cook them in.

Just like you took your eggs from the refrigerator, which is long-term storage (hold up the hard drive), *and moved them to the counter or table, which is your short-term storage area* (hold up the RAM), *raw data has to be moved to RAM so it can be processed.*

Before you can eat the eggs on your counter, you have to cook them. But we don't cook data, we process it. What do we do to data? The data you are looking at on your computer has been processed. That's why all those ones and zeroes appear to you as words. The data has been processed and now it's information. Discuss with your neighbor how processing is like cooking.

(The teacher continues with this approach with all four functions of the computer, relating the computer and its parts to the kitchen and cooking. The teacher uses realia (parts of the computer), a graphic organizer, Tell Your Neighbor, and choral response to keep the students engaged, to practice oral language, and to make the content comprehensible. There is plenty of meaningful interaction and feedback throughout. The teacher also spot-checks along the way to make sure ELs comprehend.)

PRACTICE/APPLICATION
(Meaningful activities, interaction, strategies, practice/application, feedback)

After the presentation of concepts, students work with their partners to complete the classification activity (Figure 6.2c). The class brainstorms together words and then identifies the categories. Students work to classify words into categories. After they finish, it is checked/reviewed on the big screen.

REVIEW/ASSESSMENT
(Review objectives and vocabulary, assess learning)

If there is time for the following cloze summary, students do it. If not, it is saved for review the following day.

> *The computer has _____ functions. Keeping data is the _____ function. Putting data into the computer is the _____ function. Changing raw data into information is the _____ function. Displaying or printing information is the _____ function.*
>
> *The most common input devices are the k _____ and m _____ . The monitor is an _____ device. D _____ is what the computer understands. I _____ is what humans understand. Data must be p _____ to be changed into Information.*
>
> *The two places where data is stored are the h _____ d _____ and R _____ . The hard drive is for l _____ t _____ storage and RAM is for sh _____ t _____ storage. Data must be moved from the hard drive to R _____ so it can be processed. When the processed data is saved it is moved from RAM to the h _____ d _____ .*

At the end of the period, someone in each row must tell the teacher something he or she learned. They can discuss it with their row (Four Heads Together) and when one student gives a response, the row is dismissed. The following day, students write three things they learned the day before in their learning log for focus/review activity.

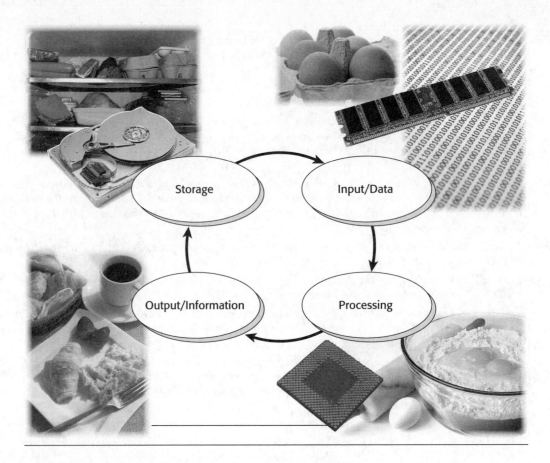

FIGURE 6.2b   *Four Functions of a Computer*

FIGURE 6.2c

Categorize This

Directions: Brainstorm words related to your topic. Place these words in the Holding Cell. Then pull your words out of the Holding Cell and put them into categories. Finally, assign your category labels and write a summary sentence (on the back) describing each category.

The Holding Cell

> *Data, Information, RAM, Hard Drive, Identify,*
> *Function, Distinguish, Relate, Classify*

STORAGE	INPUT	PROCESSING
OUTPUT	PROCESS WORDS	

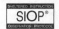

SIOP® FEATURE **17**:
Grouping Configurations Support Language and Content Objectives of the Lesson

To see an example of students working in groups, please view the corresponding video clip (Chapter 6, Module 1) on the accompanying CD.

To maximize achievement, a balance is necessary between whole-group and small-group learning in the classroom. Varying grouping configurations—by moving from whole group to small group, small group to individual assignments—provides students with opportunities to learn new information, discuss it, and process it. Organizing students into smaller groups for instructional purposes provides a learning context that whole-group teacher-dominated instruction doesn't offer. Fisher and Frey (2008) present a gradual release of responsibility model that slowly and purposefully shifts the workload from teacher to students. As seen in Figure 6.3 the teacher presents information and models "the type of thinking required to solve problems, understand directions, comprehend a text, or the like" (p. 5). The focus lesson is followed by guided instruction; the students are given an opportunity to collaborate. During this phase, students discuss ideas and information they learned during the focus lessons and guided instruction—not new information. Finally, students have acquired background knowledge from the first three phases and are ready to apply the information with independent tasks. When students aren't learning, it is often because there has not been the critical scaffolding that Figure 6.3 represents; teachers go directly from "I do it" to "You do it alone" (Fisher & Frey, 2008, p. 10).

In small guided instruction groups, the teacher naturally differentiates instruction as she works on focused skill instruction, language development, and/or assessment of student progress. Small-group instruction provides more opportunity to discuss text

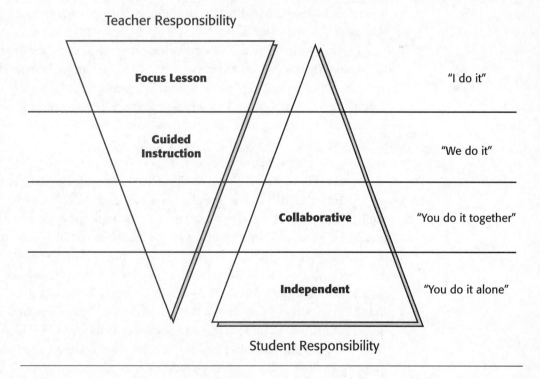

FIGURE 6.3 *A structure for successful instruction*

Source: Fisher & Frey, 2008

(Saunders & Goldenberg, 2007) and increases reading achievement (Vaughn, Linan-Thompson, Kouzekanani, Bryan, Dickson, Blozis, 2003). While the teacher is working with one group, the other students can work on familiar material in small groups, with a partner, or individually either at their desks or at work stations. Activities may include creating graphic representations of vocabulary terms or concepts, summarizing material, practicing word sorts, or reading self-selected leveled readers. These activities are purposeful, and meaningful, and lead to increased learning. In our work, we have seen this type of grouping work successfully with all ages, from kindergarten to the upper grades. In their book, *Differentiated Instruction: Grouping for Success*, Gibson and Hasbrouck (2008) provide a wealth of ideas for grouping effectively, including how to organize the classroom and schedule, and how to use a rotation chart for flexible grouping.

But not just any kind of grouping works well. Grouping by ability, which divides students for instruction based on their perceived capabilities for learning (low group, average group, high group) has serious academic and social effects for students who are not in the top group (Hiebert, 1983; Lucas, 1999; Callahan, 2005). Futrell and Gomez (2008) make this point: "We cannot ignore the fact that for more than five decades, ability grouping has resulted in separation of students by race, ethnicity, and socioeconomic status. Many studies have confirmed that minority and low-income students of all ability levels are overrepresented in the lower tracks and underrepresented in the higher tracks" (p. 76). English learners, who learn from exposure to good language models, are often shut out of the groups with rich academic learning opportunities.

When working with low-achieving groups, teachers have been found to talk more, use more structure, ask lower-level questions, cover less material, spend more time on skills and drills, provide fewer opportunities for leadership and independent research, encourage more oral than silent reading, teach less vocabulary, and allow less wait time during questioning, in addition, they spent twice as much time on behavior and management issues (Oakes, 1985; Vogt, 1989).

In many schools, it has become common practice to group English learners with low-achieving students regardless of their academic ability and performance. However, all students, including ELs, benefit from instruction that frequently includes a variety of grouping configurations. Whole-class groups are beneficial for introducing new information and concepts, modeling processes, and review. Flexible small groups promote the development of multiple perspectives and encourage collaboration. Partnering encourages success because it provides practice opportunities, scaffolding, and assistance for classmates (Flood, Lapp, Flood, & Nagel, 1992; Nagel, 2001; Tompkins, 2006).

Effective SIOP® classes are characterized by a variety of grouping structures, including individual work, partners, triads, small groups of four or five, cooperative learning groups, and whole group. Groups also vary because they may be homogeneous or heterogeneous by gender, language proficiency, language background, and/or ability. The decisions teachers make about how to group students should be purposeful, not arbitrary. A case can be made for grouping children by how well they speak English during literacy instruction (Uribe & Nathenson-Mejia, 2008). Teachers can target specific language instruction, and students are more apt to take risks in their second language. However, grouping students from very different grade levels (i.e., second through fifth grade) together based on language proficiency should be discouraged because they have very different social and academic needs (Uribe & Nathenson-Mejia, 2008). There are other times that grouping by language proficiency level is useful. For example, if a teacher's goal is for students at beginning levels of English proficiency to practice using a particular language structure within the context of a social studies lesson, such as present progressive (-*ing* form), then it may be useful to have those students grouped together for that lesson. Likewise, when developing the skills of students with low levels of literacy, it makes sense to have those with similar ability grouped together for a particular lesson. Assigning all ELs to the same group regularly is *not* good practice, especially when a bilingual aide teaches them almost exclusively. In SIOP® classes, ELs are given the same access to the curriculum and the teacher's expertise as native English-speaking students.

Using a variety of grouping configurations also facilitates learning in a number of ways. The variety of groups helps to maintain student interest because it is difficult for some students to stay focused when the teacher relies almost exclusively on whole-group instruction or having children work individually. Moving from whole group to cooperative learning groups or partners adds variety to the learning situation and increases student involvement in the learning process. Another benefit of grouping is that it provides much-needed movement for learners. When students are active, their brains are provided with the oxygen-rich blood needed for highest performance. Movement may be especially important for learners with special needs (Jensen, 2005).

It is recommended that at least two different grouping structures be used during a lesson, depending on the activity and objectives of the lesson.

SIOP® FEATURE 18:
Sufficient Wait Time for Student Responses Consistently Provided

Wait time is the length of time between utterances during an interaction. In classroom settings, it refers to the length of time that teachers wait for students to respond before interrupting, answering a question themselves, or calling on someone else to participate. Wait time varies by culture; it is appropriate in some cultures to let seconds, even minutes, lag between utterances, while in other cultures utterances can even overlap one another. In U.S. classrooms, the average length of wait time is clearly *not* sufficient. Imagine the impact of wait time on ELs who are processing ideas in a new language and need additional time to formulate the phrasings of their thoughts. Research supports the idea of wait time and has found it to increase student discourse and more student-to-student interaction (Honea, 1982; Swift & Gooding, 1983; Tobin, 1987).

Effective SIOP® teachers consciously allow children to express their thoughts fully, without interruption. Many teachers in U.S. schools are uncomfortable with the silence that follows their questions or comments, and they immediately fill the void by talking themselves. This situation may be especially pertinent in SIOP® classes where ELs need extra time to process questions in English, think of an answer in their second language, and then formulate their responses in English. Although teachers may be tempted to fill the silence, ELs benefit from a patient approach to classroom participation, in which teachers wait for students to complete their verbal contributions.

While effective SIOP® teachers provide sufficient wait time for ELs, they also work to find a balance between wait time and moving a lesson along. Some youngsters may become impatient if the pace of the class lags. One strategy for accommodating impatient students is to have them write down their responses while waiting, and then they can check their answers against the final answer.

Another way to help ELs is to allow the techniques made popular by a television show: "50-50" and "phone a friend." Students who are unsure of an answer or are unable to articulate it well might ask to choose between two possible responses provided by the teacher (50-50) or ask a classmate for help (phone a friend). However, to ensure practice with the language, the original student must give "the final answer" to the teacher.

SIOP® FEATURE 19:
Ample Opportunity for Students to Clarify Key Concepts in L1

Best practice indicates that English learners benefit from opportunities to clarify concepts in their first language (L1). In fact, the National Literacy Panel on Language Minority Children and Youth found that academic skills such as reading taught in the first language transfer to the second language (August & Shanahan, 2006). Although SIOP® instruction involves teaching subject-matter material in English, children are given the opportunity to have a concept or assignment explained in their L1 as needed. Significant controversy surrounds the use of L1 for instructional purposes, but we believe that clarification of key concepts in students' L1 by a bilingual instructional aide, peer, or through the use of materials written in the students' L1 provides an important support for the academic learning of those students who are not yet fully proficient in English.

This feature on the SIOP® may have NA circled as a score because not all SIOP® classes need to use students' L1 to clarify concepts for them (especially for advanced ELs).

However, with websites offering word translation capabilities, and the availability of bilingual dictionaries in book and computer program formats, all SIOP® classrooms should have resources in the students' native languages.

The Lesson

UNIT: Addition and Subtraction (First Grade)

The first-grade teachers in this chapter, Mr. Charles, Mrs. Lantero, and Mrs. Manvi, work in a suburban school that has a 24 percent EL population. Their classes have an even distribution of English learners, each with approximately 10 percent ELs. Most of those students are at the intermediate to advanced-intermediate levels of English proficiency and still benefit from having teachers use SIOP® techniques to increase their understanding of lessons.

The teachers in this school plan math units around the district's content standards. The lessons described in the scenarios that follow are part of a unit on addition and subtraction sums to twelve. The standards in this lesson are related to number sense and mathematical reasoning. Students are to know the addition facts (sums to twenty) and the corresponding subtraction facts and commit them to memory. The teachers each have their own methods for teaching addition, as seen in the lessons that follow. (For more examples of lesson and unit plans in with, see Echevarria, Vogt, & Short, in press.)

Teaching Scenarios

Mr. Charles

Mr. Charles began the lesson by explaining to the first-grade children that they were going to learn about different ways to do addition. He reviewed vocabulary that had been taught previously, such as addends and sums. He then engaged the children in a discussion about what information they knew about addition that had been learned previously, and he provided an adequate amount of time for the children to respond. He then asked the children when they would use addition in their everyday lives. Some of the children volunteered information about going to the grocery store or the bank and how they might have to use addition to solve problems. Mr. Charles then showed the children an addition problem on the overhead and asked them to work with a partner to figure out how they might solve the problem. He picked a student to come up to the overhead to solve one of the problems. (He chose the student by picking a name that had been written on a tongue depressor to ensure that he would call on a variety of children—not just the ones who raised their hands.) He also asked the student to underline the addends and circle the sums in the problem. To engage the whole class, Mr. Charles asked the children to raise their hands if they thought the student had the correct answer.

Mr. Charles continued the lesson by asking a volunteer to give a number from one to eight. He then had the children write the number on their paper, then draw the same number of shapes as the number they had written, using the color blue. Mr. Charles checked to make sure the children understood the directions, and he stopped at each child's desk to see how each was doing. He then asked the children to draw two more shapes, using the color yellow. He checked all students' work by circulating around the room. He asked the children to count all the blue and yellow shapes and to write an addition problem to illustrate what they had done. Mr. Charles asked the children to check with a partner to see if their problem was done correctly. He then engaged the children in a discussion of how pictures can help you find the answer to "how many in all." The discussion was balanced between the teacher and the students, and Mr. Charles asked for some examples of the kinds of pictures that they might draw to help them solve addition problems. He reminded the children to check for the addends and the sums in their problems.

Mr. Charles then had the children work in pairs. He distributed a paper plate and clothespins to each pair of students. He told the children to clip four clothespins on the top edge of a paper plate and three on the bottom. He then instructed the students to write an addition sentence for the clothespins and solve it $(4 + 3 = 7)$. Mr. Charles called on children to explain how they found the answer. He asked a child who understood the concept to model putting clothespins on the plate and writing a corresponding addition sentence. He then asked another child to answer the addition problem provided by the previous child.

Next, Mr. Charles told the children that they would be taking the clothespins off their plates and making up a new problem using a different number of clothespins. He explained that he would like one partner in the group to tell the other partner how many clothespins to place on the top and how many to place on the bottom, thus giving the children an opportunity to practice their English with each other. The children exchanged paper plates, and one partner was responsible for writing the addition problem.

Mr. Charles finished the lesson with a review of what the students had learned about addition and asked for volunteers from the class to give some examples of addends and sums.

On the SIOP® form in Figure 6.4, rate Mr. Charles's lesson on each of the Interaction features.

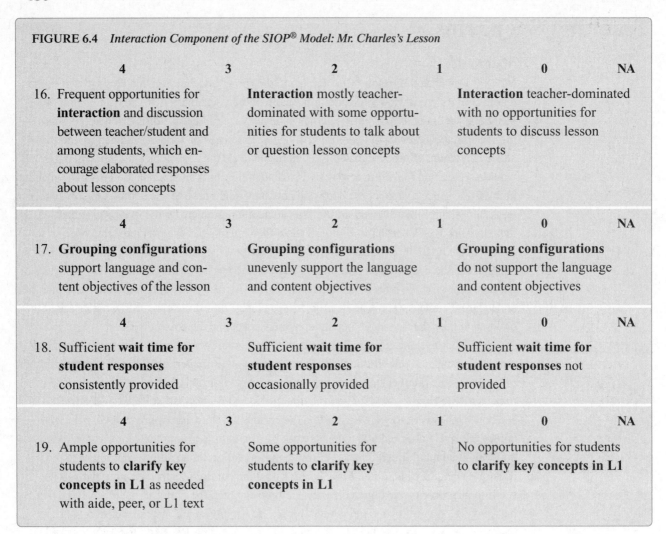

FIGURE 6.4 *Interaction Component of the SIOP® Model: Mr. Charles's Lesson*

4	3	2	1	0	NA
16. Frequent opportunities for **interaction** and discussion between teacher/student and among students, which encourage elaborated responses about lesson concepts	**Interaction** mostly teacher-dominated with some opportunities for students to talk about or question lesson concepts	**Interaction** teacher-dominated with no opportunities for students to discuss lesson concepts			

4	3	2	1	0	NA
17. **Grouping configurations** support language and content objectives of the lesson	**Grouping configurations** unevenly support the language and content objectives	**Grouping configurations** do not support the language and content objectives			

4	3	2	1	0	NA
18. Sufficient **wait time for student responses** consistently provided	Sufficient **wait time for student responses** occasionally provided	Sufficient **wait time for student responses** not provided			

4	3	2	1	0	NA
19. Ample opportunities for students to **clarify key concepts in L1** as needed with aide, peer, or L1 text	Some opportunities for students to **clarify key concepts in L1**	No opportunities for students to **clarify key concepts in L1**			

Mrs. Lantero

Mrs. Lantero introduced the lesson on addition by giving an example of how she used addition to count and add the playground equipment that they had in their classroom. On an overhead projector transparency, she drew a picture of five balls, three jump ropes, and three hula hoops. She called on students to come up to the overhead to solve the problem and demonstrate how they counted all the objects that she drew. She made an effort to call on a wide variety of students to respond and explain their answers. She asked students to explain how they answered the question "How many in all?" Several students raised their hands to volunteer. She then asked the students to give some examples of how they use addition in their everyday lives. She instructed individual students to come up to the overhead to write an addition problem using pictures to represent the numbers (e.g., four flowers + two trees). Mrs. Lantero then told the students that they were going to practice using addition to solve problems. She wrote an addition problem on the overhead ($3 + 4 = 7$). She asked the class if they could solve the problem and explain their work, then called on a volunteer to do so.

Mrs. Lantero gave a description of "counting on," a strategy that teaches what the next number is regardless of where the child starts counting. The children had previously learned this strategy. She asked the children, "How do you count on in the addition problem ($9 + 1 = $)?" She instructed the children to talk to the person next to them and gave adequate time for the discussion. Mrs. Lantero wrote some additional problems on the overhead and showed the students how to solve the various problems. Mrs. Lantero then gave the class a brief review of some of the strategies that they had used previously to solve addition problems, such as counting on and using doubles. Mrs. Lantero spent the next five minutes solving various addition problems on the overhead and calling on individual students who raised their hands to give the answer. At times she encouraged the students to elaborate on their responses and to explain how they solved the problem. After Mrs. Lantero was sure that the students had a clear understanding of addition, she had the children get into groups of three to complete the workpage from their textbook, helping one another as needed. At the end of the lesson the teacher reviewed the concepts of addends and sums and asked students to explain their answers.

On the SIOP® form in Figure 6.5, rate Mrs. Lantero's lesson on each of the Interaction features.

Mrs. Manvi

Mrs. Manvi introduced the lesson on addition by having the students open their math book to a specific page on addition. She reviewed with the class what they had learned in the previous day's lesson and picked a student in the class to tell what they had learned. She asked the students if they had any questions, and when none of the children raised their hand, she continued her lesson. Mrs. Manvi had the children count in unison from one to thirty. Then she

---

FIGURE 6.5 *Interaction Component of the SIOP® Model: Mrs. Lantero's Lesson*

4	3	2	1	0	NA
16. Frequent opportunities for **interaction** and discussion between teacher/student and among students, which encourage elaborated responses about lesson concepts		**Interaction** mostly teacher-dominated with some opportunities for students to talk about or question lesson concepts		**Interaction** teacher-dominated with no opportunities for students to discuss lesson concepts	

4	3	2	1	0	NA
17. **Grouping configurations** support language and content objectives of the lesson		**Grouping configurations** unevenly support the language and content objectives		**Grouping configurations** do not support the language and content objectives	

4	3	2	1	0	NA
18. Sufficient **wait time for student responses** consistently provided		Sufficient **wait time for student responses** occasionally provided		Sufficient **wait time for student responses** not provided	

4	3	2	1	0	NA
19. Ample opportunities for students to **clarify key concepts in L1** as needed with aide, peer, or L1 text		Some opportunities for students to **clarify key concepts in L1**		No opportunities for students to **clarify key concepts in L1**	

asked the students to come up with some examples using addition facts to add numbers and she called on two volunteers to provide examples. Next, Mrs. Manvi demonstrated some addition problems on the overhead. To engage the students in prior learning, she asked the students to provide descriptions of the word "addition." She reviewed the strategies of counting on and drawing pictures to help determine the correct answers to the problems. Mrs. Manvi tried to encourage the children to raise their hands if they did not understand how to do the addition problems. She continued the lesson, providing many examples to the children.

Mrs. Manvi had the students take out their workbooks and told them to do two pages of addition. She walked around the room to make sure that the students were on task and to see if anyone needed extra support. Mrs. Manvi realized that the students were having difficulty, so she drew some examples on the board using pictures and asked the children if they had any questions. She again encouraged the children to raise their hands if they were having problems. Mrs. Manvi then worked through the problems one at a time on the overhead and had the children check their work. She noticed that one student in particular was coming up with incorrect responses, so she focused her attention on that child and tried to help the child solve the problem correctly.

When she was confident that the students understood addition, Mrs. Manvi assigned homework that night so they could practice some more addition problems.

On the SIOP® form in Figure 6.6, rate Mrs. Manvi's lesson on each of the Interaction features.

FIGURE 6.6 *Interaction Component of the SIOP® Model: Mrs. Manvi's Lesson*

4	3	2	1	0	NA
16. Frequent opportunities for **interaction** and discussion between teacher/student and among students, which encourage elaborated responses about lesson concepts		**Interaction** mostly teacher-dominated with some opportunities for students to talk about or question lesson concepts		**Interaction** teacher-dominated with no opportunities for students to discuss lesson concepts	

4	3	2	1	0	NA
17. **Grouping configurations** support language and content objectives of the lesson		**Grouping configurations** unevenly support the language and content objectives		**Grouping configurations** do not support the language and content objectives	

4	3	2	1	0	NA
18. Sufficient **wait time for student responses** consistently provided		Sufficient **wait time for student responses** occasionally provided		Sufficient **wait time for student responses** never provided	

4	3	2	1	0	NA
19. Ample opportunities for students to **clarify key concepts in L1** as needed with aide, peer, or L1 text		Some opportunity for students to **clarify key concepts in L1**		No opportunity for students to **clarify key concepts in L1**	

Discussion of Lessons

16. *Frequent Opportunities for Interaction and Discussion Between Teacher/Student and Among Students*

    Mr. Charles: 4

    Mrs. Lantero: 2

    Mrs. Manvi: 0

Although interaction among students is important for learning new concepts and practicing English, the teachers varied in the opportunities they provided to their students. Mr. Charles planned a lesson that had frequent opportunities for interaction, so he received a "4" on the SIOP®. He used a variety of techniques that ensured participation from the whole class, such as calling on children by selecting their names on written sticks (tongue depressors); asking students to work with partners to solve problems; involving students in a discussion; and having students work in pairs for practice with addition sentences represented by clothespins, writing the sentence, and coming up with the sum.

Mrs. Lantero's lesson was heavily teacher controlled, although she did attempt to involve the children in discussion and did call on volunteers to come to the overhead. (Often it is the students who least need the practice using English that are called upon to participate in the lesson.) She also had students work in groups of three, although completing a workpage from the textbook isn't an optimal activity for interaction because it is basically an individual paper-and-pencil activity.

Mrs. Manvi used a traditional whole-group format for teaching her first graders. This format severely restricted opportunities for students to discuss the concepts and ask for clarification as needed. It is very difficult to determine the needs of students and gauge their understanding when teaching the way Mrs. Manvi did.

17. *Grouping Configurations Support Language and Content Objectives of the Lesson*

    Mr. Charles: 4

    Mrs. Lantero: 2

    Mrs. Manvi: 0

Rather than having students in structured groups interact to solve problems, Mrs. Lantero and Mrs. Manvi solved problems on the overhead in front of the whole class. Whole group instruction has a role to play, but it should not be used extensively because it limits opportunities for students to ask questions, discuss ideas, and clarify information. English learners and students who struggle academically may find whole-group instruction intimidating, as undoubtedly was the case with Mrs. Manvi's lesson. Although she asked several times if students had questions, nobody was willing to speak up in the whole-group setting.

Mr. Charles, on the other hand, was aware of the importance of having students interact with the material (creating problems and solving them) and one another (practicing English). He had students work in pairs and small groups throughout the lesson, which provided optimal opportunity for interaction.

18. *Sufficient Wait Time for Student Responses Consistently Provided*

> Mr. Charles: 4

> Mrs. Lantero: 4

> Mrs. Manvi: 0

Both Mr. Charles and Mrs. Lantero interacted with students so that they had time to formulate their thoughts and express them in English. These teachers recognized English learners' need to have a little extra time when participating in class. Mrs. Manvi, on the other hand, had students count in unison, so the pace was set by the more proficient speakers, leaving the others with no time to think about the next number. Also, when she did call on students, she was looking for specific answers to be given quickly to the whole class. Therefore, she received a "0" on the SIOP® for Wait Time.

19. *Ample Opportunities for Students to Clarify Key Concepts in L1*

> Mr. Charles: N/A

> Mrs. Lantero: 3

> Mrs. Manvi: 0

The students in Mr. Charles's class had enough contextual clues throughout the lesson— coupled with intermediate English proficiency—so they did not need to use their primary language (L1). Therefore, Mr. Charles received an N/A on the SIOP®. Mrs. Lantero permitted the students to complete the worksheet together, which provided the opportunity for discussing and clarifying concepts in the students' native language if necessary. However, because opportunities for interaction were limited, there may have been a need for students to use L1 more extensively, which is why Mrs. Lantero received a "3" on the SIOP®. Mrs. Manvi did not provide opportunities for students to interact with one another so their L1 could not be used even if it would have helped scaffold their understanding.

Summary

SIOP® teachers create ample opportunities for English learners to practice using academic English, both among themselves and with teachers. Incorporating a number of grouping configurations into lessons often facilitates using English in ways that support the lessons' objectives.

The evidence is clear that for most teachers, it is challenging to balance the interchange between themselves and their students. Effective SIOP® teachers plan for and incorporate structured opportunities for students to use English in a variety of ways.

Discussion Questions

1. Think of a content concept that you might be teaching. Describe three different grouping configurations that could be used for teaching and learning this concept. How would you organize the members of each group? How would you monitor student learning? What would you want students to do while working in their groups? How would the grouping configurations facilitate learning for ELs?

2. Either videotape your own classroom while you're teaching a lesson or observe another teacher's classroom for a 15-minute segment. Estimate the proportion of teacher talk and student talk. Given the ratio of teacher–student talk, what are some possible ramifications for English learners in the class?

3. English learners are often reticent to contribute to class discussions. An important role for a SIOP® teacher is to encourage ELs to participate in nonthreatening ways. What are some specific techniques you can use to encourage students to elaborate on their responses and express their thoughts fully? What can you do to ensure sufficient wait time for students to formulate and express their thoughts?

4. Using the SIOP® lesson you have been developing, add activities and grouping configurations to enhance interaction.

chapter 7

Practice & Application

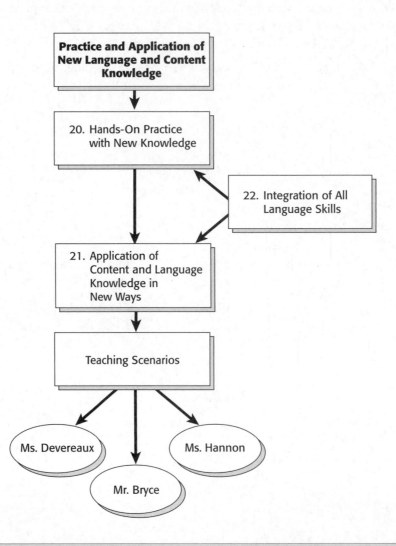

Objectives

After reading, discussing, and engaging in activities related to this chapter, you will be able to meet the following content and language objectives.

Content Objectives

Identify a variety of ways for students to enhance their learning through hands-on practice.

Create application activities that extend the learning in new ways and relate to language or content objectives.

Language Objectives

Design activities that integrate different language skills as students practice new content knowledge.

Discuss the importance of linking practice and application activities to specific lesson objectives.

One common memory that most adults share is of learning to ride an adult bike. Even after riding smaller bicycles with training wheels, most of us were unprepared for the balancing act required for us not to fall down when riding a regular bike. If you had an older brother or sister who talked you through the process, showed you how to balance, and perhaps even held on to the bike while you were steadying yourself, your independent practice time with the big bike was probably enhanced. Talking about the experience, listening to someone else describe it, observing other riders, and then practicing for yourself all worked together to turn you into a bicycle rider. That feeling of accomplishment, of mastering something new through practice and applying it to a bigger bike, or perhaps a motorcycle in later years, is a special feeling that most of us have experienced as learners.

Background

Up to this point in a SIOP® lesson, a teacher has introduced content and language objectives, built background or activated prior knowledge, introduced key vocabulary, selected a learning strategy and higher-order questions for students to focus on, developed a scaffolding approach for teaching the new information, and planned for student interaction. In the Practice & Application component, the teacher gives the students a chance to practice with the new material, and, with careful teacher oversight, demonstrate how well they are learning it. In the same lesson or a subsequent one, the teacher plans a task so students apply this new knowledge in new ways. It is well established that practice and application helps one master a skill (Fisher & Frey, 2008; Jensen, 2005; Marzano, Pickering, & Pollock, 2001).

For SIOP® instruction, however, both the practice and application tasks should also aim for practice of all four language skills: reading, writing, listening, and speaking.

For English learners, this stage of a SIOP® lesson is very important, especially for academic language development. As Saville-Troike (1984) pointed out, both language and academic learning occur through language use in the classroom. Second language acquisition research has shown repeatedly that for an individual to develop a high level of proficiency in a new language, he or she must have opportunities not only for comprehensible input (Krashen, 1985) but also targeted output (Swain, 1985), namely, oral and written practice. In the chapter on oral language development in the recent research synthesis conducted by CREDE researchers (discussed in Chapter 1), Saunders and O'Brien (2006) conclude "ELLs are most likely to use the language used to deliver instruction in their interactions with peers and teachers" (p. 41). They further explain that

> . . . while use and exposure are necessary conditions, they may not be sufficient conditions, especially when it comes to achieving higher levels of proficiency involving more academic uses of language. The content and quality of L2 exposure and use are probably of equal, if not greater, importance than L2 exposure and use per se (p. 41).

What this says to us as SIOP® teachers is that we need to carefully choose the activities we include in our lessons. The activities must support the students' progress in meeting or mastering the content and language objectives. If a language objective calls for third-grade students to argue a point of view, for example, then an activity might have the students write a letter to the editor of a school or local newspaper on the content topic of a lesson (or a related one for application), such as nutrition in school lunches for a health unit. If the class includes students with multiple proficiency levels, the Practice & Application component of the SIOP® Model is the ideal place to differentiate instruction. In the lesson we are developing here, the teacher might facilitate a whole-class brainstorming of pros and cons for the argument. Then some advanced-level students might write individual letters, intermediate-level students might write in pairs or triads, and beginners might work with the teacher to prepare a group letter.

Indeed, it is within this component that teachers can incorporate activities that explore multiple intelligences (Gardner, 1993), project-based learning, or other methods for meeting the different language needs of students (Vogt & Echevarria, 2008). As teachers plan these practice and application activities, they should consider the structure of the task and degree of difficulty for the resulting product, the grouping configurations, the type of feedback that will be provided so it is geared to proficiency level, and the expectations for student achievement (Vogt, 2000). As Tomlinson (2005) explains, instruction may be differentiated in terms of the content material, the learning process (e.g., aural versus kinesthetic), or the task and product. In *Implementing the SIOP Model Through Effective Professional Development and Coaching* (Echevarria, Short, & Vogt, 2008, pp. 152–161), we provide guidance on implementing differentiated instruction in SIOP® classrooms.

In this chapter, we discuss how sheltered teachers provide English learners (ELs) with the types of hands-on experiences, guidance, and practice that can lead to mastery of content knowledge and higher levels of language proficiency. The teaching vignettes demonstrate how three second-grade classroom teachers, all of whom have large numbers of ELs in their classes, designed science lessons on weather precipitation.

To see an example of practical application of SIOP® features, please view the corresponding video clip (Chapter 7, Module 1) on the accompanying CD.

SIOP® FEATURE 20:
Hands-On Materials and/or Manipulatives Provided for Students to Practice Using New Content Knowledge

As previously mentioned, riding a bike is usually preceded by practicing with training wheels and working with a more experienced bike rider. Obviously, the more practice one has on the bike, the more likely one is to become a good bike rider. Now think about learning to play a musical instrument.

Some years ago, an entrepreneur decided to market a piano-teaching course that included a cardboard sheet printed with piano keys. Students were supposed to practice the piano on the paper keyboard by following the directions printed in the course manual. The black-and-white keys on the keyboard were printed, and dotted lines represented where students were supposed to place their fingers during practice sessions. It was little surprise that the paper keyboards didn't catch on, even though the course manual clearly described in incremental steps how to play the piano, because even with hours of practice on the paper keyboard, students were still unable to play the piano well. In this case, it wasn't just the *practice* that was important. Without hearing the sounds during practice, learning to play the piano was an artificial and nearly impossible task.

When learning to ride a bicycle, play the piano, or write a comparative essay, students have a greater chance of mastering content concepts and skills when they are given multiple opportunities to practice in relevant, meaningful ways. Even young English learners in primary grades should have regular practice opportunities during the week to work on structured academic tasks (Gersten, Baker, Shanahan, Linan-Thompson, Collins, & Scarcella, 2007). When this practice includes hands-on experiences like manipulatives, practice sessions are enhanced. Madeline Hunter (1982), a renowned expert in teaching methods, coined the term *guided practice* to describe the process of the teacher leading the student through practice sessions prior to independent application. She suggested that we keep the following four questions (and their answers) in mind as we plan lessons involving hands-on practice for students (pp. 65–68):

1. How much material should be practiced at one time? *Answer:* A short meaningful amount. Always use meaning to divide your content into parts.

2. How long in time should a practice period be? *Answer:* A short time so the student exerts intense effort and has intent to learn.

3. How often should students practice? *Answer:* New learning, massed practice. Older learning, distributed practice. [Hunter explains that massed practice means several practice periods scheduled close together. Distributed practice means spacing practice periods farther and farther apart, such as when we review previously learned material.]

4. How will students know how well they have done? *Answer:* Give specific knowledge of results (i.e., specific feedback).

Although all students benefit from guided practice as they advance to independent work, English learners make more rapid progress in mastering content objectives when they are provided with multiple opportunities to practice with hands-on materials and/or manipulatives. These may be organized, created, counted, classified, stacked, experimented with, observed, rearranged, dismantled, and so forth. We would also include kinesthetic activities in a broad definition of this feature. Manipulating learning materials is important for ELs because it helps them connect abstract concepts with concrete experiences. Furthermore, manipulatives and other hands-on materials reduce the language load for students. Students with beginning proficiency in English, for instance, can still participate and demonstrate what they are learning.

Obviously, the type of manipulative employed for practice depends on the subject being taught. For example, in a tenth-grade geometry class in which students are learning how to solve proofs, content objectives might justify paper-and-pencil practice. However, if it is possible to incorporate hands-on practice with manipulatives, students' learning will likely be enhanced.

For a kinesthetic example, instead of having students fill out a worksheet on a timeline about Ancient China, they could form a physical timeline. Some students might have a card displaying a date; others might have one displaying an event. The students would organize themselves, first pairing the dates and events, and then forming the human timeline in the front of the room.

In *99 Ideas and Activities for Teaching English Learners with the SIOP® Model* (Vogt & Echevarria, 2008), the "Bingo" (p. 130) and the "Piece O' Pizza" (p. 148) activities offer other examples where students create the hands-on materials as part of their practice or application time. Students build a bingo chart with teacher guidance and then play the game. Individual students or small groups create a pizza slice with information that differs from their peers. They put their slices together to address the main points of a key topic.

Being told how to ride a bike or play the piano, reading about how to do so, or watching a DVD of someone else engaged in bike riding or piano playing is much different from riding down the sidewalk or listening to musical sounds you have produced yourself. Whenever possible and appropriate, use hands-on materials for practice. Fortunately, many elementary curricula recommend the use of manipulatives, and a variety of supplementary materials are widely available. Some have been designed for specific content areas, such as manipulatives and foldables for elementary math or science (e.g., Zike, 1994, 2004).

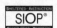

SIOP® FEATURE 21:
Activities Provided for Students to Apply Content and Language Knowledge

Think again about the relationship between actually riding a bicycle and just watching someone else ride it, or about actually playing a piano and just reading step-by-step piano-playing instructions. As Hunter (1982) said:

The difference between knowing how something should be done and being able to do it is the quantum leap in learning . . . new learning is like wet cement, it can be easily damaged. A mistake at the beginning of learning can have long-lasting consequences that are hard to eradicate (p. 71).

We all recall our own learning experiences in elementary, middle, and high school, and the university. For many of us, the classes and courses we remember best are the ones in which we applied our new knowledge in meaningful ways. These may have included activities such as writing a diary entry from the perspective of a character in a novel, creating a semantic map illustrating the relationships among complex concepts, or completing comprehensive case studies on children we assessed and taught. These concrete experiences forced us to apply new information and concepts in a personally relevant way. We remember the times when we "got it," and we remember the times when we gave it our all but somehow still missed the point. Consider this as you do the activity below.

Think about a college or graduate school course. What is one activity you remember well? What made it memorable? Did it involve different learning styles or senses? Now think about a recent lesson you taught or observed. Was there an activity that would be memorable for the students? If not, how could the activity have been more engaging and unforgettable?

For students acquiring a new language, the need to apply new information is critically important because discussing and "doing" make abstract concepts concrete. Application can occur in a number of ways, such as using graphic organizers to synthesize information, solving problems in cooperative learning groups, writing a journal, engaging in literature circles, or a variety of other meaningful activities (Peregoy & Boyle, 2005). Fisher and Frey (2008), in their model for gradual release of responsibility (by the teacher), argue that collaborative learning is an important bridging step between guided practice and independent work. They state that "collaborative learning should be a time for students to apply information in novel situations or to engage in a spiral review of previous knowledge" (p. 7). Mainly we must remember that we learn best by involving ourselves in relevant, meaningful application of what we are learning.

For English learners, application must also include opportunities for them to practice language knowledge in the classroom. Opportunities for oral interaction promote language development, and these include discussion, working with partners and small groups, and "reporting out" information orally and in writing. For example, it is appropriate, depending on students' language proficiency, to ask them to explain a process to a peer using a newly learned sentence structure. Activities such as describing the results of an experiment, specifying why a character reacted in a particular way, and justifying the steps for solving a word problem all help ELs produce and practice new language and vocabulary while they are in a supportive environment.

Consider a fifth-grade math class with mixed-proficiency ELs and native English speakers. To apply new vocabulary from the unit, the teacher might plan a scaffolded listening cloze dictation. The native English speakers might record what the teacher says as a regular dictation. The ELs might have two different dictation forms with more or fewer

FIGURE 7.1 *Scaffolded Listening Cloze Dictation Forms*

More Proficient Students	Less Proficient Students
Fill in the blanks with the missing words while the teacher reads a passage aloud. You will hear the passage twice.	Fill in the blanks with the missing words while the teacher reads a passage aloud. You will hear the passage twice.
In order to _____ two fractions, they must have the same _____. If the _____ are the same, you add the _____ together, but you don't _____ the denominator. For example, $\frac{3}{8}+$ _____ equals _____. Sometimes the answer is not in the simplest ____. In that case, you have to _____ it, or reduce it. You have to find a(n) _____ fraction. When we simplify _____, we get ____.	In order to add two fractions, they must have the same _____. If the denominators are the same, you add the _____ together, but you don't change the denominator. For example, $\frac{3}{8}+\frac{3}{8}$ equals _____. Sometimes the answer is not in the simplest form. In that case, you have to _____ it, or reduce it. You have find an equivalent _____. When we simplify $\frac{6}{8}$, we get _____.

words already written down. (See Figure 7.1.) All the students listen to the paragraph the teacher reads on adding fractions, all participate in the listening task, but the task format is slightly adjusted to the students' English abilities.

SIOP® FEATURE 22:
Activities Integrate All Language Skills

Reading, writing, listening, and speaking are complex, cognitive language processes that are interrelated and integrated. As we go about our daily lives, we move through the processes in a natural way, reading what we write; talking about what we've read; and listening to others talk about what they've read, written, and seen. Most young children become grammatically competent in their home language by age five, and their continuing language development relates primarily to vocabulary, more sophisticated grammar usage (e.g., embedding subordinate clauses), and functional as well as sociocultural applications of language (e.g., using different language registers according to their audience, and developing rhetorical styles) (Peregoy & Boyle, 2005; TESOL, 2006). Proficiency in reading and writing is achieved much later, and differences exist among individuals in levels of competence. Students in particular need to learn academic language for use in school settings (see Chapter 1 for a detailed discussion).

For English learners, students may achieve competence in written language earlier than oral language, and ELs do not need to be proficient speakers before they start to read and write (August & Shanahan, 2006a). In fact, the language processes—reading, writing, listening, and speaking—are mutually supportive. Although the relationships among the processes are complex, practice in any one promotes development in the others (Hinkel, 2006).

Effective sheltered teachers understand the need to create many opportunities for English learners to practice and use all four language processes in an integrated manner. Throughout the day, ELs benefit from varied experiences that incorporate reading, promote interactions with others, provide the chance to listen to peers' ideas, and encourage writing about what is being learned. Because students have different preferred learning styles, when teachers teach through different modalities and encourage students to practice and apply new knowledge through multiple language processes, they have a better chance of meeting students' needs and furthering both their language and content development.

We do want to clarify that, although all identified language objectives in a lesson need to be practiced and applied as the lesson advances, not all language skills that are practiced need to be tied to an objective. In other words, a language objective represents a key skill, language structure, or strategy the teacher plans to teach explicitly and intends for students to learn. In a SIOP® lesson, the teacher teaches to this objective and assesses, formally or informally, how well students are meeting it. The objective may focus on one language domain, such as writing, but in the course of the lesson, students may have additional opportunities to read, speak, and listen. These should be carefully planned but need not be assessed in the same way an objective would be.

Teachers are sometimes unsure whether to correct ELs' language errors during practice time or not (Peregoy & Boyle, 2005). In general, consider students' stages of English language development when deciding. For beginning English speakers, errors may be developmental and reflect students' native language use (e.g., not remembering to add past tense inflected endings to English verbs). Other errors may deal with placement of adjectives, sentence structure, plurals, and so forth. If errors impede communication, you can gently correct them by restating the sentence in correct form. Otherwise, leave the errors alone.

If you notice, however, that many students make the same error and it does not seem to be due to the language acquisition process, it is reasonable to plan a mini-lesson on the issue for a later day. This practice conforms to a recommendation in a research-based, practice guide for elementary ELs that "error correction needs to be focused on the instructional target of the lesson" (Gersten et al., 2007, p. 19), and to second-language acquisition research studies that offer evidence that "corrective feedback is important for learning grammar" (Ellis, 2006, p. 102).

For example, Meeli, who recently emigrated from Estonia, told her teacher, "My parents sends congratulations to you." She meant that her parents sent their greetings. In reply, Meeli's teacher responded, "Thank you. I think you mean 'greetings.' Please tell your parents I send them my greetings, too." Note that the confusion over the nouns, "congratulations" and "greetings" was corrected, but the teacher did not correct the form of the verb *send* because acquisition of these verb endings occurs later in the second language development process. What is most important is that you be sensitive to errors that confuse communication; these usually can be corrected in a natural and nonthreatening way.

The Lesson

The lesson below is intended to teach second graders about the weather. (For more examples of lesson and unit plans in science, see Short, Vogt, & Echevarria, in press.)

UNIT: Weather (Second Grade)

The three second-grade classrooms in these teaching vignettes are located in an urban elementary school in the Northeast. Approximately 40 percent of the 24 students are English learners from multiple language backgrounds, including Spanish, Cape Verdean, and Haitian Creole. They range in proficiency from beginner to advanced. The other students in the class are native English speakers.

The state does not have standards for science in grade 2 because statewide testing does not begin until grade 3. However, the district has a curriculum framework that the teachers follow. The state does have English language proficiency standards for grades Pre-K–12.

The second-grade teachers in these scenarios have been teaching a unit on the weather. They have had two days of instruction prior to the lessons described here. The students have been introduced to types of weather, the seasons, and the concept of temperature.

Teaching Scenarios

Ms. Devereaux

Ms. Devereaux entered class wearing a raincoat holding an open umbrella above her head. "What is the weather outside?" she asked. "Raining," shouted several second graders. She then took a piece of ice out of a container. "What weather does this remind you of?" "Winter" said one student. "Winter is a season," Ms. Devereaux replied. "I want to know the weather. Think about the forms of water we studied yesterday." One young girl said, "Ice." "Yes, it is ice," replied the teacher, "Can you also think of another kind of precipitation? (She paused for several seconds.) I'll give you a hint. It rhymes with tail." Sensing the students were still unsure, she told them to open their notebooks and find the weather words. One student finally said "hail" and Ms. Devereaux acknowledged he was right.

Ms. Devereaux pointed to the objectives on the board and told the students to copy them while she got supplies ready. The objectives were:

Content objective: We will identify types of weather.

Language objective: We will describe weather using adjectives.

Ms. Devereaux then showed the students the props they would use that day: a microphone, a map of their state, and a pointer. She asked the class to raise their hands if they have ever watched the news on television. Then she asked them to keep their hands up if they watched the weather broadcast. She called on one child with his hand still up to tell about a broadcast he saw. "The lady talked about the clouds and the rain." Ms. Devereaux replied, "Yes, she probably told you the temperature for the day and how cloudy it was and when the rain would come. Also she probably gave a prediction about the amount of rain and whether it would be windy or not. I bet she pointed to the weather map and showed you how a storm was moving across our state. Well, that's what I want you to do today in your groups."

She told them they could work with whomever they wanted in groups of three or four. They should prepare a two-minute broadcast about the weather, and they could decide what type of weather, they would report on. She told them that when they performed their broadcast, they could use the props and she would record them with her digital camera.

Ms. Devereaux circulated among the groups and noticed that the English learners were mostly all together in three groups. All three groups planned to do a broadcast about rain. She tried to encourage them to do another form of weather, "What about snow? Or fog?" The students said they didn't know what to say about those. "I not see snow," said a student from Cape Verde who had only been in the United States for one month.

After 10 minutes of planning, the groups began to present their broadcasts. Ms. Devereaux noticed that the groups with the ELs had very little to say. One young EL broadcaster's statements were representative of all the EL groups. "It is raining tomorrow. You get wet. Bring umbrella to school." She was disappointed that they weren't more descriptive about the upcoming weather and didn't seem excited about the activity, even though she was filming them.

On the SIOP® form in Figure 7.2, rate Ms. Devereaux 's lesson on each of the Practice & Application components.

FIGURE 7.2 *Practice & Application Component of the SIOP® Model: Ms. Devereaux's Lesson*

4	3	2	1	0	NA
20. **Hands-on materials and/or manipulatives** provided for students to practice using new content knowledge		**Few hands-on materials and/or manipulatives** provided for students to practice using new content knowledge		**No hands-on materials and/or manipulatives** provided for students to practice using new content knowledge	

4	3	2	1	0	NA
21. Activities provided for students to **apply content and language knowledge** in the classroom		Activities provided for students to **apply either content or language knowledge** in the classroom		No activities provided for students to **apply content and language knowledge** in the classroom	

4	3	2	1	0
22. Activities integrate all **language skills** (i.e, reading, writing, listening, and speaking)		Activities integrate some **language skills**		Activities do not integrate **language skills**

Mr. Bryce

Mr. Bryce reminded the second graders of the lesson they started the day before. He showed some pictures of different types of weather and had students identify the types of precipitation. He continued by reading the objectives aloud from the board:

> Content objective: We will distinguish among different forms of precipitation.

> Language objective: We will write sentences about the weather using details.

He said, "Let's think, what do our objectives mean? Who can explain them? Look at the verbs in our objectives. What does *distinguish* mean? Tell a partner." The students spoke softly in pairs and then several raised their hands.

"It means to tell them apart," said one young girl.

"Can anyone add on?" asked Mr. Bryce.

"To tell how rain and snow differ," responded a boy.

"Right" replied Mr. Bryce. "And what does our language objective tell us?"

"We are going to write today," said another boy.

Mr. Bryce extended this, "Yes. We will write sentences with the word *because*. Our sentences will give us more information, more details."

Mr. Bryce began the first activity. He asked two students—one an English learner, the other a native English speaker—to find the word cards about precipitation on the word wall that they had been studying. The children selected *rain, hail, snow, ice, mist,* and *fog* and brought the cards to him. He posted them across the board and checked that the students remembered the words by having six volunteers come up and quick-draw a picture of the water form next to the word.

Next he explained the task. The students were to choose one of these words and write a sentence using the word on an index card, which he provided. He displayed two sentence starters they could use: "I like _____ because ____." and reminded the students that they were going to write sentences with details, with more information.

He showed a transparency and revealed the first part of the sentence.

I like wind

He said, "This tells you one thing, but I want to know more. Why do I like wind?" He revealed the next word.

I like wind because _____.

He asked the students to turn to a partner and suggest a reason. After one minute he asked students to share some ideas. He acknowledged their ideas and then revealed the rest of the sentence.

I like wind because the leaves dance.

Mr. Bryce explained that using *because* gives more details. It can tell why something happened or why someone did something.

After the students had a few minutes to write their sentences, he asked them to stand and form two rows (A and B), facing each other, to perform a Conga Line. At his signal, the students took turns reading their cards to their partner in the opposite row. At the next signal, the students in Row A took one step to their left and faced a new partner in Row B to read with. Mr. Bryce repeated this process two more times and then had the students return to their seats. Because the students were familiar with the activity, the process took only eight minutes. He asked students to share one idea they heard. He also asked if any of the students changed their sentences after reading it to a partner. Two students explained how they improved their work based on feedback from a classmate. He gave the class two minutes to edit their sentence if they wanted.

Mr. Bryce introduced the next activity. In heterogeneous groups of four, the children would design a Wacky Weather! poster. They would choose a form of precipitation to depict in a wacky way. Then they would write a caption for the picture, using a sentence with *because*. He showed a sample poster of people wearing bathing suits and standing in the snow. The caption read: "The people are surprised because it is snowing at the beach." He asked the students to generate some wacky weather ideas related to the six precipitation words that he listed on the board. He then assigned a type of precipitation to each of the six groups, giving the potentially more difficult types (mist, fog) to groups with more proficient students. He told them that they could choose one of those ideas or think of a new one in their groups. He informed the materials managers of each group that once they had finished a draft poster on scrap paper, they could come to him for chart paper and markers to create the final poster. He stated that he expected they would complete the posters the next day.

On the SIOP® form in Figure 7.3, rate Mr. Bryce's lesson on each of the Practice & Application components.

FIGURE 7.3 *Practice & Application Component of the SIOP® Model: Mr. Bryce's Lesson*

4	3	2	1	0	NA
20. **Hands-on materials and/or manipulatives** provided for students to practice using new content knowledge		**Few hands-on materials and/or manipulatives** provided for students to practice using new content knowledge		**No hands-on materials and/or manipulatives** provided for students to practice using new content knowledge	

4	3	2	1	0	NA
21. Activities provided for students to **apply content and language knowledge** in the classroom		Activities provided for students to **apply either content or language knowledge** in the classroom		No activities provided for students to **apply content and language knowledge** in the classroom	

4	3	2	1	0
22. Activities integrate all **language skills** (i.e, reading, writing, listening, and speaking)		Activities integrate some **language skills**		Activities do not integrate **language skills**

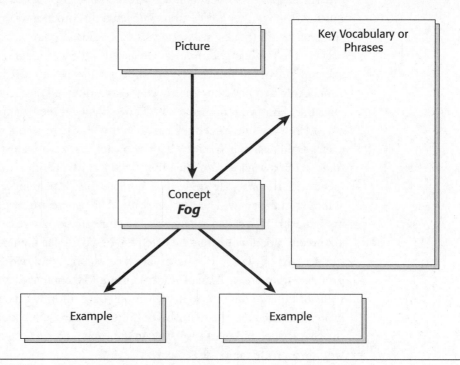

FIGURE 7.4 *Precipitation Concept Map*

Ms. Hannon

Ms. Hannon greeted her second graders when they returned from lunch and reviewed the day's objectives on weather precipitation terms by asking the students questions about types of weather and weather words. The students copied the objectives in their notebooks:

> Content objective: We will identify types of precipitation: *rain, hail, snow, ice, mist,* and *fog*.
>
> Language objective: We will write words and phrases that describe weather.

Ms. Hannon divided the class into six groups, each with at least one native English speaker and one English learner. She pointed out the six concept maps posted on chart paper around the room and explained the task. Each group would receive a concept map (see Figure 7.4). They would have five minutes to complete it and then they would place their maps back up on the walls. Next they would move around the room in a Carousel fashion, with each group having two or three minutes at each map to add ideas before moving on to the next map at her signal. "Do you remember how we did the Carousel when we studied animals?" she asked and most of the students responded "Yes."

Ms. Hannon distributed the concept maps to the student groups and they began work. As she circulated, she noticed that students had many things to write down for some maps, like those for snow and rain, but less for others. She hoped that the Carousel activity would generate more ideas. After the allotted time, she had the groups post their maps and begin the Carousel. She reminded them that when a group reached a map, the students were to discuss their ideas, and then the recorder would add to the concept map.

After about 15 minutes, the groups returned to their original map, and she asked the reporter from each group to read what was written. This process started well, but after the first two maps, the students began to fidget. To maintain order, she ended this reading aloud after the third group finished and had everyone sit down.

She told the students that for the next activity they would write about their favorite type of weather. She told them to think of the six types of precipitation they studied and choose one. In a paragraph they were to write what they liked about that type and why. They could use the words and ideas on the concept maps. The students worked on this task for about 10 minutes, although some of the English learners struggled to write even one initial sentence. She talked to several of these students individually to get them started. When the time for science ended, she told the class to complete the paragraph for homework.

On the SIOP® form in Figure 7.5, rate Ms Hannon's lesson on each of the Practice & Application components.

FIGURE 7.5 *Practice & Application Component of the SIOP® Model: Ms. Hannon's Lesson*

4	3	2	1	0	NA
20. **Hands-on materials and/or manipulatives** provided for students to practice using new content knowledge		**Few hands-on materials and/or manipulatives** provided for students to practice using new content knowledge		**No hands-on materials and/or manipulatives** provided for students to practice using new content knowledge	

4	3	2	1	0	NA
21. Activities provided for students to **apply content and language knowledge** in the classroom		Activities provided for students to **apply either content or language knowledge** in the classroom		No activities provided for students to **apply content and language knowledge** in the classroom	

4	3	2	1	0
22. Activities integrate all **language skills** (i.e, reading, writing, listening, and speaking)		Activities integrate some **language skills**		Activities do not integrate **language skills**

Discussion of Lessons

Ms. Devereaux, Mr. Bryce, and Ms. Hannon taught lessons with similar objectives in their weather unit, but they used different activities with varying results. As you read our ratings, compare them to your own and those of colleagues.

20. *Hands-on Materials and/or Manipulatives Provided for Students to Practice Using New Content Knowledge*

    Ms. Devereaux: 0

    Mr. Bryce: 4

    Ms. Hannon: 3

Ms. Devereaux's lesson was primarily an application activity, but it was evident by the outcome that her students, in particular the English learners, needed some practice time first. This lesson received a score of 0 for practice using new content knowledge. The class didn't review the weather terms other than *rain* and *hail* with Ms. Devereaux's real objects. The fact that the students didn't recall *hail* without considerable prompting should have indicated to her that they were not ready to jump into a broadcasting activity. Further, there were no occasions for students to practice descriptive words that they might associate with different types of weather.

Mr. Bryce's lesson received a 4 for hands-on practice with new content knowledge. Knowing that his second graders don't like to sit at their desks for long periods of time, he used the Conga Line technique. First, he had students practice writing sentences using a *because* clause (which had been modeled) and a precipitation term. The students thought of a term they preferred and wrote the sentence independently. Then they took turns reading their sentences to partners as they moved in the Conga Line.

Ms. Hannon's lesson received a score of 3 for hands-on practice. Her concept map activity offered the students a chance to review and organize information they had about types of precipitation. It was hands-on and kinesthetic, which is beneficial with young children, especially after lunchtime. The students focused on one type initially and then had a chance to review other groups' work and add to their maps. The activity had to be cut short during the reporting stage however because the students lost concentration when the activity lasted too long.

21. *Activities Provided for Students to Apply Content and Language Knowledge*

    Ms. Devereaux: 1

    Mr. Bryce: 4

    Ms. Hannon: 2

Ms. Devereaux's lesson received a 1 for application of language and content knowledge. Although she had an interesting plan to have the students act as weather broadcasters, she did not prepare the students well for the role. She asked a few students to talk about a weather report they'd seen on the television news, but she provided most of the details. Also she did not make sure all the students were familiar with that type of broadcast. If she had shown a brief video clip, she would have modeled the activity for the students and thus given them a greater chance at being successful. Doing so might have helped her meet the language and content objectives. As it was, no attention was given to the language objective. No practice time was devoted to reviewing adjectives that could be used with weather terms.

Mr. Bryce's lesson received a 4 for this application feature. After the Conga Line practice with the new sentence structure and the precipitation terms, he had students apply their language and content knowledge to a poster. The second graders enjoyed doing something amusing, in this case, designing a Wacky Weather! poster. It gave them a chance to consider characteristics of weather that are unexpected and also prompted them to write another sentence using a *because* clause. This activity also used hands-on materials and had students working in small groups so those with stronger academic language skills could support those with weaker ones.

Ms. Hannon's lesson received a 2 for activities that apply language and content knowledge. She asked students to write a paragraph about their favorite type of precipitation, which would have been a good application task if it had been executed well. Unfortunately, Ms. Hannon did not scaffold the writing process. She provided no model paragraphs, nor did the students, as a class or in a group, brainstorm ideas or list information that could be included. Her instructions were delivered only orally and the language objective was implicit, not explicit. The concept maps had information the students could draw from but because they remained on the walls, the students did not make much use of them. When the English learners were unable to do the task well, she did not reconsider and, for example, pull them aside to work in a small writing group with her. This situation was an obvious opportunity for her to differentiate instruction for the ELs. Instead she talked to them one by one. Finally, she moved the completion of the task to a homework assignment, which was unlikely to yield success for the ELs if they were not sure how to complete the task in class.

22. *Activities Integrate All Language Skills*
Ms. Devereaux: 2
Mr. Bryce: 3
Ms. Hannon: 3

Ms. Devereaux's lesson received a 2 for integrating all four language skills. The students focused only on listening and speaking as they prepared and then delivered their weather reports. No reading was required; even if some students wrote a transcript of what they intended to say, it was not part of the instructions to the children.

Mr. Bryce's lesson received a 3 for integrating all four language skills in the lesson. The second graders had multiple opportunities to listen and speak (during the Conga Line, while at work in their groups, when the class was generating ideas for the poster) and to write (the *because* sentence and the poster caption). There was less reading in this particular lesson, although they did read the precipitation word cards, the ideas listed on the board, and their sentences aloud. In the next lesson, they will do a Gallery Walk activity whereby each group posts its poster and the students circulate on their own to view them and read the captions. Students will put a dot sticker on two posters they think are the wackiest.

Ms. Hannon's Concept Map/Carousel activity prompted students to practice all four language skills because they had to discuss ideas for the map and record those ideas, read what others had written on their maps and extend the ideas, and then listen while some students spoke during the reporting phase. The paragraph writing task was also intended to apply writing skills to the science topic. The lesson received a 3 on this feature of the SIOP® component, however, because the reporting phase of the Carousel and the paragraph writing were not well accomplished.

Summary

With any type of new learning, practice and application of newly acquired skills are needed to ensure mastery of content concepts. Hands-on activities and materials, including manipulatives, enable students to forge connections between abstract and concrete concepts. Students make these connections most effectively when they use all language processes, including reading, writing, listening, and speaking, during practice and application.

Thematic and cross-disciplinary curricula are found more often in elementary school settings than in secondary ones, and this can be advantageous for young English learners. Being able to study, practice, and apply related information over time and/or across subjects helps expand the opportunities for academic language development and gives the children more time to reach a level of independence.

Discussion Questions

1. Compare and contrast the following two teachers' approaches to teaching a lesson on nutrition.
   a. One teacher's approach involves a lecture about the nutritious content of different foods while showing a food pyramid diagram. The teacher then gives the youngsters a list of appropriate food for each food group in the pyramid. Students are then tested about their knowledge of the food pyramid.
   b. The other teacher's approach begins with students' maintaining a food diary for a week. Copies of the food pyramid are distributed and explained, and all students must analyze their food consumption according to the recommendations on the pyramid. With a partner, students must design a nutritionally sound weekly menu for each day of the following week, and they must be prepared to defend their food choices to peer group members.

   Which of the approaches to teaching this content concept is most appropriate for English learners? How do you know? Be as specific as you can.

2. One way to ensure practice and application of new knowledge is through project-based learning. Develop a unit project that students in one of your courses can build incrementally as the series of lessons progress over several days or weeks. Identify the steps to completion that students will accomplish in each lesson of

the unit. Determine which language objectives can be taught, practiced, and applied in the project. Plan a culminating presentation or performance to enhance oral language practice.

3. English learners benefit from the integration of reading, writing, listening, and speaking. For those with limited English language proficiency, tell what may be difficult. Is it performance of all four skills or just some? What adjustments and techniques can a teacher use to provide ELs with successful experiences while they read, write, listen, and speak about new information they are learning? Include specific activities and examples in your answer.

4. With a large number of content standards in each subject area for which teachers and students are accountable, how is it possible to provide direct application and hands-on practice for lessons? What can teachers do to alleviate the conflict between "covering the content" and making it "accessible" for English learners?

5. Using the SIOP® lesson you have been developing, write some activities for students to practice and then apply the key language and content concepts.

Lesson Delivery

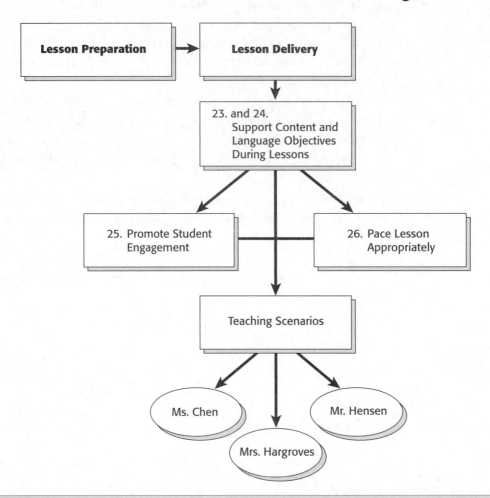

Objectives

After reading, discussing, and engaging in activities related to this chapter, you will be able to meet the following content and language objectives.

Content Objectives

Monitor lessons to determine if the delivery is supporting the objectives.

List strategies for improving student time on task throughout a lesson.

Explain how a focus on a lesson's objectives can aid in pacing.

Generate activities to keep English learners engaged.

Language Objectives

Evaluate a situation where a well-designed lesson plan is not enacted successfully and explain what might have gone wrong and what could be improved.

Compare pacing considerations in classes that have only native English speakers with classes that have English learners.

Discuss characteristics of effective SIOP® lesson delivery.

Background

To see an example of using the SIOP® Model for lesson delivery, please view the corresponding video clip (Chapter 8, Module 1) on the accompanying CD.

As we mentioned, good preparation is the first step in delivering a lesson that leads to student learning. However, a lesson can go awry, even if it is well written. Activities might be too easy or too difficult for the students. The lesson might be too long or too short. A student might ask an interesting but tangential question, and the ensuing class discussion consumes ten unexpected minutes. The Lesson Delivery component of the SIOP® Model is included to remind teachers to stay on track, and in this chapter we provide some guidance for doing so.

This chapter addresses the way a lesson is delivered, how well the content and language objectives are supported during the lesson, to what extent students are engaged in the lesson, and how appropriate the pace of the lesson is to students' ability levels. You will see that this chapter parallels Chapter 2, Lesson Preparation, because the two components are closely related. The effectiveness of a lesson's delivery—the level of student participation, how clearly information is communicated, students' level of understanding reflected in the quality of their work—often can be traced back to the preparation that took place before students entered the classroom. We will meet the teachers from Chapter 2 again and discuss how their level of preparation was executed in their lesson delivery.

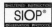

SIOP® FEATURE 23:
Content Objectives Clearly Supported by Lesson Delivery

As we discussed in Chapter 2, content objectives must be stated orally and must be displayed for students and teachers alike to see. From the content perspective, this is no longer an unusual proposition. Since the No Child Left Behind Act has raised the level of school accountability, teachers and principals are more comfortable with posting objectives tied to state standards. We caution against any inclination to list the standard in an abbreviated form, like CA History 5.2.3, as an objective because it would be meaningless to the students and is unlikely to be at the level of a lesson goal. For young learners it may appear as gibberish. Rather, written, student-friendly objectives serve to remind us of the focus of the lesson, providing a structure to classroom procedures. Written objectives also allow students to know the direction of the lesson and help them stay on task. It is helpful for teachers to make explicit connections to the objectives during the lesson at the times that children do related tasks. Throughout the lesson and at its conclusion, the teacher and students can evaluate the extent to which the lesson delivery supported the content objectives.

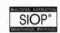

SIOP® FEATURE 24:
Language Objectives Clearly Supported by Lesson Delivery

As you now know, language objectives are an important part of effective sheltered lessons. Teachers and students benefit from having a clear language objective written for them to see and reviewed with them during the lesson. The objective may be related to an English language proficiency standard such as "Students will compare/contrast attributes of three-dimensional shapes from labeled models or charts (e.g., A _____ is like a _____ because _____.)." (WIDA Consortium, 2007, p. 35); or it may be related to teachers' scope and sequence of language skills that their own students need to develop, such as "Students will make connections between text and self, and text and world." No matter which language objective is written for a lesson, as we stated in Chapter 2, a teacher needs to address it explicitly during instruction. For example, if first-graders in a language arts lesson have to "retell a story" as their language objective with *The Hungry Caterpillar* by Eric Carle, then we expect the teacher will spend some time teaching or reviewing *how* to retell with students, perhaps using a different, familiar story, and also reviewing the number words and names of the objects that the caterpillar ate.

Meeting Content and Language Objectives

A SIOP® lesson is effective when it meets its objectives. Although we have experienced some teacher reluctance to write both kinds of objectives for each lesson and to post them and review them with students, our research results give evidence of their value. When presenting a SIOP® lesson, the objectives should be noticeable throughout—in terms of the activities students are asked to accomplish and the questions and comprehension checks the teachers perform. The objectives should always be reviewed at the end of the lesson too.

Some teachers have explained that they don't want to write out and discuss the objectives with the students because they can't write them in a manner that students understand or because they fear not completing the full lesson. Both of those arguments are easily overcome with practice and support. A SIOP® coach or a fellow SIOP® teacher can advise a teacher on writing student-friendly objectives. The students themselves will confirm if they understood the objective when it is presented in class. And as a teacher gets to know his or her students, writing for their age and proficiency level becomes easier. If the problem is that the objectives are not being met by the end of the lesson, then the teacher and students can discuss why as they review them. It may be that the activities took longer than planned or class discussions veered off track, but the presence of objectives can actually impose discipline on the pacing of each lesson. If a teacher consistently does not meet objectives, however, it may also be that too many objectives are planned for the time frame of the lesson, or time is lost during activity transitions or at the start or end of the period.

We acknowledge that it takes time to determine good objectives for every lesson, but the investment in writing them and then teaching to them pays off in student achievement.

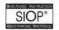

SIOP® FEATURE 25:
Students Engaged Approximately 90% to 100% of the Period

This feature in the Lesson Delivery component calls on teachers to engage students 90 percent to 100 percent of the class period. By this we mean that the students are paying attention and on task. It does not mean they need to be highly active (writing, reading, moving) the entire time, but they are following the lesson, responding to teacher direction, and performing the activities as expected. When students are in groups, all are participating. Lessons where students are engaged less than 50 percent of the time are unacceptable. This situation tends to occur when teachers have not provided clear explanations of the assignment or have not scaffolded the process well.

When children are engaged, they are involved in activities that challenge them and allow them to gain confidence. Offering choices in task, text, or partner; setting up learning centers; and differentiating instruction are key methods for accommodating classrooms with English learners of varying proficiency levels as well as classrooms with both native English speakers and English learners. It is often through such modifications to a curriculum that student engagement can be enhanced (Buck, Carr, & Robertson, 2008; Tomlinson, 2005).

Student engagement is enhanced, for example, when a teacher incorporates a **Think-Pair-Share** technique during a class discussion. Instead of asking questions of the whole class and calling on two or three students to respond, the teacher asks everyone to think of an answer, then tell it to a partner before calling on some students to share responses with the whole class. This relatively simple and quick technique gives *all* of the students a chance to think and speak, instead of two or three. Another activity called

Chunk and Chew (see Vogt & Echevarria, 2008, p. 164) encourages teachers to pause after every ten minutes of input to give students time to discuss or reflect.

English learners are the students who can least afford to have valuable time squandered through boredom, inattention, socializing, and other off-task behaviors. Time also is wasted when teachers are ill prepared, have poor classroom management skills, spend excessive amounts of time making announcements and passing out and handing in papers, and the like. The most effective teachers minimize these behaviors and maximize time spent actively engaged in instruction (Mastropieri & Scruggs, 1994). English learners who are working to achieve grade-level competence benefit from efficient use of class time. Further, many of these learners have had uneven schooling experiences, missing time in school due to circumstances beyond their control, and are then further disadvantaged by inefficient use of class time.

There are actually three aspects to student engagement that should be considered: (1) allocated time, (2) engaged time, and (3) academic learning time (Berliner, 1984). *Allocated time* reflects the decisions teachers make regarding the amount of time to spend studying a topic (e.g., math versus reading) and doing a given academic task (e.g., how much time to spend on reading comprehension versus decoding skills). As we have discussed throughout this book, effective sheltered instruction teachers plan for and deliver lessons that are balanced between teacher presentation of information and opportunities for students to practice and apply the information in meaningful ways. Effective sheltered instruction teachers use instructional time wisely.

Engaged time refers to the time students are actively participating in instruction during the time allocated. The engaged time-on-task research has consistently concluded that the more actively students participate in the instructional process, the more they achieve (Schmoker, 2006). As Bickel and Bickel (1986) explained: "Students learn more when they are attending to the learning tasks that are the focus of instruction" (p. 493). Instruction that is understandable to ELs, that creates opportunities for students to talk about the lesson's concepts, and that provides hands-on activities to reinforce learning captures students' attention and keeps them more actively engaged.

Academic learning time focuses on students' time-on-task, when the task is related to the materials they will be tested on. Creative, fun activities are not effective if they are unrelated to the content and language objectives of the lesson. According to Leinhardt and colleagues (1982):

> When teachers spend their time and energy teaching students the content the students need to learn, students learn the material. When students spend their time actively engaged in activities that relate strongly to the materials they will be tested on, they learn more of the material (p. 409).

Of course, sheltered teachers need to be explicit in their expectations and make certain that their English learners understand how activities and materials relate to standards and upcoming assessments.

In summary, effective SIOP® teachers need to plan to use the entire class period efficiently, teach in ways that engage students, and make sure students are engaged in activities that specifically relate to the material on which they will be assessed.

SIOP® FEATURE 26:
Pacing of the Lesson Appropriate to Students' Ability Levels

Pacing refers to the rate at which information is presented during a lesson. The pace of the lesson depends on the nature of the lesson's content, as well as the level of students' background knowledge. When working with ELs, it can be challenging to find a pace that doesn't present information too quickly yet is brisk enough to maintain students' interest, especially when a variety of English proficiency levels are represented in the same classroom. Finding an appropriate pace requires practice but becomes easier as teachers develop familiarity with their students' skills.

Elementary teachers know, for instance, that the attention span of a kindergartener or first-grader is much shorter than that of a fifth-grader, so they adjust their lessons accordingly. A practice activity may last only five to seven minutes in the primary grades, where in the upper grades it could last 20. When considering pacing for ELs, it is also important to chunk information in smaller conceptual units and allot time for processing the material taught in the new language between the chunks. Because many elementary teachers have a less rigid bell schedule than secondary teachers (i.e., students do not typically switch classes at the end of each period), on some days, certain lessons may extend beyond the normal time frame to cover the material. Furthermore, if the ELs have additional support from an ESL teacher, the grade-level teacher and the ESL teacher can co-plan to augment instructional time. In this way, the ESL teacher might introduce key vocabulary and build background on topics that will be covered in the regular classroom, or provide additional practice and application activities. (See Lacina, New Levine, & Sowa, 2006, for examples of ESL–elementary classroom teacher partnerships.)

In classes with native English speakers and English learners, it can take some effort and experience to establish the pacing. Using a thematic, interdisciplinary curriculum that spirals not only the content but also key language terms, functions, and sentence structures allows English learners time, over the course of a unit and across several content areas, to develop the academic English skills they need for success. Collaborative learning projects offer opportunities for peer support and tasks geared to proficiency level and interest. Differentiating instruction techniques and prorating the task are other options for managing a lesson with multiple proficiency levels. Some other related ideas can be found in *99 Ideas and Activities for Teaching English Learners with the SIOP® Model* (Vogt & Echevarria, 2008) and in *Implementing the SIOP® Model Through Effective Professional Development and Coaching* (Echevarria, Short, & Vogt, 2008).

One important fact to remember is this: If a teacher wastes five minutes of a class period daily, perhaps by starting the lesson late or finishing early, over the course of 180 days, 15 hours of instructional time will be lost! Sometimes little routines can help the pacing: a basket by the door where students deposit homework when they enter or classwork when they leave, or a materials manager for each group of desks who distributes books or worksheets to everyone in the group. It is also useful to invest in teaching routines and task procedures (e.g., how to do a Conga Line, how to create a Venn diagram) at the start of the school year. In sum, we need to maximize the way we use time when we have English learners in the classroom.

The Lesson

These Scenarios continue the lessons for Chapter 2 on the Gold Rush. (For more examples of lesson and unit plans for social studies, see Short, Vogt, & Echevarria, in press.)

UNIT: The Gold Rush (Fourth Grade)

The classrooms described in the teaching vignettes in this chapter are all in a suburban elementary school with heterogeneously mixed students. English learners represent approximately 30 percent of the student population, and the children speak a variety of languages. In the fourth-grade classrooms of teachers Ms. Chen, Mrs. Hargroves, and Mr. Hensen, the majority of the ELs are at the intermediate stage of English fluency.

As part of the fourth-grade social studies curriculum, Ms. Chen, Mrs. Hargroves, and Mr. Hensen have planned a unit on the California Gold Rush. The school district requires the use of the adopted social studies series, although teachers are encouraged to supplement the text with primary source materials, literature, and realia. The content topics for the Gold Rush unit include westward expansion, routes and trails to the West, the people who sought their fortunes, hardships, settlements, the discovery of gold, the life of miners, methods for extracting gold, the impact of the Gold Rush, and so forth.

Each of the teachers has created several lessons for this unit, beginning with a lesson plan (approximately 45 minutes per day) on routes and trails to the West. Specifically, the content of this lesson covers the Oregon Trail, the Overland Trail, and the Route Around Cape Horn.

Teaching Scenarios

To refresh your memory about the lessons on westward expansion and the Gold Rush taught by Ms. Chen, Mrs. Hargroves, and Mr. Hensen, we summarize them in the sections that follow. (See Chapter 2, Teaching Scenarios, for a complete description of the three lessons.)

Ms. Chen

Ms. Chen began the lesson on westward expansion by reading aloud the content and language objectives for the day.

Content Objectives

1. Find and label the three main routes to the West on a map.

2. Tell one or two facts about each of the three trails.

Language Objectives

1. Write sentences explaining how the three routes to the West were given their names.

2. Tell how the structure of some words gives clues to their meaning.

After a whole-class brainstorming and List-Group-Label activity about why people leave their homes and move to new locations, Ms. Chen assigned most of the class a quick-write on the Gold Rush. She then provided a "jump-start" for the English learners with very limited proficiency by introducing key vocabulary, passing around iron pyrite ("fool's gold"), looking together at a map of the trails west, and viewing several pictures of pioneers and Gold Rush characters.

FIGURE 8.1 *Lesson Delivery Component of the SIOP® Model: Ms. Chen's Lesson*

4	3	2	1	0
23. **Content objectives** clearly supported by lesson delivery	**Content objectives** somewhat supported by lesson delivery			**Content objectives** not supported by lesson delivery

4	3	2	1	0
24. **Language objectives** clearly supported by lesson delivery	**Language objectives** somewhat supported by lesson delivery			**Language objectives** not supported by lesson delivery

4	3	2	1	0
25. **Students engaged** approximately 90% to 100% of the period	**Students engaged** approximately 70% of the period			**Students engaged** less than 50% of the period

4	3	2	1	0
26. **Pacing** of the lesson appropriate to the students' ability level	**Pacing** generally appropriate, but at times too fast or too slow			**Pacing** inappropriate to students' ability levels

Following this, Ms. Chen introduced the key vocabulary to the entire class, and discussed why roads, streets, and trails have particular names. She pointed out the three trails west on the wall map, discussed their names, and explained how the Overland Trail was a compound word that gave clues to its meaning (over + land = overland).

Next, Ms. Chen distributed copies of maps and modeled on the overhead projector how to use colored pencils to color in the maps. Students worked together in small groups to complete their maps. Finally, with just a few minutes remaining in the period, Ms. Chen distributed a skeleton outline of the chapter that the students had read. The outline's headings (Locations, Characteristics, Challenges, and Advantages) provided an organizer for the information, and in groups, students began working together to fill in the outline. The lesson concluded with a review of the content and language objectives. Then several students volunteered to report on a number of facts about each of the trails.

On the SIOP® form in Figure 8.1, rate Ms. Chen's lesson for each of the features in Lesson Delivery. Be able to defend your ratings and discuss them with others, if possible.

Mrs. Hargroves

Mrs. Hargroves began her lesson on the trails west by stating, "Today you'll learn about the Oregon Trail, the Overland Trail, and the route around Cape Horn. We'll also be working on maps, and I want you to color the Overland Trail a different color from the color you use for the Cape Horn route. When you learn about the Oregon Trail, you'll complete

FIGURE 8.2 *Lesson Delivery Component of the SIOP® Model: Mrs. Hargroves's Lesson*

4	3	2	1	0
23. **Content objectives** clearly supported by lesson delivery	**Content objectives** somewhat supported by lesson delivery			**Content objectives** not supported by lesson delivery

4	3	2	1	0
24. **Language objectives** clearly supported by lesson delivery	**Language objectives** somewhat supported by lesson delivery			**Language objectives** not supported by lesson delivery

4	3	2	1	0
25. **Students engaged** approximately 90% to 100% of the period	**Students engaged** approximately 70% of the period			**Students engaged** less than 50% of the period

4	3	2	1	0
26. **Pacing** of the lesson appropriate to the students' ability level	**Pacing** generally appropriate, but at times too fast or too slow			**Pacing** inappropriate to students' ability levels

the map with a third color. By the time you're finished, you should have all three routes drawn on the map using different colors." She held up a completed map for the students to see as an example.

Following a brief lecture on westward expansion, Mrs. Hargroves directed students to the respective chapter in the text. Students looked at the illustrations and she responded to questions they had. She began reading the chapter and after a few minutes, she directed students to complete the reading independently. She circulated through the room, answering questions and helping with difficult words. After 20 minutes, Mrs. Hargroves stopped the reading, distributed colored pencils and maps, and asked students to complete the maps with partners. When the maps were completed, she collected them and assigned a brief essay on the topic "If you had been a pioneer, which trail would you have chosen? Why?"

On the SIOP® form in Figure 8.2, rate Mrs. Hargroves's lesson for each of the Lesson Delivery features.

Mr. Hensen

Mr. Hensen began his lesson by asking how many of the students had traveled to California. They discussed the various modes of transportation used by students who had visited the state, and then Mr. Hensen linked their responses to the travel modes of the pioneers. Following a video on the westward expansion, he introduced the key vocabulary for the day's lessons (Oregon Trail, Overland Trail, route around Cape Horn).

Next, Mr. Hensen read aloud two paragraphs from the textbook chapter. He then numbered students off into six groups, assigned sections of the text to the newly formed groups, and engaged them in a Jigsaw reading activity for the remainder of the chapter. ELs were partnered with more proficient English readers for the Jigsaw activity. After the Jigsaw groups completed their reading, they returned to their home groups and shared what they had learned from the assigned text. Again, English learners were paired with students with greater English proficiency.

Mr. Hensen then directed the students in their home groups to divide up the three trails, with one or two students in each group. One group was asked to draw the Oregon Trail on a map, and the other students were to draw either the Overland or Cape Horn trails. Their next task was to tell the other students in their group how to locate, draw, and color the trails on their maps, using the map in the text and their reading as a guide. Mr. Hensen circulated through the room, assisting as necessary, while the children completed the mapping activity. At the lesson's conclusion, students were directed to pass in their maps. Those maps that were not finished were assigned as homework.

On the SIOP® form in Figure 8.3, rate Mr. Hensen's lesson for each of the Lesson Delivery features.

FIGURE 8.3　*Lesson Delivery Component of the SIOP® Model: Mr. Hensen's Lesson*

4	3	2	1	0
23. **Content objectives** clearly supported by lesson delivery		**Content objectives** somewhat supported by lesson delivery		**Content objectives** not supported by lesson delivery
24. **Language objectives** clearly supported by lesson delivery		**Language objectives** somewhat supported by lesson delivery		**Language objectives** not supported by lesson delivery
25. **Students engaged** approximately 90% to 100% of the period		**Students engaged** approximately 70% of the period		**Students engaged** less than 50% of the period
26. **Pacing** of the lesson appropriate to the students' ability level		**Pacing** generally appropriate, but at times too fast or too slow		**Pacing** inappropriate to students' ability levels

Discussion of Lessons

23. *Content Objectives Clearly Supported by Lesson Delivery*

Ms. Chen: 4

Mrs. Hargroves: 1

Mr. Hensen: 3

Clearly, we believe (and our research supports it) that teachers must include content and language objectives in every lesson, not only for planning and teaching, but also for the students, especially English learners. They need to have a clear, explicit understanding of what the expectations are for a lesson. Recall that only Ms. Chen wrote her content and language objectives on the board and read them aloud for her students. While Mrs. Hargroves had a content objective (but no language objective) written in her plan book, she stated her plans for the day orally to her students, without clearly defining their learning or language objectives. Mr. Hensen had neither content nor language objectives written in his plan book, yet he appeared to have a clear idea of where he was going with his lesson. However, at the outset of the lesson, his plans may not have been clear for some students.

In this component of the SIOP® Model (Lesson Delivery), we move beyond having the content and lesson objectives written in plan books and on the board (or chart paper or transparency). Rather, the focus here is on whether the lesson delivery matches the stated (or unstated, in Mr. Hensen's case) objectives.

Ms. Chen's lesson received a "4" on Content Objectives. From the beginning of the lesson, she had a clearly defined content objective, and her lesson delivery supported it. Her focus on the three routes to the West was supported by (1) activating students' prior knowledge about why people leave their homes and move to a new location (brainstorming and List-Group-Label); (2) engaging some students in a quick-write about the Gold Rush, so that she could have a few minutes to preteach (jump-start) the English learners a topic about which they probably had little prior knowledge; (3) the shared reading of the textbook chapter; (4) the mapping activity; and (5) the skeleton outline that compared and contrasted the three trails.

In contrast, Mrs. Hargroves's lesson received a "1" on Content Objectives. As you may recall, she did not write an objective on the board and hurriedly stated what she wanted the students to do for the lesson. What is also problematic about her lesson is that the coloring of the maps seemed to be what was important to her, rather than her confirmation that each student understood the information about the trails west. Students were expected to read the chapter independently, which was most likely impossible for struggling readers and the English learners. Further, her lecture may have been difficult for her ELs to follow. The writing assignment, while a worthwhile topic ("If you had been a pioneer, which trail would you have chosen? Why?"), was not scaffolded so it may or may not have been appropriate for her students, depending on their English proficiency and their ability to access the information in the text. Therefore, her lesson delivery did not support well her intended content objective.

Mr. Hensen's lesson was rated "3" on Content Objectives. Although he did not state the objectives, they were certainly implied and supported by his lesson.

For example, at the end of the period, he asked several students to report on some differences among the trails; this initial feedback provided information about whether the students had met the day's objective. His constant monitoring, and the various grouping activities, provided additional information about who was meeting the objective and who was having difficulty. He might have added a quick group-response activity (pencils up/pencils down or whiteboard) to determine if all students understood the differences among the trails. Surely, the skeleton outline to be completed the following day would provide him with definitive information about his students' meeting of the content objectives. Had Mr. Hensen written his objectives on the board and reviewed them with his students, his lesson would have received a "4" for this feature.

24. *Language Objectives Clearly Supported by Lesson Delivery*

    Ms. Chen: 4

    Mrs. Hargroves: 0

    Mr. Hensen: 2

Ms. Chen's lesson was rated "4" on the Language Objectives feature. Objectives were clearly written and stated, and students had several opportunities to meet them. During the discussion of the street names, students had a chance to discuss why and how streets and routes were named. Additionally, students were asked to use complete sentences.

    Mrs. Hargroves's lesson received a "0" for Language Objectives. She did not write or state any language objectives, and although she did assign a reading and writing activity, for many of the students the text was inaccessible. Therefore, the writing activity would be difficult, if not impossible, for them to complete.

    Mr. Hensen's lesson received a "2" for Language Objectives. He did not write or state his language objectives, but as with the content objectives, they were implied. He engaged students in a Jigsaw activity for reading the text, and then they returned to their home groups and explained what they had learned from the reading.

25. *Students Engaged Approximately 90% to 100% of the Period*

    Ms. Chen: 4

    Mrs. Hargroves: 1

    Mr. Hensen: 4

Ms. Chen is an enthusiastic teacher who plans lessons that use each minute of class time to its fullest. As illustrated in the lesson, Ms. Chen spent time presenting materials and allowed students to work together. They eagerly participated in whole-group and small-group discussions, and Ms. Chen made sure they were on task as she walked around the room. In addition, the content of the lesson was directly related to the district's content standards on which the students will be assessed at the end of the unit.

    Her lesson received a "4" for this feature because it met all the criteria for active student engagement: She used the allocated time in an effective way, basing the lesson on the text, teaching outlining and mapping skills, providing opportunities for interaction and application of concepts, and so forth. Students were active and on task throughout, and the material was relevant to the assignment.

Mrs. Hargroves's lesson received a "1" for Student Engagement. Recall that Mrs. Hargroves read part of the text chapter aloud, which cut its substantial length. She then allotted twenty minutes for students to read the remaining portion of the text chapter. Most students completed the reading in about ten minutes. Some began talking among themselves, while others tried to finish the reading. Overall, students were engaged less than 50 percent of the period. During Mrs. Hargroves's lecture on westward expansion, many students were disengaged until she discussed the illustrations and the trails on the wall map.

Mr. Hensen's lesson received a "4" for Student Engagement. His students were actively engaged throughout the lesson. From the opening question about trips to California, through the video and the Jigsaw activity, all students were held accountable for learning the material. During the map activity, students not only located and colored a trail, but were also responsible for assisting each other in finding, drawing, and coloring the additional trails.

26. *Pacing of Lesson Appropriate to Students' Ability Levels*

   Ms. Chen: 4

   Mrs. Hargroves: 1

   Mr. Hensen: 3

Ms. Chen's lesson received a "4" for Pacing. She understood that the English learners in her class may have needed a slower pace than the native English speakers. Therefore, she provided them a jump-start that enabled them to keep up with the whole-class activities. She also moved the pace along by reading aloud and doing a shared reading of the text. In this way, she scaffolded instruction for the ELs, and all students were able to work at roughly the same pace. The groups for the map activity included four to five students with both native English speakers and ELs who assisted one another as needed.

The pacing of Mrs. Hargroves's lesson was slow and monotonous at times, especially when she lectured, yet she covered material too quickly at other times. Many students were off task because of the problematic pace of the lesson. Her lesson received a "1" for Pacing because it was inappropriate for the students' ability level— too slow to maintain interest and too quick for ELs to understand the information presented orally.

Mr. Hensen's lesson received a "3" for Pacing. With the discussions, videos, Jigsaw reading activity, group work, and map coloring, some students, especially the English learners, may have felt a bit rushed. However, he provided substantial scaffolding and did allow students to complete their maps at home.

Summary

The importance of setting and meeting objectives cannot be overemphasized. Many teachers may feel comfortable having a general objective in mind and moving along with a lesson's flow, but that approach is not helpful for English learners. Delivering a lesson geared to objectives that have been made clear to students benefits all. The teacher stays on task, and the students know what is important to focus on and remember. By incorporating a variety of techniques that engage students throughout the lesson, teachers not only give students opportunities to learn, practice, and apply information and language skills, but they also help to ensure meeting the lesson's objectives.

Pacing is another important aspect of lesson delivery, and appropriate pace is critical for English learners. Information that is presented at a pace suitable for native English speakers may render that information meaningless, especially for beginning English speakers. Finding the right pace for a lesson depends in part on the content of the lesson and students' prior knowledge about the topic. It may also depend on the task—whether the product has been prorated or whether students were able to work in cooperative groups. Investing in a slower pace in the first quarter of the year often pays off later because children then know the task procedures and classroom routines and have better academic language skills. As illustrated in the lessons here, effective sheltered teachers meet the lesson objectives while accommodating the language and learning needs of their students.

Discussion Questions

1. Reflect on a lesson that you taught or observed that did not go well. What happened? Can you identify a feature in Lesson Delivery that might have caused the lesson to be less successful? Or a feature from another SIOP® component? In retrospect, how might the lesson delivery have been improved?

2. Suppose three new fifth-graders, all with limited English proficiency, joined a social studies class midyear. The other students in the class include a few former ELs and native English speakers. What are some language objectives the teacher could write for each of the following content concepts?

    a. Trade routes across the Sahara
    b. Expansion of the Roman Empire

   How might the teacher prorate the tasks associated with the language objectives to meet the different academic development needs of the students?

3. How does an elementary teacher or supervisor determine whether a majority of students, including English learners, are engaged during a lesson? What techniques can be used to sustain engagement throughout the period? What should the teacher do if he or she senses that students are off task? Why is sustained engagement so critical to ELs' academic progress?

4. Look over a SIOP® lesson you have been working on. Write down the amount of time you expect each section (or activity) of the lesson to take. Teach the lesson and compare your expectations with reality. Do you have a good handle on pacing? If not, review your lesson for tightening or extending. Where did you lose or gain time? What can you add or take away? List some routines you can implement in your classroom so you do less talking, or less distributing and collecting. Share with a colleague your ideas for maximizing time on task and student engagement.

Review & Assessment

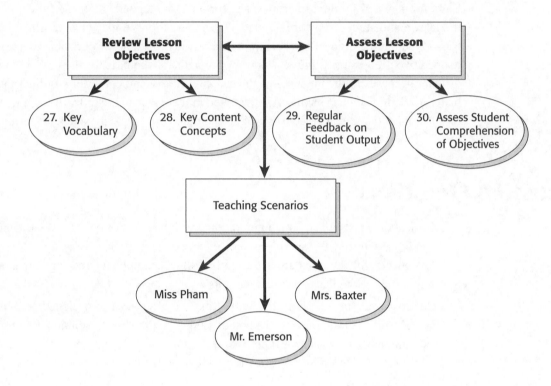

Objectives

After reading, discussing, and engaging in activities related to this chapter, you will be able to meet the following content and language objectives.

Content Objectives

Select techniques for reviewing key content concepts.

Incorporate a variety of assessment techniques into lessons.

Describe the challenges in assessing the content learning of students with limited English proficiency.

Language Objectives

Write a lesson plan that includes review of key vocabulary.

Teach a lesson with group response techniques.

Orally provide feedback to ELs that enhances language development.

Use oral, written, and physical means to provide specific feedback to students on their performance.

Over the years, teachers have asked us why Review & Assessment is the eighth component in the SIOP® Model. Usually the question is preceded by a comment such as "Shouldn't the assessment of students' strengths and needs precede any instruction?" Our response is always "Of course!" Clearly, assessment and instruction are inexorably linked (Vogt & Shearer, 2007). Effective teachers use assessment findings to plan their lessons according to student needs and strengths, and to evaluate how effectively their lessons have been delivered. Effective SIOP® teachers also realize the importance of ongoing and continuous assessment of a lesson's content and language objectives throughout the lesson. We've all experienced that feeling of frustration when we realize, sometimes too late, that students have not understood what it is we were trying to teach. That is precisely what we hope to avoid with the Review & Assessment component.

So why is Review & Assessment the eighth component? The simple answer is that other than the Preparation component, there is no particular hierarchy or order to the eight SIOP® components. For example, as you begin to write SIOP® lesson plans, you'll see that the features of Comprehensible Input are necessary from the beginning to the end of a lesson and that students must engage in Interaction throughout if they're going to learn to speak English proficiently. The components and features of the SIOP® Model are interrelated and integrated into each and every lesson. In fact, as you become more familiar with each of the components and features, you may find that you decide to implement them initially in an order other than the one presented in this book. That is just fine—as is beginning to implement them in the order presented in the SIOP® protocol. What is important is that you see that all 8 components and 30 features eventually need to be present in your lessons for English learners.

Background

The component of Review & Assessment is not only about what teachers do at the end of a lesson to see if children have learned what was intended. Rather, reviewing and assessing occur throughout each lesson and then again as the lesson concludes. During each step of a lesson, throughout each meaningful activity, we have an opportunity to assess students' progress toward meeting the lesson's content and language objectives.

For English learners, review is essential. During some elementary school lessons, ELs receive 20 or 30 minutes, and in the upper grades, perhaps 45 minutes of input in a new language. Unless the teacher takes the time to highlight and review key information and explicitly indicate what students should focus on and learn, English learners may not know what is important. Students, especially those at the early stages of English proficiency, devote considerable energy to figuring out what the teacher is saying or the text is telling them at a basic level. They are much less able to evaluate which pieces of information among all the input they receive are important to remember. That is why the teacher must take the time to review and summarize throughout a lesson and particularly as a wrap-up at the end.

To teach students effectively, teachers need information about their learning from multiple indicators. One single assessment approach is insufficient for all students, but especially those who may have difficulty articulating their level of understanding through English, their new language. As teachers gather information about what students understand or do not understand, they can adjust their instructional plan accordingly. *Scenarios for ESL Standards-Based Assessment* (TESOL, 2001) is an excellent resource for classroom assessment ideas that are linked to standards and can measure student academic performance. Effective sheltered instruction involves reviewing important concepts, providing constructive feedback through clarification, and making instructional decisions based on student response. In the end, you must have enough information to evaluate the extent to which students have mastered your lesson's objectives. This teach, assess, review, and reteach process is cyclical and recursive (see Figure 9.1).

To see an example of the relationship between assessment and instruction, please view the corresponding video clip (Chapter 9, Module 1) on the accompanying CD.

 SIOP® FEATURE 27:
Comprehensive Review of Key Vocabulary

In Chapter 2, we stated that effective teachers incorporate in their lesson plans techniques that support ELs' language development. In Chapter 3, we discussed the importance of building background through teaching academic language, key content vocabulary, language structure, and functional language. We suggested that language objectives should be identified in lesson plans, introduced to students at the beginning of a lesson, and reviewed throughout the lesson.

We can help develop academic language and key vocabulary by teaching and then reviewing terminology and concepts through *analogy*—the process of relating newly learned words to other words with the same structure or pattern. In Chapters 2 and 3, we gave the example of *photo* (meaning "light") in a lesson on photosynthesis, and suggested referring students to other words with the same morpheme (e.g., *photography*). Reviewing key vocabulary also involves drawing students' attention to tense, parts of speech, and sentence structure. Repeating and reinforcing language patterns helps children become familiar with English structures.

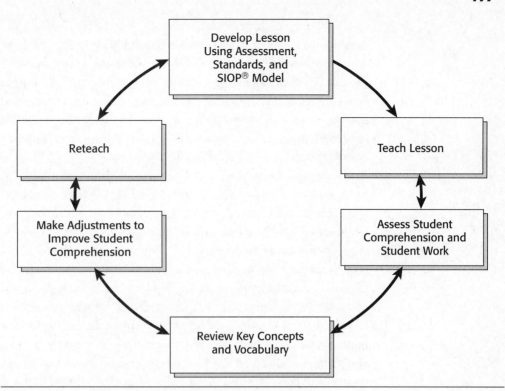

FIGURE 9.1 *Effective Teaching Cycle for English Learners*

Multiple exposures to new terminology also build familiarity, confidence, and English proficiency. Words and concepts may be reviewed through paraphrasing, such as "Remember to *share your ideas*; that is, if you have something you want to say, tell it to the others in your group." Another example of a paraphrase (and contextualized sentence) is "The townspeople were *welcoming as they invited the visitors to their home*." Paraphrasing as review provides an effective scaffold for ELs, especially after words and phrases have been previously defined and discussed in context.

Key vocabulary also can be reviewed more systematically. It is important to remember that it is ineffective to teach vocabulary through the "dreaded word list" on which students must write (or copy) dictionary definitions (Ruddell, 2007). Research findings are very clear—as stated previously, isolated word lists and dictionary definitions alone do not promote vocabulary and language development. We also know that students do not learn vocabulary words when the teacher just orally introduces and defines them and then expects students to remember the definitions. The more exposures students have to new words, especially if the vocabulary is reinforced through multiple modalities, the more likely they are to remember and use them.

An effective way to incorporate ongoing vocabulary study and review is through the use of individual Word Study Books (Bear, Invernizzi, Templeton, & Johnston, 2007). A Word Study Book is a student-made personal notebook that includes frequently used words and concepts. Vocabulary in Word Study Books might be organized by English language structure, such as listing together words with similar plural endings (e.g., *s, es, ies*). We also believe Word Study Books can be used for content study where words are grouped by topic (e.g., American Revolution words related to protest or government). Some students may benefit by creating semantic maps of the words, for example, linking events to related verbs, adjectives, adverbs, and so forth.

For young children (pre-K–grade 2), Word Study books can include the child's own illustrations as mnemonics (pictures to remember word meanings and usage), and/or rebus pictures for definitions (difficult words are represented by simple drawings, usually provided by the teacher). As children are learning to write, they can use their own Word Study books as references for spellings and meanings of the words to which they have had exposure. Usually words are organized by the alphabet, but some teachers prefer to have them organized by sounds (such as open/long sounds or closed/short sounds, initial consonants, blends, digraphs, etc.)

Helping students review and practice words in nonprint ways is beneficial as well. Students may draw a picture to depict a concept or to remember a word. They may demonstrate the meaning through physical gestures or act out several words within the context of a role-play. Pictionary and charade-like games at the end of a lesson can stimulate an engaging review of vocabulary.

Remember that we also need to help students become comfortable with academic language by introducing and modeling academic tasks throughout lessons and units. For example, if you are planning to have ELs engage in literature discussion circles, it is important to review what "discussion" means, what "turn-taking" is, what it means to "share ideas," how questions are asked and answered, and so forth. Reviewing this terminology provides the necessary scaffolding so that students understand the expectations for their participation in routine activities. This also includes language that is found in test directions or question prompts. Increasingly, our English learners need exposure, practice, and review of those types of terms and phrasings (e.g., "Which of the following is *not* a triangle?") to help prepare them for the accountability measures they will be called upon to perform.

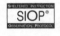

SIOP® FEATURE 28:
Comprehensive Review of Key Content Concepts

Just as it is important to review key vocabulary periodically throughout a lesson, and especially at its conclusion, it is also essential that English learners have key content concepts reviewed during and at the end of a lesson. Understandings are scaffolded when you stop and briefly summarize, along with students' help, the key content covered up to that point. For example, in a lesson on Egyptian mummification, you might say something like the following: "Up to this point, we learned that little was known about Mummy No. 1770 until it was donated to the museum. After the scientists completed the autopsy, they discovered three important things. Who remembers what they were?" This type of review is usually informal, but it must be planned carefully. It can lead into the next section of the text or to a discussion: "Let's read this next section to see what else the scientists learned." Or if predictions about an upcoming section of a text have been made or hypotheses about an experiment developed, teachers should always refer to these afterward and assess their validity with the students.

One favorite wrap-up technique of several SIOP® teachers is Outcome Sentences. A teacher can post sentence starters on the board or transparency, such as:

I wonder . . .

I discovered . . .

I still want to know . . .

I learned . . .

I still don't understand . . .

I still have a question about . . .

I will ask a friend about . . .

To see an example of assessing students' understanding, please view the corresponding video clip (Chapter 9, Module 2) on the accompanying CD.

Students take turns selecting and completing an outcome sentence orally or in writing in a journal. The students can also confer with a partner.

A more structured review might involve childern in retelling with partners, writing in a journal, or listing key points on the board. It is important to link the review to the content objectives so that you and the children stay focused on the essential content concepts. Toward the end of the lesson, a final review helps ELs assess their own understandings and clarify misconceptions. Students' responses to review should guide your decisions about what to do next, such as a summative evaluation or, if needed, additional reteaching and assessing.

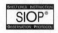

SIOP® FEATURE 29:
Regular Feedback Provided to Students on Their Output

Periodic review of language, vocabulary, and content enables teachers to provide specific academic feedback to children that clarifies and corrects misconceptions and misunderstandings. Feedback also helps develop students' proficiency in English when it is supportive and validating. For example, teachers can model correct English usage when restating a child's response: "Yes, you're right. Amelia Bedelia really does want to do what's right." Paraphrasing also supports students' understandings and validates answers if we add after the paraphrase, "Is this what you're thinking (or saying)?" If ELS are only able to respond to questions in one or two words, you can validate their answers in complete sentences: "You're right! Amelia *does* get confused, or mixed up sometimes!"

Specific feedback is generally given orally or in writing, but teachers can also provide it through facial expressions and body language. A nod, smile of support, pat on the shoulder, or encouraging look can take away fear of speaking aloud, especially for students who are beginning to develop English proficiency. Additionally, students can provide feedback to each other. Partners or groups can discuss among themselves, giving feedback on both language production and content understanding, but then report to the whole class. The teacher can facilitate feedback by providing appropriate modeling.

SIOP® FEATURE 30:
Assessment of Student Comprehension and Learning of All Lesson Objectives Throughout the Lesson

Within the context of lesson delivery for English learners, we see review and assessment as an ongoing process, especially related to a lesson's language and content objectives. Historically, educators have blurred the line between assessment and evaluation, generally using the term *evaluation* for both formative and summative judgments. The teacher's role in evaluation was primarily as a judge, one who conveyed a value on the completion of a given task. This value was frequently determined from the results of periodic quizzes, reports, or tests that served as the basis for report card grades in elementary and secondary schools.

Today, however, many educators distinguish between assessment and evaluation, (Lipson & Wixson, 2008). *Assessment* is defined as "the gathering and synthesizing of information concerning students' learning," while *evaluation* is defined as "making judgments about students' learning. The processes of assessment and evaluation can be viewed as progressive: first, assessment; then, evaluation" (McLaughlin & Vogt, 1996, pp. 104, 106).

Assessment occurs throughout a lesson, as evidenced in lesson plans and in periodic review to determine if students are understanding and applying content concepts. Assessment must be linked to the instruction, and it needs to target the lesson objectives. Just as children need to know what the objectives are, they also need also to be informed about how and what types of assessments they will have. Toward the end of the lesson, students' progress is assessed to see whether it is appropriate to move on or whether it is necessary to review and reteach. This type of assessment is *informal, authentic, multidimensional,* and includes *multiple indicators* that reflect student learning, achievement, and attitudes (McLaughlin & Vogt, 1996; O'Malley & Pierce, 1996; Lenski, Ehlers-Zavala, Daniel, & Sun-Irminger, 2006); Lipson-Wixson, 2008).

Informal assessment involves on-the-spot, ongoing opportunities for determining the extent to which students are learning content. These opportunities may include teacher observations, anecdotal reports, teacher-to-student and student-to-student conversations, quick-writes and brainstorming, or any number of tasks that occur within regular instruction and that are not intended to be graded or evaluated according to set criteria.

Authentic assessment is characterized by its application to real life, where students are engaged in meaningful tasks that take place in real-life contexts. Authentic assessment is usually *multidimensional* because teachers use different ways of determining student performance. These may include written pieces, audiotapes, student and parent interviews, videotapes, observations, creative work and art, discussion, performance, oral group responses, and so forth.

These multidimensional student performances usually involve *multiple indicators,* specific evidences related to the language and content objectives or standards. For example, a student may indicate proficiency with an objective through a piece of writing, through active participation in a group activity, and through insightful questions he or she asks during discussion. The teacher thus has more than one piece of evidence indicating the student is progressing toward mastery of the particular content or language objective.

Periodic assessments before and during lessons can eventually lead to evaluation of a student's demonstrated performance for an objective or standard. This evaluation, while summative, also may be informal and take a variety of forms. Often, rubrics (such as the SIOP® protocol) are used to ascertain a developmental level of performance for a particular goal, objective, or standard. For example, on a developmental rubric, student performance may be characterized as "emergent," "beginning," "developing," "competent," or "proficient." Other rubrics may communicate evaluative information, such as "inadequate," "adequate," "thorough," or "exceptional." Whichever rubric is used, results of assessment and evaluation are often shared with other interested stakeholders, such as parents and administrators, and with the students themselves.

As you are preparing to informally assess your English learners' oral language proficiency, reading, and writing to differentiate instruction appropriately, you may find a paucity of assessment instruments that are practical, quick, and easy to use. This represents an acute need, not only for teachers and their students, but also in terms of research findings that can guide us to assessment instruments that are reliable, valid, and appropriate for diverse students who are English learners (IRA & NICHD, 2007). Additional research is needed on how to assist teachers of ELs in becoming experts in using various assessment measures, including how to best organize all the assessment data, and how to monitor progress and design instruction based on the informal and formal assessment data (Edwards, Turner, & Mokhtari, 2008; IRA & NICHD, 2007; Mokhtari, Rosemary, & Edwards, 2008).

Assessments can be individual or group administered. Individual oral or written responses tell you how one student is performing, while group responses may quickly tell you how the entire group is progressing. Group response is especially sensitive to the needs of ELs, and there is a variety of methods for eliciting group responses, including some of our favorites:

Thumbs up/thumbs down: Generally, this is used for questions that elicit "agree/disagree" responses. (If students agree, they raise their thumbs.) It can also be used for yes/no questions or true/false statements. Older students may be more comfortable responding with "pencils up/pencils down" (point of pencil up or down). Students can also indicate "I don't know" by making a fist, holding it in front of the chest, and wiggling it back and forth. The pencil used by older students can also be wiggled to indicate that the answer is unknown.

Number wheels: A number wheel is made from tag board strips ($5'' \times 1''$) held together with a round-head brass paper fastener. Each strip has a number printed on it, with 0 to 5 or 0 to 10, or a to d, depending on your needs and students' ages. Students use their individual number wheels to indicate their answers to questions or statements that offer multiple-choice responses. Possible answers are displayed on the board, overhead, or pocket chart, and the teacher asks the questions or gives the statements orally.

For example, if you are teaching a lesson on possessives, you could write the following on the board:

1. boys
2. boy's
3. boys'

Each child has a number wheel and you say, "Show me the correct use of the word *boys* in the following sentences. Remember that you can show me a '0' if you don't know the answer. 'The little boy's dog was hungry and was barking.' Think. Get set. Show me."

Students then find the number 2 strip, and holding their number wheels in front of their chests, they display their answers. They repeat the process as you give the next sentence. Be sure to give the cues (Think, Get Set) before giving the direction, "Show me!"

Number wheels are appropriate for younger students. They enjoy working with them, and they provide you with much needed information about students' understandings of language and content concepts.

Response boards: Either small chalkboards or dry-erase boards can be used for group responses. Each student has a board and writing instrument. You ask a question, students respond on their boards, and then turn them to face you when you say,

"Show me!" Older students (grades 4–6) seem to prefer working with the dry-erase boards and will willingly use them in a classroom in which approximations are supported and errors are viewed as steps to effective learning. Dry-erase boards (12″ × 12″) can be inexpensively cut from "bathroom tile board," which is available at home and building supply stores.

Group response activities are very effective for assessing, reviewing, and providing feedback. By looking around the room, teachers can quickly gauge how many students understand what is being assessed. If students are having difficulty with language and content concepts, and this is obvious from individual answers given during a group response activity, review and reteaching are necessary.

 Number 1 to 3 for self-assessment: It's one thing for the teacher to assess student progress toward meeting objectives; it's something entirely different for students to assess their own progress and understandings. From our experience teaching students of all ages, when we ask English learners (and native speakers as well) if they have met a particular objective, the usual response is generally a grunt, a nod, or a "Yeah," often in unison. This activity (Vogt & Echevarria, 2008) is a quick and easy way to have students self-assess the degree to which they think they have met a lesson's content and language objectives. At the end of the lesson, as you review the objectives with the students, ask them to indicate with one, two, or three fingers how well they think they met them:

1 = I didn't (or can't) meet (or do) the objective; or K–2:

2 = I didn't (or can't) meet (or do) the objective, but I made progress toward meeting it; or K–2:

3 = I fully met (or can do) the objective; or K–2:

Depending on how students indicate their understandings of a lesson's key concepts (the objectives), the teacher can reteach, provide additional modeling, group students for further instruction and practice, and so forth. We have found that self-assessments that are directly related to a lesson's content and language objectives are far more informative than the typical "yeah" or "no" or "sorta" comments in response to whether objectives have been met.

STOCK MARKET (grades 3–12) (MaryEllen Vogt)

1. Stock Market is great for an end-of-unit review prior to an exam because it provides the teacher with information about student misconceptions, factual errors, etc. It's also lots of fun!

2. Prepare Monopoly or other "play" money in denominations of $5, $10, $20, $50, and $100.

3. Generate content questions (some from an actual quiz or test you're going to give) so that you can assess your students' readiness to take the test. Mix challenging and easier questions so that you'll have at least 10 to 15 to choose from, depending on the grade you teach.

4. Also write some trivia questions of interest to the grade level of your students (such as the principal's first and last name; the U.S. president's first name, the street name

where your school is located, the correct spelling of the school's name, etc.). Students also enjoy questions about popular culture, such as the names of musicians, actors, etc., but take care to ask questions on varied topics so that your immigrant English learners are not at a disadvantage because they lack background knowledge about American popular culture. On Stock Market day, group students heterogeneously (4 to 5 per group). This is very important so that all groups have a mix of children, languages, abilities, etc.

5. Provide each table group with one worksheet with two columns:
   a. for dollar "investments"
   b. for students to write answers to the questions you will be asking

6. Each group must write an "investment" dollar amount on the Stock Market handout *prior* to the teacher asking a question. Groups cannot risk more than 50 percent of what they have in their group's "bank." For example, if they have $120, the most they can invest is $60. You don't want to have any group "go broke" so they can't continue to play.

7. Ask the question (either content-related or trivia). If a group's answer is correct, the "bank" pays; if not the "bank" (you, the teacher) takes the investment.

8. Use both content and trivia questions, but don't let students know what kind of question you'll be asking. Alternate frequently, but don't let students know which type of question will be asked. If students miss several content questions in a row, you know you'll need to do some reteaching later. To keep everyone in the game, switch to a few easier trivia questions that all groups are sure to answer correctly.

9. Reward groups that are behaving well and are cooperating by giving bonuses (e.g., slipping them extra money). It's also fun to give bonuses to groups ($25 or more) for the correct spelling of answers to particular questions, either trivia or academic content. You don't need to "fine" groups for misbehavior or spelling; just reward or bonus them when they're on task, working well together, and conscientiously answering the questions.

10. If a group falls perilously behind, slip them some money so they won't go broke. If you do this discretely, no one notices and the group receiving the bank's assistance won't say a word.

11. For the final question, make it about content (not trivia) and tell groups they can invest all or some of their earnings—it's their choice. After the question is asked and answered, the group with the most money in the end is declared the winner for that day's Stock Market.

As teachers plan for formal and informal assessments, they should keep in mind that because language and content are intertwined in SIOP® classes, separating one from the other in the assessment process is difficult. It is, however, necessary to do so. When students have difficulty, teachers need to determine if it is the content that has not been mastered, or if it is a lack of English proficiency that is interfering with their acquisition and application of information.

A general rule of thumb is to plan multiple assessments. Having students perform a test on one day only provides limited information. Alternative assessment techniques balance the norm- and criterion-referenced tests teachers are required to give. These alternative techniques include performance-based tasks, portfolios, journals, and projects.

All of these assessments allow students to demonstrate their knowledge more fully than would be possible on a multiple-choice test. Although all students benefit from a wide range of assessment procedures, variety is particularly important for ELs because they (1) may be unfamiliar with the type of tests usually required in U.S. schools and (2) may need to demonstrate their knowledge in ways other than using academic English.

Teachers who are learning to implement the SIOP® Model often express concern about having varied content assessments, in part because of the perceived amount of work it takes to create them, and because some believe it is unfair if students are not assessed equally. While acknowledging this, we also believe that for English learners, adaptations must be made if teachers are to ascertain accurately the extent to which content objectives and standards are met. Often, English learners do know the information on which they are being assessed, but because of language proficiency issues, including vocabulary, reading, and writing, they are unable to demonstrate their knowledge.

The Center for Intercultural and Multilingual Advocacy (CIMA) at Kansas State University, based on recommendations made by Deschenes, Ebeling, & Sprague (1994), summarized nine types of assessment adaptations that permit teachers to more accurately determine students' knowledge and understanding. We have modified them somewhat to enable teachers to assess more accurately, and give grades when necessary, to English learners. The following are possible assessment adaptations for English learners that are congruent with the SIOP® Model and that hold high academic expectations for ELs:

- **Range:** Adapt the number of items the English learner is expected to complete, such as even or odd numbers only (see Leveled Study Guides in Chapter 2 as another example). Determine percentages of correct responses based on the number of items assessed.

- **Time:** Adapt the amount of time the English learner has for completing a task, such as providing more processing time and/or breaking tasks into manageable chunks. Unless there is a requirement to have a timed test, allowing additional time should not affect a student's score or grade.

- **Level of support:** Adapt the amount of scaffolding provided to an English learner during assessments, by asking an aide, peer assistant, or parent volunteer to read and/or explain the task, or even read aloud (and translate, if necessary and possible) the items for the assessment. Remember the difference between assessing an EL's ability to *read* and follow *written* directions and his or her ability to complete a task or answer questions about a content topic. If you are looking for a student's content knowledge (not his or her ability to read directions), it is fine to have someone else help with reading or clarifying what the expectation for the task is.

- **Difficulty:** Adapt the skill level, type of problem or task, and the process for how an English learner can approach the task, such as allowing a calculator, dictionary, or simplified instructions. Once again, you are not reducing the expectation that the English learner should know the material—you're just making it easier for him or her to demonstrate understandings.

- **Product:** Adapt the type of response the English learner is allowed to provide, such as permitting drawings, a hands-on demonstration, a verbal, and, if necessary, a translated response. Whereas native speakers may be required to write a paragraph summary or essay, it may be reasonable for an English learner to submit an illustration, poster-board explanation, or other kind of product that doesn't rely so much on sophisticated English usage.

- **Participation:** Adapt the degree of active involvement of an English learner in assessment, such as encouraging individual self-assessment, assistance in creating rubrics, and cooperative group self-assessment. As you have read often in this book, content learning is enhanced for all students, but especially for English learners, through interaction and group work. English learners can certainly be involved in their own assessment progress, particularly in the upper grades.

Finally, to the extent possible, students should be assessed on their personal progress to determine if learning has taken place. In sheltered classes in particular, where students may have different levels of language proficiency, the value of this approach becomes apparent. If teachers gather baseline data on what their students know and can do with the content information before instruction occurs and then what they know and can do afterward, teachers can identify student growth.

The Lesson

UNIT: Mathematices (Kindergarten)

Measurement and Geometry: Concepts of *shorter/taller; lighter/heavier; holds less/holds more*

The classrooms described in the scenarios in this chapter are in a small rural elementary district in the Midwest of the United States. Until recently, there were very few children whose home language was not English. However, there has been a substantial increase in the number of children coming to kindergarten with little or no English, and now approximately 30 percent of the children in the district's four elementary schools speak Spanish as their primary language. Nearly all of these children are native born, and most of their parents were immigrants from Central America and Mexico. Most of the children do not have any formal preschool experiences, although some attended the day care facility at the recently built meat-packing plant where their parents currently work. In addition to the children who live in town, a large number of children, both English-speaking and Spanish-speaking are regularly bused to school from farms and neighboring small towns. The

three kindergarten classes depicted here have an average of 25 students.

The three kindergarten teachers, Miss Pham, Mr. Emerson, and Mrs. Baxter, teach mathematics each day after the reading/language arts block. The lessons described in the vignettes were designed to meet the following state Mathematics Content Standards for Kindergarten: Measurement and Geometry

1.0 Students understand the concept of time and units to measure it; they understand that objects have properties, such as length, weight, and capacity; and that comparisons may be made by referring to those properties:

   1.1 Compare the length, weight, and capacity of objects by making direct comparisons with reference objects (e.g., note which object is shorter, longer, taller, lighter, heavier, or holds more).

(For more examples of lesson and unit plans in math, see Echevarria, Vogt, & Short, in press.)

Teaching Scenarios

The following vignettes illustrate how Miss Pham, Mr. Emerson, and Mrs. Baxter review vocabulary and key concepts, and assess student learning in their kindergarten math lessons. Each of the lessons was planned for approximately 20 to 30 minutes. The kindergarten classes are full-day with substantial Title I funding, so instructional assistants are available but not on a full-time basis. Because nearly all of the parents are employed, classroom volunteers are available infrequently.

Miss Pham

Miss Pham's lesson began with the children on the rug. She had a portable white board and markers, and she had written the following words on the board: *taller, shorter, lighter, heavier, holds less, holds more*. She had placed several objects on a table near the white board, including one large can of tomato juice, one small can of tomato juice, one large drinking glass, one small drinking glass. She introduced the words on the board by asking the children if anyone recognized any of them. Several of the English-speaking children raised their hands, and Miss Pham called on them for their responses. The selected children who speak English read some of the words they recognized. Next, Miss Pham read all of the words and asked the children to chorally read them after her. Nearly all the children were able to echo-read each of the words as the teacher pointed to them.

Then the teacher pointed to the tomato juice cans and asked the class which can was taller and which was shorter. Again, several hands were raised. Miss Pham called on these children, and one by one they came to the table. As before, all of the children who volunteered were native English speakers. The teacher asked, "Which can is taller?" and a student pointed to the large can of tomato juice. She then asked, "Which can is smaller?" and the next child pointed to the small can of tomato juice. Miss Pham smiled and said, "Very good." She then asked for two more volunteers who came to the table, and Miss Pham asked, "Which can is heavier?" and the first child pointed to the large can of tomato juice. The next child pointed to the small can when Miss Pham asked, "Which can is lighter?" The same routine was followed when the teacher asked the children, "Which of these glasses, the taller one or the shorter one will hold more tomato juice?" Again, two volunteers (both of whom speak English) came forward and each pointed to the respective glass. Miss Pham smiled warmly and said, "Good job, class!"

At this point, the children were directed to return to their desks. Miss Pham distributed a math worksheet with three lines of illustrations that were of familiar objects. The teacher orally presented the following directions while she pointed to the worksheet: "On the first line, cross out the picture of the *taller* item. On the second line, cross out the *heavier* item. On the third line, cross out the item that *holds more*. When you are finished, you may take out your crayons and color the pictures on the worksheet."

The children began working. Some made X's on the correct illustrations, while others looked around and followed the lead of the students who understood what to do. These students marked the same pictures as the other children. When some were finished and began coloring, others observed this and they also began coloring the pictures on their worksheets. When all children appeared to have marked their worksheets and were coloring, Miss Pham called the end of the period and the children turned in their work for the lesson.

One the SIOP® form in Figure 9.2, rate. Miss Pham's lesson for each of the Reviews & Assessment features.

Mr. Emerson

Mr. Emerson also began his lesson on the rug. Referring to a pocket chart, Mr. Emerson pointed to and orally read and explained the math lesson's content objective:

- We will *compare* people and objects to see which are *taller* and which are *shorter*.

FIGURE 9.2 *Review & Assessment Component of the SIOP® Model: Miss Pham's Lesson*

4	3	2	1	0
27. Comprehensive **review of key vocabulary**		Uneven **review of key vocabulary**		No **review of key vocabulary**

4	3	2	1	0
28. Comprehensive **review of key content concepts**		Uneven **review of key content concepts**		No **review of key content concepts**

4	3	2	1	0
29. Regular **feedback** provided to students on their output (e.g., language, content, work)		Inconsistent **feedback** provided to students on their output		No **feedback** provided to students on their output

4	3	2	1	0
30. **Assessment** of student comprehension and learning of all lesson objectives (e.g., spot-checking, group response) throughout the lesson		**Assessment** of student comprehension and learning of some lesson objectives		No **assessment** of student comprehension and learning of lesson objectives

He then read and explained the language objectives:

- We will learn the difference between the words *taller* and *shorter*.
- We will create a sentence using "_(blank)_ is *taller* than _(blank)_."
- We will write a sentence using "_(blank)_ is *shorter* than _(blank)_".

Mr. Emerson held up pictures of a watermelon and a tennis ball. He reminded the students that in their last math lesson, they had talked about the words *bigger* and *smaller*. He wrote the words on the white board. He then asked each child to think-think-think (they all followed his lead and tapped their index fingers on their temples) and decide which is bigger: a *watermelon* or a *tennis ball*. The unanimous decision was that the watermelon was bigger. He asked the students to think-think-think about which object was smaller; again a unanimous vote for the tennis ball. He reviewed with the children the word *compare* that they had used previously; they had just *compared* the watermelon and tennis ball to see which was *bigger* and which was *smaller*. "Today," he said, "we will *compare* people and objects, and use the words *taller* and *shorter*." He pointed once again to the words *taller* and *shorter* in the lesson's objectives.

Next, Mr. Emerson asked two of the boys (one taller than the other) to stand up. He asked the children, in pairs, to think and talk about different ways they could *compare* these two friends. He asked the partners to put their thumbs together (up high so he could see) when they were finished with the task. Mr. Emerson also asked the two boys who were standing to think and talk about the same question.

After about two minutes, Mr. Emerson asked the children what they talked about with their partners. One child said, "They're both boys." "Yes," Mr. Emerson confirmed, "they are both boys." Another student suggested, "They both have brown hair." Again, Mr. Emerson repeated the response, "Yes, they both have brown hair." One of the boys standing in front of the class said, "I'm shorter than Jed is." Mr. Emerson said, "Yes, Julio is shorter than Jed! And Jed is taller than Julio!" The children all giggled.

Mr. Emerson then asked all the children to stand with their partners. On chart paper, he had written the following: "_____ is *taller* than _____." He introduced the sentence stem and said that it could be used to *compare* two people or other objects. Mr. Emerson then asked the students to read several times (nonreaders could echo-read) the words, *is, taller, than*. Further, he explained that in English we can talk about a person as being *short* and we also talk about a person as being *tall*. He motioned with his hands what *short* would look like and then he motioned what *tall* would look like. Mr. Emerson explained that when we compare the height of two people, we can use the words *taller* and *shorter* (and he pointed again to the words in the language objectives). He used the words again in the sentence: "Jed is taller than Julio. Julio is shorter than Jed."

Next, Mr. Emerson asked the children to sit back down on the rug. He then asked all the students to stand up if they thought they were *tall*. Several students stood. Mr. Emerson then asked all the "tall children" to sit down except for two, one of whom was considerably taller than the other. He then pointed to the word *taller* as he wrote it on the white board and asked, "Who is *taller*? Raphael or Isabelle?" As he asked the question, Mr. Emerson held his hand over each child, emphasizing the difference in their heights. He asked the children to "vote" on who they thought was *taller*, Raphael or Isabelle. Mr. Emerson then asked the students on the rug to use the sentence starter, as he pointed with a pointing stick to the words on the chart paper, "I think _____ is taller than _____." He also asked Raphael and Isabelle to practice saying the same sentence, using their first names.

The children practiced with their partners saying the sentence starter several times, including Raphael and Isabelle's names. During this time, Mr. Emerson walked the perimeter of the rug and listened carefully to what the students were saying, intervening when necessary. The teacher then asked each set of partners to chorally use the sentence starter, inserting the names of the respective children, until everyone had a chance to practice the sentence in front of the other class members.

Mr. Emerson then asked two other children to stand, one of whom was considerably shorter than the other. He asked the class to talk with their partners and *compare* Graciela and Blaine, to see who was *shorter*, Graciela or Blaine. The children chatted and put their thumbs together when they were finished. Mr. Emerson flipped the chart paper and a new sentence starter appeared: "_____ is *shorter* than _____." The children repeated the earlier practice round with Mr. Emerson closely monitoring their responses, which was followed by each partner saying together the sentence with *shorter*.

Next, Mr. Emerson asked the children to return to their table groups. He provided each table group with several small trees and bushes (such as one would find in a crafts store). He asked each table group (three to four children) to sort the trees and bushes from tall to short (notice he was careful not to use *tallest* to *shortest*, at this time). Once the children had finished this task, he asked them to again use the sentence starters to *compare* the trees, but this time they were to write the words into the blanks on the sentence starters. He modeled with a tree and a bush and used the sentence starters he had written on sentence strips on chart paper: "This tree is *taller* than this bush. This bush is *shorter* than this tree."

While the children were working, Mr. Emerson walked the room, monitoring and providing feedback, such as, "You two are working so well together. Can you show your sentences to your other table group members?" "Wonderful! I just heard you use the words *taller* and *shorter* correctly. You are doing a great job of *comparing* your tree and bush!" "Oops, let's check your spelling of the word *taller*. Can you find the word on the chart? Show me . . . that's right! Now, do you see what needs fixing? Good, now it's correct!"

At the end of the lesson, Mr. Emerson brought the children back to the rug. He reviewed the meanings of the words *compare, taller,* and *shorter* with the class. Finally, he reviewed the lesson's objectives, asking the children to respond with a silent cheer for each objective if they thought they had met them. The classroom resounded with silent, kindergarten cheers. Mr. Baxter concluded the lesson with, "Yes, I agree. You all met the objectives by *comparing* the children and the trees and shrubs, by using our key words *taller* and *shorter* when you were saying the sentences. Later, you used the words in your sentences. You also worked very well with your partners and groups. Nice job, kindergartners!"

On the SIOP® form in Figure 9.3, rate Mr. Emerson's lesson for each of the Review & Assessment features.

FIGURE 9.3   *Review & Assessment Component of the SIOP® Model: Mr. Emerson's Lesson*

	4	3	2	1	0
27.	Comprehensive **review of key vocabulary**		Uneven **review of key vocabulary**		No **review of key vocabulary**
28.	Comprehensive **review of key content concepts**		Uneven **review of key content concepts**		No **review of key content concepts**
29.	Regular **feedback** provided to students on their output (e.g., language, content, work)		Inconsistent **feedback** provided to students on their output		No **feedback** provided to students on their output
30.	**Assessment** of student comprehension and learning of all lesson objectives (e.g., spot-checking, group response) throughout the lesson		**Assessment** of student comprehension and learning of some lesson objectives		No **assessment** of student comprehension and learning of lesson objectives

Mrs. Baxter

Mrs. Baxter decided to teach the math lesson using Cuisenaire Rods to develop the math concept of comparison. First, she brought the children to the rug and explained that they were going to be learning about the words *longer* and *shorter*. She didn't write the words on the board because she believed that doing so would only confuse her kindergartners, especially the English learners; they didn't know how to read English words yet. She began by introducing how Cuisenaire Rods are used, and she held up several of the colorful rods as examples. She told the students, "Some of these rods are long and others are short. Some are fat and others are thin." The children nodded in agreement. "Today we are going to compare the sizes of these rods, using the words *longer* and *shorter*." She then asked the children to return to their desks. She distributed a worksheet with drawings that represented the various sizes of the Cuisenaire Rods:

On each table was a box with some Cuisenaire Rods, and the children began dumping them onto their desks. Mrs. Baxter directed the students to find the sizes of the rods that fit into the diagrams on the worksheet. Most students did this with ease and began playing with the rods, using them to stack and sword fight. The teacher brought the kindergartners back to attention and she asked them to look at their papers with the rods. She then asked which of the rods was the *longer* one and which was the *shorter* one. One of the boys responded by pointing to the longest rod on the paper, "Teacher, this one is *longerest* and this one is *smallerest*." "Okay, let's use the words *longer* and *shorter*." She then held up two rods, one considerably longer than the other. She said, "See, this rod is taller so it is *longer* than the *shorter* one." The child persisted, "Yep, that's what I said. It's bigger." At this point, Mrs. Baxter realized the children were confused. "Okay," she said, "let's just use two rods. Pick any two off your paper and put them like this. She held two different-size rods up next to each other. "Which is *longer* and which is *shorter*?" Some of the children placed their rods like this:

FIGURE 9.4 *Review & Assessment Component of the SIOP® Model: Mrs. Baxter's Lesson*

4	3	2	1	0
27. Comprehensive **review of key vocabulary**		Uneven **review of key vocabulary**		No **review of key vocabulary**
28. Comprehensive **review of key content concepts**		Uneven **review of key content concepts**		No **review of key content concepts**
29. Regular **feedback** provided to students on their output (e.g., language, content, work)		Inconsistent **feedback** provided to students on their output		No **feedback** provided to students on their output
30. **Assessment** of student comprehension and learning of all lesson objectives (e.g., spot-checking, group response) throughout the lesson		**Assessment** of student comprehension and learning of some lesson objectives		No **assessment** of student comprehension and learning of lesson objectives

When Mrs. Baxter asked these children to move the second rod down so one looked "taller" than the other, the children became more confused. She decided at that point that kindergartners were not really ready for Cuisenaire Rods *or* superlatives in English, and they all took an early recess.

One the SIOP® form in Figure 9.4, rate Mrs. Baxter's lesson for each of the Review & Assessment Features.

Discussion of Lessons

27. *Comprehensive Review of Key Vocabulary*

Miss Pham: 2

Mr. Emerson: 4

Mrs. Baxter: 1

In Miss Pham's lesson, she introduced the challenging academic vocabulary by having those students who could already read the words do so for the other children. She also pronounced the words, followed by the children's echo-reading of the words. For the children who are native English speakers already familiar with the words and concepts Miss Pham was presenting, this quick review might have been adequate. However, for English learners and other children unfamiliar with English superlatives (e.g., *taller, tallest*), the very brief introduction was inadequate. Miss Pham did provide familiar, concrete examples with the tomato juice cans and drinking glasses to illustrate the challenging academic vocabulary, yet the only children who had an opportunity to demonstrate their understandings were the ones who clearly understood the concepts. By not providing many more opportunities for students to practice with the concrete examples, Miss Pham had little idea of which children comprehended the vocabulary and which did not. Her lesson received a 2 for this feature.

Mr. Emerson's lesson received a 4 for comprehensive review of vocabulary feature. At the beginning of the lesson, he reviewed the academic vocabulary by going over the language objectives. He reviewed the words *compare, bigger, smaller* from a previous lesson before teaching the new and related words. He provided multiple opportunities for the children to practice using the words, and while they were practicing, he was able to monitor and correct, if needed. Because all students were engaged with every part of the lesson, he had ample opportunities to observe informally which students were having difficulty with pronunciations and usage. Even though many of the kinders could not read the words in the objectives and sentence stems, Mr. Emerson provided practice in speech-to-print match, a very important prereading and vocabulary learning skill. At the end of the lesson, Mr. Emerson reviewed once again the academic vocabulary for the day when he reviewed the language objectives.

Mrs. Baxter's lesson received a 1 for this feature. Unfortunately, she did not believe that kindergarten children were ready to begin using print because many were still non-readers. Therefore, she did not have her objectives, vocabulary words, or directions for the day's activity on the board. She did, however, state the words *longer* and *shorter* for the children. However, the children did not understand why they were "playing" with the Cuisenaire Rods or why it was important to use the words *longer* and *shorter*. Instead of realizing that the children didn't understand what they were supposed to do, stopping, and going back to introduce the lesson objectives and explicitly teach the math lesson's academic language, both the teacher and children eventually gave up.

28. *Comprehensive Review of Key Concepts*

   Miss Pham: 2

   Mr. Emerson: 4

   Mrs. Baxter: 1

Miss Pham's lesson received a 2 for this feature. The worksheet activity, intended for use as an assessment of the children's understandings of the academic language and key concepts of the math lesson, was largely ineffective because, once again, the children who already understood the vocabulary and concepts zipped through it; those who did not understand were able to mimic what the others were doing. In the end, Miss Pham had little idea of whether her English learners and struggling students had made any progress toward mastering the standards that guided her lesson planning. This happens too often when teachers assess responses only from those who volunteer and when their activities, such as the worksheet, do not really provide assessment information about who understood key concepts and who did not.

Mr. Emerson's lesson received a 4 for this feature. As with vocabulary, Mr. Emerson reviewed the content concepts from the previous lesson before beginning with the new lesson. It was essential that the children understand what it means to *compare* (especially in math), so his examples were concrete and meaningful. Now that they understood the fundamentals (*bigger, smaller, taller, shorter*), they could move to the next steps (*heavier, lighter, holds more, holds less*), all of which involved more comparisons. In his lesson, Mr. Emerson carefully developed each level of learning, and he did so by continuing to review prior to moving to the next step. The practice activities, with the whole class, partners, and small groups enabled the teacher to assess on the spot and provide intervention as necessary. By continuing to develop these measurement and geometry concepts in a purposeful and sequential manner, all of Mr. Emerson's students, including his ELs and struggling learners, had the opportunity for success with the content concepts and with English language development.

Mrs. Baxter's lesson received a 1 for this feature. She made two attempts with the Cuisenaire Rods to have the students place their rods in different positions, but because she did not have clear content objectives for the lessons, the students didn't understand the purpose for what they were doing. The Cuisenaire Rods were also new to the children; they represented a novelty and seemed like blocks to play with rather than learning tools. Mrs. Baxter first could have used the rods on an overhead projector to demonstrate precisely what the children were to do with them. She could have said, "Let's *compare* these rods. Notice how this rod is *longer* than this rod. Notice how this rod is *shorter* than this rod. No matter how I place the rods, this one will always be *longer* than this rod. Watch while I move them. Now, let's *compare* them again." If Mrs. Baxter had provided explicit instruction and modeling, the children would have been able to practice with the rods, and she would have had an opportunity to review and assess their understandings.

29. *Regular Feedback Provided Students on Their Output*

Miss Pham: 2

Mr. Emerson: 4

Mrs. Baxter: 1

Miss Pham's lesson received a 2 for this feature because she did attempt to provide feedback to those students who volunteered to come to the table and point to the respective objectives. However, "Very good!" and "Good job!" are comments that are ubiquitous in many classrooms, but they provide very little information to English learners about what the children did to deserve the warm smile and congratulations. Miss Pham could have followed the accolades with specific academic feedback such as, "Good job! You listened carefully for the word *taller* and then you compared the two cans. You saw that one can is definitely *taller* than the other." Holding up the two cans of tomato juice so all students could clearly compare them would have provided even more effective and specific feedback.

Mr. Emerson's lesson received a 4 for this feature because all of his feedback to his students was specific and academic. From the beginning of the lesson, he repeated his students' responses, extending each of them. He let his students know exactly what they had done correctly so they could repeat the behavior at another time. At the end of the lesson, after the children's attainment of the objectives, Mr. Emerson paraphrased the objectives one more time, repeating and reviewing the key vocabulary and content concepts that were the goals for the lesson.

Mrs. Baxter's lesson received a 1 for this feature because she provided little academic feedback to her students. She repeated and corrected one child's incorrect English but because the other students had little opportunity to demonstrate their understandings, other feedback was not provided.

30. *Assessment of Student Comprehension and Learning of All Lesson Objectives*

Miss Pham: 2

Mr. Emerson: 4

Mrs. Baxter: 0

Miss Pham's lesson received a 2 for this feature because her objectives were not made clear to her students, and in reality, Miss Pham may not have been clear about them herself. Had she clearly thought through what her *lesson objectives* were (not just the state standards), she probably would have seen that it was unrealistic to expect her young students, especially the English learners, to be able to master the academic language and key concepts all in one lesson without considerable scaffolding. Each of the vocabulary words and math concepts should have been introduced, practiced, reviewed, and assessed, before she moved on to the other vocabulary and concepts. Additionally, while some of this lesson could have been taught effectively with the whole class, many of the students would have benefitted from differentiated, small-group instruction and practice. "Backwards planning" (thinking ahead of time about what students really need to know and be able to do in order to accomplish this day's objectives), and then assessing and reteaching when students are not understanding, are critical elements of effective SIOP® lessons.

Mr. Emerson's lesson received a 4 for this feature. Throughout the lesson, Mr. Emerson reviewed the progress his students were making toward meeting the objectives. He modeled what he wanted his students to do, he provided students with the opportunity to model with each other, he had his students work with pairs to practice further, and then the students practiced their sentences orally with the entire class. Following the oral practice, the students then wrote sentences by using the sentence starter and filling in the appropriate words (*taller, shorter*), which were listed on the board. Note also that even though he was teaching math concepts, all of his students were expected to read, write, listen, and speak during this lesson, thus developing concurrently math content and English language proficiency.

Mrs. Baxter's lesson received a 0 for this feature. Because she did not have explicit content and language objectives, her lesson was poorly designed and executed. She didn't have a clear idea of what she wanted to teach and what her students should learn. Given the short attention spans of kindergartners and the ease with which they can move off task, and without an understandable purpose for an activity, the children will create their own goals. By the end of the lesson, Mrs. Baxter underestimated both the learning capacity of her children and the potential benefits of manipulatives like Cuisenaire Rods.

Summary

Review and assessment are integrated processes, essential for all students, but they are critical to the success of English learners. Effective SIOP® teachers carefully plan for periodic review and informal formative assessment throughout lessons. This informal assessment is authentic and multidimensional, and includes multiple indicators of students' performance. Effective SIOP® teachers also design appropriate summative evaluation of key vocabulary and content concept objectives at the conclusion of the lesson. Assessment adaptations that provide for effective differentiated instruction include the time ELs need to complete a task; the level of support they need during practice and application; the difficulty level of the task and the process by which ELs can approach it; the type of response or product an EL is allowed to provide; and the degree of active participation. These adaptations do not reduce the level of cognitive involvement of English learners, but rather provide them with the opportunity to demonstrate their knowledge and understanding. Most important, review and assessment guide teaching and reteaching, inform decision making, lead to supportive feedback, and provide for fair and comprehensive judgments about student performance.

Discussion Questions

1. Many teachers introduce key vocabulary at the beginning of the lesson, but often neglect to revisit the new terms systematically throughout the lesson and review them at its conclusion. How can you ensure that a SIOP® lesson's key academic vocabulary is reviewed at the end of each lesson? Describe a variety of ways you would review the terms, as well as the techniques you could put in place to build a vocabulary review into each lesson. Which of the activities introduced in this chapter would you select? Why?

2. Research has shown that gratuitous compliments to students (e.g., "Good job" or "Keep up the good work") do little to motivate them or assist with their learning. Instead, teachers should give regular, substantive feedback to students on their verbal contributions and on their academic work. What are some ways to provide constructive, specific academic feedback to students? Consider class size and English proficiency levels as you answer this question.

3. Reflect on the ideas presented in this chapter, as well as all the other activities you have used to assess student learning of specific lesson objectives. How much time do you think you should allocate for review and assessment during each lesson? What if you discover (as is often the case) that some students are ready to move on, while others need more review and/or reteaching? Using the SIOP® lesson you have been creating, provide specific provisions for students at varying levels. Plan multiple indicators throughout the lesson that will enable you to assess on-the-spot progress toward meeting the lesson's content objectives. Then determine what you will do for (1) independent or partner work for students who are ready to move on and (2) a reteaching or review minilesson for those who need additional assistance from you. This is probably the most challenging aspect of providing differentiated instruction, not only for English learners, but for all students. How will you assess who is ready to move on? How will you assess the students in the reteaching/review group to determine if and when they're ready to move on? What will you do if a few students are still struggling? These are the *big* questions to ask (and answer) when planning for a lesson's review and assessment.

chapter 10

Issues of Reading Development and Special Education for English Learners

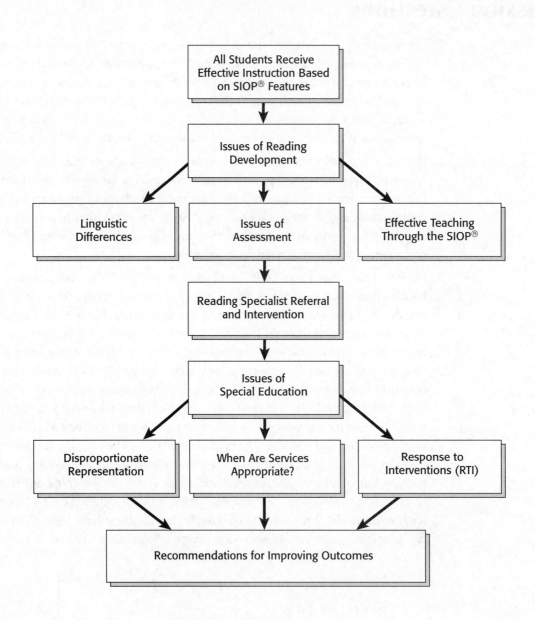

Objectives

After reading, discussing, and engaging in activities related to this chapter, you will be able to meet the following content and language objectives.

Content Objectives

Explain how linguistic differences in home languages and English can affect English learners' reading and writing development.

Describe in-class interventions that content teachers can provide to struggling readers and learners.

Delineate a sequence of steps teachers and other educators can take to ensure appropriate placement of English learners in regular and special education classes.

Language Objectives

Discuss with a group how to plan appropriate instruction for English learners who may have reading and learning difficulties.

Write a lesson plan that develops vocabulary and reading proficiency for English learners who struggle to read and learn.

In our work with teachers and administrators throughout the United States, a persistent question concerns appropriate instruction for English learners who exhibit difficulties with reading and learning. Teachers often feel ill-prepared to provide content instruction for these students because they're not sure whether a student's difficulty is due to a reading problem, a learning disability, lack of schooling, or limited English proficiency. Unfortunately, the result of this confusion has been both under- and overrepresentation of English learners in remedial and special education classes (Gunderson & Siegel, 2005). In this chapter, we discuss issues of assessment, identification, and instruction for children who may be experiencing reading and/or learning problems. It is beyond the scope of this book to provide a comprehensive treatment of this topic. (For a full discussion, see Echevarria and Graves, 2007). Instead, we hope to stimulate your thinking and discussion with colleagues about these issues, especially as they affect English learners. We begin with a discussion of reading development and assessment for English learners and then move on to issues related to special education.

Issues of Reading Development and Assessment for Children

Teachers face many challenges related to the literacy development of their English learners. The task of teaching ELs to read is made difficult in part due to the complexity of learning to read and write in a language one does not understand. However, it is not always possible for children to learn to read first in their primary language. Therefore, teachers must often find ways to help their students learn to read and write in English at the same time they are learning to speak and understand the language. "Children who are particularly likely to have difficulty with learning to read in the primary grades are those who begin school with less prior knowledge and skill in relevant domains, most notably general verbal abilities, the ability to attend to the sounds of language as distinct from its meaning, familiarity with the basic purposes and mechanisms of reading, and letter knowledge. Children . . . with limited proficiency in English . . . are particularly at risk of arriving at school with weaknesses in these areas and hence of falling behind from the onset" (Snow, Burns, & Griffin, 1998, p. 5).

Research suggests that English learners need systematic, high-quality literacy instruction from the start. According to the Report of the National Literacy Panel on Language-Minority Children and Youth (August & Shanahan, 2006), "Instruction that provides substantial coverage in the key components of reading—identified by the National Reading Panel (NICHD, 2000), such as phonemic awareness, phonics, fluency, vocabulary, and text comprehension—has clear benefits for language-minority students . . . but [these components are] . . . not sufficient—for teaching language-minority students to read and write proficiently in English. Oral proficiency in English is critical as well—but student performance suggests that it is often overlooked in instruction" (August & Shanahan, Executive Summary, p. 4, 2006).

To improve ELs' oral proficiency for reading development, the following suggestions are offered:

 Engage students in "picture walks" where ELs and native speakers take turns describing a picture book's illustrations, which they use to predict the story's content before reading (Lenters, 2005).

 Provide repeated readings of highly predictable picture books so that ELs can internalize and then orally produce the patterns, rhyming words, and rhythm.

 Record the reading of stories that can then be listened to, then retold by ELs as they refer to pictures they have drawn about the story's content.

 Using the Language Experience Approach (LEA), record on chart paper English learners' dictated short stories and/or experiences, such as what occurred during a recent field trip. After the dictation, the text is used for repeated readings, discussion, and instruction. LEA is very effective for developing oral language proficiency, vocabulary, and an understanding of English sentence structure. It is recommended that students have their own copies of the dictated texts so they can underline words they recognize each time they orally and silently reread their stories (Stauffer, 1980; Rasinski & Padak, 2004).

English learners may also need explicit instruction in the aspects of English that differ from their native languages, including the phonology, morphology, and syntax of English (Au, Garcia, Goldenberg, & Vogt, 2005; Goldenberg, 2008). Clearly, English learners benefit when they learn to read and write in both their native language and in English (August & Shanahan, 2006; Genesee, Lindholm-Leary, Saunders, & Christian, 2006; Goldenberg, 2008; Lenters, 2005; Slavin & Cheung, 2004).

An additional challenge when teaching immigrant ELs to read in English is determining their reading proficiency. Students who arrive in the United States with well-developed reading skills in their native language have mastered many of the essentials of reading (Tabors & Snow, 2005). They have learned that print carries meaning, and if their home language is alphabetic, they have learned that phonemes (sounds) are represented by graphemes (letters and letter combinations), and that when put together these graphemes create words and meaning (the alphabetic principle). They have also learned the syntax (structure) of their first language, and though they may be challenged by learning English syntax, they can use their knowledge of their first language's structure to make connections with English. Also, once students have learned what it means to strategically comprehend text in their native language, they are able to transfer these cognitive and metacognitive strategies from their home language to English (August, 2006; Gutiérrez, 2004; August & Shanahan, 2006; Genesee, Lindholm-Leary, Saunders, & Christian, 2006; Goldenberg, 2008). English learners whose first language is nonalphabetic (such as Mandarin) will need to learn an alphabetic sound–symbol system in order to speak, read, and write English, but will carry over their understandings of the reading and writing processes to their new language.

Therefore, students who read satisfactorily in their primary language do not have to relearn how to read or write. However, they do need to learn English. With comprehensible input and explicit instruction in the structure of English they have a better chance of transferring their existing reading skills to the reading of English. For example, for students whose primary language is Spanish, there are many cognates that link English vocabulary and spelling with Spanish (estudiar = study; excepción = exception). Using dictionaries in Spanish, English, French, and German as resources helps students make these connections as they explore similarities in the languages (Bear, Templeton, Helman, & Baren, 2003). It is also clear that English learners need to be immersed in print, with many opportunities to read appropriate books, stories, and informational texts, ideally in their home language as well as in English (Krashen, 2003).

In contrast to those ELs who have well-developed literacy skills in their primary language, other students enter American schools with little or no reading instruction in their primary language, or find reading and writing very difficult. These students are often referred to special education programs inappropriately, when other interventions, such as longer exposure to high-quality, scaffolded instruction; more direct, small-group, or individual instruction; or referral to a reading specialist may be more appropriate. It is important for teachers to know whether their English learners can read in their primary language and to be able to ascertain whether difficulty in content subjects may be due to a reading problem or a lack of English proficiency.

Many teachers, rightly, want to know the "reading level" of their students. This information helps the teacher match texts to students. For example, if a fifth-grade student is reading at approximately the third-grade reading level, he is likely to have difficulty comprehending his fifth-grade social studies textbook without instructional modifications and scaffolding. Either the too-difficult text will need to be adapted or the student will require considerable assistance in accessing the content information from the text. It is challenging enough to teach struggling readers who are native English speakers. With English learners, the problem of struggling readers is even more complex. According to Tabors and Snow (2005), "Knowing what a child knows—and in what language—is necessary before any informed placement or program decisions can be made. Often, however, assessment—if it occurs at all—only occurs in English, providing no information about possible early literacy strengths that have been developed in the child's first language" (p. 263).

Classroom teachers and reading specialists use a variety of assessments to determine their students' reading proficiency. However, commonly used assessments that yield a particular reading level (such as fourth grade) may be inappropriate for English learners (Jiménez, 2004). For example, a common diagnostic instrument for assessing students' fluency and comprehension is an informal reading inventory (IRI). During this assessment, a student reads silently or orally a series of increasingly difficult, leveled passages. The teacher or reading specialist marks reading errors, asks comprehension questions, and, based on a student's reading proficiency, determines approximate *independent, instructional,* and *frustration* reading levels.

Think of your own reading. If you read for pleasure and enjoy lying in a hammock with a favorite book during the summer, you'll most likely select an independent-level text that doesn't require you to look up the meaning of words, take notes, or work very hard while reading. However, if you're taking a graduate course, your textbook should be at your instructional level. You expect to have assistance from your professor, and after a lecture or class discussion on the topic, the text is more accessible for you. You may experience frustration-level reading when you read detailed and complex directions that accompany a new computer, confusing income tax forms, or a text on a subject for which you have very little knowledge or experience.

What we know is that it is futile to assign any students, native English speakers and English learners alike, text that is written at their frustration level (Snow, Burns, & Griffin, 1998). Instead, we need to select texts that are written at the student's instructional level, if possible, and that account for children's different experiential bases (Goldenberg, 2008), and then provide additional assistance so that the text becomes accessible. If this level and type of text isn't available, then we must adapt the grade-level text through rewriting, providing a detailed study guide, highlighting the key concepts, or providing detailed marginal notes. Without these, the instructional- and frustration-level texts will be largely inaccessible, especially for English learners.

It's important to remember that successful reading of any text is also dependent on a number of other variables, including familiarity with the topic being read, vocabulary knowledge, the flexible use of a variety of reading skills and strategies, motivation, and purpose-setting. For students who are reading in their native language, these variables are relatively easy to assess, and the selection of appropriate text materials can be made with a reasonable amount of confidence. However, many of our usual battery of reading assessments may not yield reliable results for English learners, and selection of appropriate texts is considerably more difficult. A student who is assessed at grade level in his native language may be assessed as reading at a considerably lower level in English. Using results from an IRI (or a standardized achievement test printed in English) in English might suggest that the child has a serious reading problem. However, if he doesn't have difficulty reading in his native language, it's unlikely he'll have a serious reading problem in his new language. Likewise, if the student has a reading problem in his first language, he may very well have difficulty reading in English.

So how do we determine whether a student's academic difficulties are due to a reading problem or English proficiency? First, we need to recognize that the phonology of a student's native language may differ substantially from that of English. Although we may teach phonics explicitly and effectively, some ELs may not hear or be able to reproduce the sounds of English because these sounds do not exist in their primary language. The consonant sounds may be considerably different, the number of vowels may vary, and such things as vowel combinations, commonly found in English (*ea, ie, oa*), may be nonexistent in the students' home languages (such as Spanish).

As an example, consider Tables 10.1 and 10.2 (Au, Garcia, Goldenberg, & Vogt, 2005). These represent just a few of the differences in consonants and vowels in English that may give speakers of other languages difficulty.

It's not just the sound system (the phonemes) that can cause difficulty for English learners. Because of English orthography (the spelling system), some ELs may have difficulty learning to read and write the language. Orthographies of various languages are described in terms of whether they are *transparent* with highly regular words that are easy to decode (such as Spanish and Italian), or they are *deep* or *opaque*, with correspondences between letters and sounds that are much less direct (such as French and English). A language like German

TABLE 10.1   *Table of Selected Consonant Sounds*

Key:

1 = Often a problem
2 = May be a problem at beginning of words
3 = May be a problem at the end of words

Consonant Sound	*Arabic*	*Chinese*	*Hmong*	*Khmer*	*Russian*	*Spanish*	*Vietnamese*
/b/		2	1		3	3	3
/ch/							1
/d/		2			3	3	3
/g/	1	2	1	1	3	3	3
/j/			1	1		1	1
/k/					2	2	2
/p/	1				2	2	2
/sh/				1		1	1
/t/					2	2	2
/th/	1			1	1		1
/th/	1	1		1	1	1	1
/v/	1	1				1	3
/z/		1		1		1	1

Adapted from Au, Garcia, Goldenberg, & Vogt, 2005, pp. R5–R6.

TABLE 10.2 *Vowel Sounds*

Key:	
Language	*Features*
Arabic	8 vowels and diphthongs (compared to 20 in English) Possible confusion: short vowels
Chinese	Fewer vowel sounds in Chinese than English Chinese is a tonal language. Each syllable pronounced with a particular tone that gives it its meaning.
Hmong	6 pure vowels and 7 diphthongs Hmong is a tonal language. Each syllable pronounced with a particular tone that gives it its meaning.
Khmer	16 vowels and 11 diphthongs Possible confusion: Short vowels that don't exist in Khmer (as in *bat, bet, bit*)
Russian	No diphthongs in Russian Possible confusion: Difficulty with /ûr/ after /w/ as in *work, word*; short vowels, such as short ă and ĕ
Spanish	5 pure vowel sounds and 5 diphthongs Possible confusion: Sounds of long ē, long ō (as in *pool*); short *oo* (as in *pull*)
Vietnamese	Complex vowel system with 11 pure vowels and many more diphthongs and triphthongs Possible confusion: May simplify long vowels in English; variations in the length of vowels in English may be confusing because in English they don't carry a difference in meaning

Adapted from Au, Garcia, Goldenberg, & Vogt, 2005, p. R12.

is considered to be *semitransparent* because its orthography lies somewhere between deep and transparent (Bear, Templeton, Helman, & Baren, 2003). The point is that some students who have a primary language that is transparent (such as Spanish) may have a difficult time learning a language that is deep (such as English). However, in some studies that compare orthographic knowledge, bilingual learners have been found to negotiate satisfactorily between their languages and literacies (Tolchinsky & Teberosky, 1998). Rather than being confused by orthographic differences, these students can apply what they know about the structure of their primary language to the language they are learning.

So what do we do about those who *are* confused, and despite appropriate instruction in English, reading, and language arts, are not making satisfactory progress? First, it's important to examine the students' present instructional context. The following questions might guide this inquiry:

1. What evidence do you have that a particular student is having difficulty with reading?

2. Do you have any evidence that this student has difficulty reading in his or her home language? If not, how might you gather some? If you are not fluent in the student's language, is there another student who is? Is there a community liaison or family member who can provide information about the student's L1 literacy development?

3. If your evidence points to a reading problem, what have you and other teachers done to accommodate the student's needs?

   a. Are the student's teachers adapting content and texts to provide greater accessibility (see Chapter 2)?

b. Are the teachers using instructional techniques that make the content and expectations understandable for English learners (see Chapter 4)?

c. Are the student's teachers incorporating cognitive and metacognitive strategy instruction in the language arts and content subjects (see Chapter 5)?

d. Are the student's teachers scaffolding instruction through flexible grouping (see Chapters 5 and 6)?

e. Are the student's teachers providing multiple opportunities for practice and application of key content and language concepts (see Chapter 7)?

f. Are the student's teachers using effective assessment to determine what the student knows and can do related to content and language objectives, and to plan subsequent reteaching lessons (see Chapter 9)?

At this point, we hope you're getting the idea that appropriate instruction for this student involves all of the components of the SIOP® Model: those listed above as well as appropriate pacing, meaningful activities, sufficient wait time, and so forth. Certainly, a child with reading problems will benefit from the effective practices advocated in the SIOP® Model, while he or she receives an appropriate intervention for the reading problems.

Will this type of instruction overcome a serious reading problem? Probably not, although recent research on effective literacy instruction for young English learners is consistent with the features of the SIOP® Model (Graves, Gersten, & Haager, 2004). But here's the key: If you (and your colleagues) have done all you can to provide effective English language development and content instruction using the SIOP® Model and a student is still struggling with reading, it is appropriate and important that the student be referred to a reading specialist. The reading specialist can do a thorough, diagnostic assessment and implement an intervention designed for the student's literacy needs. If the student is still struggling with school after the intensive intervention, then further intervention and referral to special education might be warranted (Haager, Dimino, & Windmueller, 2007).

Issues Related to Special Education

The previous discussion of reading is closely related to any discussion of special education because approximately 80 percent of referrals to special education are for reading problems. It is critically important that school personnel provide the support and assistance necessary when English learners exhibit learning difficulties and exhaust every option before considering referral to special education (see the discussion of response to intervention that follows). There has been a long history of disproportionate representation of minority students in special education, especially those from low socioeconomic backgrounds (Artiles, 1998; Dunn, 1968; Lee, 2006; Trent, Kea, & Oh, 2008). A number of factors may contribute to the disproportionate number of minority students referred to and placed in special education.

One factor is that teachers and administrators in general education often fail to provide effective instruction in reading and math—content areas basic to learning in other areas—and also fail to manage their classrooms effectively (Orfield, Losen, & Edley, 2001). This is more often the case in urban schools where students have the greatest needs. When teachers feel unprepared to work with students who struggle academically or who exhibit inappropriate classroom behaviors, referral to special education is often the first option to which they turn.

Another factor may be a mismatch between minority-learner characteristics and the materials and teaching methods presented in school, which contributes to underachievement among this group of students (Powers, 2001; Vogt & Shearer, 2007). Much of what students understand and are able to do in school is based on their culture and background, and most academic tasks and curricula reflect middle-class values and experiences (see Chapter 3 for more discussion). Reliance on paper-and-pencil tasks, independent reading of dense text in upper grades, and information presented orally are only some of the types of academic tasks that create difficulties for English learners. Also, students who are culturally and linguistically diverse may not have the requisite background knowledge and experience to perform well academically, nor do they have behaviors that are consistent with the values of school. In general, students achieve better educational outcomes if they have been reared in a culture that has expectations and patterns of behaviors that are consistent with those of the school (Comer, 1984). If that is not the case, then instruction such as that characterized in the SIOP® Model provides the best opportunity for English learners to participate successfully in the academic program of school.

Underachievement among minority youth, which often leads to special education referral and placement, may also be explained by outside factors such as the effects of poverty (Smith, 2006), low teacher expectations (Callahan, 2006), poor study habits and poor time management (Ford, 1998), cultural differences in students' and teachers' behavioral expectations (Neal, McCray, Webb-Johnson, & Bridgest, 2003; Patton & Townsend, 1999), and language differences (Cummins, 1984; Echevarria & Graves, 2007; Genesee, 1994). Obviously, all the complexities of underachievement cannot be ameliorated with good instruction alone; however, quality of instruction is a variable that makes a difference, and it is something that is under the control of school personnel.

It should be mentioned that English learners are also sometimes underreferred for special education services for many of these same reasons: (1) teachers may be unsure whether to refer ELs to special education, (2) low expectations allow ELs to languish without services, or (3) district policies require an arbitrary amount of time to pass before students can be referred for the services they need.

Teachers and administrators must understand the critical relationship between quality of instruction and student performance. For a complete discussion of these issues, see Echevarria and Graves, 2007.

Special Education Services: When Are They Appropriate?

Disproportionate representation of minority students in special education is most pronounced among the mild and moderate disability categories, such as learning disabilities and speech and language disorders. For example, more than 17 percent of Hispanic students are labeled as learning disabled, although they account for only about 12 to 13 percent of the population, while 61 percent of white students have the LD label, but they make up 75 percent of the population (Office of Special Education Programs, 2002).

The characteristics of students in these categories are not as easily identifiable as they are in students with more significant disabilities and therefore require subjective judgment. Recent research indicates that it is very difficult for school personnel to distinguish between the challenges associated with acquiring a second language and a language-based

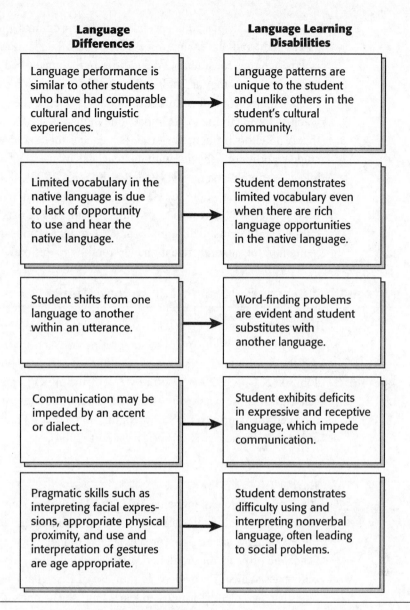

Language Differences	Language Learning Disabilities
Language performance is similar to other students who have had comparable cultural and linguistic experiences.	Language patterns are unique to the student and unlike others in the student's cultural community.
Limited vocabulary in the native language is due to lack of opportunity to use and hear the native language.	Student demonstrates limited vocabulary even when there are rich language opportunities in the native language.
Student shifts from one language to another within an utterance.	Word-finding problems are evident and student substitutes with another language.
Communication may be impeded by an accent or dialect.	Student exhibits deficits in expressive and receptive language, which impede communication.
Pragmatic skills such as interpreting facial expressions, appropriate physical proximity, and use and interpretation of gestures are age appropriate.	Student demonstrates difficulty using and interpreting nonverbal language, often leading to social problems.

FIGURE 10.1 *Causes of Confusion in Assessing Students with Language Differences and/or Language Learning Disabilities*

learning disability (Klinger & Harry, 2006; Lesaux & Geva, 2006). The distinctions can be fairly subtle, as you can see in Figure 10.1. The subjectivity of identification is exacerbated because mild to moderate disabilities do not have a clear biological cause, prompting some to argue that the disabilities themselves are socially constructed (Barnes, Mercer, & Shakespeare, 1999). What is considered "normal" is influenced by a number of factors, including culture, age, community practice, point in history, and school expectations. The labels associated with mild disabilities are assigned arbitrarily and are subject to extreme variability in identification rates. American Indians/Alaskan Native children are about one and a half times more likely to be identified as having learning disabilities than the rest of the population, while Asian/Pacific Islanders are much less likely to receive an LD label (Office of Special Education Services Programs, 2002).

All students placed in special education programs have gone through a referral, assessment, and placement process. The special education process is initiated once a child is experiencing considerable difficulties in the general education program—academic, behavioral, or both. For English learners, low English language proficiency, gaps in educational experience, and cultural differences influence the referral process. The reality is that teachers have a tremendous impact on who is referred and who is not. Research indicates that two factors influence referral: (1) teacher tolerance and (2) the interaction of perceived student ability or behavior with the teacher's own expectations and approach to instruction and classroom management (Podell & Soodak, 1993). Subjectivity is part of the evaluation process including whom to test, what test to use, when to use alternative assessments, and how to interpret the results (Losen & Orfield, 2002). So if teachers have an appreciation of cultural and linguistic differences and the modifications those differences require, intervention in the general education classroom is more likely.

Assisting Struggling Learners: Response to Intervention

Response to intervention (RTI) is a systematic schoolwide process for addressing the needs of struggling learners by integrating instruction, intervention, and assessment, which can ultimately result in higher student achievement (Brown & Doolittle, 2008; Johnson & Smith, 2008). Before we describe an RTI approach in detail, there are some related issues we want you to consider, such as the importance of early intervention and the need for improved teacher preparation, so that RTI—or any approach—can work effectively (Echevarria, Powers, & Elliott, 2004).

Earlier Intervention

Children who are experiencing difficulties require systematic interventions to enable them to participate fully in the academic and social opportunities offered by school. Currently, before students are eligible for specialized support services, they must exhibit significant academic or behavior problems. Why should children have to establish a pattern of failure before assistance is provided? In the case of ELs, many teachers delay referral so that students have ample opportunity to learn English (Limbos & Geva, 2002).

All children should be screened for potential reading problems because early identification and intervention reduces problems that are exacerbated by time and continued failure. Screening tools that identify gaps in prereading skills provide the kind of early identification and intervention students need.

Better Training

Professional preparation programs for all school personnel should address effective instruction for English learners—general education, special education, reading specialists, school psychologists, and administrators. Preparing general education and special education personnel to work together effectively with English learners begins at the preservice level. Teacher preparation programs (general and special education) that address issues of diversity, social equity, second language acquisition, culturally relevant instruction methods, and empirically supported interventions contribute to a teaching force that implements meaningful and appropriate instruction for students with differing abilities (Echevarria & Graves, 2007).

However, in the past decade, there has not been considerable progress in incorporating into preservice general education or special education programs practices for addressing diverse learners. There have been numerous calls for change but few actual changes (Trent et al., 2008). Working effectively with diverse populations should be a priority for teacher preparation programs, especially given demographic trends. In many ways, a teacher is the key to a child's success or failure. Students' interactions with their teacher can be either disabling or empowering, and the quality of teacher–student interaction has a significant impact on academic performance and classroom behavior (Kea & Utley, 1998). In a recent study on teacher–student interaction (Yoon, 2008), it was found that when teachers treat English learners with respect and have positive interactions with them, English-speaking peers follow suit. In addition, ELs participate in class to a greater extent and learning opportunities are enhanced in such settings.

Effective SIOP® teachers reflect on their practice and are mindful of the interaction between the learner and the instructional setting, materials, and teaching methods, and make adjustments as needed to facilitate learning. The importance of context to learning cannot be overstated; characteristics of the classroom and school can increase the risk for academic and behavioral problems. Teachers need training in understanding the interaction between learning and context, avoiding the deficit model that views academic and behavior problems as a within-child problem. We have empirical and anecdotal evidence that many academic and behavioral difficulties can be attributed to the impact of the instructional setting (teacher, materials, methods) on the student, rather than some inherent problem of the learner.

In fact, in our observation of classrooms, it seems that the best option for struggling students may be gifted classes. In those classes, teachers tend to capitalize on students' strengths; allow students time to interact and discuss ideas; and teach in creative, stimulating ways. Too many classes for low-performing students are devoid of an excitement for learning, and teachers seem to be simply trying to keep students in their seats.

Search for Interventions Rather Than Disabilities

When young English learners struggle in school, they are referred to a site-based team that considers the reason for the referral and makes recommendations for interventions to be implemented in the general education program (Ortiz, 2002; Rinaldi & Samson, 2008). A site-based team approach offers the best way to address problems the student is experiencing because they know the context of the school and have the potential to provide appropriate, effective instructional interventions for English learners, especially when the membership of the team is diverse, and includes parents and members who are knowledgeable about issues related to diverse learners (Klinger & Harry, 2006). Site-based intervention teams have been shown to decrease referral and special education placement (Fuchs, Fuchs, & Bahr, 1990; Ysseldyke & Marston, 1999), and even reduce disproportionate referrals of minority students to special education (Powers, 2001). Too often, when students struggle, the focus is on naming the student's problem rather than searching for solutions.

Response to intervention (RtI) is a multi-tiered service delivery model that is founded on the principle that *all children can learn*. As you can see in Figure 10.2, all students receive high-quality core instruction in general education, while some receive additional services for as long as there is evidence that they need those services. The

• Multidisciplinary team evaluates data
• May include additional interventions and/or special education assessment
- -
• Small group instruction outside general ed classroom
• 30–50 min daily; 8–36 weeks
• Weekly progress monitoring and adjustments
• Taught at students instructional level
- -
• Evidence-based practices
• Universal screening of all children
• Progress monitoring of oral language and academic language proficiency

Tier 3
Specialized Services
"Intensive Interventions"
Few
5–8%

Tier 2
Specific Interventions
"Strategic Instruction"
Some
10–20%

Tier 1
Effective Instruction Based on SIOP® Features
"Core Curriculum"
All
100%

FIGURE 10.2 *Response to Intervention for ELs*

Adapted from Echevarria & Graves (2007). *Sheltered Content Instruction*: *Teaching English Language Learners with Diverse Abilities, Third Edition.*

focus is on finding ways to change instruction (or student behaviors) so the learner can be successful, beginning in the general education classroom, using evidence-based practices that work for the individual child. RtI involves documenting a change in behavior or performance as a result of intervention and assessments. In the IDEA 2004 reauthorization (Individuals with Disabilities Education Act), RtI was approved as an option for schools to use, and resources may be allocated from a number of sources such as Title I and special education funds (Tilly, 2006).

Tier One represents general education. All students should receive high-quality, appropriate instruction and progress monitoring in their general education classroom. For English learners, that would be the type of instructional practices featured in the SIOP®. Students in Tier One who are not keeping up may need extra support, such as some of the supplemental interventions listed below. For many students, the extra attention will be enough to catch them up. However, a subset of students (approximately 10–20 percent) who have received effective instruction will require more intensive interventions to meet their learning needs (Tier Two). Interventions should, to the extent possible, be scientifically validated through research. Some examples include:

● specialized materials
● small-group or individualized instruction
● family involvement
● primary language support
● explicit teaching of learning strategies for students who need assistance in "learning how to learn"
● more intensive English language development
● modification of assignments

- counseling services
- reading specialist services
- classroom-based reading interventions
- Saturday school or after-school sessions

The difference between Tier One and Tier Two is the individualized nature of the instruction, level of intensity of the intervention, and frequency of assessments. Based on progress monitoring, the team may find some students (approximately 5–8 percent) who have had systematic, effective interventions yet do not respond (Leafstedt, Richards, & Gerber, 2004; Rinaldi & Samson, 2008). These students are eligible for Tier Three, which may include special education services. Few students would be in this category, and this consideration is based on a student's documented insufficient response to general education and Tier Two interventions and the team's informed determination that an additional level of support is needed to increase achievement.

One of the main advantages of an RtI model is its emphasis on ensuring appropriate learning opportunities for all children, beginning in the general education classroom. All students receive instruction in the core curriculum, even those who receive additional services. Using research-based interventions in an RtI model with ELs for prevention instruction has been shown to improve the early literacy skills and overall reading outcomes for these children (Linan-Thompson, Cirino, & Vaughn, 2007). By focusing on interventions rather than disability, more students' needs will be met in the least restrictive environment, and decisions about student placement will be based on documented evidence over time. The result should be that fewer children from diverse backgrounds will be inappropriately identified as disabled; for those who require special education services, their IEPs will include instructional strategies and modifications that are tailored to their demonstrated needs (Echevarria, Powers, & Elliott, 2004).

Students with Special Needs

Many of the features of the SIOP® are effective for students with learning differences. In a study with middle school students with learning disabilities, students made significant growth in writing when teachers used the SIOP® Model (Echevarria, 1998). However, it is also important to keep in mind the unique individual characteristics of students with learning and behavior problems.

- Focus students' attention by limiting the clutter and excessive visual stimuli in the classroom. While we advocate word walls and other visuals to assist students in information recall and vocabulary development, they must be used with discretion. Students with special needs are often distracted by artwork and projects hanging around the room.
- Repetition is essential. Students will retain more information if it is repeated and reviewed frequently. Poor memory is often a characteristic of students with special needs, especially memory that is associated with symbols, (e.g., letters and numbers).
- Allow extra time for students to process information. Students with learning differences are often just processing a question by the time the answer is given. Teachers

may use strategies such as asking a question, letting the student know he or she will be asked for the answer, then coming back to the student.

- Assessment should be scaffolded to measure understanding. Students' disabilities can interfere with their demonstration of knowledge and understanding. These students may have difficulty with vocabulary, expressing their ideas, or using language adequately. Rather than asking a student to write an explanation of a concept, have him list the features of the concept or label a graphic organizer that is provided, ask the student to complete an outline rather than generate a summary or essay, or select examples from a list provided rather than producing examples.

- Differentiate the curriculum to students' needs, such as modifying the number of items the learner completes, increasing the amount of personal assistance, providing different materials to meet a learner's individual needs, or allotting a different amount of time for learning, task completion, or testing.

- Be sensitive to frustration levels. Students with special needs often have a lower frustration threshold than typical learners, which may result in outbursts or giving up easily. A structured learning environment, scaffolded instruction, and opportunities to experience success help alleviate frustration.

All of these suggestions for assisting children with learning and behavior problems have commonalities: They must be used consistently, data are used to monitor student learning, student well-being is the focus, and there is a commitment to enhancing learning for all students.

Summary

One of the most critical issues facing educators is delivering an instructional program appropriate for *all* students in their classes: those with limited English proficiency, those who excel academically, those who are performing at grade level, those with low academic levels, those who find reading difficult, those who have experienced persistent failure, those who work hard but continue to struggle academically, and those with problematic behaviors.

This chapter provided an overview of issues related to reading and special education, including how linguistic differences in home languages and English may cause English learners difficulty with literacy development. When classroom teachers implement the features of the SIOP® Model, many students with reading and learning difficulties find success. Very often, students' academic difficulties have more to do with the curriculum, teaching methods, and classroom setting than with any deficit in the child. That said, some students will still struggle with reading and learning despite best practices in teaching. We recommend the kinds of interventions used in a tiered service delivery model so that appropriate supports are afforded struggling students. Most important, we want to avoid labeling students with reading problems or disabilities and instead provide them with the most appropriate and effective instructional context possible.

Discussion Questions

1. Select an English learner in your class who is having difficulty with reading and/or content learning. Reread the questions in this chapter on pages 202–203. Begin with the first question: What evidence do you have that a particular student is having

difficulty with reading? Try to provide answers to the other questions as they relate to your identified student. If questions 3.a–e are answered negatively, what are the implications for your instruction of this student, and for the other teachers who work with him or her? Now examine Figure 10.1. From your work with this student, using your best guess as well as any assessment findings you have—including a measure of English language proficiency that you may need to obtain from your school's ESL specialist—see if any of the descriptions of Language Differences and/or Language Learning Disabilities match your student. If he or she is very young (four to seven), you might want to consider this: Snow, Burns, and Griffin (1998) recommend that very young English learners who haven't learned to read in their native language should learn to speak English first before they are taught to read in English. For older English learners, what are some possible next steps for meeting students' language, literacy, and academic needs?

2. Analyze your school and/or district's assessment program in reading and language arts. Are reading specialists available to help with the assessment and instruction of students with reading problems? If not, who has the expertise for helping teachers and administrators design an effective assessment program in literacy? What happens to teachers' district-required literacy assessment results? Are they used for designing appropriate instruction for students, including English learners? Are professional development programs in place to assist teachers and administrators in increasing their knowledge and skills in teaching reading? These are critical questions to consider when planning literacy instruction for English learners (and all students, for that matter), and they should be asked when designing schoolwide and district inservice and professional development.

3. In this chapter we have discussed some of the reasons why minority children, including many English learners, are over- and underrepresented in special education. For your own school or district, determine the number (percent) of English learners who are designated as receiving special education services (this information should be available at your district office). Are there disproportionate numbers of ELs in special education compared to their percent of the population? How can RtI help ensure that English learners are receiving an appropriate education and that proper services are offered as needed?

4. How would you respond to a teacher who says, "Well, if I follow the SIOP® Model and make sure my ELs are able to access content using these activities, techniques, and approaches, my on-level kids and native English speakers will be bored." Do you agree with this statement? Why or why not? How can teachers with only a few English learners in their classrooms organize instruction so that all students' needs are met? Which, if any, of the activities, methods, or SIOP® features in this book are inappropriate for some students, such as accelerated learners? Or are all of these instructional features appropriate for all students? Obviously, we believe that all students benefit from the instruction that is integral to the SIOP® Model. But from our experience, some teachers think otherwise. Prepare a response to these teachers' concerns.

Effective Use of the SIOP® Protocol

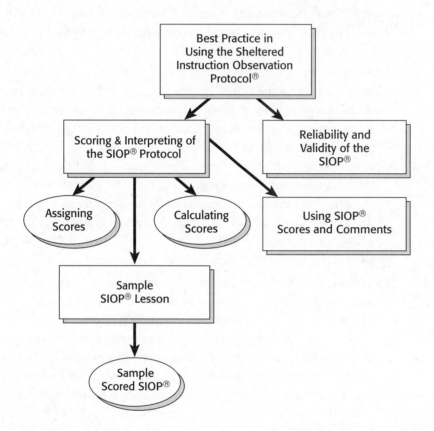

Objectives

After reading, discussing, and engaging in activities related to this chapter, you will be able to meet the following content and language objectives.

Content Objectives

Examine how all the SIOP® features fit into one lesson plan.

Use the Sheltered Instruction Observation Protocol to score and assess a teacher's lesson.

Language Objectives

Discuss SIOP® scores as a postobservation conference with the teacher whose lesson was rated.

Explain the value of observing and rating teachers over time on the SIOP®.

Since its inception, the SIOP® Model has been used as a lesson planning and instructional delivery system for teaching ELs effectively. Sample lesson plan formats can be found in Chapter 2, Appendix B, and at *www.siopinstitute.net.*

The SIOP® protocol, our observation instrument, has also been useful to educators in a number of ways. The SIOP® Model and protocol have been used in school districts and universities around the country since the 1990s with measurable success. We have interviewed many school personnel who have told us their stories of SIOP® implementation (Echevarria, Short, & Vogt, 2008). From their stories we suggest the following uses of the SIOP® protocol.

Best Practice in Using the SIOP® Protocol

Initially we developed the SIOP® protocol because we found that school personnel and researchers wanted and needed an objective measure of high-quality sheltered instruction for ELs. Over time, uses of the SIOP® protocol have expanded.

The SIOP® protocol provides a tool for gauging the quality of teaching. Qualitative and quantitative information written on the protocol documents lesson effectiveness and shows areas that need improvement. This information may be used by teachers, administrators, university faculty, and researchers.

Teachers find the SIOP® protocol useful for improving their own practice through self-reflection and/or peer coaching. Some schools reported that their teachers regularly used the protocol to reflect on their lessons, completing the protocol after they taught a specific lesson. More effective is the practice of videotaping lessons and scoring the lessons on their various SIOP® features. The objectivity the camera provides is valuable to teachers in recognizing their areas of strength and areas that need attention.

Some elementary schools used peer coaches to assist teachers in SIOP® implementation. In one school district, a coach modeled a SIOP® lesson for a group of three to five peers. Using the SIOP® protocol with the rating numbers removed, the group debriefed the lesson and discussed the components of the SIOP®. The focus of the debriefing and discussion was around the comments written on the protocol. Participants wrote what they saw the coach do and described it on the protocol under each corresponding feature. At the conclusion of the session, one of the teachers in the group volunteered to model a lesson during the following quarter (two-month period). Because of the nonevaluative nature of the feedback, it wasn't difficult to get teachers to volunteer. The coach assisted the teacher volunteer in planning the lesson that was later modeled for the group. Feedback from the group was always limited to positive comments and a discussion of how the lesson matched SIOP® features. After each teacher in the group had a turn in modeling a SIOP® lesson for the group, the individuals then became coaches for another small group of teachers. In this way, a large number of teachers learned and practiced using the SIOP® Model and had the opportunity to understand the model deeply (Echevarria, Short, & Vogt, 2008).

A number of sources have reported that schoolwide use of the SIOP® Model and protocol provides a common language and conceptual framework from which to work and develop a community of practice. School site administrators commented that the features of the SIOP® bring together in one place many of the ideas and techniques staff have learned through district professional development efforts. For example, a school staff may have received inservice training in cooperative learning, Thinking Maps, or differentiated instruction, but teachers struggle with how to incorporate these varied ideas into their daily teaching practice. The SIOP® Model provides a framework for systematically addressing and incorporating a variety of techniques into one's teaching practice.

The SIOP® protocol is useful for administrators because it provides them with a way of understanding instruction for ELs. Administrators typically do not have the same opportunity to learn about effective instruction for ELs as the teachers on their staff (Short, Vogt, & Echevarria 2008). Yet the administrator is responsible for observing and providing feedback to teaching personnel. The SIOP® protocol gives administrators a means for providing clear, concrete feedback to the teachers they observe. The format allows for rating of lessons but, more important, has space for writing comments that will be constructive for improving instruction for English learners.

University faculty have also found the SIOP® Model and protocol to be useful in courses that specifically address the needs of English learners. Faculty who supervise field experience find that the SIOP® protocol assists in providing concrete examples of techniques necessary for making instruction comprehensible for English learners. Feedback on the rating and comments sections of the instrument assists student teachers in their professional development.

Finally, the SIOP® protocol is a tool researchers can use to determine the extent to which SIOP® instruction is implemented in a given classroom. It can also be used to measure consistency and fidelity of implementation.

Scoring and Interpreting the SIOP® Protocol

The heading on the first page of the SIOP® protocol is fairly self-explanatory (see Figure 11.1). It is intended to provide a context for the lesson being observed. There is space for the observer's name and the date of the observation. Other information, such as the teacher's name, school, grade of the class being observed, ESL level of the students, and the academic content area, is also included. We recognize that an observation at one point in time does not always accurately represent the teacher's implementation of SIOP® strategies and techniques. Therefore, there is a place for the observer to indicate if the lesson is part of a multiday unit or is a single-day lesson.

In using the SIOP® protocol, we have found that it is most useful to videotape a lesson and analyze it later. Teachers, supervisors, and researchers alike have found this to be an effective way of recording and measuring teachers' growth over time. The tape number may be written on the heading to indicate its corresponding lesson.

Finally, there is a box for the total score the teacher received on the SIOP®. It is most useful to represent a teacher's score as a percentage because NA (not applicable) affects a total score number (see the next section for an explanation of scoring).

When scoring a lesson is appropriate, an observer may assign scores in a number of ways: (1) during the observation itself, as individual features are recognized; (2) after the observation, as the observer reflects on the entire lesson, referring to observational field notes; or (3) after the observation while watching a videotape of the lesson. The third option is often useful so that the teacher and observer are able to share the same point of reference when discussing the lesson.

It is important to stress that not all features on the SIOP® will be present in every lesson. However, some features, such as items under Preparation, Comprehensible Input, Interaction, and Review/Assessment, are essential for each lesson. Over the course of time (several lessons, a week), all features should be represented in one's teaching.

Assigning Scores

An observer determines the level of SIOP® implementation, guided by the scenario descriptions in this book. Each chapter's scenarios were designed to show a clear example for each feature, with scores ranging from 4 to 0. The SIOP® protocol provides a five-point scale as well as space for qualitative data. It is recommended that the observer use the "Comments" section to record examples of the presence or absence of each feature. That way, both the observer and the teacher have specific information, besides a score,

FIGURE 11.1 *SIOP® Heading*

The Sheltered Instruction Observation Protocol (SIOP®) (Echevarria, Vogt, & Short, 2000; 2004; 2008)	Observer(s): _____ Teacher: _____ Date: _____ School: _____ Grade: _____ Class/Topic: _____ ESL Level: _____ Lesson: Multiday Single-day *(circle one)*

Total Points Possible: 120 (Subtract 4 points for each NA given) _____

Total Points Earned: _____   Percentage Score: _____

Directions: Circle the number that best reflects what you observe in a sheltered lesson. You may give a score from 0–4 (or NA on selected items). Cite under "Comments" specific examples of the behaviors observed.

to use in their postlesson discussion. More information may be added to the Comments section during review of the SIOP®, documenting the content of the discussion for future reference, which is particularly useful as subsequent lessons are planned. In any case, sufficient notes with examples of how the feature was addressed should be included to provide concrete feedback with each score.

Naturally, there is an element of subjectivity to interpreting the features and assigning scores. Observers must be consistent in their scoring. For example, one person may think that for Feature #3 (Content concepts appropriate for age and educational background level of students), only grade-level materials are appropriate, while another observer may feel that the same content found in materials for lower grade levels can be used because of the students' low reading levels or because students have interrupted educational backgrounds. In either case, observers must be consistent in their interpretation and scoring across settings.

We suggest that, to assist in more accurate scoring, the observer ask the teacher for a copy of the lesson plan in advance of observing the class. Ideally, the teacher and observer would meet for a preobservation conference to discuss the lesson plan and provide the observer with background about the lesson. In this way, the observer is better able to score the lesson, especially the Preparation section, and NA items.

Not Applicable (NA) Category

The Not Applicable (NA) scoring option is important because it distinguishes a feature that is "not applicable" to the observed lesson from a score of "0," which indicates that the feature should have been present but was not. For example, Mr. Leung taught a five-day unit on the solar system. During the first few lessons of the unit, Mr. Leung concentrated on making the rather dense information accessible to his students. He adapted the text to make it understandable for them and provided ample opportunities for students to use strategies. On the final day of the unit, an observer was present. Mr. Leung wrapped up the unit by having the students complete an enjoyable hands-on activity wherein they applied the concepts they had learned. It was obvious that the students had learned the content and were able to use it in the activity. However, because of the nature of that particular lesson, there was no observed adaptation of content (Feature #5). Mr. Leung was not penalized by receiving a score of "0" because the lesson did not lend itself to that item and because Mr. Leung had covered that item on another day. A score of NA would be correct in this case.

In the case of Mrs. Nash, however, it would be appropriate to score this feature as "0." Mrs. Nash also taught a unit on the solar system. On the first day of the unit, she showed a video about the solar system and had a brief oral discussion following the movie. The next day an observer was present as she read from the text and then had students answer chapter questions. There was no evidence that any of the content had been adapted to the variety of student proficiency levels in her class. In fact, many students appeared to be confused as they tried to answer questions based on readings from the grade-level textbook.

The distinction between a "0" and "NA" is an important one because a score of "0" adversely affects the overall score for the lesson, while an "NA" does not because a percentage is to be used.

Calculating Scores

There are 30 features on the SIOP®, each with a range of possible scores from 0 to 4, or NA. After scoring each feature, the observer tallies all numeric scores. The score is written over the total possible score, usually 120 (30 features × a score of 4). So an example of a total score would be written 115/120. Because of the NA, adding the individual scores for a grand total is meaningless. It is more informative to know the total score based on the total possible score.

Let's take a step-by-step look at how a lesson's total score is calculated.

Mr. Leung's lesson received a score of 4 on 20 features, a score of 3 on 5 features, a score of 2 on 4 features, and 1 NA. The sum of those scores is 103.

$$20 \times 4 = 80$$
$$5 \times 3 = 15$$
$$2 \times 4 = 8$$
$$\text{Total score} = \overline{103}/116$$

The score of 116 was derived in this way: If the lesson had received a 4 on each feature of the SIOP® (a perfect score), it would have had a total score of 116.

$$29 \times 4 = 116$$

The number of features is 29 instead of 30 because one feature was not applicable (NA); the lesson was rated on only 29 features.

Mr. Leung's lesson received a total score of 103/116. The total score can be converted to a percentage, if that form is more useful. Simply divide the numerator by the denominator: $103 \div 116$. In this case, the SIOP® was implemented at a level of 88 percent. You can see the importance of distinguishing between a score of 0 and NA. For Mr. Leung's lesson, a 0 score would have changed the total score from 88 percent to 85 percent. Let's see how.

$$20 \times 4 = 80$$
$$5 \times 3 = 15$$
$$2 \times 4 = 8$$
$$1 \times 0 = 0$$
$$\text{Total score} = \overline{103}/120^{[1]}$$

The step-by-step process for tallying scores is shown in Figure 11.2.

FIGURE 11.2 *The Step-by-Step Process for Tallying Scores*

1. Add the lesson's scores from all features.
2. Count the number of NAs, multiply by 4, then subtract this number from 120.
3. Divide the number from step 2 into the number from step 1 (the adjusted possible score into the lesson's score).

Sample Lesson

In this section of the chapter, we will describe an entire science lesson conducted by a sixth-grade teacher and show how it was scored on the SIOP® protocol. Ms. Clark received training and has been using the SIOP® for lesson planning and delivery for

---

[1]The highest possible score on the SIOP® for all 30 features is 120 (30 items × a score of 4). If Mr. Leung's lesson were rated on all 30 features, the total score would be 103/120, or 85 percent.

about 16 months. This lesson took place at the end of the first quarter of the school year. The class consisted of beginning ESL students from varying language backgrounds and countries of origin. The class has been studying a unit on minerals and visited a local natural history museum. The students have examined rocks in class as well. Ms. Clark provided us with a lesson plan before we conducted the observation.

In the classroom, the desks were arranged in three circular groups. Some students had to turn around to see the board and overhead screen at the front of the room. The class objectives and agenda were written on a whiteboard at the side. Two bulletin boards in the back of the room displayed the students' work for a language arts project and a science project. A Spanish-speaking bilingual aide assisted the teacher and also helped newly arrived Spanish-speaking students. The class period was 45 minutes long.

The teacher began the class by complimenting the students for their performance on a test they had taken on minerals and singled out one student who received the highest A grade in the class. She then asked the students to read the objectives and activities for the day silently while she read them aloud:

Content Objective: Today we will develop an understanding of what volcanoes are and why they erupt.

- First, I will demonstrate how rocks could move and what happens when they move.
- Second, you will use a semantic web worksheet to recall what you know about volcanoes.
- Third, I will use a model to show how a volcano erupts.
- Fourth, you will make predictions about the story *Pompeii . . . Buried Alive*, and then read pages 4 to 9 silently.
- Fifth, you will refer to information on page 6 in the book to write on a worksheet the steps that happen before a volcano erupts.
- Your homework is to draw a volcano and label the parts. The vocabulary words and terms for the day are: melts, blast, mixture, rumbles, straw, pipe, shepherd, giant, peddler, crater, lava, magma, magma chamber.

The teacher then demonstrated for the class what happens when rocks move against each other, using two stacks of books. After placing the stacks side by side on a desk, she pushed against one stack so the other stack slid off the desk and scattered onto the floor. She asked the students what happens when one set of rocks moves another set of rocks. The students responded that the rocks break.

The aide distributed semantic web worksheets to the students and asked them to write "Volcano" in the center circle. Then, in the other spaces, students were to write everything they already knew about volcanoes. While the students worked, the teacher and aide circulated to monitor the students' understanding of the task and to see how they were progressing.

After the students filled in their webs, the teacher led them in a discussion of what they had written and wrote some of their comments on the whiteboard:

- Lava melts and explodes
- When it erupts, all that force comes from the middle of the earth

- Volcanoes are formed deep inside the earth
- When a volcano is under water, the lava comes out and makes an island

The teacher repeated that she was going to make a model volcano and asked the class what a "model" is. One student answered that it is an example, not a real volcano. All of the students were watching as the teacher showed them a bottle and explained it would be like the magma chamber that is inside a volcano. She poured a cup of warm water inside the bottle. While it cooled slightly, she showed the class a diagram of the model for the experiment, with the corresponding volcano parts labeled. They discussed each part of the volcano and in doing so emphasized some of the key vocabulary words and terms: crater, magma pipe, lava, magma, magma chamber, basin.

The teacher returned to the model and placed a few drops of liquid dish detergent in the warm water. Next, she picked up an object and asked the students to identify it. One student said it was a measuring spoon. The teacher measured a teaspoon of baking soda and put it into the water and detergent mixture. She asked the students to identify where she was putting it. The students responded, "magma chamber." She put in a second teaspoon of baking soda, then held up the bottle for the students to observe, and then they reviewed the ingredients. To speed up the process, she added vinegar to the bottle. She asked them, "When was the last time we used vinegar?" The students said they had used it on the previous day. The "volcano" began to erupt, and the teacher displayed the bottle so that the students could see the foam overflowing.

The class reviewed the process and the ingredients for the model volcano. Individual students were called to the front to participate in a second volcano demonstration, each one completing one of the steps to produce another "eruption." The second "lava" flow was a bit larger than the first.

The teacher asked the whole class to think about "What causes a volcano to erupt?" and added, "We used warm water. What will happen to heat in a chamber?" One student answered, "Heat rises." The teacher explained that it was not just the heat that caused the eruption and asked them to think of the other ingredients and what happened when they were mixed. The teacher went on to explain, "The mixture of gases produces carbon monoxide," and wrote "carbon monoxide" and its chemical symbol on the board. She also asked them what they knew about plants and said, "They breathe in carbon monoxide. We breathe out carbon monoxide; we breathe in oxygen." [This part was an error, but the teacher did not realize her mistake in calling carbon dioxide (for plants and humans), carbon monoxide.]

One student wanted to know why rocks come out of volcanoes and another student offered an explanation, "The volcano is inside of a mountain of rocks." The teacher commented that whatever is inside the chamber when it erupts will come out with the lava, and if they had put small bits of material inside their model, those bits also would have come out when it erupted.

The teacher and aide handed out the storybooks *Pompeii . . . Buried Alive*, to the students, and they began prereading activities. The teacher focused their attention on the title and asked them to predict what they thought the book would be about. One student said, "Volcanoes erupting." The teacher asked, "Where do you think it takes place?" Students guessed various places: Nicaragua, Rome, Greece, England. The teacher commented on the togas in the cover's picture. She then directed their attention to the back cover and read the summary aloud, stating the story took place 2,000 years ago in Italy. She asked, "Is it a true story?" Some students guessed yes; others no. "How do you know it's true?" They discussed that the term "took place" and the use of a specific time in history meant that it was true. The teacher then asked for a student volunteer to point out Italy on the wall map, and the class discussed the location of Italy in southern Europe.

The teacher asked how many of the students came from countries with volcanoes. Students from Ethiopia, El Salvador, and Guatemala said they knew about volcanoes in their countries. One student asked if it had to be a hot country to have a volcano. The teacher asked if they knew where the most recent eruption had occurred. She told them it was Montserrat in the Caribbean and that volcanoes often occur in warm countries, but not all are in warm countries. She asked if they knew about a volcano in the United States and told them about Mt. St. Helens in Washington, a state that is cold in winter. She showed them Washington on the map. One student commented on the way precipitation forms and tried to compare it with what happens in the formation of a volcano.

The teacher directed the students to read pages 4 to 9 silently for two minutes. While they were reading, she distributed worksheets with a sequencing exercise to describe what happens before a volcano erupts. The instructions told students to put the sentences in order according to what they read on page 6. They could refer back to the reading.

The teacher began to read the passage aloud slowly about three minutes later, although some students indicated that they had not yet finished reading it silently. As she read, she again displayed the transparency with the model volcano diagram on the overhead and referred to it and to the key vocabulary as she read. She also paused from time to time to ask comprehension questions. Students were able to answer questions orally, using the model and naming the parts of a volcano. They discussed unknown words in the reading, such as peddler, rumbled, and shepherd, as they went along.

As the period drew to a close, the teacher told the students they would complete the sequencing worksheet the next day. She reminded them of the homework—draw a volcano in their journal and label the parts. They were also told to place the webs they had completed in their journals. The teacher then led a brief wrap-up of the lesson, asking questions about a volcano, which students answered.

On the following pages (Figure 11.3), you will see how Ms. Clark was scored on the SIOP® items and the Comments that provide evidence for her score.

Using SIOP® Scores and Comments

Scores can be used "as is" to serve as a starting point for a collaborative discussion between a teacher and a supervisor or among a group of teachers. If lessons are rated, comments supporting the scores are essential. We have found that videotaping a lesson, rating it, and discussing it with the teacher provides an effective forum for professional growth. We also get valuable information from teachers explaining a student's behavior or why something may not have taken place despite the lesson plan that included it, for example. The discussion may take place between the teacher and the observer, or a group of teachers may meet on a regular basis to provide feedback to one another and assist in refining their teaching.

FIGURE 11.3 *The Sheltered Instruction Observation Protocol (SIOP®)*

The Sheltered Instruction Observation Protocol (SIOP®)

(Echevarria, Vogt, & Short, 2000; 2004; 2008)

Teacher: Ms. Clark
School: Cloverleaf
Class/Topic: Science
Lesson: Multiday (Single-day) *(circle one)*

Observer(s): J. Cruz
Date: 4/3
Grade: 6
ESL Level: 6

Total Points Possible: 120 (Subtract 4 points for each NA given) 120
Total Points Earned: 94   Percentage Score: 78%

Directions: Circle the number that best reflects what you observe in a sheltered lesson. You may give a score from 0–4 (or NA on selected items). Cite under "Comments" specific examples of the behaviors observed.

Lesson Preparation

④	3	2	1	0
1. **Content objectives** are clearly defined, displayed and reviewed with students		**Content objectives** for students implied		No clearly defined **content objectives** for students

Comments: Content objectives were written and stated at the beginning of the lesson.

4	3	**②**	1	0
2. **Language objectives** are clearly defined, displayed and reviewed with students		**Language objectives** for students implied		No clearly defined **language objectives** for students

Comments: No specific language objective was written or stated. Key vocabulary was listed, but the language skills to be targeted were listed and stated as activities and not written as objectives.

4	3	**②**	1	0
3. **Content concepts** appropriate for age and educational background level of students		**Content concepts** somewhat appropriate for age and educational background level of students		**Content concepts** inappropriate for age and educational background level of students

Comments: Students seemed to understand the concepts. However, several students mentioned that they studied volcanos in elementary school. It is unclear why volcanos were taught when these concepts had been introduced previously.

FIGURE 11.3   *Continued*

4. Supplementary materials used to a high degree, making the lesson clear and meaningful (e.g., computer programs, graphs, models, visuals)

④ 3 2 1 0

2 Some use of **supplementary materials**

0 No use of **supplementary materials**

Comments: Good use of supplementary materials to enhance students' understanding of volcanoes such as copies of semantic maps, pull-down maps, a book, Pompeii . . . Buried Alive, a transparency indicating the parts of a volcano, stacks of books to demonstrate rocks pushing against each other, household items to illustrate a volcanic eruption.

5. Adaptation of content (e.g., text, assignment) to all levels of student proficiency

④ 3 2 1 0 NA

2 Some **adaption of content** to all levels of student proficiency

0 No significant **adaption of content** to all levels of student proficiency

Comments: All students were given the same text with which to work. There were no specific adaptations made to the text itself to address the varying levels of language proficiency. However, the teacher had prepared a sequencing activity for students to complete where she identified sentences that explained the process of a volcanic eruption and students were required to put the steps in order. In addition, she began reading the text aloud to the students and paused frequently to ask questions and to check for clarification.

6. Meaningful activities that integrate lesson concepts (e.g., surveys, letter writing, simulations, models) with language practice opportunities for reading, writing, listening, and/or speaking

④ 3 2 1 0

2 **Meaningful activities** that integrate lesson concepts but provide little opportunity for language practice with opportunities for reading, writing, listening, and/or speaking

0 No **meaningful activities** that integrate lesson concepts with language practice

Comments: There were a lot of meaningful and interesting activities that provided students with language practice (e.g., participation in building the model volcano, discussing information from their semantic maps about volcanoes, and reading authentic text).

Building Background

7. Concepts explicitly linked to students' background experiences

④ 3 2 1 0 NA

2 **Concepts loosely linked** to students' background experiences

0 **Concepts not explicitly linked** to students' background experiences

Comments: The teacher tapped into students' understanding of volcanoes by asking them to complete a semantic mapping exercise writing everything they knew about volcanoes.

8. Links explicitly made between past learning and new concepts

4	3	2	1	0
Links explicitly made between past learning and new concepts	Few links made between past learning and new concepts	(2)		No links made between past learning and new concepts

Comments: There were few links made between past learning and its connection to new concepts. The teacher initiated the class by reminding the students of the visit to the Museum of Natural History and also reminded them of the rocks they had brought in. However, she did not explain how the visit or the collection of rocks related to that day's lesson about volcanoes.

9. Key vocabulary emphasized (e.g., introduced, written, repeated, and highlighted for students to see)

4	3	2	1	0
(4)	Key vocabulary emphasized	Key vocabulary introduced, but not emphasized		Key vocabulary not introduced or emphasized

Comments: The key vocabulary words used for this lesson were written on the board, stated to the students at the beginning of the lesson, and reiterated throughout the lesson, particularly when the teacher and students constructed the model volcano.

Comprehensible Input

10. Speech appropriate for students' proficiency level (e.g., slower rate, enunciation, and simple sentence structure for beginners)

4	3	2	1	0
(4)	Speech appropriate for students' proficiency level	Speech sometimes inappropriate for students' proficiency level		Speech inappropriate for students' proficiency level

Comments: The teacher explained tasks well and modeled the demonstrations first before the students participated.

11. Clear explanation of academic tasks

4	3	2	1	0
(4)	Clear explanation of academic tasks	Unclear explanation of academic tasks		No explanation of academic tasks

Comments: The teacher explained tasks well and modeled the demonstrations first before the students participated.

FIGURE 11.3 Continued

12. **A variety of techniques** used to make content concepts clear (e.g., modeling, visuals, hands-on activities, demonstrations, gestures, body language)

④	3	2	1	0
		Some **techniques** used to make content concepts clear		No **techniques** used to make content concepts clear

Comments: A variety of techniques were used in this lesson: the use of the overhead transparency with a diagram of a volcano and the labeled parts, brainstorming in the semantic mapping activity, demonstrating a model of a volcanic eruption, and reading about the topic after exploring it orally and visually. Used sequencing steps to check reading comprehension.

Strategies

13. Ample opportunities provided for students to use **learning strategies**

4	③	2	1	0
		Inadequate opportunities provided for students to use **learning strategies**		No opportunity provided for students to use **learning strategies**

Comments: The teacher used various strategies with students such as accessing prior knowledge and having them make predictions. Students, however, used these strategies with the teacher, not with other students.

14. **Scaffolding techniques** consistently used, assisting and supporting student understanding (e.g., think-alouds)

④	3	2	1	0
		Scaffolding techniques occasionally used		**Scaffolding techniques** not used

Comments: The teacher used various scaffolding techniques throughout the lesson to promote and assess students' comprehension of content concepts by means of questions, visuals, models, graphic organizers, prereading predictions, and demonstrations.

15. A variety of **questions or tasks that promote higher-order thinking skills** (e.g., literal, analytical, and interpretive questions)

4	③	2	1	0
		Infrequent **questions or tasks that promote higher-order thinking skills**		No **questions or tasks that promote higher-order thinking skills**

Comments: Most of the questions for this beginning level consisted of more factual/identification questions. In some cases, more elaborated responses were required of students; for example, "What happens when one set of rocks moves against another?" "Can you think of other places in the world where eruptions have occurred?" "Tell me about volcanoes in your country." "How do you know this is a true story?"

Interaction

16.

4	3	2	1	0
Frequent opportunities for **interaction** and discussion between teacher/student and among students, which encourage elaborated responses about lesson concepts	③	**Interaction** mostly teacher-dominated with some opportunities for students to talk about or question lesson concepts		**Interaction** teacher-dominated with no opportunities for students to discuss lesson concepts

Comments: The teacher engaged the students in discussions about volcanoes throughout the class period. The semantic mapping exercise, the demonstration, and the prereading activity were all means that facilitated student interaction. The majority of interactions were teacher-student.

17.

4	3	2	1	0
Grouping configurations support language and content objectives of the lesson	3	② **Grouping configurations** unevenly support the language and content objectives		**Grouping configurations** do not support the language and content objectives

Comments: Although students were seated in groups, there was little opportunity for them to interact to practice their language skills. The whole-class setting supported the demonstration about volcanic eruption.

18.

4	3	2	1	0
Sufficient **wait time for student responses** consistently provided	③	Sufficient **wait time for student responses** occasionally provided		Sufficient **wait time for student responses** not provided

Comments:: At times there were students who wanted to respond but were overlooked, perhaps because the period was running out of time. For those students selected to respond, the teacher allowed them time to articulate their thoughts.

19.

4	3	2	1	0	NA
④ Ample opportunities for students to **clarify key concepts in L1** as needed with aide, peer, or L1 text	3	Some opportunities for students to **clarify key concepts in L1**		No opportunities for students to **clarify key concepts in L1**	NA

Comments: Only a few students could be identified as using their L1 during the lesson, and they were seated in the far left corner of the classroom where the bilingual aide assisted them. The other students in the classroom did not seem to need to use their L1 text.

FIGURE 11.3 *Continued*

Practice/Application

4	3	2	1	0	NA
20. **Hands-on materials and/or manipulatives** provided for students to practice using new content knowledge	③	**Few hands-on materials and/or manipulatives** provided for students to practice using new content knowledge	1	**No hands-on materials and/or manipulatives** provided for students to practice using new content knowledge	NA

Comments: The lesson involved manipulatives. During the experiment/demonstration for the volcanic eruption, for example, the teacher used materials such as a bottle, liquid detergent, warm water, measuring spoons, baking soda, and vinegar. Only a few students, though, used these materials themselves.

4	3	2	1	0	NA
21. Activities provided for students to **apply content and language knowledge** in the classroom	③	Activities provided for students to apply either **content or language knowledge** in the classroom	1	No activities provided for students to **apply content or language knowledge** in the classroom	NA

Comments: For the most part, students applied content and language. More student–student interactions would have been beneficial and provided better opportunities for assessment.

4	3	2	1	0
22. Activities integrate all **language skills** (i.e., reading, writing, listening, and speaking)	③	Activities integrate some **language skills**	1	Activities do not integrate **language skills**

Comments: The lesson allowed students an opportunity to use all language skills (some more than others) such as listening, speaking, and reading. Writing was evident mostly in the semantic mapping activity. Some predicting and scanning for information was part of the reading skills practiced.

Lesson Delivery

4	3	2	1	0
23. **Content objectives** clearly supported by lesson delivery	③	**Content objectives** supported somewhat by lesson delivery	1	**Content objectives** not supported by lesson delivery

Comments: The demonstration and discussion along with the constant repetition of key vocabulary served to accomplish most of the content objectives for the lesson. While students seemed to indicate an understanding of what volcanoes are, it is not certain that they fully understand what causes them to erupt.

24. Language objectives clearly supported by lesson delivery — 4
Language objectives somewhat supported by lesson delivery — 3 / ②
Language objectives not supported by lesson delivery — 1 / 0

Comments: Most of the language objectives were supported by the delivery. Students did not have a chance to complete the sequencing activity based on the reading in order to assess their reading comprehension.

25. Students engaged approximately 90% to 100% of the period — ④ / 3
Students engaged approximately 70% of the period — 2
Students engaged less than 50% of the period — 1 / 0

Comments: Students were on task throughout the lesson activity.

26. Pacing of the lesson appropriate to students' ability levels — 4 / 3
Pacing generally appropriate, but at times too fast or too slow — ②
Pacing inappropriate to the students' ability levels — 1 / 0

Comments: The pacing seemed fine, but was a little rushed at times, which prevented students from completing some activities such as the individual silent reading and sequencing activity.

Review/Assessment

27. Comprehensive review of key vocabulary — 4 / 3
Uneven **review of key vocabulary** — ②
No **review of key vocabulary** — 1 / 0

Comments: Teacher reviewed key vocabulary at the beginning of the lesson and reinforced it throughout. No final review took place at the end of the lesson.

28. Comprehensive review of key content concepts — 4 / ③
Uneven **review of key content concepts** — 2
No **review of key content concepts** — 1 / 0

Comments: The key content concepts were reviewed throughout the lesson, but there was no comprehensive review to wrap up the lesson, other than the final question posed to students at the end of the class, "What is a volcano?"

FIGURE 11.3 *Continued*

4	3	2	1	0
29. Regular **feedback** provided to students on their output (e.g., language, content, work)	③	Inconsistent **feedback** provided to students on their output		No **feedback** provided to students on their output

Comments: The teacher gave positive feedback to students' responses in most cases. In some instances, when time was short, she did not always respond to students whose hands were raised. She guided the brainstorming and prereading discussions.

4	3	2	1	0
30. **Assessment of student comprehension and learning** of all lesson objectives (e.g., spot-checking, group response) throughout the lesson	3	**Assessment of student comprehension and learning** of some lesson objectives	②	No **assessment of student comprehension and learning** of lesson objectives

Comments: Throughout the lesson, the teacher checked students' understanding of some concepts and of the instructional tasks. She monitored the classroom to answer questions and to provide assistance. During the reading activity, however, students were not allotted sufficient time to read individually, and the sequencing activity was moved to the following day. Therefore, it is unclear how she was able to assess individual student comprehension before she began reading the text to students.

Teacher	Observation 1 Score/Date	Observation 2 Score/Date	Observation 3 Score/Date

FIGURE 11.4 *SIOP® Lesson Rating Form*

Scores can also be documented on a SIOP® Lesson Rating Form over time to show growth (see Figure 11.4). Using percentages, teachers can see how their implementation of the SIOP® features improves. This type of documentation is also useful for research purposes to document systematic implementation of the SIOP® and fidelity of implementation.

Further, plotting scores on a graph, as seen in Figure 11.5, is a very effective way to illustrate strong areas as well as areas that require attention, or areas teachers have highlighted as important for their own growth. If a lesson consistently shows low scores on certain features, that provides the teacher with clear feedback for areas on which to focus. Staff developers and teacher educators can use the scores to determine areas for further discussion and practice in workshops and course sessions if several teachers are having difficulty with the same feature or component.

Finally, while the SIOP® protocol is a useful tool for professional development, scores should be used with caution. Many variables affect the success or failure of a given lesson such as time of day, time of year, dynamics between students, and the like. Rather than just doing one observation and scoring of a lesson, several lessons should be rated over time for a more complete picture of the teacher's implementation of sheltered instruction.

FIGURE 11.5   *Ms. Clark's Scores*

Reliability and Validity of the SIOP®

After several years of field-testing and refining the SIOP®, a study was conducted (Guarino, Echevarria, Short, Schick, Forbes, & Rueda, 2001) to establish the validity and reliability of the instrument. The findings of the study indicated that the SIOP® is a highly reliable and valid measure of sheltered instruction (see Appendix C for a discussion of the study).

Summary

This book has been developed for teachers, supervisors, administrators, teacher education faculty, professional developers, and researchers as a resource for increasing the effectiveness of instruction for elementary English learners. We have presented a research-based, professional development model of sheltered instruction, the SIOP®, that can be used as an observation instrument, as well as a lesson planning guide.

The SIOP® Model and protocol provide concrete examples of the features of effective instruction for ELs, and the book has been written as a way to illustrate and elucidate those features by describing how real teachers might actually teach SIOP® lessons in grades K–6. The use of vignettes allows readers to "see" what each feature might look like in a classroom setting. The features of the SIOP® Model represent best practice for teaching English learners.

Discussion Questions

1. The SIOP® has a number of uses by different constituencies (e.g., teachers, supervisors, administrators, and researchers). How can you begin using the SIOP®? What additional uses might it have for you or other constituencies?

2. Reread the sample lesson on pages 218–220. Would you score this lesson differently from the sample SIOP® scores? On what items would you differ? What was the basis of your disagreement?

3. Look at the sample SIOP® protocol and change any two scores to 1. What would be the total score and percentage score on the revised and recalculated SIOP®?

4. Imagine that you and a supervisor have just watched a videotape of your SIOP® lesson. You are discussing the SIOP® rating sheet that each of you scored independently. What would be the most collaborative way to approach the discussion of your teaching? What would yield the most useful information for improving your teaching?

appendix a: The Sheltered Instruction Observation Protocol (SIOP®)

Observer(s): _____   Teacher: _____

Date: _____   School: _____

Grade: _____   Class/Topic: _____

ESL Level: _____   Lesson: Multi-day   Single-day   (*circle one*)

Total Points Possible: 120 (Subtract 4 points for each NA given: _____)

Total Points Earned: _____   Percentage Score: _____

Directions: Circle the number that best reflects what you observe in a sheltered lesson. You may give a score from 0–4 (or NA on selected items). Cite under "Comments" specific examples of the behaviors observed.

LESSON PREPARATION

4	3	2	1	0
1. **Content objectives** clearly defined, displayed and reviewed with students		**Content objectives** for students implied		No clearly defined **content objectives** for students

Comments:

4	3	2	1	0
2. **Language objectives** clearly defined, displayed and reviewed with students		**Language objectives** for students implied		No clearly defined **language objectives** for students

Comments:

4	3	2	1	0
3. **Content concepts** appropriate for age and educational background level of students		**Content concepts** somewhat appropriate for age and educational background level of students		**Content concepts** inappropriate for age and educational background level of students

Comments:

4	3	2	1	0
4. **Supplementary materials** used to a high degree, making the lesson clear and meaningful (e.g., computer programs, graphs, models, visuals)		Some use of **supplementary materials**		No use of **supplementary materials**

Comments:

(Echevarria, Vogt, & Short, 2000; 2004; 2008)

4	3	2	1	0	NA
5. **Adaptation of content** (e.g., text, assignment) to all levels of student proficiency		Some **adaptation of content** to all levels of student proficiency		No significant **adaptation of content** to all levels of student proficiency	

Comments:

4	3	2	1	0
6. **Meaningful activities** that integrate lesson concepts (e.g., interviews, letter writing, simulations, models) with language practice opportunities for reading, writing, listening, and/or speaking		**Meaningful activities** that integrate lesson concepts but provide few language practice opportunities for reading, writing, listening, and/or speaking		No **meaningful activities** that integrate lesson concepts with language practice

Comments:

BUILDING BACKGROUND

4	3	2	1	0	NA
7. **Concepts explicitly linked** to students' background experiences		**Concepts loosely linked** to students' background experiences		**Concepts not explicitly linked** to students' background experiences	

Comments:

4	3	2	1	0
8. **Links explicitly made** between past learning and new concepts		**Few links made** between past learning and new concepts		**No links made** between past learning and new concepts

Comments:

4	3	2	1	0
9. **Key vocabulary** emphasized (e.g., introduced, written, repeated, and highlighted for students to see)		**Key vocabulary** introduced, but not emphasized		**Key vocabulary** not introduced or emphasized

Comments:

COMPREHENSIBLE INPUT

4	3	2	1	0

10. **Speech** appropriate for students' proficiency levels (e.g., slower rate, enunciation, and simple sentence structure for beginners)

          Speech sometimes inappropriate for students' proficiency levels

          Speech inappropriate for students' proficiency levels

Comments:

4	3	2	1	0

11. **Clear explanation** of academic tasks

          Unclear explanation of academic tasks

          No explanation of academic tasks

Comments:

4	3	2	1	0

12. **A variety of techniques** used to make content concepts clear (e.g., modeling, visuals, hands-on activities, demonstrations, gestures, body language)

          Some **techniques** used to make content concepts clear

          No **techniques** used to make concepts clear

Comments:

STRATEGIES

4	3	2	1	0

13. Ample opportunities provided for students to use **learning strategies**

          Inadequate opportunities provided for students to use **learning strategies**

          No opportunity provided for students to use **learning strategies**

Comments:

4	3	2	1	0

14. **Scaffolding techniques** consistently used, assisting and supporting student understanding (e.g., think-alouds)

          Scaffolding techniques occasionally used

          Scaffolding techniques not used

Comments:

4	3	2	1	0

15. A variety of **questions or tasks that promote higher-order thinking skills** (e.g., literal, analytical, and interpretive questions) | | Infrequent **questions or tasks that promote higher-order thinking skills** | | No **questions or tasks that promote higher-order thinking skills**

Comments:

INTERACTION

4	3	2	1	0

16. Frequent opportunities for **interaction** and discussion between teacher/student and among students, which encourage elaborated responses about lesson concepts | | **Interaction** mostly teacher-dominated with some opportunities for students to talk about or question lesson concepts | | **Interaction** teacher-dominated with no opportunities for students to discuss lesson concepts

Comments:

4	3	2	1	0

17. **Grouping configurations** support language and content objectives of the lesson | | **Grouping configurations** unevenly support the language and content objectives | | **Grouping configurations** do not support the language and content objectives

Comments:

4	3	2	1	0

18. Sufficient **wait time for student responses** consistently provided | | Sufficient **wait time for student responses** occasionally provided | | Sufficient **wait time for student responses** not provided

Comments:

4	3	2	1	0	NA

19. Ample opportunities for students to **clarify key concepts in L1** as needed with aide, peer, or L1 text | | Some opportunities for students to **clarify key concepts in L1** | | No opportunities for students to **clarify key concepts in L1** |

Comments:

PRACTICE & APPLICATION

4	3	2	1	0	NA

20. **Hands-on materials and/or manipulatives** provided for students to practice using new content knowledge

Few **hands-on materials and/or manipulatives** provided for students to practice using new content knowledge

No **hands-on materials and/or manipulatives** provided for students to practice using new content knowledge

Comments:

4	3	2	1	0	NA

21. Activities provided for students to **apply content and language knowledge** in the classroom

Activities provided for students to **apply** either **content or language knowledge** in the classroom

No activities provided for students to **apply content and language knowledge** in the classroom

Comments:

4	3	2	1	0

22. Activities integrate all **language skills** (i.e., reading, writing, listening, and speaking)

Activities integrate some **language skills**

Activities do not integrate **language skills**

Comments:

LESSON DELIVERY

4	3	2	1	0

23. **Content objectives** clearly supported by lesson delivery

Content objectives somewhat supported by lesson delivery

Content objectives not supported by lesson delivery

Comments:

4	3	2	1	0

24. **Language objectives** clearly supported by lesson delivery

Language objectives somewhat supported by lesson delivery

Language objectives not supported by lesson delivery

Comments:

4	3	2	1	0

25. **Students engaged** approximately 90% to 100% of the period   **Students engaged** approximately 70% of the period   **Students engaged** less than 50% of the period

Comments:

4	3	2	1	0

26. **Pacing** of the lesson appropriate to students' ability levels   **Pacing** generally appropriate, but at times too fast or too slow   **Pacing** inappropriate to students' ability levels

Comments:

REVIEW & ASSESSMENT

4	3	2	1	0

27. Comprehensive **review of key vocabulary**   Uneven **review of key vocabulary**   No **review of key vocabulary**

Comments:

4	3	2	1	0

28. Comprehensive **review of key content concepts**   Uneven **review of key content concepts**   No **review of key content concepts**

Comments:

4	3	2	1	0

29. Regular **feedback** provided to students on their output (e.g., language, content, work)   Inconsistent **feedback** provided to students on their output   No **feedback** provided to students on their output

Comments:

4	3	2	1	0

30. **Assessment of student comprehension and learning** of all lesson objectives (e.g., spot checking, group response) throughout the lesson   **Assessment of student comprehension and learning** of some lesson objectives   No **assessment of student comprehension and learning** of lesson objectives

Comments:

The Sheltered Instruction Observation Protocol (SIOP®)
(Echevarria, Vogt, & Short, 2000; 2004; 2008)

Observer(s): _____ Teacher: _____

Date: _____ School: _____

Grade: _____ Class/Topic: _____

ESL Level: _____ Lesson: Multi-day Single-day (*circle one*)

Total Points Possible: 120 (Subtract 4 points for each NA given) _____

Total Points Earned: _____ Percentage Score: _____

Directions: Circle the number that best reflects what you observe in a sheltered lesson. You may give a score from 0–4 (or NA on selected items). Cite under "Comments" specific examples of the behaviors observed.

	Highly Evident		Somewhat Evident		Not Evident	
Preparation	**4**	**3**	**2**	**1**	**0**	
1. **Content objectives** clearly defined, displayed, and reviewed with students	❏	❏	❏	❏	❏	
2. **Language objectives** clearly defined, displayed, and reviewed with students	❏	❏	❏	❏	❏	
3. **Content concepts** appropriate for age and educational background level of students	❏	❏	❏	❏	❏	
4. **Supplementary materials** used to a high degree, making the lesson clear and meaningful (e.g., computer programs, graphs, models, visuals)	❏	❏	❏	❏	❏	
5. **Adaptation of content** (e.g., text, assignment) to all levels of student proficiency	❏	❏	❏	❏	❏	**NA** ❏
6. **Meaningful activities** that integrate lesson concepts (e.g., surveys, letter writing, simulations, constructing models) with language practice opportunities for reading, writing, listening, and/or speaking	❏	❏	❏	❏	❏	

Comments:

	4	**3**	**2**	**1**	**0**	**NA**
Building Background						
7. **Concepts explicitly linked** to students' background experiences	❏	❏	❏	❏	❏	❏
8. **Links explicitly made** between past learning and new concepts	❏	❏	❏	❏	❏	
9. **Key vocabulary** emphasized (e.g., introduced, written, repeated, and highlighted for students to see)	❏	❏	❏	❏	❏	

Comments:

	4	**3**	**2**	**1**	**0**
Comprehensible Input					
10. **Speech** appropriate for students' proficiency level (e.g., slower rate, enunciation, and simple sentence structure for beginners)	❏	❏	❏	❏	❏
11. **Clear explanation** of academic tasks	❏	❏	❏	❏	❏
12. **A variety of techniques** used to make content concepts clear (e.g., modeling, visuals, hands-on activities, demonstrations, gestures, body language)	❏	❏	❏	❏	❏

Comments:

	4	**3**	**2**	**1**	**0**
Strategies					
13. Ample opportunities provided for students to use **learning strategies**	❏	❏	❏	❏	❏

(Reproduction of this material is restricted to use with Echevarria, Vogt, and Short (2008), *Making Content Comprehensible for English Learners: The SIOP® Model.*)

	Highly Evident		Somewhat Evident		Not Evident	
	4	**3**	**2**	**1**	**0**	
14. **Scaffolding techniques** consistently used assisting and supporting student understanding (e.g., think-alouds)	❏	❏	❏	❏	❏	
15. A variety of **questions or tasks that promote higher-order thinking skills** (e.g., literal, analytical, and interpretive questions) *Comments:*	❏	❏	❏	❏	❏	
Interaction	**4**	**3**	**2**	**1**	**0**	
16. Frequent opportunities for **interaction** and discussion between teacher/student and among students, which encourage elaborated responses about lesson concepts	❏	❏	❏	❏	❏	
17. **Grouping configurations** support language and content objectives of the lesson	❏	❏	❏	❏	❏	
18. Sufficient **wait time for student responses** consistently provided	❏	❏	❏	❏	❏	**NA**
19. Ample opportunities for students to **clarify key concepts in L1** as needed with aide, peer, or L1 text *Comments:*	❏	❏	❏	❏	❏	❏
Practice & Application	**4**	**3**	**2**	**1**	**0**	**NA**
20. **Hands-on materials and/or manipulatives** provided for students to practice using new content knowledge	❏	❏	❏	❏	❏	❏
21. Activities provided for students to **apply content and language knowledge** in the classroom	❏	❏	❏	❏	❏	❏
22. Activities integrate all **language skills** (i.e., reading, writing, listening, and speaking) *Comments:*	❏	❏	❏	❏	❏	
Lesson Delivery	**4**	**3**	**2**	**1**	**0**	
23. **Content objectives** clearly supported by lesson delivery	❏	❏	❏	❏	❏	
24. **Language objectives** clearly supported by lesson delivery	❏	❏	❏	❏	❏	
25. **Students engaged** approximately 90% to 100% of the period	❏	❏	❏	❏	❏	
26. **Pacing** of the lesson appropriate to students' ability level *Comments:*	❏	❏	❏	❏	❏	
Review & Assessment	**4**	**3**	**2**	**1**	**0**	
27. Comprehensive **review of key vocabulary**	❏	❏	❏	❏	❏	
28. Comprehensive **review of key content concepts**	❏	❏	❏	❏	❏	
29. Regular **feedback** provided to students on their output (e.g., language, content, work)	❏	❏	❏	❏	❏	
30. **Assessment of student comprehension and learning** of all lesson objectives (e.g., spot checking, group response) throughout the lesson *Comments:*	❏	❏	❏	❏	❏	

SIOP® Lesson Plan Template 1

Date: _____ **Grade/Class/Subject:** _____

Unit/Theme: _____ **Standards:** _____

Content Objective(s): _____

_____

Language Objective(s): _____

_____

Key Vocabulary	Supplementary Materials

SIOP® Features

Preparation	Scaffolding	Grouping Options
Adaptation of Content	Modeling	Whole class
Links to Background	Guided practice	Small groups
Links to Past Learning	Independent practice	Partners
Strategies incorporated	Comprehensible input	Independent

Integration of Processes	Application	Assessment
Reading	Hands-on	Individual
Writing	Meaningful	Group
Speaking	Linked to objectives	Written
Listening	Promotes engagement	Oral

Lesson Sequence

Reflections:

(Reproduction of this material is restricted to use with Echevarria, Vogt, and Short (2008), *Making Content Comprehensible for English Learners: The SIOP® Model.*)

SIOP® Lesson Plan Template 2

STANDARDS:

THEME:

LESSON TOPIC:

OBJECTIVES:
Language

Content

LEARNING STRATEGIES:

KEY VOCABULARY:

MATERIALS:

MOTIVATION:
(Building background)

PRESENTATION
(Language and content objectives, comprehensible input, strategies, interaction, feedback)

PRACTICE & APPLICATION:
(Meaningful activities, interaction, strategies, practice/application, feedback)

REVIEW & ASSESSMENT:
(Review objectives and vocabulary, assess learning)

EXTENSION:

(Reproduction of this material is restricted to use with Echevarria, Vogt, and Short (2008), *Making Content Comprehensible for English Learners: The SIOP® Model.*)

SIOP® Lesson Plan Template 3

Topic:	Class:	Date:

Content Objectives:	Language Objectives:

Key Vocabulary:

Materials (including supplementary and adapted):

Higher-Order Questions:

Time:	Activities
	Building Background
	Links to Experience:
	Links to Learning:
	Key Vocabulary:

(Continued on next page)

Time:	**Student Activities** (Check all that apply for activities throughout lesson):
	Scaffolding: ❑ Modeling ❑ Guided ❑ Independent
	Grouping: ❑ Whole Class ❑ Small Group ❑ Partners ❑ Independent
	Processes: ❑ Reading ❑ Writing ❑ Listening ❑ Independent
	Strategies: ❑ Hands-on ❑ Meaningful ❑ Links to Objectives
	Review and Assessment (Check all that apply): Individual ❑ Group ❑ Written ❑ Oral ❑
	Review Key Vocabulary:
	Review Key Content Concepts:

(Developed by John Seidlitz. Used with permission.)

SIOP® Lesson Plan Template 4

SIOP® Lesson

Content Standards: Grade:

Key Vocabulary: Visuals/Resources:

Nigher-Order Thinking Skills (HOTS):

Connections: Prior Knowledge/Building Background/Prior Learning:

Content Objective(s): Meaningful Activities: Lesson Sequence | Review & Assessment:

Language Objective(s):

(Developed by Melissa Castillo & Nicole Teyechea. Used with permission.)

(Continued on next page)

Lesson Sequence (*continued*)

Review & Assessment (*continued*)

Wrap-up:

(Developed by Melissa Castillo & Nicole Teyechea. Used with permission.)

The original research study that developed the SIOP® Model, "The Effects of Sheltered Instruction on the Achievement of Limited English Proficient Students," was a seven-year project (1996–2003) conducted for the Center for Research on Education, Diversity & Excellence (CREDE), a national research center funded by the U.S. Department of Education, Office of Educational Research and Improvement (now known as the Institute of Education Sciences). This project worked with middle school teachers in four large metropolitan school districts—two on the East Coast and two on the West Coast—to identify key practices for sheltered instruction and develop a professional development model to enable more teachers to use sheltered instruction effectively in their classrooms. Dr. Jana Echevarria of California State University, Long Beach, and Dr. Deborah Short of the Center for Applied Linguistics in Washington, DC, were co–project investigators.

Although sheltered instruction had been widely advocated as an effective instructional strategy for language minority students, when this study began there had been little agreement among practitioners as to what sheltered instruction should look like in the classroom, and few research investigations measuring what constituted an effective sheltered lesson. This project therefore set the following goals: (1) develop an explicit model of sheltered instruction, (2) use that model to train teachers in effective sheltered strategies, and (3) conduct field experiments and collect data to evaluate teacher change and the effects of sheltered instruction on LEP students' English language development and content knowledge.

The specific research questions posed by this project follow:

1. What are the characteristics of sheltered instruction, and how does it differ from high-quality nonsheltered instruction?

2. What are the characteristics of an effective professional development program for implementing quality sheltered instruction to a high degree?

3. Does sheltered instruction improve the achievement of LEP students in content areas such as social studies?

4. Are there significant differences in achievement data (reading scores, writing samples, attendance) for students of project teachers versus students in sheltered classes whose teachers have not received SIOP® training?

This research project involved the active collaboration of practicing middle school teachers both in refining the model of sheltered instruction and in implementing it in their classrooms. In the first two years of the project we identified, based on literature review and classroom research, effective teaching strategies involved in sheltered instruction. The model began as a research observation instrument, the Sheltered Instruction Observation Protocol (SIOP®), so that researchers could determine how well teachers were including these features of effective sheltered instruction in their lessons. Drawing from the literature on best practices, the SIOP® protocol incorporated topics such as scaffolding, learning strategies, literacy techniques, and use of meaningful curricula and materials. Our goal was to determine which combination of best practices in one instructional framework, the SIOP®, would yield positive achievement results for English learners. With feedback from the teachers, the protocol evolved into a lesson planning and delivery approach, the SIOP® Model (Echevarria, Vogt, & Short, 2000, 2008; Short & Echevarria, 1999). It is composed of 30 items grouped into 8 components essential for making content comprehensible for English learners—Lesson Preparation, Building Background, Comprehensible Input, Strategies, Interaction, Practice & Application, Lesson Delivery, and Review & Assessment. The SIOP® Model shares many features recommended for high-quality instruction for all students, but adds key features for the academic success of students learning through a second language, such as including language objectives in every content lesson, developing background knowledge among the students, and attending to specific academic literacy skills. This model can be applied in ESL classes as well as all content area classes because it offers a framework for instruction that incorporates best practices for teaching both language and content.

After several years of field-testing the SIOP® protocol, a study was conducted to establish the validity and reliability of the observation instrument. It was found to be a highly reliable and valid measure of sheltered instruction (Guarino, Echevarria, Short, Schick, Forbes, & Rueda, 2001). Experienced observers of classroom instruction (e.g., teacher education faculty who supervise student teachers) who were *not* specifically trained in the SIOP® Model were able to use the protocol to distinguish between high and low implementers of the model. A statistical analysis revealed an interrater of correlation 0.99.

As part of the research design, student data in the form of a writing assessment based on the IMAGE (Illinois Measure of Annual Growth in English) Test were gathered and analyzed. The IMAGE was the standardized test of reading and writing used by the state of Illinois to measure annual growth of these skills in their limited English proficient students in grades 3–12. It was correlated to and a predictor of scores on the IGAP (the state standardized test of achievement) that was given to all students in Illinois, except those exempted for linguistic development reasons or learning disabilities. The IMAGE Writing Test provides separate scores for five features of writing: Language Production, Focus, Support/Elaboration, Organization, and Mechanics, as well as an overall score.

During the 1998–99 school year, researchers gave prompts to middle school English language learning students that required expository writing, once in the fall (pretest) and then again in the spring (posttest). Two distinct, but similar, cohorts of English learners in sheltered classes participated: students whose teachers were trained in implementing the SIOP® Model (the treatment group), and students whose teachers had no exposure to the SIOP® Model (the comparison group). The students in both groups were in grades 6–8 and represented mixed proficiency levels.

Results showed English learners in sheltered classes with teachers who had been trained in implementing the SIOP® Model to a high degree improved their writing and outperformed the students in control classes by receiving overall higher scores for the spring assessment (Echevarria, Short, & Powers, 2006). They also made greater gains from the fall to spring administrations of the test. These findings were statistically significant. The results indicated that students whose teachers implemented the SIOP® Model of sheltered instruction improved significantly in all areas of writing over students in sheltered classes whose teachers were not familiar with the SIOP® Model. These results match the findings from the 1997–98 school year when a similar administration of a writing assessment requiring narrative writing was given. Secondary analyses of the data revealed that special education

TABLE C.1 *Mean Scores, Standard Deviations, and Sample Size for Treatment and Comparison Groups*

	SIOP®(Treatment)		Comparison	
	Pretest	*Posttest*	*Pretest*	*Posttest*
Total Score				
M	13.55	16.36	14.61	15.81
SD	3.42	3.33	3.36	3.45
N	238	238	77	77
Language Production				
M	2.65	3.22	2.77	3.09
SD	.78	.79	.78	.73
N	240	240	77	77
Focus				
M	2.81	3.30	3.01	3.17
SD	.87	.98	.88	.94
N	239	239	77	77
Support/Elaboration				
M	2.65	3.26	2.83	3.18
SD	.78	.72	.70	.81
N	241	241	77	77
Organization				
M	2.77	3.31	3.16	3.21
SD	.96	.78	.92	.71
N	241	241	77	77
Mechanics				
M	2.72	3.28	2.84	3.17
SD	.88	.87	.86	.94
N	241	241	77	77

students who constituted a subset of the English learners made significant improvement overall in their writing as well, with both the narrative and expository assessments.

Specifically, with the 1998–99 assessment, analysis of treatment and comparison groups' total scores (i.e., aggregated across the five subscales) found the participants whose teachers were trained in the SIOP® Model made statistically significantly better gains than the control group in writing ($F(1,312) = 10.79$; $p < 0.05$). Follow-up analyses on student performance on the various subtests of the writing assessment found that the treatment group performed at a significantly higher level in language production ($F(1,314) = 5.00$; $p < 0.05$), organization ($F(1,315) = 5.65$; $p < 0.05$) and mechanics ($F(1,315) = 4.10$; $p < 0.05$) than those in the comparison group, whose teachers had not received the study-developed training and support in delivering sheltered instruction (see Tables C.1 and C.2). The treatment group did not make significant gains over the comparison group in their performance on the writing focus and elaboration subtests.

The project also developed and field-tested a professional development program for the SIOP® Model that incorporated key features of effective teacher development as recommended by Darling-Hammond (1998) and Garet, Porter, Desimone, Birman, &

TABLE C.2   *Analysis of Covariance of Posttest Writing Results by Treatment Condition*

Variable	df	M Square	F-ratio	p
Total Score	1	78.276	10.785	.001*
Language Production	1	2.133	5.004	.026*
Focus	1	2.904	3.706	.055
Support/Elaboration	1	1.247	2.680	1.03
Organization	1	2.842	5.651	.018*
Mechanics	1	2.065	4.101	.044*

Note: Pretest scores for each measure served as the covariate for posttest dependent measures.
* $p < .05$*

Yoon (2001). In this project, it has been found that through sustained, intensive interaction and coaching among staff developers and teachers—for at least one year—teachers can modify their pedagogy to promote both language and content learning among English learners. Two professional development videos (Hudec & Short, 2002a; 2002b), training manuals (Echevarria & Vogt, 2006; Short, Hudec, & Echevarria, 2002), and other materials have been developed to support this program, and institutes to prepare staff developers and teacher educators to coach others in the SIOP® Model have been held across the United States. (See www.siopinstitute.net for more details.)

Since the SIOP® Model was first published in 2000, the following uses for the observation tool and professional development program have been realized:

- Teacher lesson plan checklist and self-reflection guide
- Classroom observation tool for administrators
- Supervision tool for faculty to observe student teachers
- Research observation tool for fidelity of model implementation
- Program of professional development

Summary: Selected Findings from the SIOP® Research Project

- After five years of collaboration with practicing teachers, CREDE researchers developed a model of high-quality sheltered instruction, known as the SIOP® Model. This model takes into account the special language development needs of English language learners, which distinguishes it from high-quality nonsheltered teaching.
- A study conducted to establish the validity and reliability of the Sheltered Instruction Observation Protocol found that the instrument is a highly reliable and valid measure of sheltered instruction (Guarino, Echevarria, Short, Schick, Forbes, & Rueda, 2001).
- 1997–98: Researchers compared English language learning students in classes whose teachers had been trained in implementing the SIOP® Model to a high degree to a comparison group (taught by teachers not trained in the SIOP® Model) using a prompt that required narrative writing. They scored the prompt using the writing rubric of the Illinois Measure of Annual Growth in English (IMAGE) Test. The English learners in

classes whose teachers had been trained in implementing the SIOP® Model to a high degree demonstrated significantly higher writing scores than the control group.

- 1998–99: Researchers compared English learners in classes whose teachers had been trained in implementing the SIOP® Model to a high degree to a comparison group (taught by teachers not trained in the SIOP® Model) using a prompt that required expository writing. They scored the prompt using the writing rubric of the Illinois Measure of Annual Growth in English (IMAGE) Test. The English learners in classes whose teachers had been trained in implementing the SIOP® Model to a high degree demonstrated significantly higher writing scores than the comparison group and made greater gains from the pretest to the posttest. See the results in Tables C.1 and C.2.

Current and Recent SIOP® Research Studies

Since we conducted the original SIOP® research for CREDE, additional investigations have taken or are taking place. Some school districts have implemented the SIOP® Model and have evaluated their results. In addition, some large-scale quasi-experimental and experimental studies have taken place or are in progress. We describe them briefly here but encourage you to look at *www.cal.org* and *www.siopinstitute.net* for updates and final results.

Academic Literacy through Sheltered Instruction for Secondary English Language Learners was a quasi-experimental research study conducted in the two districts in New Jersey. Funded by the Carnegie Corporation of New York and the Rockefeller Foundation from 2004–07, researchers from the Center for Applied Linguistics collected and analyzed data to investigate the relationship between professional development in the SIOP® Model and the academic achievement of secondary English language learners. One school district received the SIOP® Model as the professional development treatment; the other was a comparison site. Both school districts have two middle schools and one high school with similar multilingual English learner populations. More than 500 ELs were in the treatment district, approximately 225 in the comparison site. Each district follows an ESL program design in grades 6–12 with some designated sheltered courses.

In the treatment site, math, science, social studies, language arts, ESL, and technology teachers participated in ongoing SIOP® Model training: approximately 35 teachers for 2 years (cohort 1) and an additional 25 for 1 (cohort 2). Each cohort had 7 days for workshops spread throughout the year, and cohort 1 had 3 follow-up days in the second year. The teachers in the comparison site did not receive any SIOP® Model training. The treatment teachers also had part-time on-site coaches who primarily facilitated after-school meetings and offered guidance in lesson design and material resources. Some coaches were able to make classroom visits. Ongoing support was also provided via closed Listserv, a project dedicated website, and online chats.

Researchers collected teacher implementation data (two classroom observations each year, one in the fall, the other in the spring) using the SIOP® protocol at both sites. Analyses showed that the number of high implementers of the SIOP® Model increased to a greater extent in the treatment district than the comparison district. After one year of SIOP® professional development in the treatment district, 56% of cohort 1 and 74% of cohort 2 teachers implemented the model to a high degree. After two years, 71% of cohort 1 reached a high level. In contrast, only 5% of the teachers reached a high level of implementation after one year at the comparison site and only 17% after two years (Center for Applied Linguistics, 2007).

In addition, pre- and post-SIOP® lesson plans were collected at the treatment site to measure how well teachers incorporated SIOP® Model components in their preparation. The incorporation of SIOP® features in the teachers' lesson plans improved by more than 50 percent.

The researchers collected and analyzed results on the state's English language proficiency assessment, which at that time was the IDEA Proficiency Test (IPT), for all ELs in grades 6–12 who were in ESL programs. Analyses showed that, on average, students with SIOP-trained teachers (in the treatment district) outperformed students without SIOP-trained teachers (in the comparison district) to a statistically significant level ($p < .05$) when comparing average mean scores on the IPT oral, writing, and total tests in the second year of the intervention (2005–06). There was no significant difference in first year. However, SIOP students in the treatment district made greater gains in average mean scores on all IPT tests from the baseline year (2003–04) to the final year (2005–06) than the students in the comparison district did.

An examination of student performance within the treatment district revealed that, on average, SIOP students outperformed non-SIOP students to a statistically significant level ($p < .05$) in both the first and second year of the intervention, when comparing mean scores on the IPT oral, reading, writing, and total tests (Center for Applied Linguistics, 2007).

The researchers also collected and analyzed student content area achievement data from New Jersey state tests in reading, math, social studies, and science for grades 6–7; reading, math, and science for grade 8; and reading and math for grade 11 (or grade 12 for some ELs), although this was complicated by the fact that New Jersey changed tests during the study. (In the second year, students in grades 6 and 7 had a new test, and were tested only in reading and math.) The analyses were further limited by the fact that the students in the treatment and comparison districts took these tests only once, and the number of student subjects was very small for each test; therefore, the results are not generalizable. The results showed a significant difference ($p < .05$) in mean scores in favor of SIOP students in the treatment district on six state content tests: grade 6 reading, language arts, and total proficiency score for 2004–05 and grade 6 language arts, grade 7 language arts, and grade 11 mathematics in 2005–06. There was a significant difference ($p < .05$) in mean scores in favor of students in the comparison district on one state content test, grade 7 social studies in 2004–05. There were no significant differences between groups on the other 19 content tests (Center for Applied Linguistics, 2007). The content achievement results indicate some promise for the SIOP Model, but further research and larger sample sizes are needed.

Optimizing Educational Outcomes for English Language Learners is a five-year experimental study conducted by the University of Houston, the University of Texas at Austin, the Center for Applied Linguistics, and the University of Miami (2003–08). It is supported by the U.S. Department of Education. Within this research project, the SIOP® Model is part of a larger intervention design to enhance academic language/literacy development and content knowledge in elementary school students in ESL and bilingual programs.

The project follows a longitudinal, experimental design to evaluate traditional and enhanced models of ESL and bilingual programs in grades K–3. Approximately 12 schools in one district are participating. Some offer a bilingual (Spanish-English) program model; others, an ESL program. Students have been randomly assigned to traditional or intervention classes, and the study follows the same students over four years as they progress from kindergarten to grade 3. The intervention consists of the following elements:

- Tier I (core instruction)

  –Enhanced language enrichment in English and/or Spanish for phonics and reading (grades 1–3)

  –SIOP® Model instruction with a focus on mathematics classes in English or Spanish (grades K–3)

  –Additional language development using authentic text and focusing on vocabulary in English and/or Spanish (grades K–3)

- Tier II

  –Classroom-based supplemental reading instruction (offered in small groups to identified students, grades K–3)

- Tier III

  –Intensive small-group, pull-out intervention for reading (grades 2–3)

Intervention teachers participate in professional development on all interventions. The training is distributed throughout each school year to the targeted grade level. External mentors offer ongoing mentoring with biweekly classroom visits and meetings. Additional pedagogical materials and curriculum units are developed by the research staff and given to the teachers for use in the classrooms.

Data collection consists of classroom observations using the SIOP® protocol and other researcher-developed measures to determine the teachers' level of implementation. In addition, student data is collected: pre- and post-assessments for literacy/language development in grades K–3, which include early reading (letter names, letter sounds, phonological awareness), vocabulary, word reading, and listening comprehension. When students reach grade 3, they are also assessed with the state reading and mathematics tests.

Findings from this study should be available in 2009.

The Impact of the SIOP® Model on Middle School Science and Language Learning is another five-year study funded by the U.S. Department of Education. It is one of several studies in the national Center for Research on the Educational Achievement & Teaching of English Language Learners (CREATE). This SIOP® research is conducted by researchers at California State University Long Beach, the Center for Applied Linguistics, and the University of Houston (2005–10). This study uses a randomized experimental design to investigate the impact of the SIOP® Model on student academic achievement in middle school science. Researchers are developing science curriculum units with SIOP® lesson plans and science language assessments that focus on the acquisition of science concepts and language development among English learners.

The study is being conducted in phases. Phase 1 was a pilot study designed to develop and refine science curriculum lessons that incorporate the SIOP® Model features and to field-test academic science language assessments. Phase 2 involves two one-year studies. In the first year, approximately 10 schools will participate as treatment or control sites. Treatment teachers will receive SIOP® training, the SIOP® science lessons, and coaching. In the second year, approximately 15 schools in another district will participate as Treatment 1, Treatment 2, or control sites. Treatment 1 teachers will receive SIOP® training, SIOP® science lessons, and coaching. Treatment 2 teachers will receive SIOP® training and coaching. The analyses will examine if SIOP® lessons help teachers learn the SIOP® Model faster and/or better. Phase 3 will occur in the final two years of the research center: data gathered from years 1–3 will be combined with the research findings from other CREATE research studies and will be tested as a school reform intervention for English learners in several sites across the United States.

Data collection and analyses for Phases 2 and 3 will be of teacher implementation ratings using the SIOP® protocol and student state test results in reading, science, and English language development. In addition, the researchers are collecting data from local district content tests and the project-developed science language tests.

Findings from this study should be available in 2011.

References

Center for Applied Linguistics. (2007). *Academic literacy through sheltered instruction for secondary English language learners.* Final Report to the Carnegie Corporation of New York. Washington, DC: Center for Applied Linguistics.

Darling-Hammond, L. (1998). Teacher learning that supports student learning. *Educational Leadership, 55,* 6–11.

Echevarria, J., Short, D., & Powers, K. (2006). School reform and standards-based education: An instructional model for English language learners. *Journal of Educational Research, 99*(4), 195–211.

Echevarria, J., & Vogt, M. E. (2008). *The SIOP® model SIOP® I institute training manual.* Glenview, IL: Pearson.

Echevarria, J., Vogt, M. E., & Short, D. (2000). *Making content comprehensible for English language learners: The SIOP® Model.* Needham Heights, MA: Allyn & Bacon.

Echevarria, J., Vogt, M. E., & Short, D. (2008). *Making content comprehensible for English learners: The SIOP® Model* (3rd ed). Boston: Pearson/Allyn & Bacon.

Garet, M. S., Porter, A. C., Desimone, L., Birman, B. F., & Yoon, K. S. (2001). What makes professional development effective? Results from a national sample of teachers. *American Educational Research Journal, 38*(4), 915–945.

Guarino, A. J., Echevarria, J., Short, D., Schick, J. E., Forbes, S., & Rueda, R. (2001). The sheltered instruction observation protocol. *Journal of Research in Education, 11*(1), 138–140.

Hudec, J., & Short, D. (Prods). (2002a). *Helping English learners succeed: An overview of the SIOP® Model.* [Video]. Washington, DC: Center for Applied Linguistics.

Hudec, J., & Short, D. (Prods). (2002b). *The SIOP® Model: Sheltered instruction for academic achievement.* [Video]. Washington, DC: Center for Applied Linguistics.

Short, D., & Echevarria, J. (1999). *The sheltered instruction observation protocol: A tool for teacher-researcher collaboration and professional development* (Educational Practice Rep. No. 3). Santa Cruz, CA, and Washington, DC: Center for Research on Education, Diversity & Excellence.

Short, D., Hudec, J, & Echevarria, J. (2002). *Using the SIOP® Model: Professional development manual for sheltered instruction.* Washington, DC: Center for Applied Linguistics.

glossary

Academic language: Language used in formal contexts for academic subjects. The aspect of language connected with literacy and academic achievement. This includes technical and academic terms (*see* Cognitive/Academic Language Proficiency–CALP).

Additive bilingualism: Rather than neglecting or rejecting students' language and culture, additive bilingualism promotes building on what the child brings to the classroom and adding to it.

Alignment: Match among the ESL and content standards, instruction, curriculum, and assessment.

Assessment: The orderly process of gathering, analyzing, interpreting, and reporting student performance, ideally from multiple sources over a period of time.

Basic Interpersonal Communicative Skills (BICS): Face-to-face conversational fluency, including mastery of pronunciation, vocabulary, and grammar. English language learners typically acquire conversational language used in everyday activities before they develop more complex, conceptual language proficiency.

Bilingual instruction: School instruction using two languages, generally a native language of the student and a second language. The amount of time that each language is used depends on the type of bilingual program, its specific objectives, and students' level of language proficiency.

Cognitive Academic Language Learning Approach (CALLA): An instructional model developed by Chamot and O'Malley (1987, 1994) for content and language learning that incorporates student development of learning strategies, specifically metacognitive, cognitive, and socioaffective strategies.

Cognitive/Academic Language Proficiency (CALP): Language proficiency associated with schooling, and the abstract language abilities required for academic work. A more complex, conceptual, linguistic ability that includes analysis, synthesis, and evaluation.

Communicative competence: The combination of grammatical, discourse, strategic, and sociolinguistic competence that allows the recognition and production of fluent and appropriate language in all communicative settings.

Content-based ESL: An instructional approach in which content topics are used as the vehicle for second language learning. A system of instruction in which teachers use a variety of instructional techniques as a way of developing second language, content, cognitive, and study skills, and is often delivered through thematic units.

Content objectives: Statements that identify what students should know and be able to do in particular content areas. They support school district and state content standards and learning outcomes, and they guide teaching and learning in the classroom.

Content standards: Definitions of what students are expected to know and be capable of doing for a given content area; the knowledge and skills that need to be taught in order for students to reach competency; what students are expected to learn and what schools are expected to teach. May be national, state, or local-level standards.

Cross-cultural competence: The ability to understand and follow the cultural rules and norms of more than one system. The ability to respond to the demands of a given situation in a culturally acceptable way.

Culture: The customs, lifestyle, traditions, behavior, attitudes, and artifacts of a given people. Culture also encompasses the ways people organize and interpret the world, and the way events are perceived based on established social norms. A system of standards for understanding the world.

Dialect: The form of a language peculiar to a specific region. Features a variation in vocabulary, grammar, and pronunciation.

Differentiated instruction In order to create a learning environment that addresses the diversity represented in a typical classroom, teachers change the pace, amount, level, or kind of instruction to meet the individual needs of each learner.

Engagement: When students are fully taking part in a lesson, they are said to be engaged. This is a holistic term that encompasses listening, reading, writing, responding, and discussing. The level of students' engagement during a lesson may be assessed to a greater or lesser degree. A low SIOP® score for engagement would imply frequent chatting, daydreaming, nonattention, and other off-task behaviors.

English learners (ELs): Children and adults who are learning English as a second or additional language. This term may apply to learners across various levels of proficiency in English. ELs may also be referred to as English language learners (ELLs), non–English speaking (NES), limited English proficient (LEP), and a non-native speaker (NNS).

EO: Used in some regions, English-only or EO refers to students whose native language is English.

ESL: English as a second language. Used to refer to programs and classes to teach students English as a second (additional) language.

ESOL: English speakers of other languages. Students whose first language is not English and who do not write, speak, and understand the language as well as their classmates.

Evaluation: Judgments about students' learning made by interpreting and analyzing assessment data; the process of judging achievement, growth, product, processes, or changes in these; judgments of education programs. The processes of assessment and evaluation can be viewed as progressive: first, assessment; then, evaluation.

Formative evaluation: Ongoing collection, analysis, and reporting of information about student performance for purposes of instruction and learning.

Grouping: The assignment of students into groups or classes for instruction, such as by age, ability, or achievement; or within classes, such as by reading ability, proficiency, language background, or interests.

Home language: The language, or languages, spoken in the student's home by people who live there. Also referred to as first language (L1), primary language, or native language.

Informal assessment: Appraisal of student performance through unstructured observation; characterized as frequent, ongoing, continuous, and involving simple but important techniques such as verbal checks for understanding, teacher-created assessments, and other nonstandardized procedures. This type of assessment provides teachers with immediate feedback.

Instructional conversations (IC): An approach to teaching that is an interactive dialogue with an instructional intent. An IC approach encourages thoughtful discussion around a concept or idea with balanced participation between teacher and students.

Inter-rater reliability: Measures of the degree of agreement between two different raters on separate ratings of one assessment indicator using the same scale and criteria.

L1: First language. A widely used abbreviation for the primary, home, or native language.

Language competence: An individual's total language ability. The underlying language system as indicated by the individual's language performance.

Language minority: In the United States, a student whose primary language is not English. The individual students' ability to speak English will vary.

Language objectives: Statements that identify what students should know and be able to do while using English (or another language). They support students' language development, often focusing on vocabulary, functional language, questioning, articulating predictions or hypotheses, reading, writing, and so forth.

Language proficiency: An individual's competence in using a language for basic communication and for academic purposes. May be categorized as stages of language acquisition (*see* Levels of language proficiency).

Levels of language proficiency: Students learning language progress through stages. The stages or levels are labeled differently across geographic regions. For example, the WIDA Consortium (World-class Instructional Design and Assessment) uses the terms Entering (Level 1), Beginning (Level 2), Developing (Level 3), Expanding (Level 4), and

Bridging (Level 5). Krashen and Terrell, 1983, 1984 describe the stages as the following:

Preproduction: Students at this stage are not ready to produce much language, so they primarily communicate with gestures and actions. They are absorbing the new language and developing receptive vocabulary.

Early production: Students at this level speak using one or two words or short phrases. Their receptive vocabulary is developing; they understand approximately one thousand words. Students can answer "who, what, and where" questions with limited expression.

Speech emergence: Students speak in longer phrases and complete sentences. However, they may experience frustration at not being able to express completely what they know. Although the number of errors they make increases, they can communicate ideas and the quantity of speech they produce increases.

Intermediate fluency: Students may appear to be fluent; they engage in conversation and produce connected narrative. Errors are usually of style or usage. Lessons continue to expand receptive vocabulary, and activities develop higher levels of language use in content areas. Students at this level are able to communicate effectively.

Advanced fluency: Students communicate very effectively, orally and in writing, in social and academic settings.

Limited English Proficient (LEP): A term used to refer to a student with restricted understanding or use of written and spoken English; a learner who is still developing competence in using English. The federal government uses the term *LEP*, while *EL* or *ELL* is more commonly used in schools.

Mnemonics: From the Greek *mnemon,* meaning "mindful." Mnemonics are devices to jog the memory. For example, steps of a learning strategy are often abbreviated to form an acronym or word that enables the learner to remember the steps.

Multilingualism: The ability to speak more than two languages; proficiency in more than two languages.

Native English speaker: An individual whose first language is English.

Native language: An individual's first, primary, or home language (L1).

Non–English speaking (NES): Individuals who are in an English-speaking environment (such as U.S. schools) but who have not acquired any English proficiency.

Nonverbal communication: Paralinguistic messages such as intonation, stress, pauses and rate of speech, and nonlinguistic messages such as gestures, facial expressions, and body language that can accompany speech or be conveyed without the aid of speech.

Performance assessment: A measure of educational achievement in which students produce a response, create a product, or apply knowledge in ways similar to tasks required in the instructional environment. The performance measures are analyzed and interpreted according to preset criteria.

Portfolio assessment: A type of performance assessment that involves gathering multiple indicators of student progress to support course goals in a dynamic, ongoing process. Portfolios are purposeful collections of student performance that evince students' efforts, progress, and achievement over time.

Primary language: An individual's first, home, or native language (L1).

Pull-out instruction: Students are "pulled-out" from their regular classes for special classes of ESL instruction, remediation, or acceleration.

Realia: Real-life objects and artifacts used to supplement teaching; can provide effective visual scaffolds for English learners.

Reliability: Statistical consistency in measurements and tests, such as the extent to which two assessments measure student performance in the same way.

Rubrics: Statements that describe indicators of performance, which include scoring criteria, on a continuum; may be described as "developmental" (e.g., emergent, beginning, developing, proficient) or "evaluative" (e.g., exceptional, thorough, adequate, inadequate).

Scaffolding: Adult (e.g., teacher) support for learning and student performance of the tasks through instruction, modeling, questioning, feedback, graphic organizers, and more, across successive engagements. These supports are gradually withdrawn, thus transferring more and more autonomy to the child. Scaffolding activities provide support for learning that can be removed as learners are able to demonstrate strategic behaviors in their own learning activities.

SDAIE (Specially Designed Academic Instruction in English): A term for sheltered instruction used mostly in California. It features strategies and techniques for making content understandable for English learners. Although some SDAIE techniques are research based, SDAIE itself has not been scientifically validated. (*See* Sheltered instruction.)

Self-contained ESL class: A class consisting solely of English speakers of other languages for the purpose of learning English; content may also be taught. An effective alternative to pull-out instruction.

Sheltered instruction (SI): A means for making content comprehensible for English learners while they are developing English proficiency. The SIOP® is a validated model of sheltered instruction. Sheltered classrooms, which may, in a mix of native English speakers and English learners or only ELs, integrate language and content while infusing sociocultural awareness. (*See* SDAIE and SIOP®.)

SIOP® (Sheltered Instruction Observation Protocol): A scientifically validated model of sheltered instruction designed to make grade-level academic content understandable for English learners while at the same time developing their English language. The protocol and lesson planning guide ensure that teachers are consistently implementing practices known to be effective for English learners.

Social language: Basic language proficiency associated with fluency in day-to-day situations, including the classroom. (*See* Basic Interpersonal Communicative Skills [BICS].)

Sociocultural competence: The ability to function effectively by following the rules and behavioral expectations held by members of a given social or cultural group.

Sociolinguistic competence: The degree to which a language is used and understood in a given situation. The use of appropriate comments and responses in conversation. (*See* Communicative competence.)

Standard: *See* Content standards.

Standard American English: "That variety of American English in which most educational texts, government, and media publications are written in the United States; English as it is spoken and written by those groups with social, economic, and political power in the United States. Standard American English is a relative concept, varying widely in pronunciation and in idiomatic use but maintaining a fairly uniform grammatical structure" (Harris and Hodges, 1995, p. 241).

Standards-based assessment: Assessment involving the planning, gathering, analyzing, and reporting of a student's performance according to the ESL and/or district content standards.

Strategies: Mental processes and plans that people use to help them comprehend, learn, and retain new information. There are three types of strategies—cognitive, metacognitive, and social/affective—and these are consciously adapted and monitored during reading, writing, and learning.

Subtractive bilingualism: The learning of a new language at the expense of the primary language. Learners often lose their native language and culture because they don't have opportunities to continue learning or using it, or they perceive that language to be of lower status. Loss of the primary language often leads to cultural ambivalence.

Summative evaluation: The final collection, analysis, and reporting of information about student achievement or program effectiveness at the end of a given time frame.

Task: An activity that calls for a response to a question, issue, or problem.

Validity: A statistical measure of an assessment's match between the information collected and its stated purpose; evidence that inferences from evaluation are trustworthy.

Vignette: A short sketch that gives a description of an instructional process drawn from real-life classroom experiences.

references

Abedi, J., & Lord, C. (2001). The language factor in mathematics tests. *Applied Measurement in Education, 14*(3), 219–234.

Afflerbach, P., Pearson, P. D., & Paris, S. G. (2008). Clarifying differences between reading skills and reading strategies. *The Reading Teacher, 61*(5), 364–373.

Allen, J. (2007). *Inside words: Tools for teaching academic vocabulary, grades 4–12.* Portland, ME: Stenhouse Publishers.

Alvarez, M. C. (1990). *Knowledge activation and schema construction.* Paper presented at the Annual Meeting of the American Educational Research Association, Boston, MA, 1990, 25p. [ED 317 988]

Anderson, L. W., & Krathwohl, D. R. (Eds.). (2001). *Taxonomy for learning, teaching, and assessing: A revision of Bloom's Taxonomy of Educational Objectives.* Boston: Longman.

Anderson, R. C. (1984). Role of the reader's schema in comprehension, learning, and memory. In R. C. Anderson, J. Osborn, & R. J. Tierney (Eds.), *Learning to read in American schools: Basal readers and content texts.* Hillsdale, NJ: Erlbaum.

Anderson, R. C. (1994). Role of the reader's schema in comprehension, learning, and memory. In R. Ruddell, M. Ruddell, & H. Singer (Eds.), *Theoretical models and processes of reading* (4th Ed.). Newark, DE: International Reading Association.

Artiles, A. (1998). Overrepresentation of minority students: The case for greater specificity or reconsideration of the variables examined. *Journal of Special Education, 32*(1), 32–36.

Au, K., Garcia, G. G., Goldenberg, C., & Vogt, M.E. (2005). *Handbook for English language learners.* Boston: Houghton Mifflin.

August, D. A. (2006). How does first language literacy development relate to second language literacy development? In E. Hamayan & R. Freeman (Eds.), *English language learners in school: Over 50 experts answer YOUR questions* (pp. 71–72). Philadelphia: Caslon Publishing.

August, D., & Hakuta, K. (Eds.). (1997). *Improving schooling for language minority children: A research agenda.* Washington, DC: National Academy Press.

August, D., & Shanahan T. (Eds.). (2006a). *Developing literacy in second-language learners: A report of the National Literacy Panel on Language-Minority Children and Youth.* Mahwah, NJ: Lawrence Erlbaum Associates.

August, D., & Shanahan, T. (2006b). *Executive summary. Developing literacy in second-language learners: Report of the National Literacy Panel on Language-Minority Children and Youth.* Mahwah, NJ: Lawrence Erlbaum Associates. Available at http://www.cal.org/projects/archive/nlpreports/Executive_Summary.pdf

Bailey, A. (Ed.). (2007). *The language demands of school: Putting academic English to the test.* New Haven, CT: Yale University Press.

Bailey, A., & Butler, F. (2007). A conceptual framework of academic English language for broad application to education.

In A. Bailey (Ed.), *The language demands of school: Putting academic English to the test* (pp. 68–102). New Haven, CT: Yale University Press.

Baker, L. (2004). Reading comprehension and science inquiry: Metacognitive connections. In E. W. Saul (Ed.), *Crossing borders in literacy and science instruction: Perspectives on theory and practice* (pp. 239–257). Newark, DE: International Reading Association; Arlington, VA: National Science Teachers Association (NSTA) Press.

Baker, L., & Brown, A. L. (1984). Metacognitive skills and reading. In P. D. Pearson (Ed.), *Handbook of reading research.* New York: Longman.

Barnes, C., Mercer, G., & Shakespeare, T. (1999). *Exploring disability: A sociological introduction.* Cambridge: Polity Press.

Barnhardt, S. (1997). Effective memory strategies. *NCLRC Language Resource, 1*(6), http://www.nclrc.org

Bartolome, L. I. (1994). Beyond the methods fetish: Toward a humanizing pedagogy. *Harvard Educational Review, 64*(2), 173–194.

Barton, M. L., Heidama, C., & Jordan, D. (2002). Teaching reading in mathematics and science. *Educational Leadership, 60*(3), 24–28.

Batalova, J., Fix, M., & Murray, J. (2005). *English language learner adolescents: Demographics and literacy achievements.* Report to the Center for Applied Linguistics. Washington, DC: Migration Policy Institute.

Baumann, J. F. (2005). Vocabulary-comprehension relationships. In B. Maloch, J. V. Hoffman, D. L. Schallert, C. M. Fairbanks, & J. Worthy (Eds.), *54th Yearbook of the National Reading Conference.* Oak Creek, WI: National Reading Conference, Inc.

Baumann, J., Jones, L., & Seifert-Kessell, N. (1993). Using think-alouds to enhance children's comprehension monitoring abilities. *The Reading Teacher, 47*(3), 184–193.

Bean, T. W. (2000). Reading in the content areas: Social constructivist dimensions. In M. L. Kamil, P. B. Mosenthal, P. D. Pearson, & R. Barr (Eds.), *Handbook of reading research* (Vol. III, pp. 629–644). Mahwah, NJ: Lawrence Erlbaum Associates.

Bear, D. R., Helman, L., Invernizzi, M., Templeton, S., & Johnston, F. (2007). *Words their way with English learners: Word study for spelling, phonics, and vocabulary instruction.* Boston: Merrill Prentice Hall.

Bear, D. R., Invernizzi, M., Templeton, S., & Johnston, F. (2007). *Words their way: Word study for phonics, vocabulary, and spelling instruction* (4th ed.). Upper Saddle River, NJ: Merrill Prentice Hall.

Bear, D. R., Templeton, S., Helman, L. A., & Baren, T. (2003). Orthographic development and learning to read in different languages. In G. Garcia (Ed.), *English learners: Reaching the highest level of English literacy* (pp. 71–95). Newark, DE: International Reading Association.

Beck, I., McKeown, M., & Kucan, I. (2002). *Bringing words to life: Robust vocabulary.* New York: Guilford Press.

Beck, I. L., & McKeown, M. G. (2006). *Improving comprehension with Questioning the Author: A fresh and expanded view of a powerful approach.* New York: Scholastic.

Beck, I. L., & McKeown, M. G. (2002). Questioning the author: Making sense of social studies. *Educational Leadership, 60*(3), 44–47.

Beck, I. L., Perfetti, C., & McKeown, M. G. (1982). Effects of long-term vocabulary instruction on lexical access and reading comprehension. *Journal of Educational Psychology, 74*, 506–521.

Berliner, D. C. (1984). The half-full glass: A review of research on teaching. In P. L. Hosford (Ed.), *Using what we know about teaching* (pp. 51–77). Alexandria, VA: Association for Supervision and Curriculum Development.

Berman, P., McLaughlin, B., Minicucci, C., Nelson, B., & Woodworth, K. (1995). *School reform and student diversity: Case studies of exemplary practices for LEP students.* Washington, DC: National Clearinghouse for Bilingual Education.

Biancarosa, G., & Snow, C. (2004). *Reading next: A vision for action and research in middle and high school literacy.* Report to the Carnegie Corporation of New York. Washington, DC: Alliance for Excellent Education.

Bickel, W. E., & Bickel, D. D. (1986). Effective schools, classrooms and instruction: Implications for special education. *Exceptional Children, 52*(6) 489–500.

Biemiller, A. (2004). Teaching vocabulary in the primary grades. In J. F. Baumann & J. E. Kame'enui (Eds.), *Vocabulary instruction: Research to practice.* New York: Guilford Press.

Biemiller, A. (2005). Vocabulary development and instruction: A prerequisite for school learning. In D. Dickinson & S. Neuman (Eds.), *Handbook of early literacy research,* Vol. 2. New York: Guilford Press.

Blachowicz, L. Z., & Fisher, P. (2000). Vocabulary instruction. In R. L. Kamil, P. B. Mosenthal, P. D. Pearson, & R. Barr (Eds.) *Handbook of Reading Research,* Vol. 3. (pp. 503–523). Mahwah, NJ: Lawrence Erlbaum Inc.

Bloom, B., Engelhart, M., Furst, E., Hill, W., & Krathworl, D. (Eds.). (1956). *Taxonomy of educational objectives: The classification of educational goals. Handbook I: Cognitive domain.* New York: David McKay Co.

Borko, H. (2004). Professional development and teacher learning: Mapping the terrain. *Educational Researcher, 33*(8), 3–15.

Bottle biology: An idea book for exploring the world through plastic bottles and other recyclable materials. (1993). Dubuque, IA: Kendall/Hunt Publishing Company.

Brown, R. (2008). The road not yet taken: A transactional strategies approach to comprehension instruction. *The Reading Teacher, 6*(7), 538–547.

Bransford, J. (1994). Schema activation and schema acquisition: Comments on Richard C. Anderson's remarks. In R. Ruddell, M. Ruddell, & H. Singer (Eds.), *Theoretical models and processes of reading* (4th ed.). Newark, DE: International Reading Association.

Brown, J. E., & Doolittle, J. (2008). *A cultural, linguistic, and ecological framework for response to intervention with English language learners.* The National Center for Culturally Responsive Educational Systems (NCCRESt). Retrieved December 10, 2008 from http://www.nccrest.org/

Buck, B., Carr, S., & Robertson, J. (2008). Positive psychology and student engagement. *Journal of Cross-Disciplinary Perspectives in Education, 1*(1), pp. 28–35.

Buehl, D. (2009). *Classroom strategies for interactive learning* (3rd ed.). Newark, DE: International Reading Association.

Burke, J. (2002). The Internet reader. *Educational Leadership, 60*(3), 38–42.

California Department of Education, Educational Demographics Unit. (2004). Statewide Stanford 9 test results for reading: Number of students tested and percent scoring at or above the 50th percentile ranking (NPR). Retrieved February 23, 2004, from www.cde.ca.gov/dataquest/.

Callahan, R. (2005). Tracking and high school English learners: Limiting opportunity to learn. *American Educational Research Journal, 42*(2) 305–328.

Cañado, M. L. P. (2005). English and Spanish spelling: Are they really different? *The Reading Teacher, 58*(6), 522–530.

Cantoni-Harvey, G. (1987). *Content-area language instruction: Approaches and strategies.* Reading, MA: Addison-Wesley.

Capps, R., Fix, M., Murray, J., Ost, J., Passel, J., & Herwantoro, S. (2005). *The new demography of America's schools: Immigration and the No Child Left Behind Act.* Washington, DC: The Urban Institute.

Carrell, P. (1987). Content and formal schemata in ESL reading. *TESOL Quarterly, 21*(3), 461–481.

Cazden, C. (2001). *Classroom discourse: The language of teaching and learning* (2nd ed.). Portsmouth, NH: Heinemann.

Center for Applied Linguistics. (2007). *Academic literacy through sheltered instruction for secondary English language learners.* Final Report to the Carnegie Corporation of New York. Washington, DC: Center for Applied Linguistics.

Chamot, A. U., & O'Malley, J. M. (1987). The cognitive academic language learning approach: A bridge to the mainstream. *TESOL Quarterly, 21*(2), 227–249.

Chamot, A. U., & O'Malley, J. M. (1994). *The CALLA handbook: Implementing the cognitive academic language learning approach.* Reading, MA: Addison-Wesley.

Chiesi, H., Spilich, G., & Voss, J. (1979). Acquisition of domain-related information in relation to high- and low-domain knowledge. *Journal of Verbal Learning and Verbal Behavior, 18*, 257–274.

Christen, W. L., & Murphy, T. J. (1991). *Increasing comprehension by activating prior knowledge.* ERIC Digest. Bloomington, IN: ERIC Clearinghouse on Reading, English, and Communication. [ED 328 885]

Colburn, A., & Echevarria, J. (1999). Meaningful lessons. *The Science Teacher, 66*(2) 36–39.

Collier, V. P. (1987). Age and rate of acquisition of language for academic purposes. *TESOL Quarterly, 21*(4), 677.

Coltrane, B. (2002). *English language learners and high-stakes tests: An overview of the issues.* ERIC Digest. Washington, DC: ERIC Clearinghouse on Languages and Linguistics, Center for Applied Linguistics.

Comer, J. P. (1984). Home-school relationships as they affect the academic success of children. *Education and Urban Society, 16*(3), 323–337.

Cooper, J. D., Pikulski, J. J., Au, K., Calderon, M., Comas, J., Lipson, M., Mims, S., Page, S., Valencia, S., & Vogt, M.E. (2003). *Invitations to literacy*. Boston: Houghton Mifflin Company.

Coxhead, A. (2000). A new academic word list. *TESOL Quarterly, 34*(2), 213–238.

Crandall, J. A. (1993). Content-centered learning in the United States. *Annual Review of Applied Linguistics, 13*, 111–126.

Crawford, A. N. (2003). Communicative approaches to second language acquisition: The bridge to second-language literacy. In G. G. Garcia (Ed.), *English learners: Reaching the highest level of English literacy*. Newark, DE: International Reading Association.

Crossley, S., McCarthy, P., Louwerse, M., & McNamara, D. (2007). A linguistic analysis of simplified and authentic texts. *The Modern Language Journal, 19*(2), 15–30.

Cummins, J. (1984). *Bilingualism and special education: Issues in assessment and pedagogy*. Clevedon, England: Multilingual Matters.

Cummins, J. (2000). *Language, power and pedagogy*. Clevedon, England: Multilingual Matters.

Cunningham, P. M. (2004). *Phonics they use: Words for reading and writing* (4th ed.). New York: Harper-Collins College Press.

Dale, E. (1965). Vocabulary measurement: Techniques and major findings. *Elementary English, 42*, 82–88.

Dale, E., & O'Rourke, J. (1981). *Living word vocabulary*. Chicago: World Book/Childcraft International.

Darling-Hammond, L. (1998). Teacher learning that supports student learning. *Educational Leadership, 55*(5), 6–11.

Darling-Hammond, L., & McLaughlin, M. W. (1995). Policies that support professional development in an era of reform. *Phi Delta Kappan, 76*(8), 597–604.

Davis, S. J., & Winek, J. (1989). Improving expository writing by increasing background knowledge. *Journal of Reading 33*(3), 178–181.

Day, R. (Ed.). (1986). *Talking to learn: Conversation in second language acquisition*. Cambridge, MA: Newbury House Publishers.

DeLeeuw, H. (2008). *English language learners in Washington State*. Executive Summary. Report to the Washington State Board of Education, Olympia, Washington, January 10, 2008.

Dermody, M., & Speaker, R. (1995). Effects of reciprocal strategy training in prediction, clarification, question generation, and summarization on fourth graders' reading comprehension. In K. A. Hinchman, D. Leu, & C. K. Kinzer (Eds.), *Perspectives on literacy research and practice*. Chicago: National Reading Conference.

Deschenes, C., Ebeling, D., & Sprague, J. (1994). *Adapting curriculum and instruction in inclusive classrooms: A teacher's desk reference*. Bloomington, Indiana: Institute for the Study of Developmental Disabilities, Indiana University.

Deshler, D., & Schumaker, J. (2006). *Teaching adolescents with disabilities: Accessing the general education curriculum*. Thousand Oaks, CA: Corwin Press.

Diamond, L., & Gutlohn, L. (2006). *Vocabulary handbook*. Berkeley, CA: Core Literacy Library.

Dole, J., Duffy, G., Roehler, L., & Pearson, P. D. (1991). Moving from the old to the new: Research in reading comprehension instruction. *Review of Educational Research, 61*, 239–264.

Duff, P. A. (2005). ESL in secondary schools: Programs, problematics, and possibilities. *Annual Review of Applied Linguistics*, 45–63.

Duffy, G. G. (2002). The case for direct explanation of strategies. In C. C. Block & M. Pressley (Eds.), *Comprehension instruction: Research-based best practices*. New York: Guilford Press.

Dunn, L. (1968). Special education for the mildly retarded: Is much of it justifiable? *Exceptional Children, 34*, 5–22.

Echevarria, J. (1995a). Sheltered instruction for students with learning disabilities who have limited English proficiency. *Intervention in School and Clinic, 30*(5), 302–305.

Echevarria, J. (1995b). Interactive reading instruction: A comparison of proximal and distal effects of instructional conversations. *Exceptional Children, 61*(6), 536–552.

Echevarria, J. (1998). *A model of sheltered instruction for English language learners*. Paper presented at the conference for the Division on Diversity of the Council for Exceptional Children, Washington, DC.

Echevarria, J., & Graves, A. (2007). *Sheltered content instruction: Teaching English language learners with diverse abilities* (3rd ed.). Boston: Allyn & Bacon.

Echevarria, J., Greene, G., & Goldenberg, C. (1996). *A comparison of sheltered instruction and effective non-sheltered instruction on the achievement of LEP students*. Pilot study.

Echevarria, J., Powers, K., & Elliott, J. (2004). Promising practices for curbing disproportionate representation of minority students in special education. *Issues in Teacher Education: Themed Issues on Special Needs Education, 13*(1), 19–34.

Echevarria, J., & Short, D. (in press). Programs and practices for effective sheltered content instruction. In D. Dolson & L. Burnham-Massey (Eds.). *Improving education for English learners: Research-based approaches*. Sacramento, CA: California Department of Education.

Echevarria, J., Short, D., & Powers, K. (2006). School reform and standards-based education: An instructional model for English language learners. *Journal of Educational Research, 99*(4), 195–211.

Echevarria, J., Short, D., & Vogt, M.E. (2008). *Implementing the SIOP® Model through effective professional development and coaching*. Boston, MA: Pearson/Allyn & Bacon.

Echevarria, J., & Vogt, ME. (2008). *The SIOP® model, SIOP® I institute training manual*. Glenview, IL: Pearson.

Echevarria, J., Vogt, M.E., & Short, D. (2008). *Making content comprehensible for English language learners: The SIOP® Model*. Needham Heights, MA: Allyn & Bacon.

Echevarria, J., Vogt, M.E., & Short, D. (2004). *Making content comprehensible for English learners: The SIOP® model* (2nd ed.). Boston, MA: Pearson/Allyn & Bacon.

Echevarria, J., Vogt, M.E., & Short, D. (2008). *Making content comprehensible for English learners: The SIOP® Model* (3rd ed.). Boston: Pearson/Allyn & Bacon.

Echevarria, J., Vogt, M.E., & Short, D. (in press). *The SIOP® Model for teaching mathematics to English learners*. Boston: Allyn & Bacon.

Edley, C., Jr., & Wald, J. (2002, December 16). The grade retention fallacy. *The Boston Globe.*

Edwards, P. A., Turner, J. D., & Mokhtari, K. (2008). *The Reading Teacher, 61*(8), 682–684.

Ellis, R. (2006). Current issues in the teaching of grammar: An SLA perspective. *TESOL Quarterly, 40*(1), pp. 83–107.

Erickson, F., & Shultz, J. (1991). Students' experience of the curriculum. In P. W. Jackson (Ed.), *Handbook of research on curriculum.* New York: Macmillan.

Fathman, A., & Crowther, D. (Eds.). (2006). *Science for English language learners: K–12 classroom strategies.* Arlington, VA: NSTA Press.

Fillmore, L. W., & Snow, C. (2002). What teachers need to know about language. In C. T. Adger, C. E. Snow, & D. Christian (Eds.), *What teachers need to know about language* (pp. 7–53). McHenry, IL: Delta Systems and Center for Applied Linguistics.

Fillmore, L. W., & Valadez, C. (1986). Teaching bilingual learners. In M. C. Wittrock (Ed.), *Handbook of research on teaching* (pp. 648–685). New York: Macmillan.

Fisher, D., & Frey, N. (2008a). *Better learning through structured teaching.* Alexandria, VA: Association for Supervision and Curriculum Development.

Fisher, D., & Frey, N. (2008b). *Wordwise & content rich: Five essential steps to teaching academic vocabulary.* Portsmouth, NH: Heinemann.

Fisher, D., Frey, N., & Williams, D. (2002). Seven literacy strategies that work. *Educational Leadership, 60*(3), 70–73.

Flood, J., Lapp, D., Flood, S., & Nagel, G. (1992). Am I allowed to group? Using flexible patterns for effective instruction. *The Reading Teacher, 45*, 608–616.

Ford, D. (1998). The underrepresentation of minority students in gifted education: Problems and promises in recruitment and retention. *Journal of Special Education, 32*(1), 4–14.

Fordham, D. (2006). Crafting questions that address comprehension strategies in content reading. *Journal of Adolescent & Adult Literacy, 49*(5), 391–396.

Fuchs, D., Fuchs, L. S., & Bahr, M. W. (1990). Mainstream assistance teams: A scientific basis for the art of consultation. *Exceptional Children, 57*, 128–139.

Futrell, M., & Gomez, J. (2008). How tracking creates a poverty of learning. *Educational Leadership, 65*(8), 74–78.

Gall, M. (November 1984). Synthesis of research on teachers' questioning. *Educational Leadership 42*(3), 40–47.

Gandara, P., Maxwell-Jolly, J., & Driscoll, A. (2005). *Listening to teachers of English language learners: A survey of California teachers' challenges, experiences, and professional development needs.* Santa Cruz, CA: The Center for the Future of Teaching and Learning.

Garcia, G. E., & Godina, H. (2004). Addressing the literacy needs of adolescent English language learners. In T. Jetton and J. Dole (Eds.), *Adolescent literacy: Research and practice* (pp. 304–320). New York: The Guilford Press.

Gardner, H. (1993). *Multiple intelligences: The theory in practice.* New York: Basic Books.

Genesee, F. (1994). *Educating second language children: The whole child, the whole curriculum, the whole community.* New York: Cambridge University Press.

Genesee, F. (Ed.). (1999). *Program alternatives for linguistically diverse students.* Educational Practice Report No. 1. Santa Cruz and Washington, DC: Center for Research on Education, Diversity & Excellence.

Genesee, F., Lindholm-Leary, K., Saunders, W., & Christian, D. (2006). *Educating English language learners: A synthesis of research evidence.* New York: Cambridge University Press.

Gersten, R., Baker, S., Shanahan, T., Linan-Thompson, S., Collins, P., & Scarcella, R. (2007). *Effective literacy and English language instruction for English learners in the elementary grades: A practice guide.* (NCEE 2007–4011). Washington, DC: National Center for Education Evaluation and Regional Assistance, Institute of Education Sciences, U.S. Department of Education. Retrieved May 17, 2008 from http://ies.ed.gov/ncee.

Geva, E. (2006). Second-language oral proficiency and second-language literacy. In D. August & T. Shanahan (Eds.). *Developing literacy in second-language learners: Report of the National Literacy Panel on Language Minority Children and Youth.* Mahwah, NJ: Lawrence Erlbaum Associates.

Gibbons, P. (2002). *Scaffolding language, scaffolding learning.* Portsmouth, NH: Heinemann.

Gibbons, P. (2003). Mediating language learning: Teacher interactions with ESL students in a content-based classroom. *TESOL Quarterly, 37*(2), 247–273.

Gibson, V., & Hasbrouck, J. (2008). *Differentiated instruction: Grouping for success.* New York: McGraw-Hill.

Glick, J. E., & White, M. J. (2004). Post-secondary school participation of immigrant and native youth: The role of familial resources and educational expectations. *Social Science Research, 33*, 272–299.

Goldenberg, C. (1992–93). Instuctional conversations: Promoting comprehension through discussion. *The Reading Teacher, 46*(4), 316–326.

Goldenberg, C. (2008). Teaching English language learners: What the research does and does not say. *American Educator, 32*(2), 8–23, 42–44. Retrieved June 21, 2008 from http://www.aft.org/pubs-reports/american_educator/index.htm

González, J. M., & Darling-Hammond, L. (1997). *New concepts for new challenges: Professional development for teachers of immigrant youth.* McHenry, IL: Delta Systems and CAL.

Goodlad, J. (1984). *A place called school: Prospects for the future.* New York: McGraw-Hill.

Graff, G. (2003). *Clueless in academe.* New Haven, CT: Yale University Press.

Graves, A., Gersten, R. & Haager, D. (2004). Literacy instruction in multiple-language first-grade classrooms: Linking student outcomes to observed instructional practice. *Learning Disabilities Research & Practice, 19*(4), 262–272.

Graves, M. F., & Fitzgerald, J. (2006). Effective vocabulary instruction for English-language learners. In C. C. Block, & J. N. Mangieri (Eds.), *The vocabulary-enriched classroom: Practice for improving the reading performance of all students in grades 3 and up.* New York: Scholastic.

Gray, W. S., & Leary, B. E. (1935). *What makes a book readable?* Chicago: The University of Chicago Press.

Guarino, A. J., Echevarria, J., Short, D., Schick, J. E., Forbes, S., & Rueda, R. (2001). The Sheltered Instruction Observation Protocol. *Journal of Research in Education, 11*(1), 138–140.

Gunderson, L. (1991). *ESL literacy instruction: A guidebook to theory and practice.* Englewood Cliffs, NJ: Regents/Prentice Hall.

Gunderson, L., & Siegel, L. S. (2005). The evils of the use of IQ tests to define learning disabilities in first- and second-language learners. In S. B. Barrentine & S. M. Stokes (Eds.), *Reading assessment: Principles and practices for elementary teachers* (2nd ed.). Newark, DE: International Reading Association.

Guthrie, J. T., & Ozgungor, S. (2002). Instructional contexts for reading engagement. In C. C. Block & M. Pressley (Eds.). *Comprehension instruction: Research-based best practices* (pp. 275–288). New York: Guilford Press.

Gutiérrez, K. D. (2004). Literacy as laminated activity: Rethinking literacy for English learners. In C. M. Fairbanks, J. Worthy, B. Maloch, J. V. Hoffman, & D. L. Schallert (Eds.), *53rd Yearbook of the National Reading Conference.* Oak Creek, WI: National Reading Conference.

Haager, D., Dimino, J. A., & Windmueller, M. P. (2007). *Interventions for reading success.* Baltimore, MD: Brookes Publishing.

Hakuta, K., Butler, Y., & Witt, D. (2000). *How long does it take English learners to attain proficiency?* Policy Report 2000–1. Santa Barbara: University of California, Linguistic Minority Research Institute.

Harris, T. L., & Hodges, R. E. (Eds.). (1995). *The literacy dictionary: The vocabulary of reading and writing.* Newark, DE: International Reading Association.

Harry, B. (1992). Restructuring the participation of African-American parents in special education. *Exceptional Children, 59*(2), 123–131.

Hart, B., & Risley, T. R. (2003). The early catastrophe: The 30 million word gap. *American Educator, 27,* 4–9.

Hawkin, L. (2005). Behavior programs for older students: What's helpful in secondary schools? *The Special Edge, 19*(1), 1–5.

Hayes, D. A., & Tierney, R. J. (1982). Developing readers' knowledge through analogy. *Reading Research Quarterly 17*(2), 256–280.

Helman, M., & Buchanan, K. (1993). *Reforming mathematics instruction for ESL literacy students.* NCBE Program Information Guide Series, Number 15, Fall 1993. (www.ncela.gwu.edu/ncbepubs/pigs/pig15.htm)

Henry, M. K. (1990). *TUTOR 3.* Los Gatos, CA: Lex Press.

Hiebert, E. H. (1983). An examination of ability grouping for reading instruction. *Reading Research Quarterly, 18,* 231–255.

Hinkel, E. (2006). Current perspectives on teaching the four skills. *TESOL Quarterly, 40*(1), pp. 109–131.

Honea, J. M. (1982, December). Wait-time as an instructional variable: An influence on teacher and student. *Clearinghouse, 56*(4), 167–170.

Hudec, J., & Short, D. (Prods.). (2002a). *Helping English learners succeed: An overview of the SIOP Model.* (Video). Washington, DC: Center for Applied Linguistics.

Hudec, J., & Short, D. (Prods.) (2002b). *The SIOP Model: Sheltered instruction for academic achievement.* (Video). Washington, DC: Center for Applied Linguistics.

Hunter, M. (1982). *Mastery teaching: Increasing instructional effectiveness in secondary schools, college, and universities.* El Segundo, CA: TIP Publications.

Ima, K., & Rumbaut, R. G. (1989). Southeast Asian refugees in American schools: A comparison of fluent-English-proficient and limited-English-proficient students. *Topics in Language Disorders, 9*(3), 54–77.

IRA & NICHD (2007). *Key issues and questions in English language learners literacy research.* Washington, DC: International Reading Association and National Institute of Child Health and Human Development. Retrieved July 15, 2008 from http://www.reading.org/downloads/resources/ELL_paper_071022.pdf

Jamieson, A., Curry, A., & Martinez, G. (2001). *School enrollment in the United States—Social and economic characteristics of students.* Current Population Reports, P20–533. Washington, DC: U.S. Government Printing Office.

Jensen, E. (2005). *Teaching with the brain in mind* (2nd Ed.). Alexandria, VA: Association for Supervision and Curriculum Development.

Jiménez, R. T. (2004). More equitable literacy assessments for Latino students. *The Reading Teacher, 57*(6), 576–578.

Jiménez, R. T., Garcia, G. E., & Pearson, P. D. (1996). The reading strategies of bilingual Latina/o students who are successful English readers: Opportunities and obstacles. *Reading Research Quarterly, 31*(1), 90–112.

Johnson, E., & Smith, L. (2008). Implementation of response to intervention at middle school: Challenges and potential benefits. *Teaching Exceptional Children, 40*(3), 46–52.

Kauffman, D., & Apple, G. (2000). *Oxford picture dictionary for the content areas.* Oxford, England: Oxford University Press.

Kea, C., & Utley, C. (1998). To teach me is to know me. *Journal of Special Education 32*(1), 44–48.

Keene, E. O., & Zimmerman, S. (1997). *Mosaic of thought: Teaching comprehension in a reader's workshop.* Portsmouth, NH: Heinemann.

Kindler, A. (2002). *Survey of the states' limited English proficient students and available educational programs and services. 2000–01 summary report.* Washington, DC: National Clearinghouse for English Language Acquisition.

Klinger, J., & Harry, B. (2006). The special education referral and decision-making process for English language learners: Child study team meetings and staffings. *Teachers College Record, 108,* 2247–2281.

Kober, N., Zabala, D., Chudowsky, N., Chudowsky, V., Gayler, K., & McMurrer, J. (2006). *State high school exit exams: A challenging year.* Washington, DC: Center on Education Policy.

Krashen, S. (1985). *The input hypothesis: Issues and implications.* New York: Longman.

Krashen, S. (2003). Three roles for reading for minority-language children. In G. Garcia (Ed.), *English learners: Reaching the highest level of literacy learning.* Newark, DE: International Reading Association.

Krashen, S., & Terrell, T. (1983). *The natural approach: Language acquisition in the classroom.* Englewood Cliffs, NJ: Alemany/Prentice Hall.

Kukic, S. J. (2002). *The complete school for all.* Keynote presentation at the 2nd Annual Pacific Northwest Behavior Symposium, Seattle, WA.

Lacina, J., Levine, L. N., & Sowa, P. (2006). *Helping English language learners succeed in preK–elementary schools.* Alexandria, VA: Teachers of English to Speakers of Other Languages, Inc.

Lee, J. (2006). *Teaching achievement gaps and assessing the impact of NCLB on the gaps: An in-depth look into national and state reading and math outcome trends.* Cambridge, MA: The Civil Rights Project at Harvard University.

Leafstedt, J., Richards, C., Gerber, M. (2004). Effectiveness of explicit phonological-awareness instruction for at-risk English learners. *Learning Disabilities Research & Practice, 19*(4), 252–261.

Lee, J., Grigg, W., & Dion, P. (2007). *The nation's report card: Mathematics 2007.* (NCES 2007–494). U.S. Department of Education, Institute of Education Sciences, National Center for Education Statistics. Washington, DC: U.S. Government Printing Office.

Lee, J., Grigg, W., & Donahue, P. (2007). *The nation's report card: Reading 2007.* (NCES 2007–496). U.S. Department of Education, Institute of Education Sciences, National Center for Education Statistics. Washington, DC: U.S. Government Printing Office.

Leinhardt, G., Bickel, W., & Pallay, A. (1982). Unlabeled but still entitled: Toward more effective remediation. *Teachers College Record, 84*(2), 391–422.

Lemke, J. (1988). Genres, semantics, and classroom education. *Linguistics and Education 1,* 81–99.

Lenski, S. D., Ehlers-Zavala, F., Daniel, M. C., & Sun-Irminger, X. (2006). Assessing English-language learners in mainstream classrooms. *The Reading Teacher, 60*(1), 24–34.

Lenters, K. (2005). No half measures: Reading instruction for young second-language learners. *The Reading Teacher, 58*(4), 328–336.

Lesaux, N., & Geva, E. (2006). Synthesis: Development of literacy in language-minority students. In D. August & T. Shanahan (Eds.), *Developing literacy in second-language learners.* Mahwah, NJ: Lawrence Erlbaum.

Limbos, M., & Geva, E. (2002). Accuracy of teacher assessments of second-language students at risk for reading disability. *Journal of Learning Disabilities, 34,* 137–151.

Linan-Thompson, S., Cirino, P. T., & Vaughn, S. (2007). Determining English language learners' response to intervention: Questions and some answers. *Learning Disabilities Quarterly, 30,* 185–195.

Lindholm-Leary, K., & Borsato, G. (2006). Academic achievement. In F. Genesee, K. Lindholm-Leary, W. Saunders, & D. Christian (Eds.), *Educating English language learners: A synthesis of research evidence* (pp. 176–221). New York: Cambridge University Press.

Lipson, M., & Wixson, K. (2008). *Assessment and instruction of reading and writing difficulties: An interactive approach* (3rd Ed.). New York: Longman.

Losen, D., & Orfield, G. (2002). *Racial inequity in special education.* Cambridge, MA: Harvard Education Publishing Company.

Lucas, S. R. *Tracking inequality: Stratification and mobility in American high schools.* New York: Teachers College Press.

MacMillan, D., & Reschly, D. (1998). Overrepresentation of minority students: The case for greater specificity or reconsideration of the variables examined. *Journal of Special Education, 32*(1), 15–24.

Macon, J., Buell, D., & Vogt, M.E. (1991). *Responses to literature: Grades K–8.* Newark, DE: International Reading Association.

Manzo, A. J., Manzo, U. C., & Thomas, M. T. (2005). *Content area literacy: Strategic thinking for strategic learning* (4th ed.). New York: John Wiley & Sons.

Marshall, J. (2000). Research on response to literature. In R. L. Kamil, P. B. Mosenthal, P. D. Son, & R. Barr (Eds.). *Handbook of Reading Research,* Vol. 3. (pp. 381–402). Mahwah, NJ: Lawrence Erlbaum.

Marzano, R., Pickering, D. & Pollock, J. (2001). *Classroom instruction that works.* Alexandria, VA: Association for Supervision and Curriculum Development.

Mastropieri, M. A., & Scruggs, T. E. (1994). *Effective instruction for special education.* Austin, TX: PROED.

McCormick, C. B., & Pressley, M. (1997). *Educational psychology: Learning, instruction, assessment.* New York: Longman.

McIntyre, E., Kyle, D., & Moore, G. (2006). A primary teacher's guidance toward small group dialogue. *Reading Research Quarterly, 41*(1), 36–66.

McLaughlin, M. (2003). *Guided comprehension in the primary grades.* Newark, DE: International Reading Association.

McLaughlin, M., & Allen, M. B. (2002). *Guided comprehension: A teaching model for grades 3–8.* Newark, DE: International Reading Association.

McLaughlin, M., & Kennedy, A. (1993). *A classroom guide to performance-based assessment.* Princeton, NJ: Houghton Mifflin.

McLaughlin, M., & Vogt, M.E. (1996). *Portfolios in teacher education.* Newark, DE: International Reading Association.

McLaughlin, M., & Vogt, M.E. (2000). *Creativity and innovation in content area teaching: A resource for intermediate, middle, and high school teachers.* Norwood, MA: Christopher-Gordon Publishers.

McNeil, L. M., Coppola, E., Radigan, J., & Vasquez Heilig, J. (2008). Avoidable losses: High-stakes accountability and the dropout crisis. *Education Policy Analysis Archives, 16*(3). Retrieved February 24, 2008 from http://epaa.asu.edu/epaa/v16n3/.

Menken, K. (2008). *English learners left behind: Standardized testing as language policy.* Clevedon, England: Multilingual Matters.

Miholic, V. (1990). Constructing a semantic map for textbooks. *Journal of Reading 33*(6), 464–65.

Mohan, B. A. (1986). *Language and content.* Reading, MA: Addison-Wesley.

Mohan, B., Leung, C., & Davison, C. (Eds.). (2001). *English as a second language in the mainstream.* Harlow, England: Pearson.

Mokhtari, K., Rosemary, C. A., & Edwards, P. A. (2008). Making instructional decisions based on data: What, how, and why. *The Reading Teacher, 61*(4), 354–359.

Muth, K. D., & Alvermann, D. E. (1999). *Teaching and learning in the middle grades* (2nd Ed.). Needham Heights, MA: Allyn & Bacon.

Nagel, G. (2001). *Effective grouping for literacy instruction.* Boston: Allyn & Bacon.

National Association of Secondary School Principals. (2005). *Creating a culture of literacy: A guide for middle and high school principals.* Reston, VA: NASSP.

National Center for Education Statistics (NCES). (1997). *A profile of policies and practices for limited English proficient students: Screening methods, program support, and teacher training* (The 1993–94 Schools and Staffing Survey). Washington, DC: U.S. Department of Education, OERI.

National Center for Education Statistics. (2002). *Schools and staffing survey, 1999–2000: Overview of the data for public, private, public charter, and Bureau of Indian Affairs elementary and secondary schools.* (NCES 2002–313). Washington, DC: U.S. Department of Education, National Center for Educational Statistics.

National Center for Educational Statistics (NCES). (2004). *Language minorities and their educational and labor market indicators—Recent trends,* NCES 2004–09.Washington, DC: U.S. Department of Education.

National Clearinghouse for English Language Acquisition (NCELA). (2008). *NCELA frequently asked questions.* Retrieved October 3, 2008, from www.ncela.gwu.edu/expert/faq/08leps.html.

National Commission on Teaching and America's Future (NCTAF). (1997). *Doing what matters most: Investing in quality teaching.* New York: Columbia University, Teachers College.

National Governors Association. (2005). *A governor's guide to adolescent literacy.* Washington, DC: NGA, Center for Best Practices.

National Institute of Child Health and Human Development (NICHD). (2000). *Report of the National Reading Panel. Teaching children to read: An evidence-based assessment of the scientific research literature on reading and its implications for reading instruction.* (NIH Publication No. 00–4769). Washington, DC: U.S. Department of Health and Human Services.

Neal, L., McCray, A., Webb-Johnson, G., & Bridgest, S. (2003) The effects of African American movement styles on teachers' perceptions and reactions. *Journal of Special Education, 37*(1), 49–57.

Neufeld, P. (2005). Comprehension instruction in content classes. *The Reading Teacher, 59*(4), 302–312.

New York City Department of Education. (2004). *The class of 2000 final longitudinal report: A three year follow-up study.* New York: New York City Department of Education, Division of Assessment and Accountability.

No Child Left Behind Act of 2001. 107th Congress of the United States of America. Retrieved December 1, 2002, from www.ed.gov/legislation/ESEA02/107-110.pdf.

Oakes, J. (1985). *Keeping track: How schools structure inequality.* New Haven, CT: Yale University Press.

Office of Special Education Programs (2002). *Twenty-sixth annual Report to Congress on the implementation of the Individuals with Disabilities Education Act.* Washington DC: U.S. Department of Education.

Ogle, D. (1986). K-W-L: A teaching model that develops active reading of expository text. *The Reading Teacher, 39,* 564–570.

O'Malley, J. J., & Chamot, A. U. (1990). *Learning strategies in second language acquisition.* Cambridge: Cambridge University Press.

O'Malley, J. M., & Pierce, L. V. (1996). *Authentic assessment for English language learners: Practical approaches for teachers.* Reading, MA: Addison-Wesley.

Orfield, G., Losen, D., & Edley, Jr., C. (2001). *The Civil Rights Project.* Cambridge, MA: Harvard University.

Ortiz, A. (2002). Prevention of school failure and early intervention. In A. Artiles & A. Ortiz (Eds.). *English language learners with special education needs* (pp. 31–50). Washington DC: Center for Applied Linguistics.

Palinscar, A. C., & Brown, A. L. (1984). Reciprocal teaching of comprehension-fostering and comprehension-monitoring activities. *Cognition and Instruction, 1,* 117–175.

Paris, S. (2001). Classroom applications of research on self-regulated learning. *Educational Psychologist, 36*(3), 89–102.

Paris, S. G., Lipson., M. Y., & Wixson, K. (1983). Becoming a strategic reader. *Contemporary Educational Psychology, 8,* 293–316.

Parish, T., Merikel, A., Perez, M., Linquanti, R., Socias, M., Spain, M., et al. (2006). *Effects of the implementation of Proposition 227 on the education of English learners, K–12: Findings from a five-year evaluation.* Palo Alto, CA: American Institutes for Research.

Patton, J., & Townsend, B. (1999). Ethics, power and privilege: Neglected considerations in the education of African American learners with special needs. *Teacher Education and Special Education. 22*(4), 276–286.

Peregoy, S. F., & Boyle, O. F. (2005). *Reading, writing, and learning in ESL: A resource book for K–12 teachers* (4th Ed.). New York: Longman.

Perie, M., Grigg, W. S., & Donahue, P. L. (2005). *The Nation's Report Card: Reading 2005* (NCES 2006–451). U.S. Department of Education, Institute of Education Sciences, National Center for Education Statistics. Washington DC: U.S. Government Printing Office.

Podell, D. M., & Soodak, L. C. (1993). Teacher efficacy and bias in special education referrals. *Journal of Educational Researcher, 86*(4), 247–253.

Poldrack, R., Clark, J., Pare-Blagoev, E., Shohamy, D., Creso Moyano, J., Myers, C., & Gluck, M. (2001). Interactive memory systems in the human brain. *Nature, 414*, 546–550.

Powers, K., (2001). Problem solving student support teams. *The California School Psychologist, 6,* 19–30.

Pressley, M. (2000). What should comprehension instruction be instruction of? In M. L. Kamil, P. B. Mosenthal, P. D. Pearson, & R. Barr (Eds.), *Handbook of reading research* (Vol. III, pp. 545–562). Mahwah, NJ: Lawrence Erlbaum Associates.

Pressley, M. (2002). Comprehension strategies instruction: A turn-of-the-century status report. In C. C. Block & M. Pressley (Eds.), *Comprehension instruction: Research-based best practices* (pp. 11–27). New York: Guilford.

Pressley, M. (2005). *Literacy-instructional effective classrooms and schools . . . And why I am so worried about comprehension instruction even in places like these!* Keynote address presented to the Research Institute of the 51st International Reading Association Annual Convention, Chicago, IL.

Pressley, M., Johnson, C., Symons, S., McGoldrick, J. A., & Kurita, J. A. (1989). Strategies that improve children's memory and comprehension of text. *The Elementary School Journal, 90,* 3–32.

Pressley, M., & Woloshyn, V. (Eds.) (1995). *Cognitive strategy instruction that really improves children's academic performance.* Cambridge, MA: Brookline Books.

Ramirez, J., Yuen, S., Ramey, D., & Pasta, D. (1991). *Executive summary: Final report: Longitudinal study of structure English immersion strategy, early-exit and late-exit transitional bilingual education programs for language-minority children.* (Contract No. 300087–0156). Submitted to the U.S. Department of Education. San Mateo: Aguirre International.

Raphael, T. E. (1984). Teaching learners about sources of information for answering comprehension questions. *Journal of Reading 27,* 303–311.

Raphael, T. E., Highfield, K., & Au, K. H. (2006). *QAR now: A powerful and practical framework that develops comprehension and higher-level thinking skills.* New York: Scholastic.

Rasinski, T., & Padak, N. (2004). *Effective reading strategies: Teaching children who find reading difficult.* Upper Saddle River, NJ: Pearson Merrill Prentice Hall.

Readence, J. E., Bean, T. W., & Baldwin, R. S. (2001). *Content area literacy: An integrated approach* (8th ed.). Dubuque, IA: Kendall/Hunt.

Readance, J., Bean, T., & Baldwin, R. S. (2001). *Teaching reading in the content areas* (8th ed.). Dubuque, IA: Kendall Hunt.

Reiss, J. (2008). *102 Content strategies for English learners: Teaching for academic success in grades 3–12.* Upper Saddle River, NJ: Pearson/Merrill Prentice Hall.

Rinaldi, C., & Samson, J. (2008) English language learners and response to intervention: Referral considerations. *Teaching Exceptional Children, 40*(5), 6–14.

Reutzel, D. R., & Morgan, B. C. (1990). Effects of prior knowledge, explicitness, and clause order on children's comprehension of causal relationships. *Reading Psychology 11*(2), 93–109.

Rosenblatt, L. M. (1991). Literacy theory. In J. Flood, J. Jensen, D. Flood, & J. Squire (Eds.), *Handbook of research on teaching the English-language arts.* New York: Macmillan.

Ruddell, M. R. (2007). *Teaching content reading and writing* (5th ed.). Hoboken, NJ: John Wiley & Sons, Inc.

Ruddell, M. R., & Shearer, B. A. (2002). "Extraordinary," "tremendous," "exhilarating," "magnificent": Middle school at-risk students become avid word learners with the Vocabulary Self-Collection Strategy (VSS). *Journal of Adolescent and Adult Literacy, 45*(4), 352–363.

Ruiz-de-Velasco, J., & Fix, M. (2000). *Overlooked and underserved: Immigrant students in U.S. secondary schools.* Washington, DC: Urban Institute.

Rumelhart, D. E. (1980). Schemata: The building blocks of cognition. In Rand J. Spiro et al. (Eds.), *Theoretical Issues in Reading Comprehension* (pp. 33–58). Hillsdale, NJ: Erlbaum.

Rumelhart, D. E. (2004). Toward an interactive model of reading. In R. B. Ruddell, M. R. Ruddell, & H. Singer (Eds.), *Theoretical models and processes of reading* (5th ed., pp. 1149–1179). Newark, DE: International Reading Association.

Saunders, W., & Goldenberg, C. (2007). The effects of an instructional conversation on English language learners' concepts of friendship and story comprehension. In R. Horowitz (Ed.), *Talking texts: How speech and writing interact in school learning* (pp. 221–252). Mahwah, NJ: Erlbaum.

Saunders, W., Goldenberg, C., & Hamann, J. (1992) Instructional conversations beget instructional conversations. *Teaching and Teacher Education, 8*(2), 199–218.

Saunders, W., & O'Brien, G. (2006). Oral language. In F. Genesee, K. Lindholm-Leary, W. Saunders, & D. Christian, (Eds.), *Educating English language learners: A synthesis of research evidence* (pp. 14–63). New York: Cambridge University Press.

Saville-Troike, M. (1984). What really matters in second language learning for academic achievement? *TESOL Quarterly, 18,* 117–131.

Schleppegrell, M. (2004). *The language of schooling: A functional linguistic perspective.* Mahwah, NJ: Lawrence Erlbaum Associates.

Schleppegrell, M., Achugar, M., & Orteíza, T. (2004). The grammar of history: Enhancing content-based instruction through a functional focus on language. *TESOL Quarterly, 38*(1), 67–93.

Schmoker, M. (2001) *The results fieldbook: Practical strategies from dramatically improved schools.* Alexandria, VA: Association for Supervision and Curriculum Development.

Schmoker, M. (2006). *Results now.* Alexandria, VA: Association for Supervision and Curriculum Development.

Shearer, B. A., & Ruddell, M. R. (2006). Engaging students' interests and participation in learning. In D. Lapp, J. Flood, & N. Farnan (Eds.), *Content area reading and learning* (3rd ed.). Mahwah, NJ.: Erlbaum.

Shearer, B. A., Ruddell, M. R., & Vogt, M.E. (2001). Successful middle school intervention: Negotiated strategies and individual choice. In T. Shanahan & F. V. Rodriguez (Eds.), *National Reading Conference Yearbook, 50.* Chicago, IL: National Reading Conference.

Sheppard, K. (1995). *Content-ESL across the USA (Volume I, Technical Report).* Washington, DC: National Clearinghouse for Bilingual Education.

Short, D. (1994). Expanding middle-school horizons: Integrating language, culture and social studies. *TESOL Quarterly, 28*(3), 581–608.

Short, D. (1999). Integrating language and content for effective sheltered instruction programs. In C. Faltis & P. Wolfe (Eds.), *So much to say: Adolescents, bilingualism, and ESL in the secondary school* (pp. 105–137). New York: Teachers College Press.

Short, D. J. (2002). Language learning in sheltered social studies classes. *TESOL Journal 11*(1), 18–24.

Short, D. (2006). Content teaching and learning and language. In K. Brown (Editor-in-Chief), *Encyclopedia of Language and Linguistics,* 2nd ed. (Vol. 3, pp. 101–105), Oxford: Elsevier.

Short, D., & Boyson, B. (2004). *Creating access: Language and academic programs for secondary school newcomers.* McHenry, IL: Delta Systems, Inc.

Short, D., & Echevarria, J. (2004). Teacher skills to support English language learners. *Educational Leadership, 62*(4), 9–13.

Short, D. J., & Echevarria, J. (1999). *The sheltered instruction observation protocol: Teacher-researcher collaboration and professional development.* Educational Practice Report No. 3. Santa Cruz, CA, and Washington, DC: Center for Research on Education, Diversity & Excellence.

Short, D., & Fitzsimmons, S. (2007). *Double the work: Challenges and solutions to acquiring language and academic literacy for adolescent English language learners.* Report to Carnegie Corporation of New York. Washington, DC: Alliance for Excellent Education.

Short, D., Hudec, J., & Echevarria, J. (2002). *Using the SIOP Model: Professional development manual for sheltered instruction.* Washington, DC: Center for Applied Linguistics.

Short, D., Vogt, M.E., & Echevarria, J. (2008). *The SIOP® Model for administrators.* Boston, MA: Pearson/Allyn & Bacon.

Short, D., Vogt, M.E., & Echevarria, J. (in press). *The SIOP® Model for teaching history/social studies to English learners.* Boston: Allyn & Bacon.

Short, D., Vogt, M.E., & Echevarria, J. (in press). *The SIOP® Model for teaching science to english learners.* Boston: Allyn & Bacon.

Siegel, H. (2002). Multiculturalism, universalism, and science education: In search of common ground. *Science Education, 86,* 803–820.

Silverstein, S. (1964). *The giving tree.* New York: HarperCollins.

Sirotnik, K. (1983). What you see is what you get: Consistency, persistency, and mediocrity in classrooms. *Harvard Educational Review, 53,* 16–31.

Slater, W. H., & Horstman, F. R. (2002). Teaching reading and writing to struggling middle school and high school students: The case for reciprocal teaching. *Preventing School Failure (46)*4, 163–167.

Slavin, R. E., & Cheung, A. (2004). How do English language learners learn to read? *Educational Leadership, 61*(6), 52–57.

Smith, D. (2001). *Introduction to special education: Teaching in an age of opportunity* (4th Ed.). Boston: Allyn & Bacon.

Snow, C. E., Burns, S., Griffin, P. (Eds.) (1998). *Preventing reading difficulties in young children.* Washington, DC: National Academy Press.

Snow, C. E., Cancino, H., De Temple, J. & Schley, S. (1991). Giving formal definitions: A linguistic or metalinguistic skill? In E. Bialystok (Ed.), *Language processing and language awareness by bilingual children* (pp. 90–112). New York: Cambridge University Press.

Snow, C. E., Griffin, P., & Burns, M. S. (Eds.). (2005). *Knowledge to support the teaching of reading: Preparing teachers for a changing world.* San Francisco: Jossey-Bass.

Solano-Flores, G., & Trumbull, E. (2003). Examining language in context: The need for new research and practice paradigms in the testing of English language learners. *Educational Researcher, 32*(2), 3–13.

Stahl, S., & Nagy, W. (2006). *Teaching word meanings.* Mahwah, NJ: Erlbaum.

Stanovich, K. E. (1986). Matthew effects in reading: Some consequences of individual differences in the acquisition of literacy. *Reading Research Quarterly, 21,* 360–406.

State of New Jersey Department of Education. (2006). *Preliminary analysis of former limited English proficient students' scores on the New Jersey language arts and literacy exam, 2005–2006.* Trenton, NJ: State of New Jersey Department of Education, New Jersey State Assessment Office of Title I.

Stauffer, R. (1969). *Teaching reading as a thinking process.* New York: Harper & Row.

Stauffer, R. (1980). *The language-experience approach to the teaching of reading* (2nd Ed.). New York: Harper & Row.

Stenner, A. J., & Burdick, X. (1997). *The objective measurement of reading comprehension.* Durham, NC: Metametrics.

Stoller, F. (2004). Content-based instruction: Perspectives on curriculum planning. *Annual Review of Applied Linguistics 24,* 261–283.

Sullivan, P., Yeager, M., O'Brien, E., Kober, N., Gayler, K., Chudowsky, N., Chudowsky, V., Wooden, J., Jennings, J., &. Stark Rentner, D. (2005). *States try harder, but gaps persist: High school exit exams 2005.* Washington, DC: Center on Education Policy.

Swain, M. (1985). Communicative competence: Some roles of comprehensible input and output in its development. In S. Gass & C. Madden (Eds.), *Input in second language acquisition* (pp. 235–256). Rowley, MA: Newbury House.

Swift, J. N., & Gooding, C. T. (1983). Interaction of wait time feedback and questioning instruction on middle school science teaching. *Journal of Research in Science Teaching, 20,* 721–730.

Syvanen, C. (2000). Recycling. In K. Samway (Ed.), *Integrating the ESL standards into classroom practice: Grades 3–5* (pp. 133–149). Alexandria, VA: Teachers of English to Speakers of Other Languages, Inc.

Taboada, A., & Guthrie, J. T. (2006). Contributions of student questioning and prior knowledge to construction of knowledge from reading information text. *Journal of Literacy Research, 38*(1), 1–35.

Tabors, P. O., & Snow, C. E. (2005). Young bilingual children and early literacy development. In R. B. Ruddell & N. J. Unrau (Eds.), *Theoretical models and processes of reading* (5th Ed., pp. 240–267). Newark, DE: International Reading Association.

Teachers of English to Speakers of Other Languages, Inc. (TESOL) (2001). *Scenarios for ESL standards-based assessment.* Alexandria, VA: Author.

Teachers of English to Speakers of Other Languages, Inc. (2006). *PreK–12 English language proficiency standards.* Alexandria, VA: Author.

Tharp, R., & Gallimore, R. (1988). *Rousing minds to life.* Cambridge: Cambridge University Press.

Thomas, W. P., & Collier, V. P. (2002). *A national study of school effectiveness for language minority students' long-term academic achievement.* Santa Cruz, CA, and Washington, DC: Center for Research on education, Diversity & Excellence.

Tierney, R., & Pearson, P. D. (1994). Learning to learn from text: A framework for improving classroom practice. In R. Ruddell, M. Ruddell, & H. Singer (Eds.), *Theoretical models and processes of reading* (4th Ed.). Newark, DE: International Reading Association.

Tilly, D. (2006). Response to Intervention: An overview. *The Special Edge, 19*(2), 1–5.

Tobin, K. (1987). The role of wait time in higher cognitive level learning. *Review of Educational Research, 57,* 69–95.

Tolchinsky, L., & Teberosky, A. (1998). The development of word segmentation and writing in two scripts. *Cognitive Development 13*, 1–24.

Tomlinson, C. (2005). *How to differentiate instruction in mixed-ability classrooms* (2nd ed.). Upper Saddle River, NJ: Pearson.

Trent, S., Kea, C. & Oh, K. (2008) Preparing preservice educators for cultural diversity: How far have we come? *Exceptional Children 74*(3), 328–350.

Tompkins, G. E. (2006). *Literacy for the 21st century: A balanced approach* (4th ed.). Upper Saddle River, NJ: Merrill Prentice Hall.

Uribe, M., & Nathenson-Mejia, S. (2008). *Literacy essentials for English language learners: Successful transitions.* New York: Teachers College Press.

Vacca, R. T. (2002). From efficient decoders to strategic readers. *Educational Leadership 60*(3), 6–11.

Vacca, R., & Vacca, J. A. (2004). *Content area reading: Literacy and learning across the curriculum* (7th ed.). New York: Longman.

Vaughn, S., Linan-Thompson, S., Kouzekanani, K., Pedrotty-Bryan, D., Dickson, S., & Blozis, S. (2003). Reading instruction grouping for students with reading difficulties. *Remedial and Special Education, 24*(5), 301–315.

Vogt, M.E. (1989). *A study of the congruence between preservice teachers' and cooperating teachers' attitudes and practices toward high and low achievers.* Unpublished doctoral dissertation submitted to the University of California, Berkeley.

Vogt, M.E. (1992). Strategies for leading readers into text: The pre-reading phase of a content lesson. In C. Hedley & D. Feldman (Eds.), *Literacy across the curriculum.* New York: Ablex.

Vogt, M.E. (1995). *Jumpstarting: Providing support in advance rather than remediation.* Paper presented at the Annual Conference of the International Reading Association, Anaheim, CA.

Vogt, M.E. (1997). *Intervention strategies for intermediate and middle school students: Three models that appear to work.* Paper presented at the Research Institute of the Annual Conference of the California Reading Association, Anaheim, CA.

Vogt, M.E. (2000). Content learning for students needing modifications: An issue of access. In M. McLaughlin and M.E. Vogt (Eds.), *Creativity and innovation in content area teaching: A resource for intermediate, middle, and high school teachers.* Norwood, MA: Christopher Gordon Publishers.

Vogt, M.E. (2002). *SQP2RS: Increasing students' understandings of expository text through cognitive and metacognitive strategy application.* Paper presented at the 52nd Annual Meeting of the National Reading Conference.

Vogt, M.E. (2005). Improving achievement for ELLs through sheltered instruction. *Language Learner, 1*(1), 22, 25.

Vogt, M.E., & Echevarria, J. (2008). *99 ideas and activities for teaching English learners with the SIOP® Model.* Boston: Allyn & Bacon.

Vogt, M.E., Echavarria, J., & Short, D. (in press). *The SIOP® Model for teaching English/language arts to English learners.* Boston: Allyn & Bacon.

Vogt, M.E., & McLaughlin, M. (2005). Teaching and learning in a global society: Examining changing definitions of literacy. In M. Pandis (Ed.), *Proceedings from the European Reading Conference* (Tallinn, Estonia). Newark, DE: International Reading Association.

Vogt, M.E., & Nagano, P. (2003). *Turn it on with Light Bulb Reading! Sound-switching strategies for struggling readers, 57*(3), 214–221.

Vogt, M.E., & Shearer, B. A. (2007). *Reading specialists and literacy coaches in the real world* (2nd ed.). Boston: Allyn & Bacon.

Vygotsky, L. (1978). *Mind and society: The development of higher psychological processes* (M. Cole, V. John-Steiner, S. Scribner, & E. Souberman, Eds. and trans.). Cambridge, MA: Harvard University Press.

Walqui, A. (2006). Scaffolding instruction for English language learners: A conceptual framework. *The International Journal of Bilingual Education and Bilingualism, 9*(2), 159–180.

Watson, K., & Young, B. (1986). Discourse for learning in the classroom. *Language Arts, 63*(2), 126–133.

WIDA (World-class Instructional Design and Assessment) consortium. (2007). *Assessing Comprehension and Communication in English State-to-State for English Language Learners (ACCESS for ELLs®).* Madison, WI: The Board of Regents of the University of Wisconsin System on Behalf of the WIDA Consortium.

WIDA Consortium. (2007). *English language proficiency standards and resource guide, 2007 edition, prekindergarten through grade 12.* Madison, Wisconsin: The Board of Regents of the University of Wisconsin System.

Wilen, W. (1990). Forms and phases of discussion. In W. Wilen (Ed.), *Teaching and learning through discussion* (pp. 3–24). Springfield, IL: Charles C Thomas.

Wong-Fillmore, L., & Valadez, C. (1986). Teaching bilingual learners. In M. C. Wittrock (Ed.), *Handbook of research on teaching* (pp. 648–685). New York: Macmillan.

Yoon, B. (2008). Uninvited guests: The influence of teachers' roles and pedagogies on the positioning of English language learners in the regular classroom. *American Educational Research Journal, 45*(2) 495–522.

Ysseldyke, J., & Marston, D. (1999). Origins of categorical special education services in schools and a rationale for changing them. In D. J. Reshchly, W. D. Tilly, & J. P. Grimes (Eds.), *Special education in transition: Functional assessment and noncategorical programming.* Longmont, CO: Sopris West.

Zabala, D., Minnici, A., McMurrer, J., & Briggs, L. (2008). *State high school exit exams: Moving toward end-of-course exams.* Washington, DC: Center on Education Policy.

Zike, D. (1994). *The big book of math—Elementary K–6.* San Antonio, TX: Dinah-Might Adventures.

Zike, D. (2004). *The big book of science—Elementary K–6.* San Antonio, TX: Dinah-Might Adventures.